SEPHARDIC COOKING

SEPHARDIC

COPELAND MARKS

COOKING

600 Recipes Created in Exotic Sephardic Kitchens from Morocco to India

DONALD I. FINE, INC.
New York

Library of Congress Cataloging-in-Publication Data

Marks, Copeland.
    Sephardic cooking : 600 recipes created in exotic Sephardic
kitchens from Morocco to India / Copeland Marks.
        p.   cm.
    Includes index.
    ISBN 1-55611-318-8
    1. Cookery, Sephardic.   I. Title.
TX724.M319   1992
641.5'676—dc20   91-55191
                                                                      CIP

Manufactured in the United States of America

10   9   8   7   6   5   4   3   2   1

DESIGNED BY Stanley S. Drate/Folio Graphics Company, Inc.

Contents

INTRODUCTION   vii

ACKNOWLEDGMENTS   ix

GLOSSARY   xiii

EASTERN MEDITERRANEAN   1
  Turkey   3
  Greece   35

MIDDLE EAST   63
  Kurdistan   65
  Baghdad (Iraq)   91
  Persia (Iran)   103

CAUCASUS AND CENTRAL ASIA   195
  Georgia   197
  Uzbekistan: *Bukhara and Samarkand*   249
  Afghanistan   299

INDIA   323
  Calcutta: *The Baghdadi Jews*   325
  Bombay: *Bene Israel*   353
  Cochin: *The Black Jews*   369

RED SEA   385
  Yemen   387
  Ethiopia   401
  Egypt   415

v

The Maghreb—North Africa   431
  Morocco 433
  Tangier 464
  Tunisia 471
  Libya 507

Bibliography   527

Index   529

Introduction

EXOTIC SEPHARDIC KITCHENS

Writing a cookbook about the food of unknown countries is like journeying to those countries, like a tourist who picks up a bit of language on the route, something of an unfamiliar way of life. My personal pilgrimage to four continents over a period of five years—cooking, nibbling, tasting, writing, while collecting recipes of Sephardic communities—is an experience that has changed my life, enriching it.

What is this passionate need to record the eating habits of the Jewish culinary environments in little known places? In my opinion, the preservation of ethnicity, something from the past that endures through the oral tradition, is my *raison d'être* for recording what is quite obviously disappearing. Judaic cooking became particularly fragile as individuals or groups fled, pursued out of ancient homelands by the bigotry of man. Only the strong Jewish capacity for adaptation and endurance in periods of both extravagance and denial saves culinary traditions from oblivion.

I was first drawn to the idea of recording a series of exotic communities that were Jewish in origin, by the ingathering of Jews to Israel from all corners of the world. What other country anywhere contained such a variety of nationalities within a tiny area? It seemed as though Israel would sink into the Mediterranean by the sheer weight of numbers on this small spot of historic land. Where else could one find Jews from the Maghreb, India, Greece, Ethiopia and dozens of other countries that Jews had come from, to fulfill their longing for a permanent home?

After the expulsion from Spain in 1492 and Portugal in 1497, the Spanish (read Sephardic) Jews filtered through the Mediterranean region and established communities principally in the Ottoman Empire, which was the paramount political power during that era.

Now the five hundredth anniversary of the expulsion from Iberia will be celebrated around the world, but nowhere more intensely than in Istanbul where the Jews were given refuge in the fifteenth century by Sultan Beyazit II. My focus on Turkey reveals with clarity the profound importance of that proclamation and the establishment of Sephardic life.

Not all of the countries included in this book can qualify as Sephardics according to the dictionary meaning. Jews in Yemen, Ethiopia, Soviet Georgia, Bukhara, Cochin, India are not Spanish but can be loosely considered so. Their inclusion in this book is based upon their connection with the ritual of Talmudic Baghdad and by extension, therefore, of Spain. Also, their inclusion is not only because of the exotic nature of their cooking but because they are not of the Ashkenazi of Europe.

Cooking styles, like handicrafts, identify ethnic cultures wherever they may be. In searching for a common factor in these exotic cuisines, I found kashruth as the thread that held them all together. Otherwise every community was different: depending on geography and climate. Brillat-Savarin's famous epigram states, "Tell me what you eat and I will tell you what you are." I have paraphrased this to read, "Tell me what you eat and I will tell you where you are from."

Each year, like endangered species, recipes and the folklore that goes with them disappear into the twentieth century and frequently are never to be revived in their original form. I hope that this Sephardic book will alert good cooks to the danger of that loss and the importance of keeping traditions alive by using them.

Bon Appetit!

ACKNOWLEDGMENTS

My personal pilgrimage to four continents in search of Sephardic recipes, some elusive, others easily obtained, was a labor of love. So many gave of their time—taxi drivers who tried to convince me that their elderly aunt was the best cook in town; or well-meaning citizens who directed me on wild-goose chases. Then there were the success stories with their names and communities listed below.

GEORGIA, USSR
Esther Krihely
Valentina Voloashvilli Sterling
BUKHARA AND SAMARKAND, USSR
Simcha Haimov
Meir Maximov
Miriam Abramov
COCHIN, INDIA
Solomon Mordecai Pallivathukkal, "he who lives in front of the synagogue" and his wife, Rahel
BENE ISRAEL, INDIA
Flora Samuel
Diana Abraham
Sam Daniel
CALCUTTA, INDIA
Ramah David
Flora Ezra Gubbay
Rachel Luddy Shellim
Mercia Rassaby Rembaum
Philomena Gubbay Jacob

PERSIA (IRAN)
Victoria Neydavood
Rachel Hakakian
Dolores Rabenau
MOROCCO
Esther Sellouk
Iris Kor
Jacob Ghazy
Shoshana (Suzie) Shimoni
Celine Ayash
Jeanot Cao-Ba
TUNISIA
Matilda Guez
Matilda Ktorza
Yvette Fitoussi
LIBYA
Mirella Haddad Naim
Felice Fellus
Pnina Yhaid
TANGIER
Ruth Bendayan Serels
BAGHDAD (IRAQ)
Yaffa Nuriel
Ruth Yechzkel Shiloni
Yvonne Hillel Cohen
KURDISTAN, IRAQ
Shoshana Yosef
Yochi Jacob
Shoshana Noah
ETHIOPIA
Tuvia Semani and his wife, Felagu Imar
YEMEN
Simcha Zermati
Erez Zarum
EGYPT
Shelly Shemtov

Evelina Attias
Ita Aber
GREECE
Rachel Sasson
Athena Vicos Prill
Esther Elias Abraham
Rosa Benveniste
TURKEY
Katy Halewa
Mary Cassorla Weprinsky
Viki Koronyo
Vivian Ronana
Sima Ovadya
Rita Taranto
AFGHANISTAN
Michal Kusaief

In addition, special mention must be made for Rabbi M. Mitchell Serels, Sephardic Studies, Yeshiva University, whose interest in my project was of inestimable value.

My warm thanks goes to the Beth Hatefutsoth, Museum of the Diaspora, Tel Aviv, who graciously opened their files to the melancholy view of communities no longer in existence. El Al Airlines provided practical assistance on several occasions. The staff of the Hilton Hotel, Tel Aviv, was extremely cooperative. Jeremy Frankel, formerly General Manager of the Hilton Hotel, Jerusalem, and his staff provided comfort and information above and beyond the call of duty. The Hilton Hotels in Istanbul and Athens opened their impressive professionalism to me and for this I thank them.

Also, Dalia Carmel, New York, the Sephardic Home for the Aged, Brooklyn, where I cooked with Turkish ladies; and Sephardic Jews from all walks of life on whatever continent I found them. I remember them all with affection.

I am with them a gentleman
        among savages
And a lion amidst a flock of
        apes and parrots.

—An Inquisition era poem
by a Spanish-Jewish poet

Glossary

Advieh: A powdered spice mixture containing cinnamon, cardamom, clove, ginger and sometimes pepper. Used by the Persians as the Chinese use five-spice and the Indians *garam masala*. Recipe is included.

Aloo Bukhara: Whole dried apricots complete with the seeds, looking like hard, wrinkled stones. When used in Persian cooking they are soaked in water overnight and cooked in a compote; they have a meltingly sweet flavor. Available in some Asian shops, or substitute prunes.

Barberry, Zereshk *(Berberis vulgaris)*:   The Perians like these dry tart berries incorporated in rice dishes or used as a garnish. They are expensive and not always easily obtained; a Persian friend told me to substitute dried currants.

Black Cumin *(Bunium persicum B. Fedtsch)*:   Smaller and sweeter than the standard cuminseed; the plants grow wild in the Middle East. The seeds are used in Afghanistan, Iran and Turkey. Black cuminseeds are sprinkled on Afghan bread.

Bulghur: see Wheat

Cardoon *(Cynara cardunculus)*:   Related to the artichoke, but cardoon is grown primarily for the stalks. The fleshy ribs are eaten. To some it is an esoteric vegetable, but there are those who have eaten it traditionally. The flavor is slightly bitter, the texture is similar to celery. A popular vegetable in Morocco and Tunisia, occasionally seen in New York ethnic markets.

Cocum: The very young fruit of the famous mangosteen *(Garcinia mangostana)*, one of the most fragrant and luscious tropical fruits of Asia. The young fruit, which is red and quite sour, is the basis of the sour seasoning used in Bene Israel curries of India. The skin is dried into a black, flat 1-inch object. Four or five of the skins are used to give a slightly acid flavor to curry. Since the cocum is not available to us, tamarind or lemon juice may be used as a substitute.

Cous cous: A staple in countries of the Maghreb—Morocco, Tunisia, Libya. Cous cous was prepared at home in earlier days, but now it is available packaged. It consists of semolina, salt, water and oil. The dough from this mixture is rubbed through a metal sieve, resulting in tiny globules of pasta. When steamed in a *couscousier,* cous cous expands to about three times its original size. There are those who think that it is a special whole grain, but this is incorrect. Cous cous is the name for the prepared pasta as well as for the whole dish made with it.

Couscousier: In my collection I have a beautiful copper antique *couscousier,* which is shaped like an hourglass and is in two sections. The bottom half is a container for the meat, fish or poultry stew. The top half has many round holes ¼ inch in diameter, which allow steam from the stew to permeate the cous cous deposited in the top.

Cracked Wheat: see Wheat

Cream of Wheat: see Wheat

Curry Leaf *(Murraya koenigii)*: This evergreen shrub or small tree, related to the orange, grows in the warm regions of India. It produces large flowers. The leaves, dried or fresh, are added to South Indian curries— whether vegetable, meat or fish—and add a mild aromatic flavor. Curry leaves are available in the United States and can be purchased in Indian spice shops.

Farina: see Wheat

Fava Bean *(Vicia Faba)*: Also known as broad bean. One of the most ancient cultivated vegetables, and a favorite in the Maghreb.

Fenugreek *(Trigonella foenumgraecum)*: An ancient cultivated plant known to the Greeks, Romans and Egyptians, and used for medicinal purposes. It is often an ingredient in curry powders. It has a bitter taste and the consistency of mucilage when dissolved in water, but it is rich in protein, minerals and vitamins. Both seeds and ground powder are used. Calcutta Jews prepare an interesting table hutney known as "Jewish paste" because of its viscous consistency given by the fenugreek.

Garam Masala: A combination of spices, freely translated in Hindi as "hot spice." It contains pepper, clove, cardamom, cuminseed, coriander and turmeric in proportions according to personal preference and regional taste. The mixture in my collection, in addition to the above list, includes ginger, bay leaves and nutmeg, all ground together. I bought it already ground and packaged.

Hameen: see T'fina

Harissa: A hot sauce or paste prepared at home in Tunisia and Morocco; it contains dried hot red chilies and other seasonings. Harissa is available in Middle East groceries.

Jareesha: see Wheat

Jewish Holidays

Rosh Hashanah: The high holy day that marks the beginning of the Jewish New Year. Observed September/October, a date determined by the lunar calendar. A day for family gatherings and holiday dining. Upon returning home from the synagogue, certain ritual foods are served and the diners offer prayers for the New Year. Eating apples dipped into honey will guarantee a sweet year, for instance, and pomegranate seeds will promise fertility, while beef lung will give lightness to one's life.

Yom Kippur: The Day of Atonement. Perhaps the holiest of the Jewish holy days; on this day there is complete abstinence from food and drink from the afternoon of one day until the evening of the second day. A day punctuated by the recitation of prayers and repentence of sins; observed in September/October.

Sukkoth: The Feast of the Tabernacles. This feast celebrates the harvest in autumn for 8 or 9 days depending on one's orthodoxy. It also commemorates the wandering in the desert after the Exodus from Egypt and the construction of the *sukkot*, a temporary booth or hut that represents shelter for the wanderers. In my family, the outdoor booth was covered with cornstalks, prayers were said, and food was served within.

Shavuoth: This holiday commemorates the time when God gave the Ten Commandments to Moses in the Sinai. It was also formerly connected with the harvest of barley and wheat. Dairy dishes in place of meat are the preferred foods during this time.

Hanukkah: The Feast of Lights. Candles are lighted for 8 days to commemorate the victory of the Maccabees over the Syrians. Observed in early December. Festive family foods—especially sweets—are served.

Purim: This festival celebrates the deliverance of the Persian Jews from the tyrant Haman through the intercession of the Jewish Queen Esther. Pastries are prepared, especially in Greece and Turkey, that are intended to ridicule Haman. Observed about March 1.

Passover (Pesach): This season commemorates the Exodus of the Jews from Egypt. Celebrated for 8 days, Matzoh, the unleavened cracker, is eaten and used as an ingredient in dairy, meat and sweet dishes, while bread is banished. Special foods relating to the holiday are prepared. Passover, more than any other Jewish holiday, has its own special cuisine. Observed in the spring.

Kuku: A catchy name for the much loved Persian omelets.

Limoo Amoni: The blackened dried lime about the size of a golf ball is an indispensable flavoring in Persian meat dishes. It can be used whole, in which case the lime flavor is released but the food is not discolored. At other times, it is crushed and sprinkled as ground spices are used, providing an intense citrus flavor. I have seen acres of the lime, which is similar to the Key lime of Florida, drying in the hot sun in Guatemala as they desiccate and change color from gold/green to black. Sometimes available in Arabian markets.

Mace (Myristica fragrans Houtt): Nutmeg is a tropical evergreen tree that produces two spices—nutmeg and mace. It is a native of the Molucca Islands of Indonesia, where I traveled on several occasions to do some research. Mace is the brilliant red, fleshy covering of the nutmeg shell. The mace covering is dried in the sun and is sold in pieces as it is in Morocco and ground into powder elsewhere. The pungent flavor is not as intense as nutmeg or of similar fragrance.

Maghreb: An Arabic term meaning "setting sun," the term used for the western region of North Africa. This includes the countries of Morocco, Algeria, Tunisia and Libya.

M'loukhia *(Corchorus olitorius)*:   Also known as Jews' mallow or tossa jute. The plant grows from Egypt to Japan but mostly in India and Bangladesh. Jute (burlap) is derived from the stems of the mature plant. The green leaves, fresh or dried, are used in soups and stews in Egypt and Tunisia.

Nachochi: Toasted dried chick-peas can be purchased in Middle East groceries. The chick-peas can be eaten out of hand like peanuts; they have a dry nutty consistency. Persians grind them into flour; they are used in several dishes.

Pomegranate *(Punica granatum)*:   The old Roman name for this fruit was "apple of Carthage." It is beloved by Afghans and Persian Jews, who select the largest size to be found in the markets. The fresh ripe fruit is massaged, squeezed and rolled to extract the juice from the many small seeds within the fruit. A hole of about ½ inch in diameter is then cut at one end and the tart red juice is sucked out, leaving only the juiceless seeds and pulp. I suggest that you remove several cups of seeds, store them in a plastic bag, and freeze for later use. Supermarkets sometimes carry bottled pomegranate juice or pomegranate concentrate, a thick natural syrup that can be diluted with water. During the season, fresh pomegranates are quite easy to find.

Queman: A mixture of dried spices used in Ethiopian foods, in the style of the *garam masala* of India, to which it is related.

Quince *(Cydonia vulgaris)*:   An ancient fruit of Western Asia. A large, hard acid fruit, used in preparing jam in Persia and sometimes included in meat and fish dishes in the Maghreb.

Scheena   see T'fina

Semolina: see Wheat

Sephardim, Sephardic: Sephardim are the descendants of Jews who lived in the Iberian Peninsula for centuries before the expulsion from Spain in 1492 and Portugal in 1497. Those who refused conversion to Christianity were burned at the stake as heretics. Others converted in name only but continued their Judaic religion secretly. As many as

250,000 fled to North Africa and the Middle East, especially to Turkey where they were welcomed by the Ottoman Emperor, Sultan Beyazit II.

The Spanish Jews had been in touch with the center of Jewish life in Babylonia (Iraq). The Babylonian Talmud was for them the ultimate authority in the belief and practice of Judaism.

The Sephardic Diaspora was a fifteenth- and sixteenth-century emigration. The Jews took with them the language, Judeo-Spanish or Ladino as it became known, and the songs and foods of Spain. The traditions, customs and especially their eating habits were integrated into the foods of their new homes.

Sofrito: This is a Ladino (Judeo-Spanish) word, which is translated as a sauté. Egyptians and other Sephardics prepare their regional *sofritos*.

Soojee: *see* Wheat

Sumac *(Rhus coriaria L.)*:   Also known as Sicilian sumac and tanner's sumac. The sumac shrub is grown in the Mediterranean region, around the Caucasus mountains and especially in Iran. The dried reddish powder is a condiment (not a spice but a seasoning) that is often used instead of salt; it has a citric flavor. Persians place it on the table so that it can be sprinkled over meat, rice and vegetable dishes according to taste. Recently, in Istanbul the dish of sumac mixture that was served consisted of 1 tablespoon sumac, 1 tablespoon dried mint leaves and 1 teaspoon hot red chili flakes. Hungry diners used it to sprinkle on their ravioli and salads.

Tamarind *(Tamarindus indica)*:   A legume from the tamarind tree. The pods are filled with a brown acid pulp and seeds. The pulp is soaked in water for about ½ hour and strained. It is this liquid with its unique and attractive flavor that is used in Southeast Asian dishes, especially in India and Indonesia. The tamarind tree also grows and the fruit is used in subtropical Georgia. To prepare a thick tamarind concentrate, dissolve 2 tablespoons of the paste, which can be purchased in Latin American and South Asian groceries, in ½ cup water, and strain through a metal sieve. This liquid may be reduced by half with a few minutes of boiling or it may be used as is. (In Central America the tamarind water is used to prepare a cooling summer drink.)

Teff *(Eragrostis abyssinica)*:   A tropical small-grained, drought-resistant millet grown almost exclusively in Ethiopia. The flour made from teff is used to prepare *injeera*, the Ethiopian Jewish staff of life.

Tachin: Similar to *tadiq*, but with more ingredients and less crispness. The *tachin* includes egg and yoghurt, with a result that is more or less a rice pancake, which becomes the top of the rice when the finished dish is turned upside down.

Tadiq: An essential part of Persian rice dishes. Partially cooked rice is spread over some water, oil and turmeric in a pan to complete the cooking.

Slow cooking over low heat develops a crisp bottom to the rice. Thin slices of either onion or potato may be added to the oil and water to develop an onion- or potato-flavored crust.

T'fina: A contraction of the Spanish word *adafina*, which is translated as "the stew that Spanish Jews used to place on glowing embers on Friday evening to eat on the Sabbath." *T'fina* is the modified colloquial word used by those Jews living in Tunisia and Libya. *Hameem* is the Hebrew word for this Sabbath food used in Baghdad and Calcutta. *Scheena* is the Arabic word used in Morocco.

Wheat *(Triticum aestivum* and *Triticum durum)*: Wheat, an ancient crop, is one of the most important cereals, in fact an indispensable staple of the Western diet. Flour for bread is the best-known product derived from the whole-wheat berry, but there are others. The whole-wheat berries, for example, are cooked whole in Bukhara (see Halesa in Index).
 Bulghur: This is made from wheat berries that have been partially cooked, then cracked. Bulghur may be purchased in several different sizes—large, medium, small, depending on its use and personal preference.
 Jareesha: Cracked wheat, the unprocessed berries that have been cracked into pieces but not cooked.
 Semolina: A derivative of the wheat berry, the purified middlings or the large hard particles left after the wheat has been converted to flour. It is made from durum or other hard types of wheat, rich in gluten, which are the protein fragments in wheat. The color of semolina is usually yellow but can be light eggshell. I buy yellow semolina to prepare *soojee*, the Indian dessert. Semolina is used in the Middle East, Burma, Turkey and other countries. It is also used to make bread in Italy.
 Cream of Wheat and **Farina:** These are semolina products familiar to families who prepare these supermarket cereals for children.

Yufka: These are the round sheets of dough that are used as wrappers in many ways in Turkey. I have seen round pancake sheets that are 24 inches in diameter and about ⅛ inch thick. *Borekas* of several types are prepared with *yufka*. In Izmir the *yufka* is as thin as fillo (or filo), the thin pastry dough usually associated with Greek pastries such as baklava. One can make *yufka* at home and most Jewish homes did so in the not too distant past. Whether you make or purchase it, it is interchangeable with fillo, which is easily available in Middle East groceries and many supermarkets.

In Tunisia, the fillo or *yufka* is known as *brik*; in Morocco it is called *warka*. All of these terms and uses have come from the Ottoman Empire, which had a vast influence on the cuisine of its vassal states from the thirteenth to the twentieth century.

To go one step further, the thin *yufka* are prepared by the Chinese and known as Shanghai spring-roll wrappers. I have used all of these wrappers at one time or another.

Eastern
Mediterranean

TURKEY
GREECE

Cheese maker in Turkey in the 1960s. *(Photo courtesy of Michael Tal)*

TURKEY This is a history that reads like a fable.

The general decree expelling the Jews from Spain in 1492 and its profound impact on Jewish history cannot be underestimated. It was the genesis of the Sephardic way of life throughout North Africa, the Middle East, the Baltics and parts of Europe.

That exclusively church-inspired persecution for the purpose of eradicating Judaism was led by Torquemada, the Grand Inquisitor (who was alleged to have some Jewish blood), and it resulted in conversion, confiscation of property, torture and burning the "heretics" at the stake—all in the name of religion.

In contrast, it was also in 1492 that Christopher Columbus (whose mysterious background may have included Jewish ancestors) left Spain. He, however, was outfitted with the Niña, the Pinta and the Santa Maria—to say nothing of royal support—and sailed westward, looking for India.

At that time, Turkey was the center of the Ottoman Empire, which existed from the late thirteenth century to its decline in 1924 when Kemal Ataturk, the designer of modern Turkey, abolished the Ottoman caliphate. Sultan Beyazit II, who reigned from 1482–1512, responding to the expulsion with compassion but also a degree of opportunism, rescued the Jews from the Inquisition, causing the famous sixteenth-century historian Rabbi Eliyahu Capsali to relate: "So the king of Turkey heard of all the evil that the Spanish king had brought upon the Jews and heard that they were seeking a refuge and resting place. He took pity on them, and wrote letters and sent emissaries to proclaim throughout his kingdom that none of his city rulers may be wicked enough to refuse entry to the Jews or expel them."

After that edict, Turkey, the Middle East and the Balkans opened up their borders. Tens of thousands of expelled Jews came to Turkey. (Were they the boat people of the fifteenth

3

century?) Istanbul, Salonika, Greece and Izmir (formerly Smyrna) became important centers of the Sephardim.

The Iberian Jews of Spain and Portugal were highly educated in the professions, in international trade, finance and medicine, and Sultan Beyazit, knowing this full well, welcomed this transfusion of human talent into Turkey. The Jews brought the first printing press to the Ottoman Empire, for example, and established a printing industry in 1494, two years after the expulsion.

They were not alone in their religion. They found, upon arrival in Turkey, Jews who were long-time inhabitants of the region and known as Romaniates, pre-Ottoman Empire Jews who were named thus through their early Roman connections. These Romaniates were ultimately, after some years, absorbed by the Sephardim.

The Jews lived in their own areas, maintained their own organizations, and created their own cuisine. Jewish men went forth into the cities to work, while the women for the most part remained at home—cooking? A lady from Izmir explained the Jewish cooking by saying that "The Turks borrowed from us and we from them." Cooking rules and recipes were passed down from mother to daughter and resulted in a continuity of culinary ideas throughout the centuries and to the present.

There were two components that combined to develop Sephardic cooking in Turkey—Spanish heritage and Turkish culture. (You will notice that many of these recipes still carry their Spanish or Ladino titles.) This was a gradual osmosis and not a rapid modification of existing cooking styles. The availability of fresh produce is an important factor in the creation of a cuisine and, in this case, new ideas were developed around ingredients that were available and inexpensive, like the eggplant.

Jewish desserts were strongly influenced by the extraordinary capacity for sweets so dear to the Turkish palate. Syrups are lavishly used to enrich the pastries and provide a melting texture to cakes. Strong seasonings are hardly ever used in the Sephardic cuisine except for an occasional sprinkling of hot chili flakes. Chicken, beef and lamb are the meats of choice, but in recent years less beef and lamb are used since red meat is now considered unhealthy. Cholesterol has entered the thinking of the Sephardic kitchen, and has even influenced the choice of cooking oil—sunflower has become the most popular. Duck is never eaten. I never saw a duck in Turkey (nor did I see a turkey!).

The Sephardic kitchen relies on appealing combinations of meats, vegetables or fish served up in casseroles, pies, stuffed vegetables or pastries and *Yufka* (wrapped appetizers and snacks). The tendency is to bake foods or simmer them on top of the stove. The large meat roasts of European cooking are unknown. Bread is the staff of life, and rice, in the form of seasoned and garnished dishes, is not far behind.

In the old city of Istanbul, near the Beyazit Gate of the Grand Bazaar, is the mosque of Sultan Beyazit II. The cemetery where the Sultan rests with his wives and children is nearby. From the street, alive with the fluid mass of humanity that pours in and out of the bazaar, one can see the gray stone stelae that are the tomb markers. I stopped here and wondered whether Beyazit is still remembered. Is anyone aware of his good deeds and the remarkable gesture he made in an era when such things were not done and a false step might have been his last? I got my answer the other day when reading about the plans for the five hundredth anniversary of the Spanish Jews' arrival in Turkey. As part of the quincentennial celebration in Istanbul, the Sultan's mausoleum will be restored. He has not been forgotten.

There are now about 25,000 Jews in Turkey—mostly in Istanbul, but there are small numbers also in Izmir and other cities—still living in tranquility and prosperity. This is the legacy of Beyazit.

FAJONES
Beef and White Bean Stew

Family techniques differ in preparing beans and meat. Some prefer to soak the beans overnight before cooking. Others cook the beans (without soaking) and meat together so that the beans retain their shape. The combination is Turkish home cooking.

1 pound dried white beans
1 tablespoon corn oil
2 pounds boneless beef chuck, cut into 2-inch pieces
2 medium onion, chopped (1 cup)
3 cups water
2 teaspoons paprika
1 teaspoon salt, or to taste

1. Rinse the beans in hot water, drain, and set aside. Heat the oil in a pan over low heat, add the beef and onions, and stir-fry for 5 minutes.

2. Add the water and bring to a boil. Add the beans, paprika, and salt, cover the pan, and cook slowly for about 1½ hours, or until the beans and beef are soft. Add more water if the liquid dries out too quickly.

This is a thick stew in which the beans are cooked until soft but still retain their shape.

Serve warm. Serves 8 with other dishes.

VARIATION: You may use the same amount of dried whole split peas or lentils instead of the white beans. It is not necessary to soak either one overnight, just follow the basic instructions.

HAMIM DE KASTANYA
Beef and Chestnut Stew

Chestnuts are grown in Turkey and are available from September to April. On street corners or busy thoroughfares you will find the vendors selling the roasted chestnuts from their movable carts, toasting them on metal grills. These chestnuts are purchased roasted and can be easily peeled for inclusion in the kastanya.

Hamim is a word used in Baghdad and Calcutta to indicate that the dish is being prepared for the Sabbath. I asked several Jewish ladies if they used the word or knew of its meaning, but they could not explain its use in this recipe. The recipe is an old one and time erases the fine points of its genesis.

3 tablespoons corn or sunflower oil
2 medium onions, chopped (1 cup)
2 tablespoons tomato paste
2 pounds boneless chuck, cut into ½-inch cubes
3 cups water
1 pound potatoes, peeled and cut into ½-inch cubes
1 pound chestnuts, roasted and peeled
1 teaspoon salt, or more to taste
¼ cup chopped flat-leaf parsley for garnish

1. Heat the oil in a pan, add the onions, and stir-fry over moderate heat for 2 minutes, or until they turn golden. Add the tomato paste and beef and stir-fry for 3 minutes more. Add the water, bring to a boil, cover the pan, and cook until the meat is tender, about 45 minutes, and some liquid remains.
2. Add potatoes, chestnuts, and salt and simmer over low heat for 15 to 20 minutes, adding ½ cup water if the liquid has evaporated too quickly. All the ingredients should be soft at this stage and with substantial sauce remaining.
Serve warm garnished with the parsley.
Serves 8 with Turkish pilaf.

NOTE: To toast the chestnuts so that they can be easily peeled, cut or slice out a large gash in the nutshell. They can then be baked in a 350° F. oven for 15 minutes, or in a Teflon skillet on top of the stove until charred. Cool and peel.
Sometimes I cut a large part of the shell off with a serrated knife, put the chestnuts in a pan, cover with hot water, and simmer over low heat for 15 minutes. It is then easy to drain, cool, and peel.

CODRERIO CON FAVA

Lamb and Fresh Fava Beans

The preparation of this Passover dish exemplifies the Turkish preference for the natural taste of ingredients. Only the simplest of seasonings are used here to allow the flavor of the favas to dominate.

> 3 pounds lamb shank or breast of lamb, cut into 3-inch pieces
> 4 cups water
> 3 pounds fresh fava beans
> 1 teaspoon salt, or to taste
> 2 teaspoons sugar
> 4 scallions, sliced into ½-inch pieces

1. Cook the lamb in 2 cups of the water over moderate heat for 5 minutes, stirring several times. Drain well to remove excess fat.

2. Add 2 remaining cups water to the pan, cover, and cook over low heat for 1 hour. This should tenderize the lamb.

3. Trim the fava bean pods on both ends. Cut the pods into 3 equal pieces. Add them to the lamb with the salt, sugar and scallions. Cover the pan and simmer over low heat for 20 minutes, or until the favas are tender. Adjust the salt.

Serve warm. Serves 6.

CABEZAS DE OPYO

Chicken with Celeriac

It is only the celeriac root that is eaten; the green tops are bitter and are discarded. The flavor is that of mild celery and is much appreciated during Passover when the celeriac becomes available on the vegetable stands.

> 4 celeriac roots
> 1 chicken, 3 pounds, cut into 8 pieces, loose skin and fat
>   discarded
> 1 carrot, sliced
> 1 celery rib, sliced diagonally
> 1 teaspoon salt

⅛ teaspoon pepper
2 cups water
juice of 1 lemon

1 Peel the celeriac roots and cut them into ¼-inch-thick slices. Set aside.

2. Put the chicken, carrot, celery, salt, pepper and water in a pan, bring to a boil over moderate heat, and cook, covered, for ½ hour.

3. Put the celeriac slices in a lightly oiled baking dish. Arrange the chicken pieces over the slices and the carrot and celery over that. Pour the broth and lemon juice over all. Bake in a 350° F. oven for 30 minutes.

Serve warm with matzoh and salads. Serves 6.

PESCE KOTCHU
Baked Fish

This dish focuses on the fish itself, simply flavored with tomatoes and lemon juice, a combination that the Turks enjoy.

3 tablespoons corn oil
1 pound fresh ripe tomatoes (about 3), chopped, or an equal
    amount of canned tomatoes
2 large green peppers, seeded, diced
¼ teaspoon black pepper
3 pounds mackerel, cut into 2-inch-wide slices
1 teaspoon salt
juice of 2 lemons (⅓ cup)

1. Heat the oil in a skillet, add the tomatoes, green peppers and black pepper, and sauté over low heat for 10 minutes.

2. Sprinkle the mackerel with salt and let stand for 15 minutes. Put the tomato/pepper mixture on the bottom of a baking dish. Place the fish over this and pour the lemon juice over it. Cover the dish and bake in a 350° F. oven for ½ hour. Uncover and bake for another 15 minutes.

Serve warm with rice and salad. Serves 6 to 8.

PISKADO CON UEVO I LIMON

Fillet of Fish in Egg-Lemon Sauce

T he egg-lemon sauces are classic in Greek and Turkish cooking, seeming more Greek to me than Turkish. For the American kitchen the fillet rather than the whole fish is suggested since it is more easily served. The whole fish when prepared in this recipe can be served with impressive flare and would, of course, be nearer to the old way of home cooking.

2 lemons
3 cups water
½ teaspoon salt
½ cup minced parsley
1 tablespoon corn or sunflower oil
2 pounds fillet of flounder, sea bass, or similar fish
3 egg yolks.

1. Using a pan large enough to hold all the fish in one layer, pour in the juice of 1 lemon, about 3 tablespoons, the water, salt, parsley and oil. Bring to a boil and simmer over moderate heat for 5 minutes. Arrange the fish fillets in the sauce and simmer, uncovered, for 10 minutes, basting now and then.

2. Beat the egg yolks and the juice of the other lemon together. Continue to beat as you slowly add 1 cup of warm fish sauce to the yolks. When the egg-lemon sauce thickens, add it to the pan with the fish and simmer over low heat for 3 minutes. Shake the pan several times to integrate the seasonings.

Remove the fish to a serving platter and cool the sauce.

3. Beat the fish sauce with the incorporated egg yolks and lemon juice until smooth, perhaps 2 or 3 minutes. Pour this over the fish and refrigerate for several hours before serving. The sauce, now cold, converts to a mousselike consistency.

Serve cold. Serves 8.

NOTE: My teacher in Istanbul related that her mother and grandmother did all the beating with a wooden spoon, which was arm-breaking and took much longer than a processor would. Now, of course, modern kitchen equipment gives us results that are not inferior to old-time methods. However, if you do not have a processor, I suggest you use a whisk or old-fashioned eggbeater.

YAPRAKES

Stuffed Grape Leaves

The stuffed grape leaves are eaten cold, and therefore are a vegetarian summer dish for times when the temperature rises. They may be refrigerated until ready to serve as an appetizer with drinks, or used as a snack.

¼ cup corn oil
2 medium onions, cut into small dice (1½ cups)
½ teaspoon salt
1 cup raw rice, well rinsed
1 egg, beaten
bottled grape leaves
juice of 2 lemons (⅓ cup)
1½ cups water

1. Heat the oil in a pan and stir-fry the onions and salt over low heat for 10 minutes, or until onions are golden. Remove to a bowl and cool. Add the rice and egg and mix everything together.

2. Separate the grape leaves and rinse them under cold water. Drain. Put 1 tablespoon of the rice filling on a leaf on the edge nearest you. Fold the leaf firmly over the filling, then tuck in each side and fold over into a round finger shape about 2½ inches long. Prepare all the leaves this way and arrange them in an orderly fashion in a saucepan.

3. Pour the lemon juice and water over all. Cover the pan and cook over low heat for 40 minutes. Test the rice for doneness toward the end of the time. Should the liquid dry out too quickly, add ¼ cup water and continue to cook until all has evaporated.

Cool well and serve at room temperature. Makes about 50.

CHUFLETIKOS

Leek Rolls

Leeks have been cultivated in the Eastern Mediterranean region for several thousand years and the Jews, upon arrival from Spain, found those in Turkey had extremely long leaves. The leeks

I saw in the Izmir market reminded me of the scallions I saw in Korea—with exaggerated long, green leaves and thick ends. It is the white part of the leek that is used in this recipe—ingeniously stuffed, fried, then baked in a light tomato sauce.

8 leeks, white part only
1 thick slice of white bread, softened in water and squeezed dry
     (¾ cup)
1 pound ground beef
1 teaspoon salt, or to taste
¼ teaspoon pepper
1 egg, beaten
½ cup flour
corn or sunflower oil for panfrying
½ cup beef broth
1 tablespoon tomato paste

1. Rinse the leeks well; cut each one lengthwise about halfway to the center. Cover with water, bring to a boil, and cook over moderate heat for about 10 minutes to soften the layers. Drain well. Separate the leek layers into 1 or 2 thicknesses. Set aside.

2. Mix the bread, beef, salt and pepper together. Stuff each leek layer, which is about 3 inches long, with 1 tablespoon of the meat mixture. Roll them in the egg and then in the flour.

3. Heat 3 tablespoons oil in a skillet and brown the leek rolls for about 2 minutes on all sides. Put them in an oiled baking dish. Mix the broth and tomato paste together and pour it into the dish.

Bake in a 350° F. oven for ½ hour.

Serve warm. Serves 8 with other dishes.

PATATAS KAVAKADAS
Beef-Stuffed Potatoes

The Turkish Jews trace this very old recipe to their origins in Spain in the fifteenth century. It seems to be disappearing from the repertoire and exemplifies the danger of our losing many classic ethnic recipes for good. Yet, it is an inventive and extraordinarily tasty preparation, which can be made in quantities for large groups as well as for small families. It could become popular and useful in the American kitchen.

2 pounds medium potatoes (about 8), peeled
1 pound ground beef
1 thick slice of white bread, softened in water, squeezed dry
    (¾ cup)
1 teaspoon salt
¼ teaspoon pepper
flour for dredging
2 eggs, beaten
¼ cup corn or sunflower oil for panfrying
2 cups homemade chicken broth

1. Cut the potatoes lengthwise into halves and scoop out the pulp, leaving a firm wall about ¼ inch thick.
2. Prepare the stuffing: Mix the beef, bread, salt and pepper together. Fill the potato shells with about 2 tablespoons of the mixture. Dredge them all over with flour and then dip into the beaten eggs.
3. Heat the oil in a skillet and brown the potatoes over moderate heat for 3 minutes. Put them in a pan and pour the chicken broth over them. Bring to a boil, cover the pan, and simmer over low heat for ½ hour.
Serve warm with the sauce. Serves 8 with other dishes.

SEVOYA CON CALABASA
Onion and Zucchini Sauté

H ere is another Greek/ Turkish example of a dish where simple seasonings provide a rich flavor, based upon the vegetable ingredients and the slow cooking.

1 tablespoon corn oil
1 large onion, sliced thin (1 cup)
2 ripe tomatoes, chopped (1 cup)
2 pounds zucchini (about 4), peeled, cut into 1-inch-thick slices
1 green pepper, seeded and sliced

¼ teaspoon salt
⅛ teaspoon black pepper
¼ cup raw rice, well rinsed
½ cup water

1. Heat the oil in a pan; add the onion and sauté over moderate heat for 3 minutes. Add tomatoes, zucchini, green pepper, salt and pepper, cover the pan, and simmer for 5 minutes.

2. Add the rice and water, cover the pan, and cook over low heat for 20 minutes.

Serve warm with a salad. Serves 6.

ALBÓNDIGAS DE PRASA KON NUEZ

Leek and Beef Balls with Walnuts

This is a popular and ubiquitous culinary choice of the Turkish. It goes through several stages, rinsing, chopping or slicing, boiling, squeezing, and is then mixed with ground beef and made into a meatball or an oval-shaped cutlet. In this recipe the walnuts add another texture to create something unique as an appetizer or as one of the main dishes at a meal. I enjoyed them in Istanbul for Passover, served with cheese-stuffed tomatoes.

2 pounds leeks, white part only
½ pound ground beef
¼ cup chopped walnuts
2 eggs, beaten
¼ cup matzoh meal
1 teaspoon salt, or to taste
corn or sunflower oil for panfrying

1. Cut the leeks into thin slices, rinse very well to eliminate sand, and cook them in 1 cup water over moderate heat for about 10 minutes, or until soft. Drain and press out excess liquid. Chop fine.

2. Mix the leeks, beef, walnuts, 1 beaten egg, 1 tablespoon of the matzoh meal and the salt. Mix well and prepare balls 1½ inches in diameter. Roll them first in the other beaten egg and then in the balance of matzoh meal.

3. Heat oil in a skillet and fry the balls over moderate heat for 3 minutes, or until browned. Drain on paper towels.

Serve warm. Makes about 20 balls.

VARIATION: In place of the matzoh meal, you may use regular flour for dredging; for a change, you may omit walnuts and use more leeks. In either case, the balls could be shaped as cutlets (2½ inches by ½ inch) rather than meatballs, if you wish.

QUESO CON HUEVO
Cheese and Eggs

The cheese and eggs can also be fried in an oiled skillet over low heat on top of the stove. The texture is similar but would be brown on the bottom instead of the top.

¾ pound farmer cheese, crumbled and mashed
¼ pound feta cheese, crumbled and mashed
6 eggs
¼ teaspoon black pepper
2 tablespoons corn oil

1. Mix the cheeses together. Add the eggs, one at a time, until all have been used. Stir in the pepper.

2. Oil a baking dish and pour in the egg mixture. It should be about 2 inches deep. Bake in a 350° F. oven for 30 minutes.

Serve warm or cold, cut into generous-size cubes. Serve with salad, any fish dish and bread. Serves 6.

FRITADA DE SPINAKA
Baked Spinach and Cheese

Fritada is a Ladino term that the dictionary translates as "a dish of fried food." It might have been fried in earlier days when the average Turkish home did not have an oven, but now, of course, the fritada is baked and served cold as a summer dish.

1 pound fresh spinach, leaves only, well rinsed, chopped fine
½ pound farmer cheese
¼ pound feta cheese
2 eggs, beaten
¼ teaspoon salt
⅛ teaspoon pepper
1 tablespoon corn oil
1 tablespoon grated kashkaval cheese

1. Mix the spinach, farmer and feta cheeses, eggs, salt and pepper together. Pour the oil into a skillet or pan and rub it all over. Add the spinach mixture and smooth over the surface. Sprinkle with the kashkaval cheese. Bake in a 350° F. oven for 30 minutes, or until the top is brown.

Cool well and cut into generous squares.

Serve at room temperature. Serves 6 with salads and bread.

FRITADA DE BERENJA
Baked Eggplant and Cheese

D airy dishes are paramount to the Turkish Jews, and there are many combinations that include cheese, eggs and eggplant. They are essentially summer fare, served cold. They meet our present standards for reducing or even eliminating the excessive amounts of meat that we eat.

1 pound eggplants (about 2), cut into quarters with stems
    trimmed off
½ cup water
2 eggs, beaten
½ pound farmer cheese, mashed
¼ pound feta cheese, mashed
¼ teaspoon pepper
½ teaspoon salt
1 tablespoon corn oil

1. Cook eggplants in the water in a covered pan over moderate heat for 10 minutes, or until soft. Drain well and cool. Remove the pulp and discard skin. Drain the pulp for 5 minutes on paper towels since the eggplants will have too much moisture.

2. Mix the pulp, eggs, cheeses, pepper and salt together. Oil a skillet or pan and pour in the eggplant/cheese mixture.

Bake in a 350° F. oven for 30 minutes, or until the top is brown. Cool and cut into generous squares.

Serve cold. Serves 6 with other summer dishes.

BERENJENO RELLENO CON QUESO
Stuffed Eggplant with Cheese

This meatless dish has an appealing dairy consistency that Jews favor. It may be prepared several hours in advance and then baked just in time for dining.

> 6 small eggplants (2 pounds)
> 2 teaspoons salt
> 3 tablespoons corn or olive oil
> ¼ pound feta cheese, broken up into small pieces
> ½ pound farmer cheese, pressed gently to remove excess liquid
> 2 eggs, beaten
> 4 tablespoons tomato paste
> 1 slice of white bread, soaked in milk and squeezed dry
>   (about ¾ cup)
> ¼ teaspoon pepper
> ⅛ teaspoon paprika
> 1 teaspoon sugar
> ½ teaspoon dried oregano
> ¼ cup water

1. Trim off the stems of the eggplants. Cut eggplants lengthwise into halves and scoop out most of the pulp. leaving a ¼-inch-thick wall. Sprinkle the shells and pulp with the salt and let stand for ½ hour. Gently squeeze the pulp to remove the liquid; rinse the shells with cold water and dry well, using paper towels.

2. Heat 2 tablespoons of the oil in a skillet and stir-fry the pulp over moderate heat for 2 minutes. Cool the mixture. Add the feta and farmer cheeses, eggs, 1 tablespoon of the tomato paste, the bread, pepper and paprika. Mix well. Fill the eggplant shells.

3. Prepare a sauce with the balance of the tomato paste, the sugar, oregano and water. Simmer over low heat for 5 minutes. Spoon over the tops of the stuffed eggplant.

4. Oil a heatproof glass or metal baking dish with the remaining 1 tablespoon oil, arrange the eggplants in it, and bake in a 350° F. oven for 30 minutes.

Serve warm. Serves 6 with other dishes.

ALMODROTE
Cheese and Eggplant Casserole

This *almodrote* is a first course for a traditional Friday evening dinner of the Turkish Jews.

> 2 pounds eggplants (about 3)
> ½ pound farmer cheese, mashed
> ½ pound plus 2 tablespoons kashkaval cheese, grated
> ¼ pound Cheddar or Gruyère, grated
> ¼ cup flour
> 1 slice of white bread, soaked in water, squeezed dry
>   (about ¾ cup)
> 3 eggs, beaten
> ⅛ teaspoon pepper
> 1 tablespoon corn oil

1. Bake the eggplants over charcoal or in a gas or electric broiler until they are tender, about 15 minutes. Cool, peel, chop into small pieces, and drain off any accumulated liquid.

2. Mix the eggplant pulp, cheeses, flour, bread, eggs and pepper together and put the mixture into a well-oiled heatproof glass or metal baking dish. The mixture should be about 1½ inches deep. Bake in a 350° F. oven for ½ hour, or until the top has browned.

Serve hot with hard-cooked eggs. Serves 8.

SFONGO
Baked Spinach and Potato Casserole

Vegetarian in character and assembled in the Jewish fashion, this simple yet attractive casserole is a specialty of the city of Izmir. It is difficult to trace the meaning of the word *sfongo* since the women of the city, who are the cooks, are not concerned with such trifles. It is probably one of the ancient recipes brought from Spain in 1492.

2 pounds potatoes, peeled, quartered
3 tablespoons milk
1½ cups grated kashkaval cheese
½ teaspoon salt, or to taste
6 eggs, beaten
3 pounds spinach, well rinsed in cold water, drained
corn oil

1. Cook the potatoes in water until soft. Drain, mash with the milk, 1¼ cups cheese, the salt and eggs. Mix well and set aside.

2. Chop the spinach rather fine. Mix it with half of the potato mixture. Oil a baking dish; pour in the spinach/potato mixture. Smooth over the surface. Make 6 equidistant depressions in the mixture. Fill each hole with the balance of the potato and sprinkle ¼ cup of the cheese over all.

Bake in a 350° F. oven for ½ hour, or until browned.

Serve warm with other dairy dishes and yoghurt as a side dish. Serves 6.

DOMATES YENAS DE KEZO
Cheese-Stuffed Tomatoes

The vegetables grown in Turkey are full of flavor and of great variety. Tomatoes are especially popular in salads and in this Jewish-style cheese stuffing, which is baked until golden—beautiful to look at as well as to taste. Turkey, the crossroads between Europe and Asia, was a transit point for the Spanish, discoverers of the tomato during their conquest of Mexico. They took it to

Europe and Asia, where it was incorporated into the cuisine.

> 8 medium tomatoes (about 2 pounds)
> 2 teaspoons sugar
> ½ teaspoon salt
> 2 eggs, beaten
> ¼ pound feta cheese, grated
> ¼ pound kashkaval cheese, grated
> oil

1. Cut the top off each tomato and scoop out about half of the pulp, leaving a firm wall. Sprinkle ¼ teaspoon sugar and a few grains of salt into each tomato.

2. Mix eggs and cheeses together. Fill the tomatoes almost to the top but leave room for expansion.

3. Put tomatoes in an oiled baking dish and bake in a 350° F. oven for ½ hour, or until tomatoes are soft but have not become watery.

Serve warm with other dairy dishes. Serves 8.

BAMIA
Baked Okra with Lemon

Following are two methods of preparing okra, that extraordinary plant of the cotton family. It is one of the most honored vegetables in Turkey, in Oriental cooking and also on the Indian subcontinent.

> 1 tablespoon corn oil or chicken fat
> ½ pound ripe tomato, fresh or canned, diced
> ½ teaspoon salt, or to taste
> 1 pound young okra, rinsed and trimmed ⅛ inch from stem
>   and tip
> ½ cup water
> juice of 1 or more lemons, to taste

1. Grease a heatproof glass or other rectangular baking dish with oil or fat. Spread the diced tomato over the bottom and sprinkle with salt.

2. Lay each okra flat over the tomato in one or more layers. Pour the water over all. Bake in a 350° F. oven for about 45 minutes, enough to cook the okra but not long enough to dissolve it into mush. Do not stir during the baking.

Remove the dish from the oven and pour the lemon juice over all.

Serve warm. Serves 6 with other dishes.

VARIATION: *Bamia* may be baked with chicken, a most popular combination. Just place 1 small chicken (2 pounds) or Cornish game hen, cut into 4 pieces, on top of the okra and bake as directed.

HANDRAJO
Eggplant and Zucchini Turnovers

Izmir is a beautiful city in southwest Turkey, situated on an almost perfect bay of the Aegean Sea. Here there is a Jewish community of ancient lineage. My teacher there was a Jewish lady of a certain age with a devotion to her tradition and a knowledge of Ladino and several other languages, all of which helped in the translation and explanation of these recipes. The *handrajo* is a snack or appetizer that originated in Izmir. She explained to me that the dough, as described by old time cooks, should be "as soft as the lobe of your ear."

STUFFING

> 3 tablespoons corn or sunflower oil
> 2 medium onions, chopped (1 cup)
> 2 tomatoes, chopped (1 cup)
> 1 pound zucchini, grated coarsely
> 1 pound eggplant, grated coarsely
> ¼ cup grated kashkaval cheese
> 1 teaspoon salt, or to taste
> ¼ teaspoon pepper

PASTRY

> ½ cup yoghurt
> ¼ cup corn or sunflower oil

2 tablespoons melted margarine
2 tablespoons grated kashkaval cheese
2 cups all-purpose flour, or more if needed
1 egg yolk mixed with 1 teaspoon water

1. To make the stuffing: Heat the oil in a skillet and sauté the onions over moderate heat for several minutes, until they are golden. Add the tomatoes, zucchini and eggplant and continue to stir-fry; cover the pan and simmer for 3 to 4 minutes to reduce the mixture to a paste. Uncover, add the cheese, salt and pepper, and continue to cook to evaporate all the liquid. Set aside.

2. Make the pastry by mixing the yoghurt, oil and margarine in a bowl. Add the cheese and enough flour to produce a soft smooth mixture. Prepare the dough on a well-floured board. Cut off pieces the size of a walnut, and roll out flat cakes 3 or 4 inches in diameter. Put 1 tablespoon of the stuffing on the lower half of each cake and fold over into a half-moon. Bend the two side edges down to round out the shape and seal the edges with the tines of a fork. Paint the surface with the egg yolk. Put the pastries on an oiled baking sheet and bake in a 350° F. oven for ½ hour.

Serve warm or at room temperature, anytime with tea or Turkish coffee.

Makes 25 to 30 turnovers.

TAPADA
Eggplant Pie

There are many, many eggplant recipes in Turkey—perhaps more than in any other culture. They have the long, slender eggplants similar to the Asian variety and the rounded, deep purple type, preferred for this recipe since they are meatier. *Tapada* is a Spanish word and comes from the verb *tapar*, meaning to cover up. We therefore assume that this 2-crust, or covered up, pie has Spanish origins.

2 pounds large eggplants (2 or 3)
1 cup chopped or grated feta cheese
1 cup grated kashkaval cheese
¼ teaspoon pepper
1 recipe Handrajo pastry (preceding recipe)
1 egg yolk mixed with 1 teaspoon water

1. Bake the eggplants over an open gas flame or under an electric broiler for about 15 minutes, long enough to char the surface and add a smoky flavor to the pulp. Turn eggplants around several times during this procedure. Cool; remove and discard charred skin. Chop the pulp fine and let it drain in a colander for 15 minutes, gently pressing out as much of the liquid as you can. Mix in the cheeses and pepper and set aside.

2. Oil a 2-quart rectangular metal or heatproof glass baking dish. Prepare the pastry and roll out half to fit the bottom of the dish and still have enough left to turn up the sides and provide a crust. Add the stuffing and cover with the other half of the pastry. Paint the surface with the egg yolk.

3. Bake in a 350° F. oven for ½ hour, or until the surface of the pie is golden brown.

Serve as a first course in a lunch or dinner or during the tea or coffee hour. Serves 8.

VARIATION:

2 tablespoons corn or sunflower oil
2 medium onions, chopped (1 cup)
1 pound beef, lamb or chicken, ground
1 garlic clove, chopped fine
1 teaspoon salt, or to taste
¼ teaspoon pepper

1. Heat the oil in a skillet and sauté the onions over moderate heat for several minutes, until golden. Add the meat of your preference, garlic, salt and pepper. Stir-fry until the meat changes color. Cool slightly and follow the same directions as for the eggplant stuffing.

SAMSADAS DE QUEZO
Cheese Triangles

Samsadas make admirable appetizers or luncheon items. They may be frozen. To reheat, remove from the freezer and allow to remain at room temperature for 1 hour. Then warm in a 350° F. oven for 10 minutes to renew the crispness.

¼ pound feta cheese, well mashed
1 pound farmer cheese
4 large eggs, beaten
2 tablespoons bread crumbs or matzoh meal
fillo sheets
corn oil
1 egg, beaten, mixed with 1 teaspoon water

1. Mix cheeses, eggs and bread crumbs together well. Set aside. This is the filling.

2. Take 1 fillo sheet and cut it down the center into halves. Fold 1 half together in 3 equal lengths, which leaves the sheet about 2½ inches wide.

3. Put 1 tablespoon of the filling on the bottom of the folded sheet and fold it up to the right edge, then to the left edge, back and forth, until you reach the top of the sheet, making a triangle with each fold. Make certain that the fillo covers the cheese filling. Paint each triangle with beaten egg.

4. Bake in a 350° F. oven for 30 to 40 minutes, or until the triangles are brown.

Serve warm. Makes about 15 triangles.

BULEMAS
Spinach Rolls in Fillo

I have been unable to discover the origin of the title of this recipe, bulemas. Like so many food names, it has been lost in the mists of time. One cook told me the shape was that of a rose but in my opinion it is more like that of a snail.

1 pound spinach, well rinsed and drained
2 eggs, beaten
¼ pound feta cheese, grated or chopped fine
¾ cup grated kashkaval cheese
20 fillo dough sheets
1 egg yolk, mixed with 1 teaspoon water

1. Cut the spinach into thin slices and toss well to dry. Let the spinach air-dry on a kitchen towel for about ½ hour. Then mix it with the eggs and cheeses.

2. Cut the fillo sheets into triangles, the base of which should be 4 to 5 inches. Keep them covered with a damp cloth since fillo dries out quickly. Put 2 tablespoons of the spinach/cheese filling on the bottom edge of the triangle and spread it along the length. Roll the fillo tightly away from you to the point of the triangle. Then turn the roll, which is about ¾ inch thick, around on itself in a circle like a snail, or rose if you wish.

3. Put the *bulemas* on an oiled baking sheet, paint the surface with the egg yolk, and sprinkle a few fragments of grated kashkaval on the top of each snail. Bake in a 350° F. oven for ½ hour.

Serve warm on Friday evenings for the Sabbath with hard-cooked eggs, also known as Huevos Haminados (see Index).

Makes about 20 *bulemas*.

OJALDRES
Light, Crispy Spinach Rolls

The Jewish ladies of Izmir in southwest Turkey are good cooks and follow the traditions of their ancestors. Ladino, the Judeo-Spanish, is still spoken here now and then, and well-bred people also speak French as well as Turkish. There was a thriving Jewish community in Izmir (formerly Smyrna) for centuries but now it is reduced to a handful. The *ojaldres* that I tasted were characteristic of all pastry made by the light hand of a good cook.

The lady in Izmir emphasized the importance of the spinach being dry before mixing it into the filling. She suggested slicing the spinach and letting it dry in the kitchen overnight to eliminate as much moisture as possible (or see directions for Bulemas).

½ pound fresh spinach, sliced very thin, rinsed well and drained
1 egg, beaten
¼ teaspoon salt
2 tablespoons plus 1 teaspoon grated kashkaval or
    Parmesan cheese
1 teaspoon corn or sunflower oil, plus oil for the fillo
10 fillo sheets, 12 × 17 inches
1 egg yolk, beaten with 1 teaspoon water

1. Mix the spinach, egg, salt, 2 tablespoons grated cheese and the 1 teaspoon oil together. Toss the mixture to integrate the ingredients. Set aside.

2. Divide the fillo sheets lengthwise into 3 parts. They will be 4 inches wide and 17 inches long. Oil each sheet lightly with a pastry brush and fold over lengthwise so that each sheet is about 2 inches wide.

3. Put 1 tablespoon of the spinach mix at one narrow end of the fillo and roll it up the length of the sheet. Put the roll on an oiled baking sheet, paint with egg yolk, and sprinkle with a few grains of the 1 teaspoon grated cheese. Bake in a 350° F. oven for 15 minutes, or until brown and crisp.

Serve warm or at room temperature with sweet Turkish coffee. Makes 20 rolls.

PITA DE ZEBOYA
Onion Pie

Fillo sheets are delicate and must be handled with care so that they do not crumble. Dribbling a few drops of oil here and there on the sheets encourages crispness.

> 3 tablespoons corn oil
> 1 pound onions, peeled, coarsely chopped
> ¼ teaspoon pepper
> ¼ pound feta cheese, mashed up
> ¼ cup bread crumbs
> 2 large eggs, beaten
> 7 sheets of fillo
> oil for painting fillo

1. In the 3 tablespoons corn oil, sauté the onions and pepper in a covered pan over low heat for about 20 minutes so that the onion will cook down. Stir the mixture now and then. Cool for 15 minutes.

2. Mix in the cheese, bread crumbs and all but 1 tablespoon of the beaten eggs. Set aside.

3. Oil a heatproof glass or metal baking dish. Take 3 fillo sheets, one at a time, oiling and fitting one after the other on the bottom of

the baking dish, and bringing each sheet up around the inside of the dish as though it were a piecrust. Pour the onion/cheese mixture into the dish. Cover with 4 fillo sheets, oiling each one with a pastry brush as before. Oil the last sheet up to and around the edges. Paint the entire top with the remaining tablespoon of egg.

Bake in a 350° F. oven for about 40 minutes, or until the top is crisp and brown. At this stage it is possible to lift up one corner of the pie with a metal spatula to see if the fillo bottom has browned.

Serve warm, cut into slices or squares. Serves 6.

PITA DE SPINAKA
Spinach Pie for Passover

In my opinion, substituting sheets of matzoh in place of the fragile sheets of fillo (which are not kosher for Passover) is ingenious. It results in a different taste and is an admirable solution for the kosher kitchen.

1½ pounds fresh spinach
3 eggs, beaten
½ teaspoon salt
⅛ teaspoon pepper
¼ cup matzoh meal
4 sheets of matzoh
2 tablespoons corn oil
1 tablespoon chopped walnuts

1. Wash the spinach well to remove sand and drain it. Coarsely chop the stems and leaves. Mix with the eggs, salt, pepper and matzoh meal. Set aside.

2. Moisten the sheets of matzoh with cold water, just enough to soften but not so much that they break up.

3. Rub a heatproof glass or metal baking dish about 9 × 6 × 2 inches with all but 1 teaspoon of the oil. Put 2½ sheets of moist matzoh—big enough to turn up around the edges—on the bottom of the dish. Add the spinach mixture and cover with 1½ sheets matzoh for the pie cover. Brush with 1 teaspoon oil and sprinkle the walnuts over the top.

Bake in a 350° F. oven for 30 minutes.

Serve warm, cut into generous squares or triangles. Serves 6.

VARIATIONS:

1. Mix ½ pound ground beef with the spinach, eggs, salt, pepper and matzoh meal, and proceed as for the spinach pie.

2. Or chop ¼ pound farmer cheese and ¼ pound feta cheese. Mix this with the spinach, eggs, salt, pepper and matzoh meal, and proceed as for the spinach pie. This cheese variation could be (but is not, traditionally) eaten during Passover, but it is usually prepared for other days.

PASTEL DE CARNI
Meat Pie for Passover

A popular Passover dish for the Seders or for any day. Moist matzohs are shaped to provide a piecrust. Meat, onion, eggs and seasonings are combined as a filling and the entire production is baked.

> 1½ pounds boneless beef chuck, cut into 2-inch pieces
> 4 medium onions, coarsely cut (2 cups)
> 1 teaspoon salt
> ¼ teaspoon pepper
> 1 cup water
> ¼ cup matzoh meal
> 3 eggs, beaten
> 4 sheets of matzoh
> 1 tablespoon corn oil
> ½ cup strong hot chicken broth

1. Put the beef, onions, salt, pepper and water in a pan, cover, and cook over low heat for 45 minutes to tenderize the meat and evaporate almost all the liquid. Cool the mixture and grind it coarsely. Mix this with the matzoh meal and eggs. Set aside.

2. Soften each sheet of matzoh with just enough cold water so that you can handle them without breaking them. Cut one of the matzoh sheets into 1-inch strips.

3. Oil a heatproof glass or metal baking dish that is about 9 × 6 × 2 inches with 2 teaspoons oil. Fit the matzoh strips tightly around the inside edges of the dish to prepare the piecrust. Fit 1½ sheets of matzoh on the bottom of the dish and fit tightly against the edges.

4. Pour in the meat mixture. Cover this with 2 matzohs or as many as needed to make the top of the pie. Brush the top with 1 teaspoon oil.

Bake in a 350° F. oven for 40 minutes. Remove from the oven and pour over the chicken broth, which will be absorbed immediately.

Serve warm. Serves 8 with other dishes.

PANJAR OR SHALGAN
Beet Salad

The origins of this salad are Spanish, Sephardic and Turkish. If you ask the origin of a Greek or Turkish Jew, he will frequently reply, "Spanish." Their language is Ladino, the Spanish/Sephardic/Judeo language of those who left Spain in 1492.

¼ cup wine vinegar
2 tablespoons olive oil
2 teaspoons sugar
1 garlic clove, chopped fine
1 small onion, cut into thin slices (⅓ cup)
2 pounds canned beet slices, well drained
¼ cup stuffed olives

1. Mix the vinegar, oil, sugar and garlic together well.
2. Put the onion, beets and olives in a salad bowl. Pour the dressing over and toss the salad several times.

Served chilled or at room temperature. Serves 8.

TEZPISHTI
Passover Nut Cake in Syrup

This wonderful cake is a Passover favorite for visiting friends and foreigners from New York. Like so many Turkish sweets, the cake is bathed in a syrup that keeps it moist but not soggy. The cool syrup is poured over the hot cake when it is removed from the oven. Almonds are the nut of choice but there are those who prefer the flavor of walnuts.

SYRUP

> 2 cups sugar
> 2 cups water
> 2 teaspoons lemon juice

CAKE

> 5 eggs
> 1 cup sugar
> ¼ cup corn or sunflower oil
> juice and grated rind of 1 orange
> 2 teaspoons ground cinnamon
> 1¼ cup Passover fine matzoh cake meal
> 1¼ cup finely chopped blanched almonds

1. First make the syrup. Mix the sugar and water together in a pan and bring to a boil. Add the lemon juice and simmer over low heat for 10 minutes. Cool the syrup.

2. To make the cake, beat the eggs until frothy, add the sugar, and continue to beat until golden and well mixed.

3. Add all the other ingredients, one at a time, and stir them into the batter. Pour into an oiled and floured cake pan, 13 × 9 × 2 inches, and bake in a 350° F. oven for 30 minutes. Test the doneness with a toothpick.

4. Remove the cake from the oven and pour the cooled syrup over it. Let it stand for 2 hours before serving to allow the syrup to be absorbed.

Serve at any Passover event, but especially with Turkish coffee. Makes 1 cake, about 18 pieces.

BOREKAS DE NUEZ U DE ALMENDRA
Walnut or Almond Turnovers

Turkish Jews have innumerable variations of turnovers both as sweets and savories—the stuffing determines which. In this case, personal preference indicates whether one should use walnuts or almonds or half of each. The *borekas* are a popular sweet for Purim and can be prepared in large quantities to be frozen after baking. Let them thaw out for 1 hour before gently warming in the oven.

PASTRY

> 2 eggs, beaten
> ½ cup sugar
> ¼ cup corn oil
> 2 tablespoons margarine, melted
> 2 cups flour (about)
> 1 egg yolk mixed with 1 teaspoon water (for painting surface)

STUFFING

> ½ pound shelled walnuts or almonds, chopped fine in a
>   processor
> 1 egg yolk
> 1 tablespoon sugar
> 2 tablespoons strawberry, cherry or raspberry jam
> ⅛ teaspoon ground cinnamon

1. Mix all the pastry ingredients (except for the egg yolk mixed with water) together and prepare the pastry. Knead well for a soft, manageable dough, adding enough flour to produce the proper consistency. Cover and set aside. Mix stuffing ingredients together thoroughly.

2. Roll out about 1 heaping tablespoon of the pastry on a lightly floured board to 3 or 4 inches in diameter for each *boreka*. Put 1 tablespoon of the nut mixture on the bottom half of each pastry round. Fold the top over to shape a half-moon. Press down firmly with the tines of a fork to seal. Paint the surface of each *boreka* with the egg yolk and water mixture.

3. Put them on an ungreased baking sheet and bake in a 350° F. oven for ½ hour, or until lightly brown.

Serve at room temperature with tea or Turkish coffee.

Makes about 20.

SEMOLA
Semolina Pudding

Milk puddings are frequently seen served in restaurants and for sale in pastry shops in Istanbul where I first encountered this dessert. It is a dairy dish and should not be served after meat since that would contravene the dietary laws.

1 cup sugar
1 cup milk
4 cups water
grated rind of 1 lemon
1 cup semolina flour
cinnamon for garnish

1. Mix the sugar, milk, water and grated lemon rind together in a pan large enough to hold all ingredients. Bring to a boil and continue to simmer over low heat.

2. Gradually add the semolina, stirring continuously with a wooden spoon for about 10 minutes. When the mixture becomes thick, pour it into a serving bowl and lightly sprinkle with cinnamon.

Refrigerate and serve cold. Serves 6 to 8.

VARIATION: During Sukkoth the *semola* is prepared with all milk rather than a mixture of milk and water. This provides a richer, smoother consistency, which you may prefer any time during the year.

COMPOTE DE FRUTA SECA
Compote of Dried Fruits

There are not many desserts served at Passover but a fruit compote, especially with the very fine Turkish dried fruit, is especially popular.

1 pound mixed dried fruits such as apricots, figs, pears, raisins
3 cups water
2 tablespoons sugar
juice of 1 lemon

1. Rinse the fruits and drain. Cover with the water in a bowl and soak for 4 to 6 hours.

2. Put the fruits, soaking liquid and sugar in a pan, bring to a boil, and cook, covered, over low heat for about 35 minutes. Remove the pan from the heat, add the lemon juice, and let stand for 2 hours to absorb the liquid. Refrigerate.

Serve cold. Serves 6.

BIMBRIO
Quince Jelly

During the month of March that I spent in Turkey on one of my cooking sprees, the large golden quince was a common sight on fruit barrows and in shops. The markets and sidewalk vendors of Izmir were displaying the beautiful yellow fruit, and eager buyers were making their purchases. This recipe is from Izmir where I first tasted this jelly made from one of my favorite fruits. In New York, large knobby quinces are available during October and November.

2 pounds quinces (2 or 3)
1 teaspoon lemon juice
water to cover
enough sugar to equal the amount of pulp

1. Do not peel the quinces but cut them into 1-inch cubes. Discard the cores. Cover with water in a large enough pan and cook over moderate heat until soft enough to mash, about ½ hour.

2. Pour off excess liquid and push the soft quince pulp through a colander or strainer. Measure the pulp and add an equal amount of sugar. Three cups of pulp would require 3 cups of sugar. Put the pulp, sugar and lemon juice into a pan and cook over low heat, stirring frequently, until the mixture is thick and firm. This should take about ½ hour.

Turn out the jelly into small bowls or glass dishes. Cool well. Serve this clear, translucent jelly with tea or coffee as a sweet.

N O T E : If the jelly does not jell firmly enough to slice, then it can be used as a breakfast jam. In any event, the taste of quince, an ancient fruit once admired by the Romans, can be appreciated in any condition.

MUSTACHUDO
Almond Sweet for Passover

These nut sweets are usually prepared in advance of Passover and served during the days of the Seders and afterward.

1 cup sugar
1 cup water
2 cups ground almonds or walnuts, or half and half
1 egg, beaten
confectioners' sugar

1. Mix the sugar and water together in a pan and bring to a boil. Simmer over low heat for 5 to 10 minutes.

2. Add the almonds and continue to cook for 5 minutes or a little more so that the mixture will become firm. To test this, take 1 teaspoonful, cool it enough to handle, and roll it in a ball to see if it holds together. If it does not, cook the mixture for another 2 or 3 minutes.

3. Remove the pan from the heat, let it cool for 2 minutes, then pour the egg into the mixture and stir it in rapidly. Cool well, then shape the paste into balls 1 inch in diameter. When the balls are completely cool, roll them in confectioners' sugar.

Serve with Turkish coffee. Makes about 25 balls.

HAROSETH PARA PESACH
Passover Haroseth

The Ashkenazi Jews of Europe use the word *haroseth* for this Passover ritual dish. The Indians and Persians call it *halek*.

¾ cup dark raisins
2 pounds seeded dates
1 apple, peeled and sliced
1 cup red wine, not too dry

1. Grind the fruits together. Add the wine and mix well.
Place on the Seder table.
Makes about 6 cups.

GREECE
The Jewish presence in the Aegean dates back at least to the third century B.C., when they experienced the "glory that was Greece." Large communities of Jews were found on the islands of Rhodes and Crete, and also in Thessalonika, after the Roman destruction of the Second Temple in Jerusalem in 70 A.D. About 110,000 Jews lived in Greece in the early second century. The Jews were always moving or fleeing during those days, and Asia Minor was a tempting and not-too-distant refuge from Palestine.

On the island of Rhodes there was an ancient community, both Hellenistic and Roman, dating from the Roman era (142 B.C.), and continuing through the Christian Byzantine Empire and the Arabic Islamic conquest. During the benevolent Ottoman empire in the thirteenth century, Rhodes became an important Sephardic center with a population ranging from two to four thousand Jews. In 1912 Rhodes fell under Italian rule. In World War II, the Nazis destroyed the community. The Jews of the pre-Islamic Byzantine Empire were called Romaniates, or those who were citizens at the time of the Romans. But most of the Greek Jews can trace their origins to the 1492 expulsion from Spain, when their ancestors found a haven in Turkey and Greece.

Jews arrived in Salonika about 140 B.C. For several centuries under the Ottoman Empire Salonika was the principal religious and cultural center of the Jews for Judaic studies and was an example for all other Sephardic communities. It was a Greek city but with a population of about 60,000 Jews who influenced all walks of life.

There was an overlapping, rather than a sharp differentiation, between Jewish life in Greece and Turkey. Both countries were of the Ottoman Empire and there was a homogenization of both culinary and cultural Judaic activities. Without doubt, the Ottoman was the single strongest influence on the cooking—with emphasis on the sweets. But the native recipes

Jewish fruitseller in Salonika.

were supplemented by those brought from Spain by the Jews, and those recipes continued to carry Ladino titles.

As in Turkey, the cooking consists largely of casseroles in the ovens, stews on top of the stove, and preparations wrapped in fillo (culminating in the great classic Spanakopeta). Vegetables are important ingredients in this cooking, stewed or enrobed in fillo. Strong seasonings are even less important to the Greek palate than to the Turkish. The flavors result from the natural combinations of poultry, lamb, or fish and a variety of herbs and greens. The reign of the eggplant in Greece and Turkey is permanent. There are those who say that Greek cooking is no more than a satellite of the Turkish, but I am not of this opinion.

No cuisine is established in isolation nor is Sephardic cooking in Greece a carbon copy of that found in Turkey, although both clearly show the Ottoman influence. The Greek dishes found in these pages are inventive and compelling, and the people of the Greek Sephardic community are just as chauvinistic and nostalgic for the foods eaten during the lost days of youth as are any other people.

At the time of writing this book (1991) there are about 6,000 Jews in all of Greece, with 1,000 in Athens and the balance principally in Salonika. The Holocaust was responsible for the destruction of 96%, or over 100,000 Jews in Greece alone.

HUEVOS HAMINADOS
Jewish Eggs

I can only refer to *haminados* as Jewish eggs since no other culture that I know of prepares them this way. I have eaten them in Calcutta among the Baghdadis, in Izmir and Istanbul, Turkey, Greece, Tunisia and Morocco. The eggs in their shells are served in Turkey at the Passover Seders as well as on other days. In Calcutta, they are roasted overnight with the chicken and so they are known as Sabbath eggs.

Eggshells are porous and absorb the flavors of the medium in which they are cooked. The longer one cooks them at very low heat, the softer they become instead of the reverse. In this Greek recipe from Salonika the outer shells become dyed to a rich maroon color and the inner egg white also takes on some of the color. They can be served with salads, eaten out of hand with drinks, or connected with a ritual as they are on Passover.

    6 raw eggs in the shell, at room temperature
    1 teaspoon salt
    ⅛ teaspoon pepper
    ½ teaspoon tea leaves
    ½ teaspoon coffee grounds
    3 or 4 onion skins for color
    1 teaspoon corn oil
    1 teaspoon vinegar

1. Put everything into a pan and cover the eggs well with water. Bring to a boil, cover the pan, reduce the heat to low, and cook for at least 5 hours, preferably 6. Add water now and then as it evaporates. Then drain, rinse the shells, and refrigerate.

Remove the shells and serve when wanted.

FASOLADA
White Bean Soup

"**M**eat is money," they say, and therefore a meatless soup means money in the bank. This substantial winter soup provides enough sustenance to feed a large family (with a shortage of cash).

    2 pounds dried white beans
    1 teaspoon salt
    ¼ teaspoon pepper
    8 cups water
    1 pound potatoes (about 4), quartered
    ¼ pound celery heart with leaves, cut into thick slices
    ¼ cup tomato paste

1. Cover the beans with water and soak overnight, then drain.

2. Put the beans, salt, pepper and 8 cups of water in a large pan. Bring to a boil, then simmer over low heat, covered, for 1½ hours.

3. Add the potatoes and celery and cook for ½ hour more. Add the tomato paste and simmer over low heat for 15 minutes.

Serve hot with black olives. Serves 6 to 8.

KOTO SUPA AVGOLEMONO
Chicken Egg-Lemon Soup

Egg-Lemon Soup with chicken (I have also had it with a lamb base) is probably the most typical if not the national soup of Greece. It has worked its way into the Jewish kitchens and a friend in Athens told me that in her family it always broke the fast at the end of Yom Kippur. One can only hope that the following recipe helps it achieve the status of a culinary icon in the American kitchen, since it is a classic.

1 whole chicken, 3 pounds, loose skin and fat discarded
8 cups water
several whole sprigs of flat-leaf parsley
1 whole medium onion, peeled
1 teaspoon salt
⅓ cup raw rice, well rinsed
2 eggs
juice of 2 lemons
2 teaspoons cornstarch, dissolved in 3 tablespoons cold water
chopped parsley
ground pepper

1. Put the whole chicken, water, parsley, onion and salt in a large pan and bring to a boil. Spoon off and discard the foam that accumulates. Cover the pan and let the soup simmer over moderate heat for 45 minutes, long enough to create a broth and tenderize the chicken. Remove the chicken and parsley, cut the meat off the bones, discard the bones, and cut meat into cubes. Set aside.

2. Add the rice to the broth and continue to cook for 10 minutes. Remove the onion, mash it well, and return it to the soup.

3. Beat the eggs; slowly add the lemon juice and the cornstarch mixture while continuing to beat. Turn off the heat under the soup. Take 1 cup of the hot soup and add it tablespoon by tablespoon to the eggs, beating all the time until the whole cup has been incorporated.

4. Add the cup of egg-lemon mixture to the pot, stirring it into the soup in the same direction as you have beaten the eggs. This is to prevent the eggs from curdling.

5. Add several cubes of cooked chicken per person to the soup pot—a taste of chicken for each serving.

Serve hot, garnished with chopped parsley and pepper to taste. Serves 6.

KIFTE DE PRASA
Leek and Beef Patties

The *kifte* are served on Passover by both Greek and Turkish communities. As a convenience, the patties are prepared in advance of dining, even several hours, then reheated in the hot broth. Of course, the *kifte* may be prepared for serving at any other time during the year, in which case bread crumbs may be used instead of matzoh meal.

4 large leeks, well trimmed and rinsed to remove sand
1 pound ground beef
½ teaspoon salt, or to taste
¼ teaspoon white pepper
¼ cup matzoh meal
2 large eggs, beaten
oil for panfrying
⅓ cup hot chicken broth

1. Cut the leeks into thin slices and cook them in ½ cup water in a covered pan for about 10 minutes, or until soft. Do not overcook since they become mushy. Drain well and press out the liquid gently.

2. Mix the leeks, beef, salt, pepper, matzoh meal and eggs together. Using about ⅓ cup of the mixture, shape a round patty ½ inch thick. Shape patties of all the mixture.

3. Heat the oil in a skillet and fry the patties over moderate heat until done, about 3 minutes. Fry all the patties in this way and set aside in the pan until ready to be served. Pour the hot chicken broth over the patties and cook over moderate heat until all the broth has evaporated.

Serve warm. Makes 10 patties.

NOGADA (KEFTIKA)
Meatballs in Walnut Sauce

There are not many beef dishes in a country that emphasizes lamb. This Jewish preparation is from Salonika, which was the center of Jewish life in Greece from the fifteenth century until World War II.

MEATBALLS

1 pound ground veal
2 slices of Italian-style bread, well moistened and squeezed dry
    (about ⅔ cup)
1 small onion, grated (⅓ cup)
¼ cup chopped flat-leaf parsley
1 teaspoon salt, or to taste
¼ teaspoon pepper
⅛ teaspoon ground allspice
1 egg, beaten
1 cup water
1 teaspoon lemon juice

SAUCE

2 tablespoons chopped flat-leaf parsley
¼ cup shelled walnuts, coarsely chopped
1 tablespoon bread crumbs
salt

1. Mix all the ingredients for the meatballs together except the water and lemon juice. Prepare meatballs 1½ inches in diameter.

2. Bring the water and lemon juice to a boil in a pan. Add the meatballs one at a time and simmer over low heat for 20 minutes. Remove the balls and set aside. Reserve the liquid.

3. Add enough additional water to the reserved liquid from the meatballs to make 1 cup. Bring this to a simmer in a pan over low heat. Add the parsley, walnuts, bread crumbs and salt to taste. Cook for 5 minutes to allow the bread crumbs to thicken the sauce. Add the meatballs and cook for 5 minutes more.

Serve warm. Serves 6 with other Sephardic dishes.

DOMATES KE PIPRIYA
Meat-Stuffed Peppers

    6 medium-size green peppers
    1 pound ground beef
    ½ cup raw rice, well rinsed
    ½ cup chopped parsley, leaves only
    1 teaspoon salt
    ¼ teaspoon pepper
    1 cup water
    2 tablespoons tomato paste

1. Cut out the stem end of each pepper, and scoop out and discard seeds and ribs.

2. Mix together the beef, rice, parsley, salt and black pepper. Stuff each pepper about ¾ full to allow for the expansion of the rice. Put the peppers in an oiled baking dish.

3. Mix the water and tomato paste together and pour it into the pan. Cover and bake in a 350° F. oven for 45 minutes. Uncover and bake for 10 minutes more. There is very little sauce.

Serve warm.

VARIATIONS:

TOMATO

Use 6 medium-size ripe but firm tomatoes. Cut ¾ of the way through the top of each tomato, leaving the top attached. This is the lid that one lifts up to scoop out most of the inside, leaving a firm wall. Mix the tomato centers with the beef, rice, parsley, salt, and black pepper. Stuff the tomatoes, put into a roasting pan, and pour the sauce around. Bake in a 350° F. oven for 45 minutes; uncover and bake for 10 minutes more.

EGGPLANT

Use 6 small eggplants weighing a total of about 1½ pounds. Cut the blossom ends of each eggplant (not the stem ends) crossways, 3 inches deep, so that you have an opening with 4 prongs. Bring 2 cups water to a boil in a large pan, add the eggplants, cover, and cook for 8 to 10 minutes. Drain well and cool. Open the prongs of each eggplant and stuff it with about ½ cup of the same meat/rice stuffing used for all the vegetables. Put the eggplants in a baking dish and follow the same steps as for other vegetables.

SQUASH

Yellow summer squash or zucchini. Cut off the stem ends of the squashes. Scoop out and discard the interior, leaving a firm wall. Use the same stuffing and system of cooking as for the green peppers.

QUARTICO
Beef and Matzoh Pie for Passover

The Ladino name of this dish, quartico, as explained to me by a Jewish lady in Athens, was used because the pie was cut into squares or pieces. Words that were used for centuries without the etymology being recorded have a tendency to become vague in their translation. In any event, this richly made Passover pie, although a one-dish meal, is usually served with Huevos Haminados (see Index) and a simple salad of cucumber and tomato.

BROTH

1 pound beef bones
8 cups water
2 teaspoons salt
1 large handful of flat-leaf parsley sprigs.

STUFFING

1 pound ground beef
2 medium onions, chopped (1 cup)
3 or 4 large sprigs of flat-leaf parsley, chopped (¼ cup)
½ teaspoon pepper
1 teaspoon salt
½ cup water
1 egg yolk

PIE

10 to 12 sheets of matzoh
⅓ cup chopped walnuts
3 eggs, beaten
1 tablespoon corn oil

1. Put broth ingredients into a large pan or pressure cooker and prepare about 6 cups of broth. Simmer over low heat for at least 1 hour—or 2. Strain the broth and set aside until it is cool.

2. Make stuffing: Put the beef, onions, parsley, pepper and salt in a dry pan and stir-fry over moderate heat for 3 minutes, until the color of the beef changes. Add the water and cook until all the liquid evaporates, about 15 minutes. Cool the mixture and stir in the egg yolk.

3. Assemble the pie: When the broth cools, moisten the matzohs in it for 1 minute—don't let them disintegrate. Put a double layer of the matzoh, 4 sheets, on the bottom of a well-oiled heatproof baking dish, 8 × 12 × 2 inches. Break the sheets if necessary to fit the bottom. Cover the matzoh with half of the beef stuffing. Scatter over it 3 tablespoons walnuts.

4. Add 4 more sheets of the moistened matzoh to cover the stuffing. Add the balance of the stuffing and 3 more tablespoons walnuts. Add 2 sheets of matzoh, a single layer, to cover the top of the pie, and pour the beaten eggs over it. Sprinkle 2 tablespoons walnuts over all.

5. Carefully pour 2 cups beef broth and the corn oil over the top. Bake the pie in a 325° F. oven for 1 hour. Every 15 minutes pour 1 cup of broth over the top to soften the interior.

The pie should be brown and soft with a crisp top.

Serve warm or cool. Serves 8 to 10 with other dishes.

KLEFTIKO
Patriot's Roast Lamb

This dish originated during the eighteenth century when Greek patriots under the Turkish occupation hid out and prepared their food in the hills. They dug a hole in the ground in which they fitted a clay pot known as a *pithari*. The lamb and other ingredients were put into the pot, which was covered tightly. Hot charcoal bricks were placed below and above the pot, which was then covered with earth and the contents baked for a number of hours—well concealed from the Turkish troops. Nowadays this simple, nourishing pot roast can be reproduced in an oven with very slow cooking.

    4 pounds lamb shank, cut into 3-inch pieces
    6 small whole onions (1 pound), peeled
    6 small whole potatoes (1½ pounds), peeled
    6 to 8 bay leaves
    2 teaspoons salt
    ¼ teaspoon ground pepper

1. Preheat the oven to 375° F. for 15 minutes.
2. Put all the ingredients in a heatproof glass dish or ceramic pot that has a cover. I also seal the top with aluminum foil. Bake in a 250° F. oven for 4 to 5 hours. Uncover and serve hot immediately.
Serves 6.

ARMIKO
Lamb Innards for Passover

This sauté is a typical Jewish dish for Passover. The Pascal lamb is associated with the Seder ritual, as it is with the Christian Easter ritual, both holidays occurring at similar times. The innards are one of my favorite foods although I may be in the minority.

This is a dish from Athens, where the Jewish food is regionally different from that found in Salonika, yet a common theme exists.

1½ pounds lamb liver, heart and kidneys
1 bunch of scallions (5 or 6), chopped
½ cup chopped fresh dill
2 tablespoons corn oil
1 teaspoon salt, or to taste
¼ teaspoon pepper
3 cups water
⅓ cup chopped walnuts
½ cup matzoh meal

1. Cut the innards into ½-inch cubes. Put them in a pan with the scallions and dill and stir-fry without oil over moderate heat for 3 to 4 minutes to sear them. Add the oil, salt, pepper and half of the water. Bring to a boil and add the rest of the water. Cook, covered, for about 1 hour to tenderize everything.

2. Add the walnuts and matzoh meal, which absorbs the liquid. Stir the mixture well for a minute.

Serve hot during Passover. Serves 6.

GALLINA AL HORNO
Roast Chicken for Passover

This is a simple roast for Passover. It is usually served with the Kifte de Prasa (see Index). It should be noted that some Greek families did not eat boiled potatoes on Passover since they consider that a cooked potato "rises up" like leavened bread. Rice is another food that is forbidden on Passover, yet the Jews of India do eat rice throughout the year. The Passover laws vary from region to region, each community establishing its own tradition.

1 large carrot, sliced
2 celery ribs, leaves and stems, sliced
1 chicken, 3 pounds, quartered, loose skin and fat discarded
1 teaspoon salt, or to taste
¼ teaspoon white pepper
1 cup water

1. Put the vegetables on the bottom of an oiled roasting pan; place the chicken on top. Sprinkle with salt and pepper and pour the water around.

2. Cover the pan and bake in a 350° F. oven for ½ hour. Uncover and bake for about ½ hour more to brown the chicken. Baste now and then.

Serve warm with rice or boiled potato. Serves 4.

PRASA MI KOTA
Chicken Roast with Leeks

The natural flavor of a quantity of leeks combined with lemon and chicken is what gives this dish a characteristic Greek flavor.

1 chicken, 3½ pounds, cut into 8 serving pieces, most of the skin
  and fat discarded
1 cup water
1 teaspoon salt
¼ teaspoon pepper
5 large leeks, white part only, well rinsed to remove sand
3 tablespoons fresh lemon juice
¼ teaspoon paprika

1. Put the chicken pieces in a heatproof glass or metal baking dish. Pour the water in and sprinkle with salt and pepper. Bake in a 350° F. oven for ½ hour.

2. Cut the leeks into ¾-inch pieces and cover the chicken with these. Pour the lemon juice over the leeks and sprinkle the paprika over all. Cover the roasting pan with aluminum foil or the pan cover and continue to bake for 20 minutes. Remove the cover, baste well, and bake for another 15 minutes. Much of the liquid may evaporate; the leeks become soft and the chicken is lightly browned.

Serve warm. Serves 6 with other dishes.

PAPOUTSAKIA

Stuffed and Baked Eggplant

The Greek title means "small shoes" and thereby indicates the Greek origin of the recipe. Otherwise, most of the recipes that are in a direct line from Spain to the Ottoman Empire are usually titled in Ladino, the Judeo-Spanish language. To complicate the matter further, an Athenian told me they were known as "Jewish boats" because of their shape.

> 2 pounds small Italian eggplants, 3 to 4 inches long
> 1½ teaspoons salt
> ½ pound feta cheese, crumbled
> 3 eggs
> ½ cup matzoh meal or bread crumbs
> 1 tablespoon chopped flat-leaf parsley
> ½ teaspoon pepper
> ¼ cup corn or sunflower oil

1. Bring 6 cups of water and ½ teaspoon of the salt to a rapid boil in a large pan. Cut the eggplants lengthwise into halves, add them to the pan, and cook over moderate heat for 10 minutes, or long enough to soften the pulp. Drain well and cool.

2. Scoop out most of the pulp from each eggplant half, leaving a firm wall. Combine the eggplant pulp, cheese, eggs, matzoh meal or bread crumbs, parsley, the remaining 1 teaspoon salt, the pepper and 2 tablespoons of the oil and mix well. Fill each eggplant boat with some of the mixture.

3. Oil a baking dish with the remaining 2 tablespoons oil. Place the filled eggplant halves skin side down. Bake in a 350° F. oven for ½ hour, or until a crust forms on top.

Serve cool, preferably at room temperature.

Makes 14 to 16 halves.

NOTE: Matzoh meal is used during the entire year, not only on Passover. In our Ashkenazi family, it was often used, as it is in the *papoutsakia*, instead of bread crumbs since it provides a firmer texture.

MOUSSAKA
Vegetarian Eggplant and Cheese

This Jewish-style *moussaka* does not have meat since the kosher laws prohibit mixing meat and milk together. The result is a complete vegetarian dish with considerable dimension.

2 pounds eggplants (about 4), stems removed
2 teaspoons salt
¼ cup corn oil
4 garlic cloves, chopped fine
½ cup tomato sauce
6 ounces tomato paste
1½ cups water
2 eggs, beaten
½ pound mozzarella cheese, grated

1. Cut each eggplant lengthwise into 3 equal slices. Sprinkle with the salt and let stand for 20 minutes. Dry the slices on paper towels to absorb the liquid that accumulates. Set aside.

2. Heat 1 tablespoon oil in a pan and stir-fry the garlic over moderate heat until golden, about 2 minutes. Add the tomato sauce, tomato paste and water and mix well. Simmer the sauce over low heat until it becomes thickened, about 15 minutes.

3. Heat the remaining 3 tablespoons oil in a skillet. Dip the eggplant slices into the beaten eggs and fry over moderate heat for 2 minutes. Fry all the slices this way.

4. Assemble the *moussaka* in this manner: Put a layer of eggplant in a heatproof glass or metal baking dish. Cover with about ½ cup of cooked tomato sauce. Sprinkle with about 2 tablespoons of the grated cheese. Cover this with another layer of eggplant, then sauce, then cheese. The last layer (there should be three) ends with the cheese.

Bake in a 350° F. oven for ½ hour.

Serve warm. Serves 6 with spaghetti or other dishes.

ARMEKO
Onion and Tomato Stew

This extremely tasty preparation is completely vegetarian. It may possibly have its origin in Spain as a Sephardic import after the Expulsion. In Greece, it was prepared by cooking slowly over wood fires. The armeko can be served with either meat or dairy dishes since it is neutral.

¼ cup corn oil
3 pounds large onions, coarsely cubed, rinsed in cold water
1 cup canned tomato sauce
1 pound ripe tomatoes, coarsely cubed
3 large green peppers, seeded, cubed
½ teaspoon salt, or to taste
½ cup raw rice, rinsed, drained

1. Heat the oil in a large pan, add the onions, and simmer over low heat for 15 minutes, stirring now and then. Add the tomato sauce, tomatoes, green peppers and salt. Mix well, cover the pan, and cook very slowly for 1 hour.

2. Add the rice, stir well, and continue to simmer over very low heat for ½ hour. If too much liquid has accumulated, remove the cover and simmer for 10 minutes more. The mixture is moist with very little sauce.

Serve warm. Serves 8 with other dishes.

KULUKIF TREMENO
Baked Zucchini Pudding

Dairy dishes in the Greek community are popular, common and diversified.

2 pounds zucchini (4)
3 eggs, beaten
½ pound farmer cheese or pot cheese, coarsely mashed
½ teaspoon salt
¼ cup bread crumbs or matzoh meal (during Passover)
2 tablespoons butter

1. Peel off the thin green skin of the zucchini. Grate them on the coarse side of a hand grater or in a processor. Mix this with the eggs, cheese, salt and crumbs. Pour the mixture into a well-buttered heatproof glass or metal baking dish, 8 × 8 × 2 inches. The mixture should be about 2 inches deep.

2. Bake on the middle rack of a 350° F. oven for ½ hour or until brown.

Cut into 3-inch squares and serve warm. Serves 6 with other dishes.

TOMAT Y PIMENTON
Tomato and Pepper Salad

A simple daily salad from Greece and Turkey, to be eaten with good crusty bread.

3 large sweet red peppers
3 ripe tomatoes, cut into 6 wedges each
3 sour gherkins, cut into long slices
¼ cup wine vinegar
2 tablespoons olive oil

1. Broil the whole peppers all around to char the skin. Put them in a paper bag for 10 minutes, which will steam them and thereby loosen the skin. Remove the skin and rinse off under cold water. Cut open the peppers, discard seeds, stem and ribs. Cut the flesh into long strips ½ inch wide. Arrange them on a platter in a circular design.

2. Arrange the tomato wedges and gherkin slices among the pepper slices. Mix the vinegar and oil together and pour it over the vegetables.

Serve at room temperature. Serves 6.

TARATOR
Yoghurt and Cucumber Salad with Garlic

Although my teacher is a Sephardic lady from Athens, she savors this recipe from the Romaniate community in Ioannina near the Albanian border. Thus do recipes cross Jewish lines in the same country—via personal preference.

> 5 garlic cloves, put through a press
> 1 teaspoon salt
> 3 tablespoons cider vinegar
> ⅓ cup shelled walnuts, almonds or hazelnuts, chopped fine
> 1 pound yoghurt
> 2 tablespoons olive oil
> 2 young (Kirby) cucumbers, not peeled, cut into ¼-inch cubes
> 1 tablespoon chopped fresh dill

1. Mix the garlic, salt and vinegar together, then add the nuts of your choice. Fold in the yoghurt and olive oil and mix well.

2. Wrap the diced cucumber in a towel; press very lightly to dry the cubes. Add to the yoghurt mixture. Chill the salad in the refrigerator for 3 to 4 hours.

Garnish with the dill.

Serve as a dip with bread. Also, serve with Spanakopita (see Index). Serves 8.

PASTICHIO
Noodle Pie

This is a fine dairy dish for meatless days.

> 1 pound ¼-inch-wide dry egg noodles
> 1½ pounds farmer cheese, at room temperature
> ½ pound cream cheese, at room temperature
> 4 eggs
> ¼ teaspoon salt
> 2 tablespoons butter or margarine
> 1 cup milk

1. Bring a large pot of water to a boil and cook the noodles over moderate heat for 15 minutes, or according to box directions. Drain, rinse under cold water, drain well.

2. Mix the two cheeses, beat three of the eggs and the salt together, and combine. Butter a heatproof glass or metal baking dish, about 7 × 11 inches, with 1 tablespoon of the butter. Put half of the noodles on the bottom, spread the cheese mixture over this, and cover with the balance of the noodles. Scatter 1 tablespoon butter, cut into small cubes, over the noodles. Bake in a 350° F. oven until light brown on top, about 20 minutes. Remove from the oven.

3. Beat the remaining 1 egg and the milk together and pour it over the noodles. Return the dish to the oven and bake for 15 minutes more or until it is golden brown.

Cut the pie into generous squares.

Serve warm. Serves 6 to 8 with other dishes.

FIDES
Angel-Hair Noodles in Sauce

Greek Sephardic women learn how to cook from their mothers and grandmothers. It was a feminine activity at home while the men were off to work. In this Athens family, my teacher told me that the *fides* were known as "grandmother's noodles" since she was the source. Nowadays, the noodles are purchased, but in the past even these fine, hairlike noodles were made at home.

¼ cup corn or sunflower oil
1 pound angel-hair noodles
8 cups homemade chicken broth
1 cup tomato juice
1 teaspoon dried oregano
¼ teaspoon pepper
½ teaspoon salt
1 tablespoon chopped fresh flat-leaf parsley, or 1 teaspoon dried.

1. Heat the oil in a pan, add the bundles of noodles and fry them over moderate heat for about 3 minutes until golden.

2. In another pan put the broth, tomato juice, oregano, pepper, salt and parsley. Bring to a boil and simmer over moderate heat for 10 minutes. Add the noodles and 1 tablespoon oil from the pan in which they were fried. With 2 forks separate the softened clumps and simmer for 15 minutes as the liquid is absorbed. Separate the noodles now and then as the cooking continues.

Serve hot as a side dish with meat or chicken.

Serves 6.

VARIATION FOR PAREVE STYLE: For those who follow the dietary laws, *pareve* is the neutral status of a dish, being neither milk nor meat, and so can be served with either one.

Instead of chicken broth, which limits the Fides to meat dishes, use 4 kosher vegetable soup cubes, to prepare 8 cups of pareve broth.

Follow the recipe as above, using the same system of preparation. Garnish the angel-hair noodles with grated Parmesan or kashkaval cheese, which then changes it to a dairy dish.

NOTE: Certain commercial foods have crept into the Sephardic cooking of Greece and Turkey. The first is the use of meat or vegetable cubes that are available in stores catering to kosher clients. The other is the use of margarine, which is also *pareve*, to replace butter, which is a dairy food. If one comes from a kosher household, as I do, it becomes a simple matter to analyze a situation and make a *pareve*, meat or dairy decision quickly.

BOEREKAS
Cheese Turnovers

It seems that all the Greek and Turkish ladies I met knew how to make *boerekas*, and would make them to keep on hand for daily as well as fiesta use. They are justifiably popular since they quickly fill the need for an appealing snack. *Boerekas* may be frozen in plastic bags until needed. Thaw out for 1 hour, then reheat in a 350° F. oven for 10 minutes.

PASTRY

¼ cup corn oil
¼ cup cold water
2 cups flour
¼ teaspoon salt

FILLING

¼ pound farmer cheese, mashed
¼ pound feta cheese, mashed
¼ teaspoon pepper
1 egg, beaten

TURNOVER

1 egg, beaten
2 tablespoons grated kashkaval cheese
oil for baking sheet

1. Mix the pastry ingredients together with enough water to make a soft, pliable dough. Knead for several minutes to produce this consistency, dusting with flour when necessary. Cover and set aside.

2. Mix filling ingredients together until smooth. Set aside.

3. Divide the pastry into walnut-size pieces, rolled in a ball. Roll out each ball into a disc about 4 inches in diameter. Put 1 tablespoon of the cheese filling onto the end nearest you, fold it over, moisten the rim with water, and press down the edges all around.

Using an empty can with a diameter of 3 to 4 inches, press down over the folded turnover to cut off the excess dough and seal the edges. This is a home-style method and you can, of course, use a round metal cookie cutter. I prefer the can.

4. Brush the top of each *boereka* with the beaten egg. Dip the moist brush in the grated kashkaval and rub this over the top. Bake on an oiled baking sheet in a 350° F. oven for 35 to 40 minutes, or until both the top and bottom of the *boerekas* are light brown. Remove and cool.

Serve as a snack or appetizer at room temperature. Makes 22.

SPANAKOPETA
Spinach and Feta Cheese Pie

The Jewish community in Greece has incorporated this great national spinach and cheese pie into their kitchens although it does not have Sephardic origins. No one should be intimidated by the use of the thin and fragile fillo sheets since a little experience will resolve all problems.

> 10 scallions, chopped
> ½ cup olive oil
> 2 packages, 10 ounces each, frozen chopped spinach, completely
>   defrosted, or 1 pound fresh spinach, leaves only, chopped
> ¼ teaspoon pepper
> 1½ ounces fresh dill, chopped
> 1 pound feta cheese, crumbled or mashed
> ¼ cup olive oil, slightly warmed to facilitate spreading with a
>   pastry brush
> 1 package (1 pound) fillo sheets

1. Sauté the scallions in the oil in a skillet over moderately low heat until wilted, about 2 minutes. Firmly press out the liquid from the defrosted frozen spinach. Add the spinach and pepper to the skillet and sauté for 5 minutes, mixing everything thoroughly. Add the dill and stir for 5 minutes more to evaporate the moisture. Mix and toss the contents. Remove the skillet from the heat, turn out into a mixing bowl, and cool. Stir in the feta cheese and set aside. (At this stage the mixture may be refrigerated for several hours until ready to use.)

2. Oil a heatproof glass or metal baking pan, 13 × 9 × 2 inches, on the bottom and sides with a pastry brush. Open the package of fillo and spread it out flat. Cover the sheets with a slightly damp, but not wet, cloth kitchen towel since fillo dries out quickly and must be protected. Fit 1 fillo sheet into the pan; cut off the excess at one end. Save the pieces. Oil the sheet lightly. Put down 10 sheets this way, dabbing each sheet with the oil and touching the corners and center with the brush.

3. Use the cut pieces of fillo as the eighth sheet, if you wish, fitting them in as best you can. The tenth sheet should be whole. Cover this with the filling. Cover the filling with 10 more lightly oiled fillo sheets. Oil the top sheet completely.

4. With a sharp knife, cut the top fillo sheet just through in a 2-

inch-size diamond shape diagonally across the pan. Do not cut deeply.

Bake in a 350° F. oven for 40 to 45 minutes, or until the top is uniformly light brown.

Serve warm or at room temperature as an appetizer or as an accompaniment to the main courses.

Serves 8 to 10.

RODANCHAS
Eggplant Snails

Fillo dough sheets are the quintessential Greek wrappers, regardless of the religious community. In years past, fillo was prepared by hand in enormous sheets stretched out to the thinnest possible thickness. Now it is commercially available everywhere, but especially in Middle East groceries. This Jewish recipe is from Salonika.

2 pounds large eggplants (about 2)
½ pound feta cheese, chopped or crumbled
1 medium potato, peeled, quartered, cooked and mashed
¼ teaspoon pepper
⅛ teaspoon grated nutmeg
3 eggs
fillo sheets, all-purpose, 12 × 17 inches
corn oil

1. Broil the eggplants under a gas or electric broiler for about 15 minutes to char the skin and soften the pulp. Turn them now and then so that they are quickly and uniformly baked. Cool, then peel and discard the skin. Let the pulp drain in a colander and gently press out the liquid. Then chop coarsely.

2. Mix the eggplant, cheese, potato, pepper, nutmeg and 1 egg at a time to a smooth filling.

3. Cut a number of sheets of fillo lengthwise into halves. Brush each half lightly with oil. Put about 2 tablespoons of the filling mixture along the length of the oiled fillo sheet and roll it away from yourself in a long tube. Pinch the ends closed. Turn the tube around itself like a snail so that the *rodanchas* are about 4 inches in diameter. Brush the top of each snail with oil.

4. Put the snails on a lightly oiled baking sheet and bake in a 350° F. oven for 20 minutes, or until brown and crisp.

Serve warm as a snack or appetizer with ouzo, the anise-flavored Greek drink. Makes about 20 snails.

VARIATION FOR ROSH HASHANAH: To usher in the New Year this sweet *rodancha* is prepared in Salonika.

> 2 pounds pumpkin, peeled and cut into 1-inch cubes
> ¼ teaspoon salt
> ¾ cup sugar
> ½ cup honey
> 1 tablespoon ground cinnamon
> 3 tablespoons chopped walnuts

1. Rinse the pumpkin pieces and put them into a dry pan with salt and only the water that clings to the pumpkin. Cover the pan and simmer over low heat for about ½ hour, or until soft. The liquid must evaporate.

2. Add sugar and honey, mix well, and continue to simmer until the mixture is dry and comes away from the pan. Add the cinnamon and walnuts; mix. Remove from the heat and cool. Prepare the snails with fillo as with the eggplant mixture.

PASTEL DE BERENJENA
Eggplant Pie from Salonika

One day I shall attempt to record the many ways in which eggplant is prepared in Greece and Turkey. In these two countries it has become a Sephardic standby. The crust of the pie is similar to that of European pies but the filling is absolutely Greek. The Ladino word, *pastel,* is used for savory foods and not for sweet desserts as it is in present-day Spain.

> ¾ cup margarine
> 1 teaspoon butter
> 3 cups flour
> ½ teaspoon salt
> 1 tablespoon corn oil

½ cup milk, or more as needed
1 eggplant/cheese recipe from Rodanchas (preceding recipe)
1 egg yolk mixed with 1 teaspoon water
2 teaspoons sesame seeds

1. Cut the margarine and butter into the flour and salt. Combine until the mixture has a crumbled look. Add the oil and rub this into the flour. Add milk, a little at a time, until you have a soft pastry. Cover and refrigerate overnight or let it rest for 3 to 4 hours at least.

2. Roll out half of the pastry into a round shape that will fit a 9-inch pie pan with sufficient dough to reach up the sides. Poke a number of holes into the bottom with the tines of a fork.

3. Add the filling and cover with the remaining half of the pastry. With your finger push a hole or chimney into the center of the pie to the bottom, to allow steam to escape. Paint the pie top with the egg yolk and sprinkle with sesame seeds.

Bake in a 350° F. oven for ½ hour, or until light brown.

Serve warm or at room temperature as the main dish in a meal.

Serves 6 with other Greek Sephardic dishes.

GALATOPTA
Baked Egg Custard

A very simple sweetened custard served after dairy meals.

6 eggs
¾ cup sugar
1 quart milk

1. Beat the eggs until creamy, add the sugar, and continue to beat until well integrated. Beat in the milk until well mixed.

2. Pour into an 8-inch square heatproof glass or metal baking dish. Bake on the center rack of a 350° F. oven for about 45 minutes, or until the top is brown.

Cool, then refrigerate.

Serve cold. Serves 6.

KURBIETES
Butter Cookies

These simple, traditional cookies rely on fresh butter and the correct amount of flour for their melting texture. Using the paper cups, as called for here, is not a necessity, but it does provide a neat way for both the dusting and serving.

> 1 pound sweet butter, at room temperature
> 6 tablespoons confectioners' sugar
> about 1½ cups flour
> 2 teaspoons vanilla extract
> confectioners' sugar for dusting

1. Cream the butter and sugar together. Gradually add the flour, stopping when you have achieved a soft dough, then incorporate the vanilla. Do not add too much flour or the dough will not be manageable and the cookies may be hard.

2. Shape the dough into a rolling pin shape, a long roll 1 inch in diameter. Cut the roll diagonally into 2-inch-wide pieces. Put pieces on an ungreased cookie sheet and bake at 350° F. until light brown, about ½ hour.

3. Remove the cookies from the sheet, cool well, put each one into a paper cup, and dust with confectioners' sugar.

Serve with tea or Greek coffee.

Makes 30.

TAJITOS DE BIMBRIO
Quince Sweets

This old Sephardic recipe is from the Jewish city of Salonika. The title is in Ladino and not in Greek as one might expect. Formerly, at the end of cooking time the quince paste was dumped on a marble slab and spread out to a thickness of 1 inch, then cut into 2-inch diamond-shaped pieces. This can still be done but the newer style is to prepare balls 1 inch in diameter decorated with a walnut half. My Jewish teacher, who now lives in Athens but was born and raised in Salonika, admitted to me that her personal preference is the modification of this old classic.

2 pounds quinces (2 or 3 large fruit)
½ cup water
⅛ teaspoon salt
sugar, an amount equal to the measured quince pulp
1 tablespoon lemon juice
walnut halves

1. Cut each quince, with the skin, into slices. Discard the cores. Add the water and salt, cover the pan and cook over low heat for about 30 minutes. When the quince is soft, process the pulp until smooth. Measure the pulp and add an equal amount of sugar. Mix well in the pan and let the mixture stand, covered, in the kitchen at room temperature overnight.

2. Add the lemon juice and put the pan over low heat. Stir frequently until the liquid has completely evaporated and the pulp comes away from the sides of the pan in a ball. Cool well enough to handle.

3. Roll 1 heaping teaspoon of the pulp into a ball. Press a walnut half into the top and set aside. Prepare all of the quince paste this way.

Serve any time of year. Makes about 30 balls.

Middle East

KURDISTAN

BAGHDAD (Iraq)

PERSIA (Iran)

Jewish Kurdish peddler in a transit camp, organized by the Jewish Agency for Refugees, prior to making Aliyah to Israel. Teheran, 1950. (Photo courtesy of Moshe Shapiro)

KURDISTAN

The history of the Kurds could be called a murder story. From ancient times to the present, they have been a people without a champion in a country without borders.

Benjamin of Tudela, the adventurous Jewish traveler from Spain, reported during his travels to the Middle East (1166–1171) that Mosul, the center of present-day Kurdistan in Iraq, was a very large and ancient city on the Tigris river and "here dwell about 7,000 Jews."

There are no accurate statistics on the Jews of Kurdistan, that multinational, multilingual, transnational people of Turkey, Iran, Iraq and Syria. Kurdish, the language of an ancient people, is of the Persian branch of the Indo-European languages. The Kurdistan Jews who lived mainly in Iraq spoke Aramaic interspersed with Turkish, Persian, Kurdish, Arabic and Hebrew. This Judaic language is known as Targum and is consistent with the multinational character of the Kurds whether they are Jews or Muslims.

Historically, the story goes that Shalmaneser, the king of Assyria, exiled the ten tribes of Israel during the period 858–824 B.C. An ancient tradition relates that the Jews of Kurdistan are the descendants of several of the tribes, specifically Dan, Naphtali and Benjamin.

The early Kurds were craftsmen such as weavers, gold- and silversmiths, dyers, tanners, carpenters and cobblers—occupations of medieval times. Weaving was an especially Jewish occupation and no Jewish home in Kurdistan was without a loom. But the Jews were mainly farmers, known for their strength and sturdiness, who cultivated wheat, rice, lentils and tobacco. They owned fruit orchards and vineyards. There were no bankers. In Israel, I observed that Kurdish families had planted grapevines in the yards of their modest homes in memory of their origins on the banks of the Tigris.

65

Nevertheless, Kurdish Jews lived in economic distress and in isolation from the outside world. Murder was common. Jews were sold into servitude until the beginning of the twentieth century! A trickle of emigration to Palestine started in 1912 after a series of brutal murders. The Great Exodus, as it is known, from Iraq to Israel took place in 1950–51, and the Iraqi portion of Kurdistan was emptied of its Jews.

However, the food and traditional eating habits they took with them. It is essential to remember that nostalgia is one of the principal reasons that authentic recipes of a culture endure. They are not subject to planned obsolescence and the memories linger on.

The *koobe* (dumpling) in all of its manifestations is the unique specialty of Kurdish cooking. *Koobe* means "dome" in Arabic and describes the rounded dome shape of the dumplings. Some are round balls, others are flattened half-moons and are prepared in several sizes from a 1-inch ball to the large *chamo*, which is 3 inches in diameter. All of them are stuffed with chicken or meat and are served on the Sabbath, holidays or any time at all.

Bulghur, cracked wheat, is a staple in Jewish homes and is possibly more important to the cooking than rice. Seasonings are not exotic and will not challenge a newcomer to Kurdish cooking. Simple, honest ingredients—onion, garlic, celery, tomato paste, pepper and lemon juice—combined in a range of dumplings (the *koobe*) make up the Kurdish Jewish style. Dumplings are also prepared in Baghdad and traveled from there to Calcutta.

The delicious varieties of the *koobe*, delicious and tantalizing, evolved in a region where wheat was available. The Kurdistan Jews introduced it into their kosher repertoire and now, in these pages, it is available to all adventurous cooks.

MAZEERA KOOBE
Cream Soup with Dumplings

Dairy foods have an importance in Jewish cooking in both religious observances and climatic considerations. Shavuoth is a holiday when meat is frequently omitted from menus and replaced with dairy dishes that have substance and culinary interest. The *mazeera* is one example of such a dish; it is especially popular during hot summer days.

SOUP

1 pound farmer cheese
½ pound whipped cream cheese
¼ pound regular cream cheese
7 cups water
1 teaspoon salt, or to taste
1 tablespoon corn oil (optional)
⅔ cup raw rice, well rinsed

DUMPLINGS

2 cups farina
1 tablespoon corn oil
½ cup water, or enough to prepare a malleable dough
½ pound cream cheese

1. Combine the cheeses for the soup and mix well with 1 cup water. Add the balance of the water, the salt and oil and bring to a boil. Simmer over low heat for 10 minutes.

2. Mix the farina, oil and water together to prepare a *koobe* dough that can be handled and will hold together. Take 1 heaping tablespoon dough and roll it into a ball. Push a 1-inch-deep depression into the ball and fill it with ½ teaspoon cream cheese. Close the dough around the cheese and again roll it into a ball. Press the ball down into a slightly flattened disc about ½ inch thick. Use all the dough in this way,.

3. Add the rice to the simmering soup and let it cook for 10 minutes, stirring now and then to prevent its sticking to the bottom of the pan. Add the dumplings (*koobe*) one by one, and let them simmer over low heat for 15 minutes, which should be long enough to cook the rice and dumplings.

Cool the soup and refrigerate it for several hours.
Serve cold. Serves 6, with 2 dumplings each.

MARAG KOOBE

Chicken Soup for the Passover Dumplings

Soup and dumplings is a standard if not required dish for Passover. Note that the casing of the dumpling is made of rice and finely chopped chicken breast. Rice is acceptable for Passover in the Kurdistan ritual although it is not acceptable by the Ashkenazi Jews of Europe. The rest of the year the casing of *koobe* is prepared from semolina alone without incorporating chicken.

> 1 chicken, 3½ pounds, cut into 6 pieces, include the giblets
> ½ teaspoon ground turmeric
> 1 teaspoon salt
> 12 cups water.

1. Put all the ingredients into a large pan, bring to a boil over moderate heat, then cover and simmer at low heat for ½ hour.

2. Add the prepared *koobe* (dumplings) one by one and cook them over low heat for ½ hour. The pan should be large enough to contain about 70 *koobe* and all the soup.

Serve the dumplings in the hot soup.

Serves 10 or more.

KOOBE

Kurdish Chicken Dumplings for Passover

Both the dough and stuffing may be prepared one day in advance and refrigerated separately. The dumplings can be prepared when ready to dine.

DOUGH

3½ cups raw rice
1¼ pounds chicken breast, chopped fine
about ½ cup water

STUFFING

1¼ pounds ground lamb
¼ cup raw rice, rinsed and dried
3 medium onions, grated (2 cups)
1 teaspoon salt
1 teaspoon pepper
1 teaspoon ground turmeric
3 tablespoons corn oil

1. Rinse the rice in cold water and dry well. Then grind rice in a food processor to a fine consistency. Mix this with the chicken and moisten with enough water to prepare a moist dough for the shell of the dumplings. Set aside.

2. Mix stuffing ingredients together.

3. Take a walnut-size bit of the dough and roll it into a ball. Push your thumb into the ball to make a hole for the stuffing. Put in 1 heaping teaspoon of the stuffing, pinch the opening together, and roll the dough into a ball. Set dumplings aside to be cooked in the chicken soup.

Makes about 100 dumplings (*koobe*).

KOOBE
Semolina and Rice Dumplings in Soup

The recipes found here are from Jewish Kurds of the Mosul region, in Iraq near the Turkish border. This is a classic Kurdistan preparation for Friday evening dinner after the prayers at the synagogue and for the Sabbath noon meal. The *koobe* are traditionally served with a platter of radishes, parsley, fresh coriander sprigs and scallions. I have also been served olives and dill pickles as an accompaniment and contrast.

STUFFING

    1 pound boneless beef chuck, ground
    3 onions, chopped (1½ cups)
    ½ teaspoon pepper
    ⅛ teaspoon paprika
    1 teaspoon salt
    2 tablespoons tomato paste

SOUP

    3 tablespoons corn oil
    2 medium onions, chopped (1 cup)
    1 pound chicken parts, 2 legs and thighs
    10 cups water
    ⅛ teaspoon ground cuminseed
    pinch of paprika
    1 teaspoon salt, or to taste
    ¼ teaspoon pepper
    ¼ cup tomato paste

DOUGH

    3 cups cream of wheat or farina
    2 cups soft cooked white rice
    1 teaspoon salt
    1¼ cups water

1. Mix all stuffing ingredients together and set aside.
2. Heat the oil for the soup in a large pan, add the onions, and

stir-fry over moderate heat until the onions become golden, about 2 minutes. Add the chicken pieces and fry for 2 minutes more to change their color. Add the water, cuminseed, paprika, salt, pepper and tomato paste. Mix well and bring to a boil. Simmer for 15 minutes.

3. With moist hands, mix all the dough ingredients together. Knead the dough for 2 or 3 minutes to ensure that it is well mixed. Cover the dough so it won't dry out.

4. Take 1 heaping tablespoon of the dough and press it out in your palm to make a circle ¼ inch in thickness. Add 2 teaspoons stuffing and fold it up into a round ball 2 inches in diameter. The dough should completely seal the inner meat. Keep the hands moist with cold water to smooth the outer surface and keep the dough malleable.

5. Bring the soup to a boil, add the dumplings one at a time, and cook them over low heat for 45 minutes to 1 hour. After 15 minutes or so, move any dumplings around that may have stuck to the bottom of the pan. Cover the pan as the broth simmers and the *koobe* and chicken complete cooking.

Serve warm—the *koobe*, broth and chicken all together.

Serves 8 to 10.

MARAG KOOBE
Vegetable Soup with Dumplings

Several cultures prepare the *koobe* in their own way, differing in the shell or filling. This Kurdish style is a grand dish that can be the basis for a substantial lunch or the first course in a celebratory dinner. Both soup and dumplings may be prepared one day in advance and rewarmed briefly before serving. I was told by the cook that in the event bulghur was not available, the shell of the dumpling could be made with only semolina. But the bulghur gives an additional texture and flavor.

SOUP

3 tablespoons corn oil
1 large onion, chopped (¾ cup)
4 celery ribs and leaves, sliced thin (4 cups)
4 garlic cloves, chopped fine
1 teaspoon salt
1 teaspoon lemon juice
1 tablespoon sugar
¾ cup tomato purée
¼ teaspoon pepper
10 cups water

FILLING

2 tablespoons corn oil
2 medium onions, chopped (1 cup)
3 garlic cloves, chopped fine
2 teaspoons paprika
¼ teaspoon pepper
¾ cup chopped celery
2 pounds beef chuck, chopped but not fine

DUMPLINGS (KOOBE)

2 cups bulghur, soaked in 1 cup water for 15 minutes
5 cups semolina
1 cup water
2 teaspoons salt

1. To make the soup, heat the oil in a large enough pan, add the onion and stir-fry over moderate heat for 2 minutes. Add all the other ingredients to the pan, bring to a boil, then reduce to low and simmer, covered, for ½ hour. Set aside.

2. Now make the filling. Heat the oil in a large skillet and stir-fry the onions and garlic over moderate heat for 2 minutes. Add the paprika, pepper, celery and beef and stir-fry for 10 minutes. Set aside and cool.

3. Mix a soft dough with the bulghur, semolina, water and salt. Take 1 heaping tablespoon of the dough and press it thin (not more than ¼ inch) in the palm of your hand. Put 1 heaping teaspoon of the filling in the center, fold it over, and round it out to 2 inches in diameter. Prepare all the dumplings this way. Makes 60 dumplings,

4. Bring the soup to a boil over moderate heat; add the dumplings one by one. Reduce the heat to low, cover the pan, and simmer for 45 minutes.

Serve warm soup and dumplings together. Serves 12.

NOTE: This is a rather large recipe and you may prefer to prepare half of the amount.

KUTEL PISHRA
Stuffed Fried Dumplings

The Kurds use a mixture of bulghur and semolina to prepare a dough that provides a firm casing full of wheat flavor when fried. They make an admirable appetizer with drinks or as an additional dish in a Kurdish buffet.

STUFFING

1 tablespoon corn oil
2 medium onions, chopped (1 cup)
½ pound ground beef
¼ teaspoon pepper
½ teaspoon salt
⅛ teaspoon ground allspice
¼ cup chopped celery

DOUGH

1 pound small-grain bulghur, soaked in water for 1 hour,
    drained
1 cup semolina
1 cup water
½ teaspoon salt
2 tablespoons tomato paste
oil for deep-frying

1. Heat the tablespoon of oil in a skillet and stir-fry the onions over moderate heat for 1 minute. Add the beef, pepper, salt and allspice and stir-fry for 2 minutes. Add the celery and fry for 1 minute more. Cool well.

2. Mix the dough ingredients together, then take an egg-size piece of the dough and flatten it out into a circle ¼ inch thick. Add 1 heaping teaspoon stuffing. Close the dumpling and press it into a rounded egg shape.

3. Heat the oil and brown the dumplings over moderate heat for 5 minutes. Drain on paper towels.

Serve warm. Makes 20 dumplings.

KOOBE CHAMO
Dome-Shaped Dumplings in Soup

This particular *koobe* is a large one with a high rounded dome and a flat bottom. It is a filling, meat-stuffed, dumpling, to be served in a rich chicken broth.

STUFFING

> 1 pound ground beef
> 4 medium onions, chopped (2 cups)
> ½ teaspoon pepper
> ¼ teaspoon hot red chili flakes or cayenne
> 1 teaspoon Hawaish (see Index)
> 2 teaspoons tomato paste
> ½ teaspoon salt
> 2 tablespoons corn oil

DOUGH

> 3 cups of jareesha, medium-fine bulghur
> 2 cups cream of wheat or farina
> 1 cup water
> 1 teaspoon salt

SOUP

> 2 tablespoons corn oil
> 1 medium onion, chopped (½ cup)
> 6 cups homemade chicken soup, or 6 cups water with a ½-ounce
>   bouillon cube
> ½ teaspoon ground turmeric
> ¼ teaspoon salt
> 2 tablespoons tomato paste

1. Mix all the stuffing ingredients together except the oil. Heat the oil in a skillet, add all the ingredients, and stir-fry over low heat for 10 minutes. Let cool for 5 minutes, then drain the mixture through a metal sieve to remove the fat and liquid that accumulates. Cool the stuffing and set aside.

2. Mix the *jareesha* and cream of wheat together. Add the water and salt, and mix well into a moist but firm dough that can be easily handled.

3. Take 1 heaping tablespoon of the dough and press it out to a pancake 3 inches in diameter and ¼ inch thick. This is the bottom of the dumpling. Put about ¼ cup of the stuffing in a rounded heap on the pancake. Prepare another pancake 3½ inches in diameter and cover the stuffing, pinching the two cakes together to seal in the stuffing, and shaping a rounded dome. Prepare all the dumplings this way and set aside. Makes about 12 *koobe*.

4. To make the soup, heat the oil in a large enough pan, add the onion, and stir-fry over moderate heat for 2 minutes. Add the soup, turmeric, salt and tomato paste and bring to a boil. Add the *koobe*, one at a time, and cook for 15 to 20 minutes.

Serve hot—1 or 2 *koobe* and soup for each portion. Serves 6 to 8.

KOOBE CHAMUSTA
Friday Lunch Dumplings in Soup

This dish is prepared and served on the Friday lunch before the Sabbath. On the Friday evening dinner, the beginning of the Sabbath, there is generally another menu that often includes another dumpling and soup preparation.

Koobe are the finest of Kurdistan dishes and there are several of them. They are an indispensable selection for family dinners. The Chamusta-style *koobe* is cooked in a richly endowed soup of celery, leek, garlic and lemon juice, with meat broth. The *koobe* itself is always solid, dense and filling. The shell of the *koobe* is a complete wheat product of bulghur and farina, the supermarket breakfast food called cream of wheat, which is a fine-ground semolina.

SOUP

1 large leek, ½ pound

2 tablespoons corn oil
1 cup fine-chopped celery
2 medium onions, chopped fine (1 cup)
5 garlic cloves, chopped fine
6 to 7 cups water
1 teaspoon salt
1 tablespoon lemon juice, or to taste

FILLING

2 tablespoons corn oil
¼ pound boneless beef chuck, cut into ½-inch cubes
½ cup fine-chopped celery
3 garlic cloves, chopped fine.

1 recipe for dough (see Koobe Chamo)

1. Cut the leek lengthwise into halves; trim off the root end and
about 3 inches of the green leaves. Separate all of the leaves, and
soak them in cold water for 10 minutes, rinsing them carefully to
remove the soil that has accumulated. Drain. Cut leaves and stems
into 4-inch pieces. Set aside.

2. Heat the oil in a large pan, add the leek, celery, onion and
garlic and stir-fry over moderate heat for 3 minutes. Add the water
and bring to a boil, then add the salt and lemon juice. Simmer over
low heat for 20 minutes.

3. To make the filling, heat the oil in a skillet and stir-fry the
meat over moderate heat until it starts to become brown, about 10
minutes. Cool. Chop coarsely in a processor, adding the celery and
garlic at the last moment to mix together.

4. Take about ⅓ cup of the dumpling (koobe) dough and roll it in
a ball in the palms of your wet hands. Push a deep depression into
the ball with your thumb and add 1 heaping teaspoon of the filling.
Close the hole and, pressing firmly, flatten the ball out into a disc 3
inches in diameter—a little higher in the center and thinner at the
edges. Prepare all the dumplings this way. Makes about 10.

5. Drop the koobe into the simmering soup one at a time and
cook over moderate heat for 20 minutes. Add 1 cup of water if too
much liquid has evaporated. There should be enough of this green,
lemon-flavored soup to serve 5 persons, with 2 koobe for each.

Serve warm. Serves 5 or even 6.

KOOBE MATFUNIYA
Red Dumplings

The title is mine. The tomato paste turns the soup and *koobe* red, but the basic technique of preparing the *koobe* is the same as in other recipes. The Red Dumpling soup is an anyday preparation during the week or on the Sabbath. A family preference.

DUMPLINGS (KOOBE)

½ pound boneless beef chuck, cut into ¼-inch cubes
1 medium onion, chopped (½ cup)
¼ cup chopped flat-leaf parsley
¼ teaspoon pepper
1 recipe koobe dough (see Koobe Chamo)

SOUP

3 tablespoons corn oil
1 medium onion, chopped (½ cup)
½ cup tomato paste
10 cups water
½ teaspoon salt, or to taste
1 teaspoon lemon juice
10 to 12 fresh okra

1. Mix the beef, onion, parsley and pepper together to make the stuffing and set aside.

2. Take 1 heaping tablespoon dough, about the size of an egg, and roll it into a ball. Push in a hole with your thumb and add 1 heaping teaspoon stuffing. Close the hole and roll the *koobe* into a ball. Do this with all the dough and meat stuffing. Makes about 25 *koobe*.

3. Heat the oil for the soup in a large pan, add the onion, and stir-fry over moderate heat for 2 minutes. Add the tomato paste and continue to fry for 2 minutes. Add the water, salt and lemon juice and bring to a boil. Simmer the soup over low heat for 15 minutes. Add the *koobe*, one at a time, and cook for 15 minutes. Add the okra and cook for 10 minutes more, which is enough to soften them but not turn them into a gelatinous mass.

Serve hot. Serves 8.

KOOBE MASLOCKA
Yellow Dumplings

Turmeric, a most popular spice of India, is the important component of flavor and color to this dumpling and soup dish.

1. The dumpling dough and stuffing are the same as the Koobe Matfuniya. The tomato paste, lemon juice and okra are omitted in this soup and replaced with 1 teaspoon turmeric and 1 large zucchini (1 pound) cut lengthwise and each half cut into half-moons. The zucchini is added with the *koobe* for the last 15 minutes of cooking.

Should you prefer to make the soup more intense you may use 5 cups chicken broth and 5 cups water. Or, in the modern and popular method, add ½ ounce bouillon cube to the water.

Serve hot. Serves 6 to 8.

KOOBE SHIFTE BI TOMATE
Meatballs in Tomato Sauce

Ground beef in any form has universal appeal. These Kurdish meatballs feature allspice, which is known by the name of "English pepper."

MEATBALLS

> 1½ pounds ground beef
> 2 medium onions, chopped (1 cup)
> 3 garlic cloves, chopped
> ½ cup chopped celery ribs and leaves
> 2 eggs, beaten
> ⅓ cup bread crumbs
> ¼ teaspoon pepper
> ¼ teaspoon ground allspice
> 1 teaspoon salt

TOMATO SAUCE

> 2 tablespoons corn oil
> 1 medium onion, chopped (½ cup)

1 pound ripe tomatoes, chopped fine, or equal amount canned
    (2 cups)
¼ teaspoon ground allspice
¼ teaspoon salt
¼ teaspoon pepper
2 cups water.

1. Grind together the beef, cup of chopped onions, garlic and celery until well mixed. Add the eggs, bread crumbs, pepper, allspice and salt. Prepare meatballs 1½ inches in diameter and set aside.

2. For the sauce, heat the oil in a large skillet and stir-fry the onion over moderate heat for 2 minutes, or until golden. Add the tomatoes, allspice, salt and pepper and simmer for 10 minutes. Add the water and bring to a boil.

3. Add the meatballs, one by one, to the sauce and cook for 15 minutes, basting frequently.

Serve warm. Serves 4 to 6 with other dishes.

OREZ CHAMUTZ
Lemon-Flavored Beef and Rice

Here is an everyday Kurdistan preparation for family dining. The lemon juice should be used to taste and so additional juice can be served on the side for anyone who wants to emphasize the flavor.

5 cups water
1 pound beef chuck, cut into 2-inch pieces
2 cups ½-inch pieces of celery
2 medium onions, chopped (1 cup)
1 teaspoon salt, or to taste
2 tablespoons corn oil
2 garlic cloves, chopped fine
3 tablespoons fresh lemon juice
2 cups raw rice, well rinsed

1. Put the water, beef, celery, onions, salt, oil, garlic and lemon juice into a large pan. Bring to a boil, then reduce heat to low, cover the pan, and cook for 1 hour, or until the meat is tender. Remove the beef and keep warm.

2. Put the rice in the same pan, bring to a boil, and reduce the heat to very low. Cover the pan and cook for about 45 minutes. The liquid will be absorbed by the rice.

Serve the meat and rice separately.

Serve warm. Serves 4.

SESA HAMEEN
Sabbath Chicken

In some Middle Eastern communities, an ingenious electric plate oven is used for *hameen*. This is a round dish, about 30 inches in diameter with the heating element underneath. An inner plate supports the pans or anything else that is being cooked, roasted or baked. A tight cover seals in the heat. The plate oven is usually left on the floor of the kitchen. The electricity can be controlled from very low to hot and is an ideal method of cooking the *hameen* overnight. The traditional Kurdistan food was formerly cooked over charcoal fires.

2 whole chickens, 3 pounds each
1 cup raw rice, rinsed and drained
1 pound ripe tomatoes, chopped (2 cups), or an equal amount
    canned
½ teaspoon salt
½ teaspoon ground turmeric
1 teaspoon paprika
⅓ pound boneless chicken breast, cut into ½-inch cubes
1 tablespoon raw chicken fat (optional)

1. Rinse the chickens in cold water. Dry, and discard the skin and fat.

2. Prepare a stuffing with the rice, tomato, salt, turmeric, paprika, cubed chicken breast and fat. Mix together. Stuff the chickens and sew up the openings.

3. Put the chickens in a pan large enough to hold both, and just cover them with water, about 3½ cups. Cover the pan and bring to a boil over moderate heat on top of the stove. Then bake the chicken in the oven in very low heat, about 200° F., from just before Sabbath on Friday to noon the next day.

The very slow cooking over many hours produces a meltingly rich concoction of chicken and rice.

Serve warm. Serves 6 to 8.

VARIATION: Use ½ pound of ground lamb in place of the chicken breast for a more meaty stuffing.

KALISERKET KODET KSESA
Roast Chicken Livers

Charring liver slightly over or under an open flame makes it kosher. It is the device of ritual.

2 pounds chicken livers
3 tablespoons corn oil
1 pound onions (about 3), sliced
2 cups thin-sliced celery ribs and leaves
½ teaspoon ground allspice
½ teaspoon pepper
1 teaspoon salt

1. Char the chicken livers under a flame in a broiler or over charcoal for 3 minutes. Cut them into ½-inch pieces.

2. Heat the oil in a skillet and stir-fry the onions over moderate heat for 3 minutes. Add the livers, celery, allspice and pepper. Cover the pan and cook over low heat for 10 minutes.

3. Uncover the pan, add the salt, and stir-fry over moderate heat for 2 minutes more.

Serve warm. Serves 8 with other dishes.

SCHACKSHOUKA
Eggs and Sauce

Several Sephardic communities, Tunisia for example, prepare a *schackshouka*. Here is the Kurdish version.

 3 tablespoons corn or olive oil
 1 medium onion, chopped (½ cup)
 2 pounds fresh ripe tomatoes, chopped, or an equal amount
     canned
 1 sweet red pepper, chopped (½ cup)
 1 teaspoon salt
 ¼ teaspoon black pepper
 2 teaspoons paprika
 5 eggs

1. Heat the oil in a large skillet. Stir-fry the onion over moderate heat until it turns golden. Add all the other ingredients except the eggs, and simmer, covered, over low heat for ½ hour. Stir now and then as it cooks.

2. Break each egg into a small depression you make in the sauce. Cook for 10 minutes, basting the eggs with the sauce, to produce poached eggs in a red sauce. You may add up to 8 eggs for this amount of sauce.

Serve warm. Serves 5 for breakfast or lunch.

PORPACHINA JAJIK
Spinach and Sour-Cream Spread

Literally creamed spinach with onion, this simply seasoned table spread is generously lathered on the Arabic breads of the region, or on a bagel in our own cities, and it is an attractive breakfast food. It is also a dairy spread for those times, such as Shavuoth, when meat is excluded from the diet.

 ½ pound fresh spinach, chopped
 1 large onion, chopped (⅔ cup)
 ½ teaspoon salt
 1 cup sour cream
 ½ cup whipped cream cheese

1. Blanch the spinach in boiling water for 5 minutes. Drain and firmly press out the liquid. Mix the onion and salt together and let stand for 10 minutes. Then firmly squeeze out the liquid in a kitchen towel.

2. Mix the spinach, onion, sour cream and cheese together and whip it briskly. Refrigerate.

Serve as a spread on bread or crackers. Makes about 2 cups.

YAPRACH (ALE GEFEN IN HEBREW)
Stuffed Grape Leaves

Grapevines are one of the oldest of the cultivated plants originating in Western Asia. Grapes were used to make wine several thousand years ago, especially by the Greeks and Romans. It is quite possible, therefore, that a recipe for stuffed grape leaves originated in Western Asia many years ago and proliferated throughout these regions including Kurdistan.

It would be fortuitous if one had a supply of fresh, young grape leaves, but those sold in Middle Eastern shops in jars will do quite well.

   3 cups raw rice, well rinsed, drained
   2 cups chopped tomatoes, fresh or canned
   2 tablespoons chopped onion
   1 cup chopped dill leaves and young stems
   1 cup chopped celery leaves
   ½ pound ground lamb
   ¼ cup corn or olive oil
   2 teaspoons paprika
   1 tablespoon lemon juice
   2 teaspoons salt.
   80 grape leaves, or more

1. Mix the ingredients together except for the grape leaves and 2 tablespoons oil.

2. Take 1 heaping tablespoon of the stuffing and put it in the center of each grape leaf. Roll it into a small bundle about 2 inches long and ¾ inch thick. Pack the leaves tightly in layers in a pan.

Add 2 tablespoons of oil to the pan and pour in 2 to 3 cups hot water, enough just to cover the leaves. Cover the leaves with a ceramic plate to hold them under the water. Bring to a boil over moderate heat and cover the pan. Cook over low heat for 1 hour. Should the water evaporate too quickly, add another ½ cup.

Serve warm or at room temperature. Makes about 80.

VARIATION: Here is another stuffing.

3 cups raw rice
1 cup chopped celery
2 medium onions, chopped (⅔ cup)
½ cup chopped parsley
½ pound ground beef
1 teaspoon salt
½ teaspoon pepper
½ cup chopped tomatoes, fresh or canned
1 tablespoon curry powder
¼ cup corn or olive oil
grape leaves

1. Mix and cook as directed in the basic recipe.

GURGUR
Tomato Bulghur

Bulghur is a staple in Kurdistan, perhaps even more than rice. Here is a standard way of preparing a seasoned bulghur that is, in effect, a rice substitute and can be served with meat or dairy dishes.

3 tablespoons corn oil
1 medium onion, chopped (½ cup)
1 cup fresh tomatoes, chopped fine, or 2 tablespoons tomato paste
4 cups water
¼ teaspoon salt, or to taste
2 cups medium-size bulghur (see Glossary)

1. Heat the oil in a pan, add the onion, and stir-fry over moderate heat for 2 minutes, or until translucent. Add the tomato, water and salt and bring to a boil.

2. Add the bulghur, cover the pan, and simmer over low heat for 20 minutes. Stir now and then during this time.

Serve warm, especially with chicken or meat dishes.

Serves 4 to 6.

BAMYA
Okra with Sauce

Okra is a popular and ubiquitous vegetable throughout North Africa, the Middle East and India. It may be surprising to learn that this unique vegetable is a plant of the thistle family.

1 pound young okra, whole
3 tablespoons corn oil
1 small onion, chopped (¼ cup)
2 garlic cloves, sliced
1 pound ripe tomatoes, chopped (3 cups), or an equal amount canned
½ teaspoon salt
¼ teaspoon pepper

1. Trim ¼ inch off from the stem end of the okra pods.

2. Heat the oil in a pan and stir-fry the onion and garlic over moderate heat for 2 minutes. Add the okra and fry for 2 minutes more.

3. Add the tomatoes, salt and pepper. Mix well, cover the pan, and simmer over low heat for 15 minutes.

Serve warm. Serves 6 with other Kurdish dishes.

TERSHID MECHALAL
Turnip and Beet Pickle

1 pound white turnips, peeled
1 pound fresh beets, peeled
1 tablespoon coarse salt
3 garlic cloves, peeled, left whole
3 cups water

1. Cut the turnips and beets into quarters if they are small and eighths if large.

2. Mix all ingredients together including the water and put the mixture into a glass or pottery jar. Cover and let stand at room temperature for 2 to 3 weeks before serving. Note that the liquid should cover the vegetables.

At the end of the pickling time, refrigerate and use when needed as a table condiment with Kurdish or other Middle East foods.

Makes 2 quarts.

ZALATET KALAM SMOKA UCHWARA

Red and White Cabbage Salad

Contrasting colors make this an attractive salad. What we call white cabbage is really the tender inner leaves of a regular green cabbage. But all parts of the cabbage may be used.

> 1 pound red cabbage, shredded
> 1 pound white cabbage, shredded
> ¼ cup lemon juice
> ¼ cup olive oil
> 2 teaspoons salt, or to taste

1. Toss everything together. Refrigerate for at least 1 hour before serving.

Serve cool. Serves 8.

TURSHI KURDI

Pickled Cabbage with Chili

Chili, vinegar and garlic galvanize taste buds in a traditional Kurdistan pickle of tender inner cabbage leaves. Served with any kind of Oriental or Middle Eastern food.

2 pounds white inner cabbage leaves (no outer green leaves), cut
    into 2- to 3-inch pieces
3 garlic cloves, chopped fine
1 large celery rib, cut into 1-inch pieces (about 1 cup)
½ teaspoon hot red chili flakes
1 teaspoon salt
2 to 3 cups white vinegar

1. Blanch the cabbage in boiling water for 5 minutes. Drain well
in a colander and gently press out excess water.

2. Mix the cabbage with the garlic, celery, chili and salt and fit it
into a glass jar with a tight cover. Pour in enough vinegar just to
cover the cabbage mixture. Let it stand at room temperature for 1
day before serving. After serving, refrigerate.

Makes about 2 quarts.

KASMAY
Stuffed Cookies

Stuffed cookies, sambusack, *empanadas* or *boerekes* are the names in several
cultures for a baked or fried half-moon turnover. They can
be of a delicate cookie size or plate size like the panfried
Kurdistan Kadey Shavuoth.

These *Kasmay* are filled with a sweet cinnamon, spiced
peanut and coconut stuffing.

STUFFING (MAHAJUN)

¼ cup sugar
2 teaspoons ground cinnamon
½ cup roasted peanuts, coarsely chopped
¼ cup sweetened coconut slivers

DOUGH

1 package dry yeast (¼ ounce, 7 grams)
1½ cups warm water
5 cups flour
¾ cup sugar
¾ pound (3 sticks) margarine, melted

1 egg, beaten
2 tablespoons sesame seeds

1. Mix stuffing ingredients together and set aside. (If there is extra stuffing it may be stored in a jar with a tight cover.)

2. Dissolve the yeast in ½ cup warm water and let it proof for 10 minutes.

3. Prepare the dough. Mix the flour and sugar together. Make a well in the center and all at once add the yeast mixture and melted margarine. Add the remaining 1 cup water, a little at a time, until you have formed a soft, easily handled dough. Dust with flour and knead until smooth, about 5 minutes. Cover the dough in a bowl and let rise for 1 hour.

4. Punch down the dough ball, then cut off a piece of dough the size of a small egg. Roll it out into a circle on a lightly floured board to about 3½ inches in diameter. Put 2 teaspoons of the nut stuffing on the lower half of the circle. Moisten the edge with water and fold the top over, pressing top and bottom together firmly. Then press firmly all around the edge with the tines of a fork to seal in the contents. (Another method is to pinch and turn over the entire edge of the cookie.) Brush the tops of the cookies with beaten egg and sprinkle with sesame seeds.

5. Put the cookies on an ungreased cookie sheet and bake in a 400° F. oven for about 15 minutes, or until they are a light tan color.

Cool completely and store in plastic bags. Makes 50.

KADEY SHAVUOTH
Cheese Pancake for Shavuoth

Shavuoth is that holiday when dairy foods are uppermost in the minds of Kurdistan housewives. Here is one example, prepared with a yeast dough and stuffed with feta cheese.

1 package dry yeast (¼ ounce)
2 cups warm water
6 cups flour
¼ teaspoon salt
1 tablespoon corn oil
3 to 4 tablespoons margarine
1 pound domestic or imported feta cheese, grated or chopped

1. Mix the yeast in ½ cup of the water and let it proof for 10 minutes.

2. Make a well in the flour, add the yeast mixture, salt and oil and mix all together, using enough of the balance of the water to form a soft, moist dough. Knead the dough for 5 minutes, dusting with flour now and then.

3. Take ½ cup of the dough and roll it out into a pancake 8 inches in diameter and about ¼ inch thick. Rub the pancake with about ½ teaspoon of margarine and sprinkle over the lower half 2 generous tablespoons of the feta cheese. Moisten the bottom edge of the pancake with water and fold over to shape a half-moon. Pinch the edges together and press down firmly with the tines of a fork, or turn over the edge every ½ inch in a twisting movement.

4. Melt 1 teaspoon margarine in a skillet and brown both sides of the pancake over moderate heat for about 3 minutes.

Serve warm. Makes from 18 to 20 pancakes.

VARIATION: Prepare the pancakes in the same way as for the cheese stuffing. Roll out a pancake and rub it all over with ½ teaspoon margarine. Sprinkle the surface with 1 generous teaspoon sugar, fold it over, seat it, then brown in margarine as described. Serve warm with tea or coffee.

HALIK
Grape Haroseth for Passover

When the grape juice has been reduced to a syrup it is then known as honey. Mixed with nuts, it is an extraordinary concoction that can be served any time of the year over ice cream or even as a breakfast jam. A similar *halik* made from dates is prepared by the Jews of Calcutta, India.

4 pounds juicy white grapes
⅓ cup toasted sesame seeds
⅓ cup toasted walnuts

1. Squeeze out the grape juice by hand or with an automatic juicer that removes the juice and discards a dry pulp.

2. Cook the juice down to a maple syrup consistency, ending with about ⅓ of the total amount of juice. The syrup should be thick but still liquid. Cool.

3. Grind the sesame seeds and walnuts separately in a processor, but not too smoothly. Add this to the grape syrup and mix well. This is the *haroseth* of the Kurds.

VARIATION: The same thing can be done with bottled pure white grape juice, which can be purchased in supermarkets. Simmer the juice over low heat until it has been reduced by half, about 15 to 20 minutes. Cool and mix with the sesame seeds and walnuts.

Should you wish to cook the juice for 5 to 10 minutes longer, it will become a firm breakfast jam.

CHAI KURDI
Kurdish Tea

The Kurds like this sweet, aromatic tea. The cubes of sugar are dissolved in the mouth as the tea is drunk, the sweeter the better.

1 tablespoon India tea leaves
1 cinnamon stick, 4 inches
2 cups boiling water
sugar cubes

1. Put the tea and cinnamon in a teapot and pour in the boiling water. Allow to steep for 5 minutes.

Serve hot with sugar cubes. Serves 4.

BAGHDAD (Iraq)

Baghdad, the Great City, was founded in 762 and Jews have resided there from the beginning. The traveler, Benjamin of Tudela (1166–1171), recorded in his diary that there were about 40,000 Jews in Baghdad, dwelling "in security, prosperity and honour under the great Caliph." There were 28 synagogues at this time, supporting wise men, philosophers and magicians who were expert in witchcraft—a great center of Judaic learning and a factor in spreading education and progress in Iraq. The people studied Judaic lore and spoke a Judeo-Arabic language. The Jews were traders bringing silk and spices from China, but also dealt in textiles, indigo, liquor, medicine and precious stones.

From the ninth to the seventeenth century the vicissitudes of political disputes and tribal controversies were menacing. The conquest of Baghdad, first by the Mongols in the thirteenth century, followed by Tamerlane, and then the Ottoman Empire's struggle with the fanatical Persians, brought about a political seesaw of prosperity and denial for the Jews, always at the whim of the incumbent ruler.

Starting with the British administration during World War I and for some years afterward, conditions improved for the Jews. During this mandate the Jewish population swelled to 100,000. Pro-Axis activity during 1947 reduced the numbers to about 77,000.

But through it all, the food was a constant and uniting factor, since favorite dishes travel with the community wherever it may go. The Baghdadi specialize in soups, a variety of dumplings and rice dishes—the same as many other communities. The difference is in the seasonings—hot chili and the intense spice mixes have been replaced by the herbal seasonings of the Middle East. Judaic ritual is followed, resulting in many slow-cooked preparations. Otherwise, as elsewhere,

Jewish poultry vendor in a Baghdad market, 1920s. *(Photo courtesy of David Petel)*

local produce and ingredients are used to make exotic fare from humble recipes.

When the state of Israel was established, most of the Baghdadis moved there to resettle. The Jewish presence departed from Baghdad, but the food lives on in communities established in the Western world to remind us of a unique and ancient community that no longer exists.

BEIDH B'LAHAM
Egg and Meat Patties

Ground beef, chicken or lamb may be used depending upon personal taste. My teacher preferred chicken since it has less fat and produces a lighter patty. On the other hand, I prefer lamb since it is closer to the Baghdad tradition and the flavor appeals to me. And so it goes.

½ pound ground beef, chicken or lamb
2 medium onions, chopped (about 1 cup), or the equivalent in
    thin-sliced scallions
1 cup fine-chopped celery leaves or Italian flat-leaf parsley
5 eggs, beaten
1 teaspoon salt, or to taste
½ teaspoon pepper
sufficient corn oil for panfrying

1. Mix everything together except the oil.
2. Heat about ¼ cup corn oil in a skillet and drop in 1 full tablespoon of the egg/meat mixture. Flatten the patty slightly with the back of the spoon. Fry over moderate heat until golden brown on both sides. Continue until all the patties are fried.

Drain on paper towels.

Serve as an additional dish for dinner with other Baghdad foods. Makes an excellent appetizer with drinks or sandwiches for the children.

Serve warm or cold. Makes about 20 patties.

KOOBE HAMOOTH (SOLET)
Stuffed Dumplings in Soup

The preparation of koobe (the dumplings) for the Sabbath is the quintessential culinary activity of Baghdad cooking. How could one greet the sabbath without *koobe*? During my early days, the Calcutta Jews, whose origin was Baghdad, also prepared *koobe* much like this one. *Koobe* means "dome" and these rounded stuffed dumplings fit the name.

DOUGH

2 cups semolina
1 slice white bread, soaked in hot water, squeezed dry (⅔ cup)
¼ teaspoon salt
⅛ teaspoon pepper
¾ cup water

STUFFING

½ pound ground beef
1 small onion, chopped fine (¼ cup)
2 tablespoons chopped parsley
¼ teaspoon salt
⅛ teaspoon pepper

SOUP

3 tablespoons corn oil
1 medium onion, chopped (½ cup)
8 cups water
¼ cup tomato paste
2 teaspoons salt
⅛ teaspoon pepper
juice of 1 lemon
1 large celery rib with leaves, cut into ½-inch pieces
1 zucchini, about ½ pound, cut into ½-inch cubes

1. Mix all dough ingredients together to form a malleable dough. Set aside.
2. Mix stuffing ingredients together and set aside.
3. To make the soup, heat the oil in a large pan, add the onion,

and stir-fry over moderate heat until golden, about 3 minutes. Add the water and bring to a boil. Add the tomato paste, salt, pepper, lemon juice, celery and zucchini. Boil uncovered for 10 minutes.

4. Press the dough into a roll about 1 inch thick. Cut off walnut-size pieces and roll each one into a ball. Moisten your thumb in cold water and push it into each ball nearly to the end. Push about 1 teaspoon stuffing into the hole and roll the dough into a ball to close the hole. Moisten hands with cold water to facilitate this step. Prepare all the dumplings this way.

5. When the soup has boiled for 10 minutes, add 10 dumplings at a time and let simmer over moderate heat for 2 minutes. Add all of them this way. Cover the pan and simmer over low heat for 45 minutes. Makes 40 *koobe* (dumplings).

Serve the hot soup and dumplings with bread. Serves 8.

VARIATIONS:

CHOLO CHAMAD
Sweet-and-Sour Beet Soup

> 2 tablespoons corn oil
> 1 small onion, chopped (¼ cup)
> juice of 2 lemons (about ⅓ cup), or more to taste
> 3 tablespoons sugar
> 1 teaspoon salt
> 10 cups water
> 1½ pounds fresh beets, cooked, peeled and sliced, or equal
>   amount of canned beets

1. Heat the oil in a large pan, add the onion and stir-fry until golden, about 3 minutes over moderate heat. Add the lemon juice, sugar, salt and water. Bring to a boil. Add the fresh beets at this time and simmer for 5 minutes.

2. Add the dumplings, 10 at a time, as described. Add all the *koobe* (dumplings) this way. (If you choose to use canned beets, add them with the *koobe*.) Cover the pan and cook over low heat for 45 minutes. Adjust the sweet-and-sour taste.

PUMPKIN WITH DUMPLINGS

1. Prepare the soup and *koobe* as in Sweet-and-Sour Beet Soup. Instead of beets, use 2 pounds pumpkin or calabasa, cut into 2-inch cubes. All other sweet and sour steps are the same. Add *koobe* (dumplings) 10 at a time to the soup and cook over low heat for ½ hour. Add the pumpkin cubes and simmer over low heat for ½ hour. Adjust lemon and sugar if you wish for a more intense flavor.

PUMPKIN AND MEATBALL SOUP
Sweet-and-Sour

1. Prepare the meatballs with the same mixture and quantity as in the basic recipe. Shape meatballs 1 inch in diameter. Cook them with ½ cup water in a covered pan over moderate heat for 5 minutes.

2. Prepare the same sweet-and-sour soup as in Pumpkin with Dumplings but omit the dumplings. Add ¼ cup raisins to the soup, cook for 10 minutes, then add the cooked meatballs and the liquid. Total cooking time should be about 45 minutes over low heat.

SAMBUSAK
Stuffed Chick-Pea Turnover

DOUGH

3 cups flour
¼ teaspoon salt
about 1 cup water

STUFFING

2 tablespoons corn oil
2 medium onions, sliced very thin (1 cup)
2 cups cooked chick-peas (canned are satisfactory), puréed
¼ teaspoon salt
2 teaspoons ground cuminseed
oil for deep-frying, about 1 cup

1. Mix flour, salt and water together into a soft dough, adjusting flour and water to achieve a manageable consistency. Set aside, covered, for ½ hour.

2. To make the stuffing: Heat the oil in a skillet, add the onions and stir-fry over moderate heat until just turning light brown. Add the chick-pea purée, salt and cuminseed and continue to stir-fry over low heat until the mixture is quite dry. Turn out into a dish and cool well.

3. Prepare a round disc from the dough according to the size you like. In family-style restaurants, the disc is about 8 inches in diameter and ¼ inch thick. Fill this size with ½ cup stuffing, fold over into a half-moon shape, and seal the dough with a wet finger. Heat the oil until moderately hot and fry the turnover on both sides until golden brown. Drain on paper towels.

These can be served warm as appetizers or cooled and frozen in plastic bags for future use. Makes 6 large turnovers.

The turnovers can be made in a smaller cocktail size—3 to 4 inches of thinly rolled out dough. Fill with 1 tablespoon stuffing, seal with a wet finger, and deep-fry.

Makes about 20 turnovers.

KHINTA

Wheat Porridge with Stuffed Beef Pocket

The khinta is a winter dish for the Sabbath, substantial and filling. The stuffed pockets can be made any size from 3 inches square to 6 inches. The wheat and 1 small pocket per person can be served for lunch. For a completely different taste experience, add 6 hard-cooked eggs in the shell to the pan to cook along with the wheat and beef. The eggs should be served for Sabbath breakfast.

POCKETS

1 pound boneless chuck or similar meat, cut into very thin
    slices about 4 inches square
⅓ cup half-cooked rice
½ cup assorted meat bits—beef, chicken, gizzards—cut into
    small dice
⅛ teaspoon ground cinnamon
⅛ teaspoon pepper
½ teaspoon salt
1 teaspoon beef or chicken fat, cut into small dice (optional)

WHEAT

1 cup whole-wheat grains, covered with cold water for 2 hours
2 tablespoons corn oil
2 medium onions, chopped (1 cup)
3 cups boiling water
1 teaspoon salt
1 tablespoon tomato paste
½ teaspoon ground turmeric

To prepare pockets:

1. Take 2 slices of the beef and sew up 3 sides with a needle and strong thread to prepare a pocket for stuffing. Mix the rice, meats, cinnamon, pepper, salt and fat together as the stuffing. Stuff the pockets and sew up the open end. Set aside. Make 2 or more pockets; double the recipe if necessary.

2. Drain the wheat well after soaking.

3. Heat the oil in a pan and stir-fry the onions for 3 minutes, or until light brown. Add the boiling water, salt, tomato paste, turmeric and wheat grains. Place the stuffed pockets on top. Cover the pan well and bake in a very low oven, 200° F., for 10 hours. Do not stir. During this interval, should the liquid evaporate too quickly, add another ½ cup boiling water.

Serve warm for Sabbath lunch. Serves 6.

N O T E : The khinta may be cooked at any time during the week as I often do. Prepare all the steps and put the pan in the oven at about 8 A.M. Bake for 10 hours. Dine at 7 P.M.

KWARMA
Layered Beef and Vegetables

Traditionally in old-time Baghdad the food was cooked on wood fires, which were renewed from time to time. The cooking was slow but the results were an improvement in flavor and meat tenderness. With all of today's inventions, it is hard to reproduce the dishes they prepared with the simplest of cooking utensils, kitchen equipment and stoves.

4 tablespoons corn oil
4 large onions, sliced (4 cups)
1 pound boneless beef chuck, cut into 1-inch cubes
1 teaspoon salt, or to taste
¼ teaspoon black pepper
1 pound eggplant (1 or 2), peeled, cut into 2-inch cubes
1 pound small tomatoes, halved
1 sweet red pepper, cut into long thin slices
1 sweet green pepper, cut into long thin slices
1 or 2 dried whole hot red chilies, to taste
3 tablespoons lemon juice
1 teaspoon sugar
¼ cup hot water

1. Select a pan about 10 inches in diameter and 4 inches deep. Heat the oil in the pan, add the onions, mix, and fry very slowly over low heat, covered, for 15 minutes, or until the onion has turned a melting golden. Add the meat, salt and black pepper, mix, cover the pan, and cook for 30 minutes. The meat should be approaching tenderness.

2. Now add in layers, first the eggplant, to cover the onion and meat to the edge of the pan. Over that place the tomato halves, skin side up, to cover the eggplant. Scatter the sweet peppers over all. Push the hot chili into the mixture.

3. Mix the lemon juice, sugar and hot water together and pour over all. Cover the pan and cook over very low heat for 2 or 3 hours (some say 4 hours), depending upon the quantity in the pan. Use a heat dispersal pad to allow very slow cooking during the last hour.

The meat will be tender, the vegetables cooked down and softened, and the liquid almost evaporated.

Serve warm with white rice. Serves 6 with other dishes.

TABIT
Chicken and Rice

This *tabit* may also be prepared as a *hameen* for the Sabbath, in which case the chicken and rice are put into an oven turned to the lowest heat and baked overnight from Friday afternoon to Saturday. It is more common to prepare this dish on top of the stove at the regular speed, as directed here.

2 tablespoons corn oil
1 medium onion, chopped (½ cup)
1 chicken, 3 pounds, cut into 6 pieces, loose skin and fat
    discarded
3½ cups water
1 teaspoon salt, or to taste
⅛ teaspoon pepper
2 tablespoons tomato paste
2 cups raw rice, well rinsed

1. Heat the oil in a pan, add the onion and chicken, and sauté over moderate heat for 10 minutes to brown. Add the water, salt, pepper and tomato paste and bring to a boil.
2. Add the rice, turn heat to low, cover the pan, and cook for about 1 hour without stirring. Test the rice for doneness, and if too firm add 2 or 3 tablespoons water. Turn heat off and let stand for 10 minutes before serving.
Serve warm. Serves 6.

SHABAT HAMEEN

Old-Style Oven Chicken for Sabbath

I have had various versions of *hameen*, that ubiquitous Sabbath chicken and rice whose origin is Baghdad. The Calcutta (India) Baghdadis have another style of *hameen* and there have been many modern modifications that have cropped up according to family tastes. This is an old-style version.

1 chicken, 3 pounds, wing tips and excess fat removed
1 cup recipe for Khinta Pockets (see Index)
2 cups raw rice, well rinsed
4 cups homemade chicken broth
1 tablespoon tomato paste
½ teaspoon salt
4 eggs, hard-cooked for 10 minutes

1. Stuff the chicken with the *khinta* stuffing and sew up the aperture.

2. Put the rice, chicken broth, tomato paste and salt in a large pan and bring to a boil, then simmer over low heat for 10 minutes. Place the chicken in the center of the pan and place the eggs in their shells around it. Tightly cover the pan and put in a 200° F. oven. Bake for 5 hours. (Traditionally this dish was placed in an oven for about 10 hours, overnight, on Friday afternoon and served for the Sabbath lunch.)

The rice should be dry but still have some moisture and the chicken should be brown.

Serve warm—rice, chicken and eggs all together. Serves 4.

HAMEEN II
Slow-Cooked Chicken and Rice

Another *hameen*, or slow-cooked chicken and rice dish for the Sabbath, this is a contemporary recipe. It can be prepared at any time as long as it is baked slowly and thoroughly. There are great advantages in today's busy world in having a one-dish meal that can be prepared and put in the oven 5 hours before dinner time.

2 tablespoons corn oil
1 medium onion, chopped (½ cup)
1 chicken, 3 pounds
1 cup chopped tomato, fresh or canned
2 cups raw rice, well rinsed
1 cup dried chick-peas, covered in water overnight, drained
1 teaspoon salt
⅛ teaspoon pepper
¼ teaspoon paprika
3 cups water

1. Heat the oil in a pan large enough to hold all the ingredients. Add the onion and stir-fry over low heat until golden, about 3 minutes. Add the chicken and brown lightly on all sides for 5 minutes.

2. Add the tomato and fry for 2 minutes. Place the rice all around the chicken, and add the chick-peas, salt, pepper, paprika and water. Cover the pan tightly, bring to a boil, and simmer on top of the stove for 5 minutes. Then bake in a 200° F. oven for 5 hours—the longer, the better. The chicken will become quite tender, the rice will be cooked but still moist.

Serve warm. Serves 6.

PICKLED CUCUMBERS

2 pounds young, small, thin cucumbers, well scrubbed
4 whole garlic cloves, peeled
5 sprigs of fresh dill
1 quart water, mixed with ¼ cup salt

1. Fit the cucumbers in a 2-quart glass jar. Push in the garlic and dill. Pour in the salted water. Place a clean stone or other neutral weight over the cucumbers to keep them submerged.

2. Place the jar in a sunny window for 4 to 5 days to mature as the color changes to a dull green. At this stage the cucumbers can be tasted, then refrigerated thereafter. For a stronger taste, let the cucumbers mature for 7 days before tasting.

PERSIA (Iran)

The history of the ancient Persian empire is studded with tales of their kings—Darius, Cyrus, Xerxes, Artaxerxes—and the movement of their armies. They rode into Greece, north and west into Central Asia, and from the Nile eastward to the Indus River, causing their influence to be spread over an enormous area.

The Persians were an Indo-European people and were Zoroastrians. They followed the religion of their prophet, Zarathushtra (Zoroaster), who preached that there was only one God, Ahura Mazda, and they believed in the worship of the sun.

Little is known about early contacts between Persians and Jews, but the Jews retained a favorable memory of their Persian rulers. The Book of Esther relates the story of King Ahasueras, his Jewish Queen Esther and how she thwarted the plot of the tyrant Haman to murder all the Jews. The holiday of Purim celebrates this ancient deliverance. It was King Cyrus who allowed the Jews to return from the Diaspora to their Judean homeland in 538 B.C. Jewish colonies, established in Persia during this era, have not been disturbed to the present.

In 642 A.D. invading Arab Muslims conquered Persia. The Persian Zoroastrians fled to western India and established there a community known today as the Parsis. But the Jews stayed on.

Persian Jews were engaged as weavers, dyers, gold and silversmiths, spice merchants, bankers and moneylenders. The status of the Jews among the Muslim rulers allowed complete freedom of movement and economic opportunities. Various colonies of Jews were established within the Persian realm. Cultural and religious leadership, however, was in the hands of the Jewish authorities in Baghdad.

103

Distribution of pita bread in a bakery which was supported by the Jewish Joint Distribution Committee (JJDC). *(Photo courtesy JDC, New York)*

Historical information over the centuries reveals that Jewish communities proliferated in widely scattered towns throughout the Persian borders—from ancient times through the twentieth century, but with the largest numbers in Teheran, Isfahan and Shiraz. Persia (modern Iran) had an estimated Jewish population of 95,000 in 1948, but emigration to Israel during the recent Zionist expansion reduced the number to about 72,000.

An ancient people, the Jews, living in an ancient enclave, Persia, assumed the characteristics of the land. In a culinary way the Persian Jewish cuisine follows closely the cooking of their Muslim neighbors. The dietary laws of kashruth are followed with the only differences those based on family preferences.

The Persian style of cooking must be included in the list of the world's greatest cuisines. It is cooking flavored with herbs without the sting of chilies or the overpowering essence of garlic. Their spice mix (Advieh) is described below but the quantity, quality and variety of herbs is the outstanding characteristic of their cooking.

I naturally compare the cooking of Persia with that of India where I lived for many years, since they are both Indo-European peoples and geographical neighbors. The Indians opted for hot foods using many spices to develop a pungency that is altogether addictive for some. Persian cooking has been more partial to herbs and it resulted in a more understated cuisine than the Indian. Both have their aficionados. The surprise is that people of the same race developed cuisines with completely opposite emphases.

Rice is the dominant grain in Persia and the Persians are the world's greatest rice cookers. No other cuisine produces such a variety of unconventional rice combinations. Fruits and vegetables are both used in combination with rice. Spice seeds are added to provide crunch and texture; herbs are generously added to rice dishes to complement egg and dairy foods, and there are sweet rices eaten with meat. What other cuisine has the ingenuity and adventurous spirit to adorn rice with a sweetened melange of cherries, dried orange peel and almonds? (See Albaloo Polo.)

In the Persian stew, Khoresht, small amounts of meat and poultry are glorified with a variety of chopped herbs. Herbs both well known and esoteric are added by handfuls to their recipes. All of these herbs and spices are used in Persian cooking: basil (rayhon), black pepper (felfel), cardamom (hail), celery (karafs), chive (tareh), cinnamon (darchin), coriander (tochme gishneez), cuminseed (zeere), dill (shevit), fenugreek (chambaliley), leek (tareh faranghi), marjoram (golpar), mint (nano), oregano (osha), parsley, large-leaf (jafaree), saffron (saffron), savory (marzey), scallion (piaz cheh), sumac (sumac), tarragon (tarchum), turmeric (zardchubeh).

Onion, but not garlic, is ubiquitous. The Persians in antiquity thickened their savory or sweet dishes with powdered walnuts and the idea (disseminated through conquest) was taken up with alacrity by the Arabs and Romans. Fesenjan, a world class stew of walnuts, pomegranate and meat or poultry, is extraordinary.

Unfortunately, politics has a way of interfering with the spread of culinary information and so Persian cooking is relatively unknown these days. Because the Jews benefited from the knowledge available to them as ancient citizens, it can now be utilized by others interested in the recipes included in this book.

Persian Jewish food, with its preoccupation with herbs, vegetables and moderate amounts of meat, is a relevant cuisine for our day. Cooking without excessive reliance on fats and oils is a hallmark of the Persians. I hope that once the air clears in that country the culinary history and knowledge of their cooking will achieve the applause it deserves. The Jewish community still exists in Iran.

ADVIEH
Persian Spice Mixture

The Chinese have a mix called five-spice and the Indians have *garam masala*. The Persian *advieh* is an aromatic mixture that can be heightened by doubling the amount of ginger. I prefer the proportions given here, which are balanced and will intensify the herbal flavor in the various dishes to which it is added.

1 teaspoon ground cinnamon
¼ teaspoon ground cardamom
¼ teaspoon ground cloves
¼ teaspoon ground ginger

Mix everything together and store in a jar with a tight cover for use when needed.

ADASEE
Lentil Stew

This lentil stew is traditionally eaten for breakfast. It is nourishing, filled with protein and flavored in the Persian style with a number of herbs. It is compatible with any kind of rice.

1 cup dried lentils (green/brown), well rinsed
3 cups water
¼ teaspoon salt, or to taste
¼ teaspoon pepper
¼ teaspoon oregano
1 tablespoon butter or margarine
fresh or dried marjoram, chopped, for garnish

1. Put the lentils and water in a pan, bring to a boil, then cook over low heat for 15 minutes. Add the salt, pepper and oregano and continue to cook for about 30 minutes to soften the lentils and evaporate some of the liquid.
2. Toward the end of this process stir in the butter if you are having a dairy meal, or margarine if you are having a meal with

meat. Mash a few tablespoons of the lentils against the side of the pan to thicken the stew.

Serve warm. Let each diner garnish with marjoram to taste.

Serves 4 with other dishes.

AASH RECHTE
Winter Noodle Soup

This rich, hearty soup is most enjoyed in cold weather when snow is on the ground. It is vegetarian yet satisfying and the absence of meat is not important or even noticed.

1½ pounds dried white beans, soaked in water overnight, drained
8 cups water
3 medium onions, coarsely chopped (1½ cups)
2 white turnips, sliced (1 cup)
½ pound fresh spinach, chopped
1 bunch (¼ pound) flat-leaf Italian parsley, chopped
1 bunch (¼ pound) fresh coriander, chopped
1 bunch (¼ pound) fresh dill, chopped
2 teaspoons salt, or to taste
½ teaspoon pepper
¼ teaspoon ground turmeric
3 tablespoons corn oil
1 pound fresh egg noodles, cut into 3-inch strips

1. Put beans and water in a large pan, cover, and cook over low heat for about 1 hour, or until soft but still firm.

2. Add all the other ingredients except the noodles and bring to a boil. Cook over low heat for ½ hour. Add the noodles and cook in the uncovered pan for 15 minutes more.

Serve hot. Serves 8.

ABE GUSHT GONDHI NOCHODI

Veal and Chick-Pea Dumpling in Chicken Soup

The title does not do justice to the nuances and importance of this dumpling and soup dish, assembled in the Persian manner. This is a popular recipe for festivals and special occasions when large quantities of food are needed. The dumpling plate is beautifully decorated with scallions, sliced tomatoes and green pepper strips.

SOUP

10 cups water
¼ teaspoon ground turmeric
⅛ teaspoon pepper
1 teaspoon salt, or to taste
3 pounds chicken parts—legs, thighs, breast—loose skin and fat discarded
1 cup dried chick-peas, soaked in water overnight, drained

DUMPLING

1¼ cups ground, toasted chick-peas (nachochi; see Glossary)
1 pound lean veal, ground
1 tablespoon corn oil
¼ teaspoon pepper
⅛ teaspoon ground turmeric
½ teaspoon ground cardamom
1 teaspoon salt
1 medium onion, grated (½ cup)
2 to 3 tablespoons water as needed

1. Bring the water for the soup to a boil in a large pan and add all the other ingredients. Cook over moderate heat for 35 minutes in preparation for the dumplings. Remove the chicken pieces and set aside.

2. Mix all the dumpling ingredients together preferably by hand, to make a moist but firm dough. Prepare dumpling balls 2 inches in diameter. This makes 10 balls. Add these one at a time to the simmering soup and cook, uncovered, over low heat for 20 minutes.

Serve the warm soup, chicken and dumplings separately but at the same time. Serves 8.

VARIATION: One pound of ground chicken equally divided between breast and dark meat or ground beef may be substituted for the veal.

MORGH E TU POR
Stuffed Chicken in Broth

The Jewish-style stuffed chicken is served on the Sabbath after returning from the synagogue at midday. The chicken can be embellished in several ways. The first is to cook dumplings, the Gondhi Nochodi, in the broth, which strengthens it substantially. Another method is to cook serving pieces of beef in the chicken broth. A substantial Sabbath meal could consist of the stuffed chicken, dumplings, beef, the broth, white rice and several kinds of table pickles.

3 tablespoons raw rice, rinsed
1 tablespoon yellow split peas, rinsed
½ teaspoon ground cuminseed
1 medium onion, chopped (½ cup)
¼ teaspoon ground turmeric
¼ cup chopped fresh dill (optional but recommended)
½ teaspoon salt
⅛ teaspoon pepper
1 chicken, 3 pounds, loose fat discarded
7 to 8 cups homemade chicken soup
1 cup cooked chick-peas, fresh or canned

1. Cook the rice and split peas together in 2 cups water over moderate heat for 10 minutes. Drain and set aside.

2. Mix the cuminseed, onion, turmeric, dill, salt and pepper together and add it to the rice/pea mixture. Mix well; use it to stuff the chicken and sew up the aperture.

3. Put the chicken soup in a pan large enough to hold everything, then add the chickpeas and the stuffed chicken. Bring to a boil, cover the pan, and cook over low heat for 1 hour. Baste now and then.

Serve warm, the chicken and the broth with chick-peas separately.

Serves 6 with white rice.

KOOFTEH TABRIZI
Herbed Meat and Rice Balls

This recipe for Koofteh, a specialty of the city of Tabriz, is an aromatic preparation in the Persian fashion in which a variety of herbs, combined artfully, flavors the food without the intensity of spices and hot chili. Preferred accompaniments for the meat and rice balls are table pickles and bread. The rice balls are often made in a large size, that is to say the size of a tea saucer, and stuffed with hard-cooked eggs.

HERBED BALL

1 pound ground beef or veal or a combination
1½ cups raw rice, well rinsed
1 teaspoon salt, or to taste
¼ teaspoon ground turmeric
¼ teaspoon pepper
2 tablespoons dried tarragon
2 large bunches of flat-leaf Italian parsley, chopped fine in a
    processor, about 3½ cups
1 cup fine-chopped fresh leeks, both green and white parts
½ cup chopped fresh dill
1 medium onion, chopped fine (½ cup)

BROTH

3 tablespoons corn oil
2 medium onions, sliced (1 cup)
¼ teaspoon ground turmeric
1 cup chopped tomatoes, fresh or canned
1 teaspoon salt
5 cups water
1 cup green peas, fresh or frozen

1. Mix all the meatball ingredients together and roll into balls, 2½ inches in diameter, firmly packed. Refrigerate them for 1 hour.

2. To make the broth, heat the oil in a pan or soup kettle, add the onions and turmeric, and stir-fry over moderate heat until light brown, about 3 minutes. Add the tomatoes and salt and stir-fry for 2 minutes more. Add the water and bring to a boil.

3. Moisten your hands with cold water. Take each herbed ball and roll it firmly; add the balls to the broth very carefully, one at a time, so that they do not fall apart. The water should just cover the balls. Cover the pan and cook over moderately low heat, without stirring, for 45 minutes. Add the green peas and cook for 10 minutes more. The broth will reduce somewhat, the balls swell considerably due to the expansion of the rice.

Serve warm—with the meatballs in the broth. Makes 12 balls. Serves 6 to 8.

KORMA SABZI
Herbed Meat with Prunes

A korma is a stew and this version traditionally uses the golden sour prune. The standard black prunes are a legitimate substitute since they too are somewhat tart. Note that the portions of parsley and spinach should be equal and since bunches of parsley differ in size, just use common sense in evaluating the volume.

1 tablespoon corn oil
2 pounds boneless beef chuck or lamb, cut into 1-inch cubes
2 leeks, white part only, sliced thin
2 packages, 10 ounces each, frozen chopped spinach, defrosted, liquid well pressed out, or 1 pound fresh spinach, chopped fine
3 or 4 bunches of fresh flat-leaf Italian parsley, chopped fine
¼ teaspoon ground turmeric
1 teaspoon salt
¼ teaspoon pepper
2 cups water
1½ cups prunes, soaked in 1 cup water for 1 hour

1. Heat the oil in a pan and add the beef and leeks and stir-fry over moderate heat for 5 minutes.

2. If you use frozen spinach, run it through the processor once more to produce a finer consistency and add it to the beef with the parsley, turmeric, salt and pepper. Stir well for 3 minutes.

3. Add the water, bring to a boil, and cook the mixture over low heat for 1 hour. Add the prunes with soaking liquid and continue to cook for ½ hour more. Should the liquid evaporate too quickly, add ¼ cup water so that there will be a thick sauce. The sauce will be green.

Serve warm with white rice. Serves 8 with other dishes.

KHORESHT BAMIEH
Beef and Okra Sauté

Okra is a very popular vegetable but requires special care in cooking so that it does not disintegrate into a mush. The beef sauté and its seasonings, especially the unique flavor of the dried lime, enhances the okra's unconventional flavor.

1½ pounds boneless beef chuck, cut into 2-inch cubes
½ pound soup bones (optional but helpful)
2 medium onions, sliced (1 cup)
2 tablespoons corn oil
¼ teaspoon ground turmeric
¼ teaspoon pepper
1 teaspoon salt, or to taste
3 cups water
1 cup chopped tomato, fresh or canned
3 dried limes (limoo amoni, see Glossary), opened, powdered, seeds discarded
1 tablespoon lemon juice
1 cup yellow split peas, covered with water for 2 hours, drained
½ pound fresh okra, ⅛ inch trimmed from top and bottom

1. Put the meat, bones and onions into a large pan and stir-fry without oil over low heat for 10 minutes. This will evaporate the moisture so meat can be browned. Add 1 tablespoon oil and stir-fry for 10 minutes more, which will brown the meat and onions. Add the turmeric, pepper and salt during this process.

3. Add the water, bring to a boil, cover the pan, and cook over low heat for ½ hour to tenderize the meat. Add the tomato and continue to cook for ½ hour more. Add the powdered limes, lemon juice and split peas. Cook for 15 minutes.

3. Put the remaining 1 tablespoon oil in a skillet and stir-fry the okra over moderate heat for 5 minutes. Add okra to the meat pan when the peas become soft but not mushy. Cook everything together for 10 minutes more.

Serve warm with any kind of Persian rice. Serves 8.

KHORESHT BAY
Beef and Quince Stew with Pomegranate Sauce

Imaginative culinary minds were at work when this fine combination was invented. Fresh quinces are seasonal; to make them available all year round, prepare as follows: Peel the quinces and cut the fruit into small finger-size sticks. Put them into a plastic bag and freeze; they can be stored for up to 1 year. Another method is to stir-fry the quince sticks (1 large quince) in 1 tablespoon corn oil for 3 minutes. This will reduce the bulk. Cool and freeze.

> 3 tablespoons corn oil
> 1 large ripe quince, peeled, cut into sticks 2 inches by ¼ inch
> 1 medium onion, chopped (½ cup)
> 1½ pounds boneless beef chuck, cut into 3-inch pieces
> 4 cups water
> ½ teaspoon salt
> ⅛ teaspoon pepper
> ½ cup aloo bukhara (see Glossary)
> 2 tablespoons tomato paste
> ½ cup pomegranate concentrate, or 2 cups fresh juice (see Note)

1. Heat 1 tablespoon oil in a pan and stir-fry the quince over moderate heat for 2 minutes. Remove and set aside.

2. Heat 2 tablespoons oil in the same pan, add the onion, and stir-fry over moderate heat until it becomes golden. Add the beef and brown for 5 minutes. Add the water, salt and pepper, bring to a boil and cook, covered, for 15 minutes. Add the *aloo bukhara* and continue to cook until the beef is almost tender, about 45 minutes.

3. Add the tomato paste and pomegranate concentrate and cook for 5 minutes. Lastly, add the prefried quince and cook for 3 minutes more. The finished dish should have a substantial amount of sauce.

Serve warm with rice. Serves 6 with other dishes.

VARIATION: Lamb, chicken, turkey can also be prepared with the same flavorings. Timing is different according to the type of meat. The time for lamb and beef is the same, about 1 hour and 15 minutes with 4 cups of water.

The time for chicken and turkey is the same; use parts such as thigh and breast with 3 cups water and cook for 1 hour. The *aloo bukhara* should be added to the pan at the same time as the poultry.

NOTE: Should you use pomegranate juice, which is available bottled, reduce the water to 2 cups.

KHORESHT BAMIEH LAPE
Meat, Okra and Yellow
Split-Pea Stew

Here is another Persian stew, one of an endless array of combinations that have proven the test of time. Okra, popular in Persia, enhances any dish, and ½ pound of eggplant may be broiled and added for a variation.

3 tablespoons corn oil
½ pound fresh okra
1 medium onion, chopped (½ cup)
¼ teaspoon ground turmeric
½ pound boneless beef or lamb, cut into 1-inch cubes
½ cup yellow split peas, rinsed well
3 cups water
1 teaspoon salt
⅛ teaspoon pepper
⅔ cup canned or fresh tomato sauce
¼ teaspoon Advieh (see Index) or ground cinnamon
2 teaspoons lemon juice

1. Heat 1 tablespoon of oil in a skillet, add the okra, and stir-fry over moderate heat for 3 minutes, to brown lightly. Set aside.

2. Heat 2 tablespoons oil in a pan, add the onion and turmeric, and stir-fry over moderate heat for 3 minutes to brown lightly. Add the meat cubes and stir-fry for 3 minutes more. Add the yellow split peas and stir-fry for another minute.

3. Add the water, salt and pepper and bring to a boil; cover the pan and simmer over low heat for 1 hour. Add the tomato sauce, Advieh and lemon juice and continue to simmer for 15 minutes. Add the okra and cook for 10 minutes more. The rich red sauce is thick with peas and tender meat and the okra is not overcooked.

Serve warm with white rice. Serves 4 to 6 with other dishes.

KHORESHT CHOGONDAR
Beet, Beef and Fruit Stew

Surprisingly there are no herbs in this preparation. The stew relies on the slightly tart taste provided by the prunes and quince. The beets provide their natural sweetness and color and the combination with tender beef is a winner.

3 tablespoons corn oil
⅛ teaspoon ground turmeric
2 medium onions, sliced (1 cup)
2 pounds boneless beef chuck, cut into 1-inch cubes
2 cups water
1 teaspoon salt, or to taste
⅛ teaspoon pepper
1 pound cooked beets, peeled, sliced ¼ inch thick
1 pound prunes, just covered in water for 1 hour

1. Heat the oil in a pan, add the turmeric and onions, and stir-fry over moderate heat for 2 minutes. Add the beef cubes and stir-fry for 5 minutes to brown.

2. Add the water, salt and pepper and bring to a boil. Cover the pan and simmer over low heat for 15 minutes. Add the beets, quince, prunes and the soaking liquid and cook slowly for 2 hours. There should be some sauce left at the end of cooking time.

Serve warm with rice, bread and table pickles
Serves 6 to 8 with other dishes.

KHORESHT ZARDALOO
Veal and Apricot Stew

The important flavorings of this stew are the fruits. A tart accent is provided by the dried lime *(limoo amoni)* and a suggestion of sweetness exerted by the honey and apricots. The result is not quite sweet-and-sour.

Should quince not be available, omit it and double the amount of apricots.

1 cup dried apricots
3 cups water
1 pound boneless veal, cut into 2-inch cubes
1 cup ½-inch slices of celery
2 dried limes (limoo amoni), broken into large pieces
¼ cup tomato paste
¼ teaspoon ground turmeric
1 teaspoon honey
1 teaspoon salt
1 fresh quince, peeled, sliced into 3-inch lengths ¼ inch thick

1. Soak the apricots in 1 cup water for 2 hours.
2. Put all the ingredients into a large pan, including the soaked apricots and liquid. Bring to a boil and simmer over low heat for about 1½ hours to tenderize the veal. The liquid will evaporate somewhat but there should be substantial sauce.

Serve warm with white rice.
Serves 4 to 6 with other dishes.

KHORESHT GARCH
Veal and Mushroom Stew

This is a favorite Passover dish in the family where I was being taught. It was the rainy season in the mountains near Teheran and wild mushrooms were brought in by the peasants who could tell the difference between those edible and poisonous. In the absence of authentic wild mushrooms, large meaty domestic types can be substituted to good account.

3 tablespoons corn oil
¼ teaspoon ground turmeric
2 medium onions, chopped (1 cup)
2 pounds boneless veal, cut into 1½-inch cubes
1 teaspoon salt
⅛ teaspoon pepper
1 large bunch of flat-leaf Italian parsley, chopped (3 cups)
2 large leeks, white and green parts, chopped (3 cups)
3 cups chopped tender celery leaves and ribs
1½ cups water
2 pounds domestic or wild mushrooms, halved or quartered

1. Heat the oil in a large pan; add the turmeric and onions and stir-fry over moderate heat for 2 minutes. Add the veal, salt and pepper and stir-fry for 5 minutes to brown.

2. Add the parsley, leeks and celery leaves and stir-fry for 3 minutes to reduce. Add the water, bring to a boil, cover the pan, and simmer over low heat for 45 minutes to tenderize the veal. Add the mushrooms and simmer, covered, for 15 minutes more.

Serve warm with any kind of rice. Serves 6 to 8 with other dishes.

KHORESHT NANO, JAFAREE, ALOO BUKHARA

Lamb Stew with Mint, Parsley and Prunes

Certain culinary rules are to be followed in this aromatic stew. One is that the chopped herbs are very lightly fried before any liquid is added. This intensifies their flavor and reduces the bulk. The fruit provides another texture to the mixture and the stew is a perfect blend of flavors with no one flavoring too sharp or sweet.

3 tablespoons corn oil
¼ teaspoon ground turmeric
2 medium onions, chopped (1 cup)
1 pound boneless lamb, cut into 2-inch cubes
1 small bunch of fresh chives, chopped (1 cup)

¼ cup chopped fresh mint leaves
1 large bunch of Italian flat-leaf parsley, chopped (2 cups)
1 teaspoon salt
⅛ teaspoon pepper
2 cups water
1 cup prunes, soaked in 1 cup water for 1 hour

1. Put the oil, turmeric and onions in a pan large enough to hold everything and stir-fry over moderate heat for 3 minutes to brown the onion lightly. Add the lamb and fry for 1 minute. Add the chives, mint, parsley, salt and pepper and stir-fry for 2 minutes.

2. Pour in the water, bring to a boil, cover the pan, and cook over low heat for ½ hour. Add the prunes and soaking liquid and continue to cook until the meat is tender, about ½ hour more. There will be a generous amount of herb sauce.

Serve warm. Serves 4 to 6 with other dishes especially *Chelo* (white rice) with *tadiq* and table pickles.

KHORESHT GREMEH LAPE

Tomato and Split-Pea Stew with Meat Cubes

Tomatoes are not often a paramount ingredient in Persian cooking since the vegetable was a latecomer here. The Spanish, who discovered this marvelous fruit in the Valley of Mexico and Guatemala, bypassed Persia on their way through Southeast Asia. However, in this stew the tomato fulfills the requirement for tart seasoning, which Persians enjoy. The *limoo amoni* (dried lime) is cooked whole, providing additional tartness to the other ingredients. Crushing the *limoo* would discolor the stew—which is inadvisable.

1½ cups yellow split peas
3 tablespoons corn oil
1 medium onion, chopped (½ cup)
1 pound boneless lamb or beef, cut into 2-inch cubes
¼ teaspoon ground turmeric
¼ teaspoon Advieh (see Index)
2 cups water

4 or 5 dried limes (limoo amoni; see Glossary) to taste, pierced
    with a fork in 1 or 2 places
2 cups crushed tomatoes, fresh or canned
1 large potato, about 2 cups, prepared as for french fries

1. Rinse the peas and drain well. Heat 1 tablespoon oil in a pan
and stir-fry the peas over moderate heat for 2 minutes. Remove and
set aside.

2. Add the balance of the oil (2 tablespoons) to the pan, add the
onion and meat, and stir-fry over moderate heat for 2 minutes. Add
the turmeric, Advieh, water and limes. Mix and bring to a boil.
Cook for 20 minutes, then add the split peas and tomatoes and
continue to cook for ½ hour more, or until the meat is tender. The
peas should retain their shape.

3. Fold in the french fries, prepared in advance, and cook for 5
minutes more. There is ample sauce in the stew.

Serve warm with your pilau of choice. Serves 6 with other
dishes.

KHORESHT KARAFS
Beef and Celery Stew

The English transla-
tion of this khoresht does not begin to describe the nuances
found here, as so often happens in Persian cooking. A list of
the herbs and seasonings suggests the subtlety of the flavoring, and that the stew will be aromatic rather than spicy.
The unexpected addition of prunes identifies it as a Jewish
version.

2 tablespoons plus 2 teaspoons corn oil
2 pounds boneless beef or veal, cut into 3-inch pieces
1 pound beef or veal bones
1 medium onion, coarsely cut (about ¾ cup)
1¼ teaspoons salt
8 cups water
8 cups 2-inch pieces of tender celery ribs
½ cup chopped celery leaves
2 bunches of flat-leaf Italian parsley, chopped (4 cups)
1 tablespoon dried mint leaves, or ¼ cup chopped fresh

2 teaspoons crushed dried lime (limoo amoni; see Glossary)
2 tablespoons tomato paste
12 medium prunes, covered with ½ cup water for 1 hour

1. Put 1 tablespoon of the oil in a soup kettle, heat, and add the meat, bones, onion and ½ teaspoon salt. Sauté over low heat for 15 minutes, or until light brown. Add the water, bring to a boil, and cook over low heat for 1 hour.

2. While the meat is simmering, heat another tablespoon of the oil in a skillet, add the celery and ½ teaspoon salt, and stir-fry over moderate heat for 5 minutes to soften slightly. Put in a dish and set aside. In the same skillet, add the 2 teaspoons of corn oil, heat, and add the celery leaves, parsley, mint and remaining ¼ teaspoon salt. Stir-fry over moderate heat for 3 minutes. Set aside.

3. When the soup has cooked for 1 hour, add the celery, herbs, dried lime, tomato paste, prunes and soaking liquid. Simmer over low heat, covered, for 45 minutes more. Remove and discard the meat bones. There should be ample sauce, thick with herbs and meat.

Serve warm with rice. Serves 8 to 10 with other dishes.

KHORESHT KORME SABZI
Veal Sauté with Herbs

Veal used with red kidney beans, flavored with herbs and crushed *limoo* confirms the ingenuity of Persian cooks. Notice the absence of sugar—it is the tart combinations that are characteristic of Persian cooking. Fenugreek leaves are frequently found in Indian food but only occasionally in the stews of Persia.

3 pounds veal breast or shoulder with bone, cut into 3-inch pieces
2 medium onions, coarsely cut (1 cup)
6 tablespoons corn oil
6 cups water
1 cup dried red kidney beans, soaked in water overnight, drained
6 scallions, sliced thin
2 bunches of Italian flat-leaf parsley, chopped (3 cups)
1 large leek, both white and green parts, sliced thin
1 tablespoon chopped fresh mint

2 teaspoons salt, or to taste
2 tablespoons tomato paste
1 tablespoon dried fenugreek leaves (optional) (see Glossary)
1 tablespoon crushed dried lime (limoo amoni, see Glossary)

1. Put the veal, onions and 3 tablespoons oil into a pan and stir-fry over low heat for 10 minutes to brown lightly. Add the water and beans and bring to a boil. Cook over moderately low heat, covered, for 1 hour, to tenderize the meat and beans.

2. Heat the remaining 3 tablespoons oil in a skillet, add the scallions, parsley, leek and mint, and stir-fry over moderate heat for 10 minutes to reduce the bulk and lightly sauté the herbs. Add the sautéed herbs, salt, tomato paste, fenugreek and lime (limoo) to the veal and bean mixture at the end of the hour. Simmer over low heat for ½ hour more, to integrate the flavors. Total cooking time is about 1½ hours. This stew has ample sauce.

Serve warm with any Persian rice. Serves 8 to 10.

VARIATION: Three pounds of beef chuck with or without bone, or ribs of beef, can be substituted for the veal. Both veal and beef are traditionally used.

SHIFTE KADOO
Pumpkin and Lamb Kebob Sauté

Pumpkin is a common vegetable in Persia and is popular with the Jews. This dish, the shifte kadoo, is a good example of the unusual combinations that rely on various seasonings and flavors rather than an assortment of the vivid spices used in India.

1 cup dried green mung beans, soaked in 2 cups water overnight
1 pound ground lamb
1 medium onion, grated (½ cup)
1 teaspoon salt
¼ teaspoon pepper
¼ teaspoon ground turmeric
2 tablespoons corn oil
2 medium onions, chopped (1 cup)
1 pound pumpkin, peeled, cut into 3-inch pieces

*1 cup dried apricots (aloo bukhara), soaked in 1 cup water for 1
    hour*
1 cup water

1. Stir the soaked mung beans briskly to remove the skins. Scoop off the skins with a slotted spoon and discard them. Put the beans and soaking liquid in a large pan.

2. Mix the lamb, grated onion, salt, pepper and turmeric together by hand or in a processor. Set aside.

3. Heat the oil in a skillet and stir-fry the chopped onions over low heat for about 4 minutes to turn them golden and light brown on the edges. Pour this into the pan with the beans. Add the pumpkin pieces, the apricots (aloo bukhara; see Glossary) and liquid, and the 1 cup water and bring everything to a boil.

4. Take 1 heaping tablespoon of the lamb mix for each kabob and shape cylinders 2 inches long and 1 inch thick. Put these into the bean and pumpkin pan one by one. Cover the pan and cook over low heat, without stirring, for 15 minutes, or until all ingredients are tender but not mushy. Cook for 5 to 10 minutes more if too firm.

Serve warm with the ample sauce. Serves 6 to 8 with rice and salad.

KOOFTEH BERENJI
Herbed Rice Balls in Broth

These aromatic rice balls have all the characteristics of Persian cooking: rice (berenji in the Farsi language), the meat of your choice, combined with a plethora of herbs such as parsley, dill, tarragon, leeks—with basil and peppery savory optional but highly recommended. Turmeric and cuminseed add extra zip.

RICE BALLS

*½ pound ground veal or lamb mixed with 2 tablespoons
    chopped onion*
1 cup raw rice, soaked in water for 1 hour, drained
1 tablespoon corn oil
1 tablespoon dried tarragon

½ cup chopped fresh dill
1 medium leek, chopped fine (¾ cup)
1 cup chopped Italian flat-leaf parsley
1 teaspoon chopped basil (optional)
1 teaspoon chopped savory (optional)
1 teaspoon salt
¼ teaspoon pepper
¼ teaspoon ground cuminseed
1 egg, beaten
6 dried apricots
¾ teaspoon ground dried lime (limoo amoni; see Glossary)

BROTH

1 tablespoon corn oil
1 medium onion, chopped (½ cup)
1 cup dried lima beans, soaked in 3 cups water overnight
2 cups water
½ teaspoon salt
⅛ teaspoon pepper

1. Mix together well the meat, rice, oil, tarragon, dill, leek, parsley, basil, savory, salt, pepper, turmeric, cuminseed and egg. Prepare balls 2½ inches in diameter. Push your thumb to the center of each ball and stuff each with 1 apricot and ⅛ teaspoon lime. Firmly roll it closed. Prepare all the balls this way and refrigerate them on a plate for 1 hour, or until ready to cook.

2. To prepare the broth, heat the oil in a large pan, add the onion, and stir-fry over moderate heat until the onion is light brown, about 3 minutes. Add the lima beans, soaking water and the additional 2 cups water, the salt and pepper. Bring to a boil and cook over low heat for 15 minutes.

3. Carefully add the rice balls to the pan, cover, and cook over low heat for ½ hour. This should be sufficient to soften the beans and cook the meat and rice.

Serve warm. Each serving is 1 meatball in about 1 cup broth. Serves 6 with other dishes.

SHAMI GONDHI
Ground Lamb Balls in Prune Sauce

This fine preparation shows its Persian heritage by the use of carrot and cardamom in the meat, by the use of toasted chick-pea flour and the whole colored with turmeric. All this is a strong sauce strengthened with the prunes, either golden or black.

LAMB BALLS

    1 pound ground lamb
    2 medium onions, chopped (1 cup)
    3 carrots, grated
    2 cups ground toasted chick-pea flour (nachochi; see Glossary)
    1 teaspoon salt
    ¼ teaspoon pepper
    ½ teaspoon ground cardamom
    ¼ teaspoon ground turmeric
    ½ teaspoon baking soda
    2 or 3 tablespoons cold water

SAUCE

    1 cup dried apricots (aloo bukhara; see Glossary) or medium
        black prunes
    4 cups water
    2 tablespoons corn oil
    1 medium onion, chopped (½ cup)
    ¼ teaspoon ground cardamom
    ⅛ teaspoon pepper
    ½ teaspoon salt
    ⅛ teaspoon ground turmeric

1. Mix lamb ball ingredients together into a manageable consistency, using as much water as necessary. Prepare round balls 2 inches in diameter. Set aside. This step may be done several hours in advance and the lamb balls refrigerated. Makes 20 balls.
2. Soak the aloo or prunes in water for 1 hour. Bring to a boil in a large saucepan and cook over low heat for 10 minutes.
3. Heat the oil in a skillet, add the onion, and stir-fry over moderate heat for 2 minutes. Add this to the prune sauce with

cardamom, pepper, salt, and turmeric. Bring to a simmer and carefully add the lamb balls, one at a time, to the pan, cover, and cook over low heat for 20 minutes. This makes a generous amount of sauce or broth.

Serve everything together in a soup dish.

Serves 6 with white rice and other dishes.

SHAMI KEBAB
Ground Lamb and Carrot Cutlet

The Persians artfully combine chick-pea flour (also a common ingredient in India) with meat and vegetables in this substantial cutlet. Chick-pea flour is dry and can only be integrated into the meat mixture with liquid. The moist onion, carrot and cold water provide this. I also prefer to refrigerate the mixture for ½ hour before cooking—long enough to let the seasonings blend with the moisture—or it could be prepared several hours in advance to ease the pressure of last-minute assembly.

1 pound ground lamb
2 medium onions, chopped
3 carrots, grated
1 cup ground, toasted chick-pea flour (nachochi; see Glossary)
1 teaspoon salt, or to taste
¼ teaspoon pepper
½ teaspoon ground cardamom
¼ teaspoon ground turmeric
¼ teaspoon baking soda (optional)
2 or 3 tablespoons cold water
oil for panfrying

1. Mix everything together except the oil, adding enough water to provide an easily handled batter,

2. Prepare round or oblong cutlets 3 inches in diameter, ½ inch thick. Heat about 3 tablespoons oil in a skillet and brown the cutlets, covered, over moderately low heat for 3 minutes on each side. Drain briefly on paper towels.

Serve warm. Serves 4 to 6. Makes about 10 cutlets.

DEEZEE
Meat Roast in a Clay Pot

The deezee is a stew that is very slowly cooked in its clay pot. The *limoo amoni*, dried Persian limes, are poked with the tines of a fork or skewer to allow a little soup liquid to enter and pick up the flavor. If the lime were crushed or broken into pieces, its flavor would be overwhelming. Subtlety is more important. *Deezee* is sold in public eating houses in small or large pots for 1 or 2 orders. Of course, the religious Jew would patronize a kosher eating house if one were available.

In the Jewish community, when the deezee is prepared in a pan on top of the stove it is known as *Ab Shust*. The same recipe can be modified slightly by adding either 3 sliced small beets or 2 sliced small white turnips.

¾ cup dried chick-peas, covered with water and soaked overnight
1½ pounds lamb shank, cut into 4 pieces, including bone
¼ cup yellow split peas
¼ cup skinless dried lima beans, soaked in water overnight
1 teaspoon salt
⅛ teaspoon pepper
¼ teaspoon ground turmeric
4 whole small potatoes, peeled (about ¾ pound)
1 or 2 dried limes (limoo amoni, see Glossary), pierced in 2 places
1 whole small eggplant (¼ pound) or 1 medium carrot, halved
1 small ripe tomato, quartered

1. Drain the chick-peas, cover with water again, and bring to a boil. Cook over moderate heat for about 20 minutes, which will soften but not disintegrate the peas. Drain.

2. Put the lamb, partially cooked chick-peas, split peas, lima beans, salt, pepper and turmeric in a 2-quart clay pot. Cover with water almost up to the top, about 5 cups. Bake in a 350° F. oven for 15 minutes, reduce to 275° F., and bake for 2 hours.

3. Add the potatoes, lime, eggplant or carrot and tomato. Cover the pot slightly and continue to bake slowly for 1 hour more.

Strain the broth and serve it as a separate course. Remove and discard the lamb bones. The meat and vegetables are served together on a platter as another course.

Serve warm. Serves 4 to 6 with bread, salad and pickles.

KHOREKE ZABON
Tongue and Potato Fry

This hearty, home-style cooking uses tongue in a different way. The chick-pea soup may be served as part of the meal or on a separate occasion, but I recommend serving it with the tongue and potato fry.

5 cups water
1 cup dried chick-peas, soaked in water overnight, drained
1½ pounds veal tongue
3 medium onions, sliced (1½ cups)
1 teaspoon salt
¼ teaspoon ground turmeric
⅛ teaspoon pepper
1 dried lime (limoo amoni, see Glossary), pierced with a fork, without breaking up fruit
1 pound potato, peeled, sliced as for french fries
¼ cup corn oil
1 cup green peas, fresh or frozen
3 tablespoons tomato paste

1. Bring the water to a boil in a pan with the chick-peas, tongue, 1 sliced onion, salt, turmeric, pepper and lime (limoo). Cook over moderate heat, covered, for 1 to 1½ hours, or until the tongue is completely tender. Remove it and peel off the skin. Cut tongue into ¼-inch-thick slices. Set aside. Reserve the chick-peas in the broth.

2. Dry the sliced potatoes on a towel. Heat the oil in a skillet and fry the potatoes over moderate heat until crisp and brown, about 6 minutes. Remove and set aside.

3. In the same skillet, reheat the oil, add remaining 2 sliced onions, and stir-fry over moderate heat for 3 minutes. Add the tongue slices and mix. Add the green peas and fry for 2 minutes more. Add the potatoes and tomato paste, mix well, and continue to fry the mixture for 2 minutes more.

Serve warm. Serves 6 to 8 with bread, pickles and the chick-pea soup, if wanted.

KHORKE MAGHZ
Veal Brain and Potato Sauté

H
ome-style cooking doesn't always find itself in the mainstream of ethnic cooking. Brain, for example, one of my favorite foods, is not universally popular although it is so in my teacher's Persian home.

1 pound veal brain
salt
3 tablespoons corn oil
2 potatoes (½ pound), peeled, sliced as for french fries
2 medium onions, sliced (1 cup)
¼ teaspoon ground turmeric
⅛ teaspoon pepper
3 tablespoons tomato paste, dissolved in 1 tablespoon hot water

1. Soak the brain in cold water with 2 teaspoons salt for 1 hour. Drain and remove all the membranes. Set aside.
2. Heat 2 tablespoons oil in a skillet, add the potatoes, and stir-fry over moderate heat for about 5 minutes, or until potatoes are brown and soft. Set aside.
3. Heat the remaining 1 tablespoon oil in a skillet, add onions, 1 teaspoon salt, the turmeric and pepper and stir-fry over moderate heat for 2 minutes. Add the brain and fry carefully (so that it does not break up) over low heat for 6 minutes, turning over once. Push the brain to one side of the skillet and add the potatoes on the other side. Sprinkle the tomato paste and water over all and fry for 5 minutes more.

Serve warm with the brain and potato arranged separately on the same platter. Serves 6 with other dishes.

JOOJEH ANOR
Chicken Stuffed with
Pomegranate Seeds

This is a Jewish recipe using the fresh red seeds of the pomegranate. The simple stuffing has a light fruity flavor.

2 tablespoons corn oil
1 young chicken, 1½ pounds, or Cornish game hen
1 medium onion, chopped (½ cup)
3 tablespoons fresh pomegranate seeds (see Glossary)
3 tablespoons raw rice, cooked in water for 5 minutes, drained
½ teaspoon salt
⅛ teaspoon pepper
1 tablespoon lemon juice
2 tablespoons water

1. Heat the oil in a pan and brown the chicken on all sides over moderate heat for 5 minutes. Remove the chicken.

2. In the same pan, stir-fry the onion for 3 minutes, or until golden. Remove the onion and mix it with the pomegranate seeds, rice, salt and pepper, and use this to stuff the chicken. It is not necessary to sew it up. Put the chicken back in the same pan, mix the lemon juice and water, and pour it around over the chicken. Cover the pan and bake in a 350° F. oven for 45 minutes. Baste now and then with the juices.

Serve warm. Serves 4 with other dishes.

FESENJAN I
Meatball Stew in Pomegranate
and Walnut Sauce

This is probably the most celebrated and popular dish in the Persian repertoire. It is respected, glorified, embellished with adjectives, and it deserves it all. My Persian teacher told me it was "a dish for gentlemen," meaning that it is expensive to prepare. The vital ingredient is the pomegranate juice (concentrate), which is available bottled.

Fesenjan is eclectic but chicken is the most popular. Duck, turkey, lamb, beef, veal may also be used as boneless cubes, poultry parts with the bone, or meatballs. All have their aficionados and are enhanced by the sauce. Wild duck, when available in Iran, is cooked whole in the *fesenjan* sauce. A Long Island duckling is a reasonable substitute. This is considered to be a winter dish since its dense, richly flavored sauce and meat are overpowering during the summer heat.

MEATBALLS

2 pounds ground lamb, beef, veal or turkey
1 medium onion, grated (½ cup)
1 teaspoon salt
¼ teaspoon pepper
5 tablespoons corn oil
2 medium onions, chopped (1 cup)
2 cups shelled walnuts, toasted

SAUCE

¼ teaspoon ground turmeric
⅓ cup pomegranate concentrate, or 2 cups fresh juice (if using
    fresh juice, reduce water to 1 cup)
2 cups water
½ cup tomato paste
1 cup dried apricots (aloo bukhara; see Glossary) or medium
    prunes, soaked in 1 cup water for 2 hours
1 teaspoon Advieh spice mixture (see Index, optional)

1. Mix the meat, grated onion, salt and pepper together. Prepare miniature meatballs 1 inch in diameter. Heat 3 tablespoons of the oil in a large skillet and brown the meatballs on all sides for 3 minutes so that they hold their shape. Set aside.

2. Heat remaining oil in a large pan and stir-fry the chopped onions over moderate heat until light brown, about 3 minutes. Add the meatballs to the pan and set aside. Grind the toasted walnuts fine in a processor and add to the onion and meatballs.

3. Put all the sauce ingredients in the pan with the meat and walnuts. Bring to a boil and mix carefully so as not to break up the meatballs. Turn the heat to low, cover the pan, and cook for 1 hour.

Stir now and then to prevent burning. The oil will rise to the top when the *fesenjan* is ready.

The sauce will become very dark and thick. Some cooks prefer to continue the cooking for up to 2 hours, more suitable when using the meat chunks and poultry pieces. There should be plenty of sauce.

Serve warm with white rice and *tadiq*. Serves 6 to 8 with other dishes.

NOTE: To toast the walnuts, place them in a dry skillet over moderate heat for about 2 minutes, stirring continuously so that they do not scorch, or toast them on a baking sheet in a 350° F. oven for 5 minutes.

VARIATIONS: Using the same ingredients and proportions for the sauce, try any of the variations listed. The exception is the duck, where it is necessary to increase seasonings by half. Note that all meats must be browned in oil with the onion.

Dried fruit is an admirable addition to the *fesenjan* and the American kitchen will have 3 traditional choices: dried apricots, the yellow prune or medium black prunes. The addition of the fruit is a matter of personal preference but is recommended.

Fresh pomegranate juice is sometimes available in Middle East markets.

DUCK

Use a duck weighing about 4½ pounds, cut into 8 pieces, loose skin and fat discarded. Since American ducks are fat it is suggested that the *fesenjan* be prepared 1 day in advance, refrigerated, and the congealed fat discarded. Then rewarm.

TURKEY

Two pounds of boneless turkey cut into 2- or 3-inch pieces produces an excellent and relatively fatless *fesenjan*.

LAMB

Persians eat a lot of lamb since it is the most available meat in that country. Use 2 pounds boneless lamb cut into 3-inch pieces, or use other parts of the lamb with bone, such as the shank, cut into 2-inch rounds.

FESENJAN II
Chicken in Pomegranate, Walnut and Prune Sauce

Here is another, perhaps simpler, version of the *fesenjan*, using chicken parts.

2 tablespoons corn oil
2 medium onions, sliced (1 cup)
3 pounds chicken parts—legs, breast, thigh—8 pieces, loose skin
    and fat discarded
2 cups shelled walnuts, ground fine
2 cups water
1½ cups medium prunes, covered with water for 2 hours
1 teaspoon salt, or to taste
¼ teaspoon ground turmeric
⅓ cup pomegranate concentrate (see Glossary)

1. Heat the oil in a pan, add the onions, and stir-fry over moderate heat for 2 minutes. Add the chicken, cover the pan, and brown for 5 minutes, turning the pieces now and then.
2. Add the walnuts, mix well, cover the pan, and cook over low heat for 5 minutes. Stir several times to prevent sticking. Add the water and continue cooking for ½ hour.
3. Add the prunes and liquid, salt and turmeric and simmer for 15 minutes. Lastly, add the pomegranate concentrate and simmer for 10 minutes more. Total cooking time should be about 1 hour.
Serve warm with white rice. Serves 6 to 8 with other dishes.

JOOJEH BAADEM JAN
Chicken Stew with Green Beans and Eggplant

Thick eggplant steaks and tomato add delicious flavor to chicken in this recipe. This is a big party preparation, served at Jewish weddings when something special is required. Lemon juice heightens the seasonings and the beans contribute texture.

2 pounds eggplant (about 2)
salt

4 tablespoons corn oil

3 pounds chicken parts—thighs, legs, breast—8 pieces, loose skin
     and fat discarded

2 medium onions, sliced (1 cup)

¼ teaspoon ground turmeric

¼ teaspoon pepper

1 large ripe tomato, chopped (¾ cup), or equal amount of canned

1 pound green beans, cut into 2-inch pieces

½ cup tomato paste, dissolved in 1½ cups hot water

2 tablespoons lemon juice

1. Peel the eggplants and cut them lengthwise into ½-inch-thick slices. Soak them in 3 cups water and 1 tablespoon salt for ½ hour. Drain; rinse well in cold water and dry the slices on a towel. Heat 2 tablespoons oil in a skillet and fry the eggplant on both sides over moderate heat for 3 minutes, to soften. Cover the pan during this step. Remove slices to a plate and set aside.

2. Heat remaining 2 tablespoons oil in a large pan and over moderate heat brown the chicken pieces for 10 minutes. Add the onions, 1 teaspoon salt, the turmeric and pepper, mix well, cover the pan, and fry for 5 minutes more. Add the fresh tomato and beans and cook, covered, for 5 minutes more.

3. Add the tomato paste dissolved in water and mix everything together. Place the eggplant slices on top of the mixture but do not stir. Cover the pan and cook over low heat for 15 minutes.

There should be ample thick sauce. Adjust the salt and pepper to taste. Sprinkle the lemon juice over all, cover the pan, and simmer slowly for 5 minutes more.

Serve warm with white rice and its crust (the tadiq, see Glossary). Serves 8.

VARIATION: Lamb or beef may be used instead of chicken. For this recipe use 2 pounds of boneless meat cut into 2-inch cubes, browned with the onion, salt, turmeric and pepper for 20 minutes. Proceed as for the chicken but extend the total cooking time to about 1 hour, long enough to tenderize the meat.

KEBAB DIGI
Pan Kebabs

Persian rice served with meat kebabs is the national dish and is called *chelo kabab*. There are variations from one family to another but the kebabs are essentially lightly seasoned meats, marinated as long as is convenient, and grilled over the hot ashes of charcoal. The meats can be prepared in advance, refrigerated or not, and grilled for family or friends when wanted.

> 2 pounds boneless chicken or turkey, cut into 2-inch cubes
> 1 teaspoon salt
> ¼ teaspoon pepper
> ¼ teaspoon whole saffron, crushed with ¼ teaspoon sugar,
>   dissolved in 1 teaspoon warm water
> 2 tablespoons lemon juice
> 1 medium onion, grated, then squeezed out to make the liquid for
>   the marinade (use onion pieces in soup)

1. Mix everything together and marinate overnight.

2. The next day put 4 or 5 cubes of chicken on each of 10 skewers. Oil a pan large enough so that the skewers fit flat on the bottom. Put in the filled skewers, cover the pan, and cook over low heat for 10 minutes. This will partially cook the chicken.

3. Remove the skewers from the pan and put them under a gas or electric broiler for 5 minutes or a bit more to ensure that the chicken is cooked through. The skewers of chicken may also be grilled over charcoal.

Serve warm with Persian Rice (Chelo, see Index). Serves 6 with other dishes.

VARIATIONS:

BEEF

Use 2 pounds flank or sirloin steak cut into kebab strips 2 inches wide and 5 inches long. Score the steak horizontally every inch along the entire length. Soak in the same marinade as the chicken overnight. Fit 1 beef strip on each metal skewer and grill directly in a gas or electric broiler or over charcoal.

GROUND BEEF

1 pound ground beef
1 medium onion, grated (½ cup)
½ teaspoon salt
¼ teaspoon pepper
½ teaspoon ground cuminseed
¼ teaspoon baking soda

1. Mix everything together and let sit for several hours, overnight, or for just a few minutes.

2. The modern way would be to oil a shallow metal baking dish, put the kebab mixture into the pan and flatten out to about ¾ inch thick. Then separate the meat with a spatula or knife into strips 1 inch wide and 5 inches long. Leave ½-inch space between the ground meat strips. This is to simulate the idea of the meat being fitted on metal skewers (known as *seekhs*). Broil for about 6 minutes, turning over once.

Serve warm with rice. Makes 4 or 5 pan kebabs.

KHORESHT KARI
Mushroom and Chicken Curry Persian-Style

Curry powder is used in Persia as well as in India. The difference is that the amount and intensity is more restrained. Mushrooms and boneless cubes of chicken give this curry a refinement that is not often found in India. Note that the mushrooms and chicken cubes should be about the same size.

3 tablespoons corn oil
⅛ teaspoon ground turmeric
2 medium onions, chopped (1 cup)
⅛ teaspoon ground cinnamon
1 teaspoon mild curry powder, or ½ teaspoon hot powder
1 pound boneless chicken breast, cut into 1-inch cubes
¾ cup water
1 teaspoon salt
1 pound small whole mushrooms, well rinsed

1. Heat the oil in a pan, add the turmeric and onions, and stir-fry over moderate heat for 3 minutes to brown lightly. Add the cinnamon and curry powder and mix well, then add the chicken cubes and stir-fry over moderate heat for another 2 minutes.

2. Add the water and salt, bring to a simmer, add the mushrooms, cover the pan, and cook over low heat for 15 minutes more. Stir once or twice during this process. There will be only a modest amount of sauce.

Serve warm with white rice and table pickles. Serves 4 to 6 with other dishes.

TACHIN JOOJEH

Layered Chicken, Rice, Egg and Yoghurt

Tachin, which means "what is put on the bottom layer of a casserole" (a loose but close translation), is one of the most interesting and perhaps easily adaptable Persian dishes for the American kitchen. It can be made in large casseroles, an ideal situation for entertaining groups. The *tachin*, which has a firm crust at the bottom of the casserole, is one of the culinary novelties that make Persian cooking unique. This is the non-kosher version since chicken and yoghurt are combined.

CHICKEN

> 1 tablespoon corn oil
> 1 medium onion, sliced (½ cup)
> ⅛ teaspoon ground turmeric
> ⅛ teaspoon pepper
> 1 pound boneless chicken breast and thigh, cut into 2-inch cubes
> 1 teaspoon salt
> 2 tablespoons water

TACHIN

> 1 egg, beaten with ⅛ teaspoon salt, ⅛ teaspoon pepper
> ½ cup yoghurt

¼ teaspoon whole saffron, crushed with ¼ teaspoon sugar, using
   mortar and pestle
2 cups raw rice, well rinsed and cooked for 8 minutes
3 tablespoons corn oil
2 tablespoons margarine
2 tablespoons barberries (zereshk) (see Glossary), or dried
   currants (optional garnish)

1. Heat the oil in a skillet, add the onion, turmeric and pepper, and stir-fry for 3 minutes. Add the chicken and salt, mix well, and cover the pan. Cook over low heat for 10 minutes, then add the water to lubricate the mixture and cook for 5 minutes more. Set aside.

2. Mix the beaten egg, yoghurt and saffron together well. Add half of the half-cooked rice and mix well.

3. Prepare a 1½-quart casserole, round or rectangular, preferably heatproof glass, by adding the oil and swirling it around. Add the *tachin* mixture and spread over the casserole. Over that arrange the chicken cubes and onions. Over that spread the balance of the rice. Dot with margarine. Cover the casserole with aluminum foil or the casserole cover and bake in a 400° F. oven for about 45 minutes, or until you can see that the bottom *tachin* has become quite brown and crisp. Do not burn.

4. Remove casserole from the oven and turn it upside down on a platter. Cover this with a cloth towel for about 3 minutes. The entire contents will descend into the platter with the *tachin* as a firm crust overall. Stir-fry the barberries in hot oil *off the heat* for 1 minute, which turns them quite red. Sprinkle over the *tachin* as a garnish.

Cut through the crust to make 3- or 4-inch serving pieces.
Serve warm. Serves 6.

VARIATION: To prepare Tachin Joojeh in kosher style, do not cook yoghurt and chicken together. For those who keep a kosher home this preparation can be modified in a very simple manner, in other words how to have your cake and eat it. In the step preparing the *tachin* omit the yoghurt and replace it with 1 tablespoon fresh lemon juice. Beat the egg, lemon juice, salt, pepper, saffron and 2 tablespoons water together. Add half of the rice to this mixture and put it into the oiled casserole. Continue to completion as in the basic preparation.

NOTE: *Zoch* is a Farsi word that means an unpleasant aroma associated with foods. Persians say that using pepper and turmeric with meat, poultry and fish removes that aroma during cooking. Turmeric especially has this characteristic and so is used in almost all dishes.

BORANEE
Spinach and Egg Fry

The important feature of this dish is its simplicity—a spinach and egg combination, bright with the yellow of turmeric and green of the spinach. Using fresh and tender spinach is the key.

> 2 pounds fresh spinach, well rinsed, drained and coarsely cut
> ¼ cup water
> 2 tablespoons corn oil
> 2 medium onions, sliced thin (1 cup)
> ½ teaspoon salt, or to taste
> ⅛ teaspoon ground turmeric
> ⅛ teaspoon pepper
> 6 eggs

1. Put the spinach and water in a pan, cover, and cook over low heat for 5 minutes. Let stand for 5 minutes more to reduce the bulk. Cool and press out the liquid that accumulates. Set aside.

2. Heat the oil in a large skillet. Add the onions, salt, turmeric and pepper and stir-fry over moderate heat for 3 minutes. Add the spinach and stir-fry for 3 minutes more. Remove skillet from the heat.

3. Make 6 depressions in the spinach. Break 1 egg into each depression and return the skillet to low heat. Fry for 5 minutes, or enough to set the eggs firmly.

VARIATION: For smaller quantities, that is to say half of the recipe, beat the eggs and scramble them together with the spinach after it has been steamed, squeezed, and stir-fried with the onions and seasonings.

JEGER E JOOJEH GELIE TOCHM

Chicken-Liver Sauté with Potato and Egg Garnish

This is family-style cooking, which relies on the simple flavors of the basic ingredients without the embellishment of strong spices or herbs.

    3 tablespoons corn oil
    2 medium onions, chopped (1 cup)
    1 pound chicken livers, divided into lobes
    1 teaspoon salt, or to taste
    ¼ teaspoon pepper
    2 medium potatoes, cut and cooked as french fries
    4 eggs

1. Heat the oil in a large skillet, add the onions, and stir-fry over moderate heat for 2 minutes. Add the livers, sprinkle with salt and pepper, and stir-fry for 5 minutes.

2. Fold in the french fries, which have been cooked in advance. Shape 4 depressions in the skillet mixture and break 1 egg into each depression. Fry, without stirring, for 3 minutes.

Serve the combination in the skillet

Serve warm. Serves 4 to 6 with white rice.

TOCHMEH CHORMA

Date and Egg Breakfast

Persian housewives would purchase a box of dates containing several pounds and have them available for everyday use. As a family-style dish, the dates and eggs were prepared this way for breakfast. Nourishing and tasty.

    3 tablespoons corn oil
    1 medium onion, chopped (½ cup)
    1 cup pitted dates
    ¼ teaspoon pepper
    4 eggs
    ½ teaspoon salt

1. Heat the oil in a skillet and stir-fry the onion until golden. Add the dates and pepper and stir-fry over low heat for 3 minutes.

2. Make 4 depressions in the date/onion mixture and add 1 whole egg to each depression. Sprinkle with salt and fry for 3 minutes to cook the eggs.

Serve warm, with 1 egg and some dates to each person. Serves 4.

KUKU SABZI I
Herb Omelet or Patty

Herbs are the national Persian addiction; this combination of herbs and eggs may be prepared as several small patties or as a single omelet. A more modern way would be to bake it in the skillet in a 375° F. oven for 15 minutes. You may or may not turn the omelet over to brown on both sides.

> 2 ounces each of fresh coriander, Italian flat-leaf parsley and dill,
>   chopped together
> 6 eggs, beaten
> 1 teaspoon flour
> 1 teaspoon salt
> ¼ teaspoon pepper
> oil for panfrying

Mix everything together except the oil. Heat the oil in a skillet. Scoop up 1 heaping tablespoon of the mixture for each individual omelet and fry each one over moderate heat for 2 minutes on each side.

Serve warm with yoghurt and white rice. Serves 4.

KUKU SABZI II
Green Herb Omelet

> 3 tablespoons corn oil
> 2 medium onions, chopped (1 cup)
> ⅛ teaspoon ground turmeric
> ½ cup chopped fresh spinach
> ½ cup chopped fresh leaf lettuce

½ teaspoon salt
⅛ teaspoon pepper
2 scallions, chopped
1 teaspoon dried tarragon
1 teaspoon dried basil (optional)
1 teaspoon dried savory (optional)
¾ cup chopped fresh flat-leaf Italian parsley
2 tablespoons dried dill
4 eggs, beaten
¼ teaspoon baking soda

1. Heat 2 tablespoons oil in a skillet, add the onions and tur-meric, and stir-fry over moderate heat for 3 minutes, or until the onions become light brown. Add the spinach and lettuce and stir-fry for 2 minutes.

2. Add salt, pepper, scallions, tarragon, basil, savory, parsley and dill. Mix well and stir-fry for 2 minutes. Remove skillet from the heat and cool the mixture somewhat. Mix this with the eggs and baking soda.

3. Return the mixture to the skillet, cover the pan, and fry over low heat for 5 minutes. Turn the omelet over, slipping 1 tablespoon oil into the skillet, and fry, covered, for 2 minutes more.

Serve warm, sliced like a pie. Serves 4.

NOTE: Fresh herbs are not as effective and aromatic as the dried and so although either may be used, if you are using fresh herbs, double the amount given for the dried quantity—for example, 1 teaspoon dried tarragon or 2 teaspoons fresh chopped.

KUKU SIBZAMINI
Egg and Potato Omelet

Perisans are devoted to omelets and therefore there is an abundance of recipes. This combination may be eaten for breakfast, lunch or dinner with or without other dishes. Note that a little salt is added to the oil in the belief that it makes it easier to turn the omelet over. For a thinner, crisper omelet, prepare this recipe as two, using half of the quantity for each. There are those who prefer the drier, thinner style.

¾ pound potatoes (about 3), cooked in their jackets, peeled
4 eggs, beaten
1 large onion, grated (1 cup)
1 teaspoon salt, or to taste
⅛ teaspoon pepper
⅛ teaspoon paprika
¼ teaspoon ground cuminseed
¼ teaspoon ground cardamom
2 tablespoons corn oil
⅛ teaspoon ground turmeric

1. Grate the potatoes on the coarse side of a hand grater. Mix with the eggs, onion, ¾ teaspoon salt, pepper, paprika, cuminseed and cardamom.

2. Heat 1 tablespoon oil in a skillet. Add the turmeric and sprinkle with the remaining ¼ teaspoon salt; shake the pan briskly to mix. Pour in the egg mixture, smooth over the surface, cover the skillet, and brown over moderately low heat for 5 minutes.

3. Hold the cover firmly over the skillet and turn the omelet onto the cover. Add the balance of the oil, 1 tablespoon, to the skillet and slide the omelet into the oil. Cover and continue to brown for 5 minutes more. Slice the omelet in the skillet like a pie.

Serve warm. Serves 4 to 6.

KUKU GUSHT
Ground Meat Omelet

The Persian kuku, made with meat, eggs, vegetables, herbs and other seasonings, comes in many variations and guises and is an ideal dish for the American kitchen. Easy to prepare for small lunches or as an adjunct to a dinner menu, this meat kuku is an omelet or, if you wish, a patty.

2 tablespoons corn oil
2 medium onions, chopped (1 cup)
1 pound ground lamb or beef
½ teaspoon salt
¼ teaspoon pepper
¼ teaspoon baking soda
6 eggs, beaten

1. Heat the oil, less 2 teaspoons, in a skillet. Add the onions and stir-fry over low heat for 3 minutes, or until golden. Cool somewhat and add them to the meat with the salt, pepper and baking soda in a mixing bowl. Add the eggs and mix briskly.

2. Pour half of the mixture into a 10-inch skillet, cover, and fry over low heat for 5 minutes. Turn the omelet over, slip the 2 teaspoons oil into the pan, and slide omelet into the oil. Cover, and fry for 3 minutes more. Prepare another omelet with the balance of the egg and meat mixture.

Serve warm, sliced like a pie. Serves 6.

VARIATION: A potato and carrot can be added to the meat omelet to give it more substance, as follows:

1 medium potato, cooked in its jacket until soft
1 medium carrot, cooked whole until soft

1. Peel the potato and grate it on a metal grater. Grate the carrot. Mix them with the meat and eggs of the Kuku Gusht and prepare 2 omelets. You may have to increase the amount of oil by 1 table-spoon to brown the omelets on both sides.

ANOTHER VERSION: Techniques and ingredients differ from one family to another when preparing one's favorite *kuku*. Here is another version of the ground meat omelet with additional spices and more onion.

¾ pound ground beef or lamb
4 eggs, beaten
1 large onion, grated (1 cup)
1 teaspoon salt
¼ teaspoon pepper
¼ teaspoon paprika
¼ teaspoon ground cuminseed
¼ teaspoon ground cardamom
2 tablespoons corn oil
⅛ teaspoon ground turmeric

1. Mix the beef, eggs, onion, ¾ teaspoon salt, pepper, paprika, cuminseed and cardamom together. Heat 1 tablespoon of oil in a skillet, add ¼ teaspoon salt and the turmeric, and shake the pan briskly to mix. Pour in the omelet mixture, cover the pan, and brown over moderate heat for 5 minutes.

2. Turn the omelet over, add 1 tablespoon oil to the skillet, and slide omelet into the oil. Brown the other side, covered, for 3 minutes more.

Serve warm. Serves 4 to 6.

KUKU PIAZ
Onion Omelet

Onions fried to just the right consistency and in some quantity are a potent combination with eggs, a textural marriage. The baking soda will provide a light leavening action.

2 tablespoons corn oil
1 pound (about 3 cups) onions, chopped
5 eggs, beaten
½ teaspoon salt
⅛ teaspoon ground turmeric
¼ teaspoon pepper
¼ teaspoon baking soda

1. Heat 2 tablespoons oil, reserving 1 teaspoon, in a skillet, add the onions, and stir-fry over moderate heat for 3 minutes, or until they are translucent with a touch of brown. Cool slightly; set aside.

2. Beat the eggs, salt, turmeric, pepper and baking soda together. Stir in the onion and pour back into the skillet. Cover and fry over low heat for 5 minutes. Turn the omelet over onto the cover, a slightly gymnastic movement, add the 1 teaspoon oil to the skillet, and slide in the omelet. Cover the pan and fry over moderate heat for 3 minutes.

Serve warm, sliced like a pie. Serve with salad and bread.
Serves 4 to 6.

KUKU KADOO
Zucchini Omelet

The ubiquitous zucchini provides one of the most flavorful omelets in color and texture.

    2 tablespoons corn oil
    2 medium onions, chopped (1 cup)
    ½ teaspoon salt, or to taste
    ⅛ teaspoon pepper
    ½ teaspoon curry powder
    ¼ teaspoon baking soda
    1 small potato cooked in its jacket, peeled, grated
    ½ pound zucchini, grated
    4 eggs, beaten

1. Heat the oil, reserving 1 teaspoon, in a skillet and stir-fry the onions over low heat for 3 minutes, or until golden. Set aside.

2. Put the salt, pepper, curry powder, baking soda, potato and zucchini into a bowl and mix well. Add the fried onions and the eggs and mix briskly. Turn the mixture into the skillet, cover, and fry over low heat for 5 minutes. Turn the omelet over, slip the reserved 1 teaspoon oil into the skillet, and slide in the omelet. Cover and fry for 3 minutes more.

Serve warm, sliced like a pie. Serves 4.

KUKU BAADEMJAN
Baked Eggplant Omelet

This is one of the finest omelets that Persian Jews are fond of preparing. The omelet is fried and steamed at the same time, giving a soft texture. The baking soda creates a leavening action that is elevating, no pun intended. It is vegetarian and dairy if served with yoghurt, and would be fine for hot weather dining anywhere.

    2 eggplants (about 1 pound)
    2 tablespoons corn oil
    2 medium onions, chopped (1 cup)

4 eggs, beaten
½ teaspoon salt, or to taste
¼ teaspoon pepper
⅛ teaspoon ground turmeric
¼ teaspoon baking soda

1. Bake the eggplants under an oven broiler until cooked and slightly charred, about 15 minutes. Remove, peel off and discard the skin, and chop coarsely. Drain any liquid that has accumulated.

2. Heat all but 1 teaspoon oil in a skillet and stir-fry the onions over low heat until translucent and just beginning to turn brown on the edges. Add onions to the eggplant. Add the eggs, salt, pepper, turmeric and baking soda to the mixture and mix well. Turn this mixture into the same skillet.

3. Cover the pan and fry over low heat for 5 minutes. Using the cover of the skillet, turn the omelet over on it, add the reserved 1 teaspoon oil, and return the omelet. Cover and fry over low heat for 3 minutes.

Serve warm, sliced like a pie. Serves 4 with side dishes of plain yoghurt.

KUKU ESFINADGE
Spinach Omelet

Spinach and eggs have been combined with the peppery savory, another herb in the Persian firmament.

½ pound spinach, well rinsed, coarsely chopped
2 tablespoons corn oil
2 medium onions, chopped (1 cup)
1 teaspoon dried savory, or 1 tablespoon chopped fresh
½ teaspoon salt
⅛ teaspoon pepper
4 large eggs, beaten

1. Put the spinach in a pan with ¼ cup water, cover, and cook over moderate heat for 5 minutes to wilt. Drain, cool, and press out the excess liquid firmly. Set aside.

2. Heat all but 1 teaspoon oil in a skillet, add the onions, and stir-fry over moderate heat until they turn golden, about 3 minutes. Add this to the spinach in a mixing bowl. Add the savory, salt, pepper and eggs. Mix well.

3. Turn the mixture into the same skillet, cover, and fry over low heat for 5 minutes, which should brown the bottom of the omelet. Turn it over, slip the reserved teaspoon of oil into the skillet, and return omelet to the pan. Cover, and fry for 3 minutes more.

Serve warm, sliced like a pie. Serves 4 to 6 with other dishes.

VARIATION: One 10-ounce package frozen chopped spinach may be used when the fresh is not available. Thaw out completely, press out the liquid, and use as directed.

KUKU HAVIDGE
Carrot and Potato Omelet

Vegetarians will appreciate this omelet, which is not only flavorful but substantial.

    3 medium carrots (½ pound)
    2 potatoes (¼ pound)
    2 tablespoons corn oil
    2 medium onions, chopped (1 cup)
    ½ teaspoon salt, or to taste
    ¼ teaspoon pepper
    4 large eggs, beaten

1. Cook the carrots in water until they are soft but still firm. Cook the potatoes in their jackets in water until soft. Cool and peel. Grate both vegetables.

2. Heat all but 1 teaspoon oil in a skillet and stir-fry the onions over moderate heat for 3 minutes, or until onions have turned golden and slightly brown on the edges. Set aside.

3. Mix the carrots, potatoes, fried onions, salt, pepper and eggs together. Pour the mixture into the skillet, cover, and fry over low heat for 5 minutes. Turn the omelet over, slip the 1 teaspoon reserved oil into the skillet, and return omelet to the pan. Cover, and fry for 3 minutes more.

Serve warm, sliced like a pie. Serves 4 to 6 with other dishes.

KUKU MAGHZ
Lamb Brains Omelet

Those who like brains will find this omelet a fine method of preparing it. The Persians prefer the small lamb brains from their most popular meat.

1 lamb brain
½ cup water
⅛ teaspoon ground turmeric
½ teaspoon salt
⅛ teaspoon pepper
1 medium onion, chopped fine (½ cup)
2 tablespoons corn oil
3 eggs, beaten

1. Rinse the brain in cold water and remove the veins and membrane. Put the ½ cup water, turmeric, salt, pepper and 1 tablespoon chopped onion in a pan with the brain. Cover and cook over low heat for 15 minutes to soften the brain and reduce the liquid to about 2 tablespoons. Cool the brain and chop in the liquid.
2. Heat all but 1 teaspoon of the oil in a skillet. Stir-fry remaining onion over moderate heat until translucent. Cool slightly and add to the eggs. Stir in the brain and liquid. Turn the mixture into the skillet, cover, and fry over low heat for 5 minutes to brown the bottom. Turn the omelet over, slip in the reserved 1 teaspoon oil, and return the omelet to the pan. Cover and fry for 3 minutes more.

Serve warm. Serves 4 with other dishes.

GONDHI BERENJI
Ground Meat, Rice and Herbs

Rice, vegetables and herbs predominate in this fine example of Persian cooking. The beet tints the mixture pink, the potato adds substance, and the herbs provide fragrance and color. There are no complicated cooking techniques in this family-style one-dish meal.

3 tablespoons corn oil
2 medium onions, chopped (1 cup)
¼ teaspoon ground turmeric
½ pound ground veal or lamb, mixed with 2 tablespoons fine-
    chopped onion
4 cups water
1 medium beet, cooked and sliced
1 teaspoon salt
⅛ teaspoon pepper
2 cups raw rice, soaked in water for ½ hour, drained
½ cup chopped fresh dill
1 bunch of flat-leaf Italian parsley, chopped (1½ cups)
1 large leek, well rinsed, chopped
1 tablespoon dried tarragon, or 2 tablespoons fresh
1 medium potato, peeled, cut into 6 pieces
1 cup lima beans, fresh or frozen

1. Heat the oil in a pan, add the onions, and stir-fry over moderate heat until light brown. Add the turmeric and stir-fry for 1
minute. Add the meat and stir-fry for 2 minutes.

2. Add the water, beet, salt and pepper and bring to a boil over
moderate heat. Add the rice, dill, parsley, leek, tarragon and potato
and mix well. Cover the pan and cook over low heat for 10 minutes.

3. Stir in the lima beans, cover, and cook for 15 minutes. The
completed dish is a substantial, thick gruel.

Serve warm. Serve 6 to 8 with salads and pickles.

OSHEMAST
Spinach, Herb and Rice Stew

The oshemast is a
dairy dish with considerable herbal flavor; it is served
during hot Persian summers.

¼ cup corn oil
3 small onions, sliced thin (1 cup)
1¼ cups raw rice, rinsed, drained
5 cups water
2 bunches of Italian flat-leaf parsley, coarse chopped (4 cups)
1 fresh leek, well trimmed and rinsed, sliced thin

½ pound fresh spinach, chopped coarse, or 10 ounces frozen
    chopped spinach, thawed and squeezed dry
1 teaspoon salt, or to taste
¼ teaspoon pepper
1 tablespoon dried dill
1 tablespoon chopped fresh mint, or 1 teaspoon dried
1 cup green peas, fresh or frozen
2 cups yoghurt

1. Heat the oil in a skillet and over low heat fry the onions for about 5 minutes, until they begin to turn brown. Remove them with a slotted spoon and set aside. Reserve the oil. This is the garnish.

2. Boil the rice in 2 cups of the water in a large pan over moderate heat for 10 minutes, which is long enough to half-cook it. Do not drain, but add the parsley and stir well. Add the remaining 3 cups water, the leek, spinach, salt and pepper, bring to a boil, and cook the mixture, covered, over low heat for 10 minutes. Add the dill, mint and green peas and continue to cook for 15 minutes. The stew will be thick and aromatic.

Cool, then refrigerate since the stew is eaten cold. Stir in the yoghurt before turning out into a serving bowl. Garnish with the fried onions and a few drops of the frying oil for additional flavor.

Serve cold. Serves 8.

OSHE ANOR

Rice, Barley, Herbs with Meatballs

The Persians have no fear of herbs in quantity or variety, as is exemplified in this stew or gruel. Combined with rice and barley, intensified with small meatballs, this dish is a fine family-style preparation. It is essentially fat free and can be vegetarian if the meat is omitted.

MEATBALLS

1 pound ground lamb or beef
1 medium onion, grated (½ cup)
½ teaspoon salt
¼ teaspoon pepper

STEW

> 1 cup raw rice, soaked in water for ½ hour, drained
> ½ cup raw barley, soaked in water for ½ hour, drained
> ½ pound fresh spinach, chopped, or 10 ounces frozen chopped
>   spinach, thawed and squeezed dry
> 1 cooked beet, peeled, sliced thin
> 2 tablespoons dried dill
> ¼ cup parsley flakes
> 2 tablespoons dried leeks
> 2 tablespoons dried mint
> 1 tablespoon dried tarragon
> ¼ cup chopped fresh coriander
> 1 cup chopped fresh beet greens (optional)
> 6 cups water
> 2 to 3 tablespoons lemon juice, to taste
> 2 teaspoons sugar
> 1 teaspoon salt

1. Mix meatball ingredients together and prepare small meat-balls about 1½ inches in diameter. Set aside.

2. Put all stew ingredients into a pan large enough to hold everything, and bring to a boil. Mix well, reduce heat to low, cover the pan, and cook for ½ hour, stirring now and then to prevent sticking. Add the meatballs, one at a time, to the simmering gruel and cook over low heat for another ½ hour.

Serve warm in bowls as a thick stew. Serves 8.

VARIATION: Fresh pomegranate juice is the traditional flavoring, providing color and a slightly astringent flavor. When this is available use ½ cup fresh juice instead of the lemon juice and sugar. If you have extracted the juice from the fruit, you will have the seeds left over to use. Put the seeds and 1 cup warm water into a blender and process for 1 minute. Strain the milky liquid, known as pomegranate milk, discard the pulp, and add the milk to the rice/herb mixture.

HALEEM
Lamb and Whole-Wheat Gruel

Persians are rice eaters ordinarily, and so this preparation, using wheat kernels, is a rarity for them. Extra meat, up to 3 pounds, may be used for a richer broth, in which case the meat is served separately.

    2 cups whole-wheat kernels
    8 cups water
    1 pound lamb, turkey or chicken parts with bone
    1 teaspoon salt
    ¼ teaspoon pepper
    sugar and cinnamon garnish (1 tablespoon sugar to 1 teaspoon
        cinnamon), or chopped onion garnish

1. Soak the wheat in 4 cups of the water overnight. Drain. Process the kernels in a processor for 2 or 3 seconds to crack them lightly.
2. Put the wheat, balance of the water (4 cups), meat, salt and pepper in a large enough pan. Bring to a boil, then reduce to low heat, and cook for about 1 hour to tenderize the meat. Remove the meat from the gruel and pull out and discard all bones.

Serve the gruel warm with the meat or serve the meat separately.

Sprinkle with the sugar/cinnamon mixture or onion, whichever is wanted.

CHELO
Basic Persian Rice

The first step in preparing rice in Persia is always the same—rinsing, soaking and cooking for 8 minutes. From there on you may choose from several recipes, but they all include a crusty bottom layer and a dome of perfectly cooked rice resting on top. The crust is formed by the bottom layer (plain rice or slices of potato or onion) browned in the oil and turmeric covering the bottom of the container. This is called a *tadiq*. A slightly less-crisp crust is attained when egg and yoghurt are added to the bottom layer, and that is called a *tachin*. The perfection of the rice is assured by the initial half-cooking, and then by steaming it slowly over low heat. This "dome" section may be varied by adding dates, carrots, currants, raisins, herbs, red kidney beans or whatever suits your fancy. Whatever your choice, this way of cooking is called the Chelo Method. Examples of each type follow.

Persian rice is rather like Basmati. It is soaked in water for 6 hours or longer, but American-grown rice does not require such lengthy soaking and ½ hour in lightly salted water should be sufficient.

> 2 cups raw rice
> salt
> 4 cups water
> 4 tablespoons corn oil
> ⅛ teaspoon ground turmeric
> 2 tablespoons water
> 1 medium potato, peeled, cut into ¼-inch-thick slices

1. Rinse the rice well, then cover with lightly salted water and let soak for ½ hour. Pour off nearly all the water, leaving about ½ cup.

2. Bring the 4 cups water to a boil over moderate heat; add the rice and remaining liquid. Cook for 8 minutes, drain, and rinse under cold water. Set aside.

3. Put 3 tablespoons of the oil in a large enough pan, add the turmeric and 2 tablespoons water, and shake the pan briskly to mix. Put the potato slices in a single layer in the pan.

4. Pour the rice over the potato and heap it into a pyramid shape. Cover and cook over low heat for 10 minutes. Sprinkle the remaining tablespoon of oil over it, and cover the pan with paper kitchen towels or a cloth towel. Cover that with the pan cover. Cook over low heat for 20 minutes to allow the bottom crust to become crisp and brown.

Serve the rice and *tadiq* (bottom crust) warm. Serves 6 with other dishes.

VARIATION: The *tadiq* is often made with only rice rather than potato or onion. Simply omit the potato and pour the half-cooked rice over the oil and turmeric in the bottom of the pan and continue the usual steps. The rice itself will develop into a crust.

ZEERA KISHMISH POLO
Cumin and Currant Pilau

This is a wonderfully aromatic rice, flavored with cuminseed and the slightly sweet and acid currants. In the event that currants are not available, then dark raisins may be used, making the pilau somewhat sweeter.

2 cups raw rice, well rinsed
4 cups water
4 tablespoons corn oil
2 tablespoons homemade chicken broth or water
⅛ teaspoon ground turmeric
1 medium onion, cut into ¼-inch-thick slices
⅔ cup dried black currants
2 teaspoons cuminseed

1. Soak the rice in lightly salted water for ½ hour. Pour off nearly all the water. Bring 4 cups water to a boil and add the rice and liquid. Cook over moderate heat for 10 minutes. Drain in a metal sieve and rinse under cold water. Set aside.

2. Put 2 tablespoons oil in a pan; add the chicken broth and turmeric. Shake the pan briskly to mix.

3. Arrange the onion slices over the bottom of the pan in an orderly fashion. Cover this with ½ cup of the partially cooked rice.

4. Mix the balance of the rice, the currants and cuminseed together. Pour this over the plain rice and shape the top into a pyramid. Cover the pan and cook over low heat for 10 minutes. Add the balance of the oil (2 tablespoons), then cover the rice with paper kitchen towels and the metal pan cover. Continue to cook over low heat for 15 to 20 minutes to develop a crust on the rice. The paper towels will absorb the steam and rice will not become gummy but remain in individual grains.

Invert on a platter and serve warm. The brown onion *tadiq* (crust) will provide an attractive topping for the rice.

Serves 4 to 6 with other dishes.

POLO HAVIDGE LOOBIA
Rice Pilau with Carrot and Red Kidney Beans

There are variations of variations in the artful combinations of Persian rice. Here is one that, with very few ingredients, manages to encompass a wide range of seasonings and flavors.

⅓ cup dried red kidney beans
½ pound carrots, cut into ¼-inch cubes
½ teaspoon sugar
5 tablespoons corn oil
4¼ cups water
2 cups raw rice, covered with lightly salted water for ½ hour
1 medium potato, peeled, cut into ¼-inch-thick slices
½ teaspoon ground cinnamon

1. Cover the beans with water and soak them overnight. Drain. Cover beans with water again and cook, covered, over moderate heat until they are soft but still whole, about ½ hour. Drain and set aside.

2. Put the carrots, sugar, 1 tablespoon of the oil and the ¼ cup water into a pan and cook over low heat for 5 minutes, or until the liquid evaporates. Be careful not to burn the carrots. Set aside.

3. Bring remaining 4 cups water to a boil in a pan. Drain nearly all the water from the rice and add rice to the boiling water. Cover the pan and cook over moderate heat for 10 minutes. Drain, run the rice under cold water, and drain again.

4. Put 2 tablespoons of the remaining oil in a pan large enough to spread out the potato slices flat on the bottom. Sprinkle over this 1 tablespoon water. All the other ingredients are to be added in layers as follows: Add ½ cup rice over the potato. Cover this with carrots and a few sprinklings of cinnamon. Cover with the beans. Continue in this manner, one layer after another, ending with beans. Sprinkle cinnamon lightly over each layer. Shape the top layer into a pyramid.

5. Cover the pan and cook over low heat for 10 minutes. Spoon the balance of the oil (2 tablespoons) over the rice, and cover the pan with kitchen towels and metal pan cover. Continue to cook over low heat for 15 minutes more.

The rice, carrots and beans will be cooked through and the potato and oil will develop their own crisp crust on the bottom.

Serve warm. Serves 4 to 6 with other dishes.

ADAS POLO
Lentil Pilau

Lentils and rice are a remarkably compatible combination. The crunch of the coriander seed, lightly browned in the oil on the bottom of the pan, adds a surprising taste and texture to this, one of the most attractive of Persian rice dishes.

1 cup dried lentils
2 cups water
2 cups raw rice, well rinsed
salt
3 cups boiling water
4 tablespoons corn oil
2 tablespoons chicken broth or water
⅛ teaspoon ground turmeric
1 teaspoon coriander seeds
1 large potato, peeled, cut into ¼-inch-thick slices

1. Soak the lentils in 2 cups water for 2 hours. Bring to a boil, then cook over low heat for about ½ hour just to soften the lentils. Most of the water should evaporate. Set aside.

2. Soak the rice in lightly salted water for ½ hour. Pour off nearly all the water. Put the rice and remaining soaking water in a pan with 3 cups boiling water. Cook over moderate heat for 10 minutes to partially cook the rice. Drain and rinse under cold water. Drain and set aside.

3. Put 2 tablespoons of the oil in a pan large enough to hold potato slices in a single layer. Add the broth, turmeric and coriander seeds and shake the pan briskly to mix. Fit the potato slices over the oil in the bottom of the pan.

4. Mix the lentils and rice together and spread the mixture over the potato slices, shaping a pyramid at the top. Cover the pan and cook over low heat for 10 minutes. Sprinkle the balance of the oil (2 tablespoons) over the rice, cover the pan with paper kitchen towels, and place the pan cover on top. Cook over low heat for 15 to 20 minutes more to develop the crust.

Serve the warm rice mixture together with the crisp crust. Serves 4 to 6 with other dishes.

VARIATION: For a slightly sweeter dish, omit the coriander seeds and add ⅔ cup raisins to the lentil and rice mixture.

ALBALOO POLO
Cherry Pilau with Chicken

Cherries and rice make one of the most unexpected and exotic combinations, especially when supplemented with orange peel and almond slivers.

Fresh sour cherries are rare and seasonal, but when they are available they can be pitted and frozen for future use. Canned pitted sour cherries are always available in supermarkets.

CHICKEN

2 pounds chicken parts—legs, thighs, breast—loose skin and fat
  discarded
1 medium onion, sliced (½ cup)
¼ teaspoon ground turmeric
½ teaspoon salt
⅛ teaspoon pepper
2 teaspoons corn oil
¼ cup water

CHERRY PILAU

⅓ cup juice from canned cherries
¼ cup sugar
¼ cup toasted blanched almonds
⅓ cup dried orange peel slivers, soaked in hot water
1 cup sour cherries

1 recipe Chelo (Basic Persian Rice) (see Index)

1. Put the onion on the bottom of a saucepan, and cover with the chicken, turmeric, salt, pepper, oil and water. Cover the pan tightly and cook over low heat for 25 minutes. Stir once or twice during this period to prevent burning. Should the pan dry out too quickly add 2 or 3 tablespoons water. Cook until the chicken is tender and the liquid evaporated. Set aside.

2. Mix ingredients for cherry pilau together in a saucepan, bring to a boil, and simmer for 3 minutes to prepare the syrup.

Serve the rice and pass cherry mixture and chicken separately. Serves 4 to 6.

NOTE: Fine slivers of orange peel may be prepared at home. Cut off the outer rind of the orange peel, then scrape off and discard the white pulp. Cut the peel with scissors into very thin julienne, 1-inch-long slices. Put them on a tray in a sunny window or other warm place and let them dry for several days. Toss them now and then to ensure the drying is uniform. Store in a jar with a tight cover. When preparing for use, soak in hot water for 2 or 3 minutes.

SHEREEN POLO I
Almond, Carrot, Orange Pilau

Shereen (which means sweet) Polo is one of the grandest Persian rice dishes, and a fine example of culinary virtuosity. The spices, seasonings, nuts and sweetening, artfully combined, are highly admired. This dish is served only on special occasions. The simple chicken stew is a traditional accompaniment.

The best saffron is grown and harvested in Meshed, Iran. In the public markets where the saffron is located, a sweet, overpoweringly fragrant floral aroma permeates the area. The wealthy use this most expensive of all spices and seasonings at the drop of a hat. Those who cannot afford saffron are content to use turmeric, which also provides a yellow color and subtle flavor.

SUGAR SYRUP

½ teaspoon sugar
½ teaspoon whole saffron
¼ teaspoon ground cardamom
2 tablespoons corn oil
3 cups julienned carrots
½ cup dried orange peel slivers (see Albaloo Polo, Note)
½ cup water
½ cup blanched almond slivers
2 tablespoons rosewater, or to taste
3 tablespoons shelled pistachios

RICE WITH TADIQ

2 cups raw rice, well rinsed
1 teaspoon salt
4 cups hot water
5 tablespoons corn oil
¼ teaspoon ground turmeric

1. Grind the ½ teaspoon sugar and whole saffron together, using mortar and pestle, until they are quite fine. Add the cardamom and grind everything together smoothly. Set aside.

2. Heat the oil in a pan, add the carrots, and stir-fry over low heat for about 5 minutes, stirring frequently to brown them slightly. Set aside in the pan.

3. Cover the orange peel with boiling water for 2 minutes. Drain and set aside.

4. Put the 1 cup of sugar and the ½ cup water in a pan and simmer over moderate heat for 2 minutes to dissolve the sugar. Add the almonds, cooked carrots and orange peel and continue cooking for 2 minutes more.

5. Remove the melange from the heat and stir in the rosewater, pistachios and the saffron mix. Set aside.

6. To prepare the rice, cover it with cold water and salt; let soak for ½ hour. Pour off nearly all the lightly salted water, leaving about ½ cup. Bring the 4 cups water to a boil over moderate heat, and add the rice and remaining liquid. Cook for 8 minutes, drain, and rinse under cold water. Set aside briefly.

7. Put 3 tablespoons oil in a large enough pan with the turmeric. Shake the pan briskly to mix. Pour in the rice to cover the oil and shape the top into a pyramid. Cover the pan and cook over low heat for 10 minutes.

8. Uncover and sprinkle remaining 2 tablespoons oil and 2 tablespoons water over the rice. Cover the pan with a cloth kitchen towel and the pan cover. Cook over very low heat for ½ hour to allow the rice crisp *(tadiq)* to form. Some cooks let the *tadiq* form by cooking for 1 hour but the lesser time seems to work.

Serve the rice on a platter, decorated around the top with pieces of *tadiq*, which must be scooped out from the pan bottom. The warm sugar syrup melange is served separately. Each diner spreads as much of the melange as he wants over the rice.

Serve warm with the chicken stew (Albaloo Polo). Serves 6 with other dishes.

SHEREEN POLO II
Orange-Flavored Rice

Here is another version of the famous orange/nut rice to be served at weddings or other special occasions. I had been cautioned when learning this dish not to use too much saffron since it is reputed to bring on fits of laughter.

½ cup dried orange peel slivers (see Albaloo Polo, Note)
2 tablespoons corn oil
¼ cup blanched almond slivers
¼ cup pistachio nuts, shelled
1 tablespoon sugar
¼ teaspoon whole saffron, dissolved in ¼ cup hot water
2 cups raw rice, well rinsed

1. Bring 1 cup water to a boil, add the orange peel, and simmer over low heat for 2 minutes. Drain and set aside.

2. Heat the oil in a skillet, add the almonds and pistachios, and stir-fry over low heat until the almonds becomes light brown, about 3 minutes. Add the drained orange peel and stir-fry for 1 minute more. Mix in the sugar and saffron liquid, cover the skillet, and simmer for 3 minutes. Set aside.

3. Prepare 2 cups rice with *tadiq* in the same way as Shereen Polo I.

4. When adding the partially cooked rice to the pan, cover the oil and turmeric with 1 cup rice, then with half of the orange/nut mixture, then more rice, then orange/nut mixture, ending with rice. Shape the top into a pyramid. Proceed as for the Shereen Polo I until the rice is fully cooked. Serve warm by mixing all the rice and layers together.

Serves 6 with other dishes.

SABZI POLO MOHEE
Herbed Rice with Fish

Fried fish fillets are served with this style of herbed pilau as one of the traditional combinations. The fish is a white-fleshed variety found in the Caspian Sea and is cooked as a fillet rather than with the bone. In the Persian fashion, the more herbs there are the better the flavor, so that precise measurements are not so vital. Even the sprouted garlic, which can be found in New York's Chinatown, is included. A green madness.

> 2 cups raw rice, well rinsed, covered with salted water
>   (2 teaspoons) for ½ hour
> 1 bunch of chives
> 1 bunch of fresh dill
> 1 bunch of Italian flat-leaf parsley
> 1 bunch of fresh coriander
> 1 green stalk from sprouted garlic (optional)
> 1 teaspoon dried fenugreek leaves (optional see Glossary)
> 4 tablespoons corn oil
> ¼ teaspoon ground turmeric

1. Pour off almost all the liquid from the rice. Bring 3 cups water to a boil and add the rice with its remaining lightly salted liquid. Cook over moderate heat for 6 minutes. Drain, rinse the rice under cold water, drain again, and set aside.

2. Trim, rinse, and pat dry the chives, dill, parsley, coriander and garlic sprout. Chop fine by hand or in a processor. Stir this into the partially cooked rice with the fenugreek.

3. Put 3 tablespoons of the corn oil in a pan with the turmeric and 2 tablespoons water. Swirl around to mix. Pour the rice over it, shaping a pyramid at the top. Cover the pan and cook over low heat for 10 minutes. Sprinkle over the rice the balance of the oil (1 tablespoon). Cover the top of the pan with paper kitchen towels, then the pan cover. Cook over low heat for 20 minutes more to develop the herbed crust.

FISH

> 1 pound fillet of sole, flounder or similar white fish, cut into 4
>   pieces
> ½ teaspoon salt
> ⅛ teaspoon pepper
> flour for dusting
> oil for panfrying

1. Rub the fish with the salt and pepper. Dredge with flour. Heat oil in a skillet and over moderate heat lightly brown the fish, about 5 minutes. Drain briefly on paper towels.

Serve the rice and fish separately. Serves 4 to 6.

ISTAMBULEE POLO
Turkish Rice with Tomato

The title and the tomato in the recipe reveal, perhaps, the origin of this pilau. The seasonings and assembly of the rice, meat, yellow split peas are absolutely Persian, but the addition of tomatoes reflects the influence of Istanbul.

MEAT

2 tablespoons corn oil
1 medium onion, chopped (½ cup)
1 pound boneless lamb, cut into 1-inch cubes
¼ teaspoon ground turmeric
¼ teaspoon pepper
½ teaspoon salt
½ teaspoon Advieh (mixed spice, see Index)
2 cups water
1 cup yellow split peas, rinsed under cold water
2 cups crushed tomatoes, preferably canned

RICE

2 cups raw rice, rinsed, covered with lightly salted water for ½
    hour, drained
4 tablespoons corn oil
⅛ teaspoon ground turmeric, or ½ teaspoon whole saffron
    ground with ½ teaspoon sugar
1 small potato, peeled, cut into ¼-inch-thick slices

1. Heat the oil in a pan, add the onion, and stir-fry over moderate heat for about 3 minutes, or until the onion is light brown. Remove onion and set aside.

2. Reheat the oil remaining in the pan, add the lamb, turmeric, pepper, salt and *advieh* and stir-fry for 1 minute. Add the water, cover the pan, and simmer over low heat for ½ hour. Add the split peas, and mix and cook for 20 minutes more. Test the peas for tenderness; they should be soft but still retain their shape.

3. Stir in the fried onion and crushed tomatoes; mix. Cook for 10 minutes more. Most of the liquid should have evaporated, leaving about ¼ cup. Continue cooking until this is achieved. Set aside.

4. Bring 5 cups water to a boil, add the rice, cover the pan, and cook over moderate heat for 8 minutes. Drain, rinse the rice under cold water, and drain again.

5. Put 2 tablespoons oil in a large pan with 2 tablespoons water. Add the turmeric or saffron and shake the pan to mix. Put the slices of potato in the oil in an orderly manner. Arrange ½ cup of rice over the potato. Add one third of the meat mixture over that, then in layers more rice, then meat, and rice as the final layer on top. Shape the top in a pyramid.

6. Cover the pan and cook over low heat for 10 minutes. Add the balance of the oil, 2 tablespoons, cover the top of the pan with paper kitchen towels, then the pan cover over that. Cook over low heat for 15 minutes more to establish a firm, crisp *tadiq*.

Serve warm. Serves 6 to 8 with salad and table pickles.

POLO GREMEH LAPE
Pilau with Cubed Meat, Yellow Split Peas and Dates

There is no end to ingenuity in Persian cooking. Here are entirely unpredictable ingredients combined and coming out smelling like roses. Everything here is compatible and the sweetness provided by the dates is an original and unexpected touch. Lamb or beef may be used but lamb is the most popular traditionally.

MEAT

3 tablespoons corn oil
1 medium onion, chopped (½ cup)
1 pound boneless lamb or beef, cut into ¾-inch cubes
¼ teaspoon ground turmeric
¼ teaspoon pepper
½ teaspoon salt

½ teaspoon Advieh (mixed spice, see Index)
2 cups water
1 cup yellow split peas, rinsed in cold water

RICE

5 cups water
3 cups raw rice, covered with water and soaked with 2 teaspoons
    salt for ½ hour
5 tablespoons corn oil
⅛ teaspoon ground turmeric or ¼ teaspoon whole saffron,
    crushed together with ¼ teaspoon sugar
1 small potato, peeled, cut into ¼-inch thick slices
10 whole dates, with or without seeds

1. Heat the oil in a pan, add the onion, and stir-fry over moderate heat for about 3 minutes, or until the onion is light brown. Remove onion and set aside.

2. Reheat remaining oil, add the meat, turmeric, pepper, salt and advieh, and stir-fry for 1 minute. Add the water and simmer over low heat for 1/2 hour. Add the peas, mix, and cook in a covered pan for 20 minutes more. Test the peas for tenderness; they should be softening but still retain their shape. Add more water, about 1/4 cup, if the mixture becomes too dry.

3. Stir in the fried onion. Test to see that both meat and peas are almost tender and the liquid has nearly evaporated, leaving 1 or 2 tablespoons. Set aside.

4. To prepare the rice, bring 5 cups water to a boil. Drain the rice and add to the boiling water. Cover the pan and cook over moderate heat for about 8 minutes. Drain, rinse the rice under cold water, and drain again.

5. Put 3 tablespoons oil in a pan with 2 tablespoons water. Add the turmeric and shake the pan briskly to mix. Arrange the slices of potato in the oil in an orderly manner. Spoon about ½ cup rice over the potato. Add one third of the meat mixture, 3 dates, more rice, then dates, then meat, in layers with rice the final layer on top.

6. Cover the pan and cook over low heat for 10 minutes. Spoon the balance of the oil (2 tablespoons) over the rice, cover the top with paper kitchen towels, then with the pan cover. Cook over low heat for 20 to 25 minutes to establish a firm, crisp tadiq. To test, plunge a fork handle into the rice to the bottom to feel a firm crispness.

Serve warm. Serves 6 to 8 with salad and table pickles.

RESHTE POLO

Rice and Noodle Pilau with a
Whole Chicken

Τhe combination, rice, noodles and chicken, in this celebratory pilau, is served on Rosh Hashanah. The accent on sweetness, with the orange peel and raisins, is to ensure that everyone will have a sweet year.

Dry, Jewish-style egg noodles are available in supermarkets, but originally and traditionally (as was done during my childhood) fresh egg noodles were made at home and dried before using.

> 1 cup dry thin egg noodles, broken into 1-inch pieces
> ¼ cup corn oil
> 1 small onion, sliced (¼ cup)
> ⅛ teaspoon pepper
> ¼ teaspoon ground turmeric
> 1 teaspoon salt
> 1 chicken, 2 pounds, or Cornish game hen, whole
> ½ cup water
> 2 cups raw rice, well rinsed
> 1 tablespoon dried orange peel slivers (see Albaloo Polo, Note)
> 1 cup raisins or currants
> 1 teaspoon coriander seeds

1. Put the noodles in a large dry skillet and very lightly toast them over moderate heat for 2 minutes. Remove and set aside.

2. Heat 1 tablespoon oil in a pan, add the onion, pepper and ⅛ teaspoon turmeric, and stir-fry over moderate heat for 1 minute. Add the chicken, sprinkle with salt, and brown the chicken on all sides for 5 minutes. Add the water, cover the pan, and cook for 10 minutes more to evaporate the liquid completely. Set aside.

3. Prepare the rice as in Basic Persian Rice (Chelo, see Index), but cook the rice and orange peel together for 6 minutes. Add the toasted noodles and cook for 2 minutes more. Drain under cold water and mix with the raisins and coriander seeds.

4. Put the balance of the oil (3 tablespoons) in a pan with 2 tablespoons water and ⅛ teaspoon turmeric and swirl around to mix. Cover this with half of the rice mixture. Bury the chicken in the center and cover with the balance of the rice in a pyramid shape. Cover the pan and cook over low heat for 45 minutes up to 1 hour to produce the crisp *tadiq*.

Serve rice and chicken together, carving the chicken at the table. Serve warm. Serves 6.

HAVIGE POLO CHORMA
Carrot Pilau with Dates

Dates, raisins and carrots are sweet ingredients in this unexpected combination with Persian rice. The neutral flavor of rice absorbs and complements the sweet mixture.

> ½ pound carrots, cut into ¼-inch dice
> 1 medium onion, chopped (½ cup)
> 4 tablespoons corn oil
> 2 cups raw rice
> 1 teaspoon salt
> 3 cups water plus 2 tablespoons
> ⅛ teaspoon ground turmeric
> 3 tablespoons dark raisins
> 12 pitted dates

1. Mix the carrots and onion together. Heat 1 tablespoon of the oil in a skillet and stir-fry the carrot mixture over moderate heat for 3 minutes. Remove and set aside.

2. Rinse the rice well; cover with water and salt. Soak for ½ hour. Pour off nearly all the water. Bring 3 cups water to a boil in a pan and add the rice and remaining salted liquid. Cook over low heat for 8 minutes. Drain, rinse under cold water, and set aside.

3. Put remaining 2 tablespoons oil in a large pan. Add 2 tablespoons water and the turmeric. Shake the pan briskly to mix.

4. Mix the partially cooked rice, carrots and onion, raisins and dates together. Spread this over the oil mixture in the pan and shape the top into a pyramid.

5. Cover the pan and cook over low heat for 5 minutes. Then sprinkle over the balance of the oil (1 tablespoon); cover the pan with several paper kitchen towels or a cloth towel and the pan cover. Cook/steam over low heat for about 20 minutes to develop a crisp rice layer on the bottom of the pan.

Serve warm. Serves 4 to 6 with other dishes.

SABZI POLO
Herb and Rice Pilau

The lady of the house prepared an unusual *tadiq* with eggs, rice and a large pinch of dissolved saffron to develop some color. There was a little disagreement between husband and wife as to the approximate length of time to soak the rice: he claimed it needed overnight soaking, while she asserted that a short time was enough. My own opinion is that it depends on the rice, with American long-grain rice requiring no more than ½ hour, while Basmati rice needs several hours' soaking, which develops the grain and tenderness in the pilau.

¼ pound Italian flat-leaf parsley
¼ pound fresh coriander (Chinese parsley)
¼ pound fresh dill
2 cups raw rice, covered in salted water for ½ hour (1 teaspoon salt)
4 tablespoons corn oil
1 egg, beaten
¼ teaspoon whole saffron, crushed with ¼ teaspoon sugar and dissolved in 1 teaspoon water

1. Chop the parsley, coriander and dill together in a processor. Set aside.

2. Bring 4 cups water to a boil in a pan. Drain nearly all the water from the rice and add rice with its remaining liquid to the boiling water. Cover the pan and cook over moderate heat for 8 minutes. The rice will swell but still be firm. Drain the rice and rinse under cold water. Set aside.

3. Cover the bottom of a large pan with 3 tablespoons oil. Mix ½ cup of the half-cooked rice, the egg and saffron liquid together. Heat the oil lightly in the pan and add the rice/egg mixture and smooth over the top. Fry over low heat for 5 minutes. Remove pan from the heat and slice the *tadiq*, like a pie, into 4 pieces to ease its removal later on.

4. Mix the chopped herbs and the balance of the rice together. Spread it over the *tadiq* and shape the top into a pyramid. Sprinkle the balance of the oil, 2 tablespoons, over the rice; cover the pan with paper towels and the pan cover. Cook the rice over low heat for

15 to 20 minutes to produce the crisp *tadiq* on the pan bottom, the crisper the better.

Serve warm rice and *tadiq*. Serves 6 with other dishes.

TACHIN BADEMJAN
Layered Eggplant

Here is a layered casserole that is completely vegetarian. All the same steps and techniques are used as in other *tachin* recipes. The smooth, meaty eggplant slices contrast with the crispness of the yoghurt-flavored *tachin*.

> 2 cups raw rice, prepared as in Basic Persian Rice (Chelo, see Index), cooking for 8 minutes
> 1 pound eggplant
> salt
> ¼ cup plus 3 tablespoons corn oil
> 2 eggs, beaten with ⅛ teaspoon salt, ⅛ teaspoon pepper
> 1 cup yoghurt
> ¼ teaspoon whole saffron, crushed with ¼ teaspoon sugar, using a mortar and pestle
> 3 tablespoons corn oil
> 2 tablespoons margarine

1. Cut the eggplant horizontally into ⅜-inch thick slices or in pieces 2 inches wide and 3 inches long; either will do. Lightly salt all the slices and let stand for 15 minutes. Wipe off the liquid that accumulates.

2. Heat ¼ cup oil in a large skillet and fry the slices over moderate heat for about 3 minutes. Remove them and set aside.

3. Mix the beaten eggs with the yoghurt and saffron. Add half of the precooked rice and mix well.

4. Prepare a 2-quart casserole, round or rectangular, preferably heatproof glass, by adding and swirling around 3 tablespoons oil. Add the rice and yoghurt mixture and smooth over the surface. Over that spread the slices of fried eggplant and cover with the remaining plain rice. Dot with the margarine. Cover the casserole with aluminum foil and bake in a 400° F. oven for about 45 minutes.

5. Remove the casserole from the oven and turn it upside down on a platter. Cover this with a cloth towel for about 3 minutes. The contents will descend into the platter with the crusty bottom making an attractive browned topping.

Cut through the crust into 3- or 4-inch serving pieces.

Serve warm. Serves 6.

VARIATION:

TACHIN GARCH
Layered Mushrooms

Substitute 1 pound of small fresh mushrooms for the eggplant. Stir-fry the whole mushrooms in 1 tablespoon oil with 1 small onion, sliced (¼ cup), ¼ teaspoon salt and ¼ teaspoon pepper for 5 minutes. If the mushrooms are large, halve them. Prepare the *tachin* in the casserole in the same way as for the eggplant; cover with the mushrooms and the balance of the rice. Bake in a 400° F. oven for 45 minutes.

Another variation is to use ½ pound of eggplant slices and ½ pound mushrooms, fried, layered and baked.

DOLME BARGEH
Stuffed Grape Leaves

Persians stuff grape leaves in two ways: shaped the standard way, like a cigar about 3 inches long and ½ inch thick, or shaped in a rectangle about 1½ inches long and 1 inch wide. Each should be made with 1 grape leaf only (found in the jars packed in California), as using more than 1 leaf creates a rather tough package. Following are two stuffings; one is sweet and the other herbal.

DOLME SHEREEN
Sweet Stuffing

½ cup raw rice, rinsed and drained
1 tablespoon yellow split peas, rinsed
1 tablespoon corn oil
1 medium onion, chopped (½ cup)
1 tablespoon barberries (zereshk), see Glossary (optional)
2 tablespoons dried currants
1 teaspoon crushed dried lime (limoo amoni), see Glossary
¼ teaspoon pepper
½ teaspoon salt
½ teaspoon ground cuminseed
½ cup ground lamb (3 ounces)

1. Cook the rice in water for 5 minutes and the yellow split peas for 15 minutes, separately. Drain each one and put into a mixing bowl with all the other ingredients. Mix well.

2. Use about 1 tablespoon of the mixture to stuff each grape leaf in whichever style you wish, tightly folding the leaf over the filling. Do not overstuff since the leaf may open up. Put 1 or 2 flat grape leaves in the bottom of a pan and arrange the stuffed leaves in layers. Cover the leaves with a plate that will fit into the pan and hold them down. Pour in 1 cup water. Cover the pan, bring to a boil, and cook over low heat for ½ hour. If the water evaporates too quickly, add another ¼ cup to prevent scorching. At the end the water should be completely evaporated.

Serve warm as an appetizer. Makes about 22 of the cigar-shaped leaves or 18 in the rectangular shape.

The stuffed leaves may be refrigerated for 2 or 3 days. They are best eaten when warm and can be lightly reheated.

VARIATION:

DOLME SABZI
Herbal Stuffing

To make an Herbal Stuffing, just substitute 1 tablespoon dried dill, 1 tablespoon dried parsley, 1 teaspoon dried tarragon and 2 chopped scallions for the barberries, currants and *limoo*. Proceed as with the Sweet Stuffing.

NOTE: Since fresh herbs are not always available, I have substituted the dry. When using fresh dill, parsley or tarragon, simply double the quantity noted. For example, 1 tablespoon dry dill or 2 tablespoons chopped fresh.

DOLME KADOO
Stuffed Pumpkin

Anything that can be hollowed out or rolled up can be stuffed and a pumpkin is especially festive. Use either the Dolme Shereen—Sweet Stuffing or the Dolme Sabzi—Herbal Stuffing (see Dolme Bargeh, preceding recipe). Take into account that the larger the pumpkin the more stuffing and larger pan you will need.

> 1 pumpkin, 3 or 4 pounds
> 1 recipe stuffing
> 1 hard-cooked egg, shelled
> 1 cup water

1. Cut a 3-inch disc in the top of the pumpkin; remove it and reserve for the cover. Scoop out and discard the seeds and loose strings. The flesh of the pumpkin remains intact.

2. Put half of the stuffing into the pumpkin, fit the egg on top, and cover almost to the top with the balance of the stuffing. Fit the disc over this as the cover.

3. Put the pumpkin on a sheet of aluminum foil and fit it into a large pan that will more than contain it. Pour the water around it. Cover the pan and bake in a 350° F. oven for 1 hour. Since the rice and peas are partially cooked this should be sufficient to cook the stuffing and bake the pulp of the pumpkin. The water may evaporate almost completely and the foil will protect the pan from scorching.

Carefully remove the pumpkin from the pan, uncover, and serve stuffing and pulp together.

Serve warm. Serves 4 to 6 with other dishes.

DOLME KADOO HALVOEE
Stuffed Pumpkin for Sabbath

This is a grand Jewish dish that is assembled on Friday afternoon and cooked the entire night on the lowest heat. It is served on the Sabbath noon after returning from the synagogue.

The pumpkin is put in a colander or, if nothing else is available, may be tied up in a kitchen towel for cooking. After cooking slowly for many hours, the pumpkin in the towel can be easily lifted from an outsize pan without disintegrating, so that it may be served intact. There may be some liquid in the pan after hours of cooking and this is often served as a sauce.

To prepare the Dolme Kadoo on a weekday, simply cook over moderately low heat, covered, for 3 to 3½ hours—long enough to cook all the stuffed ingredients.

A stuffed grape leaf is a *dolme* and so is this pumpkin a *dolme*. The difference is that the wrapper is a large, firm pumpkin instead of a small, flexible leaf.

2 cups raw rice, well rinsed, soaked in 4 cups water with 1
    teaspoon salt for 4 hours, drained
½ cup yellow split peas, soaked in 1 cup water for 4 hours,
    drained
1 pumpkin (3 to 4 pounds)
2 tablespoons corn oil
2 medium onions, chopped (1 cup)
1 teaspoon ground cuminseed
½ cup raisins
¼ cup barberries (zereshk), see Glossary (optional but
    traditional)
1 tablespoon ground dried lime (limoo, see Glossary)
¼ teaspoon pepper
1 pound ground lamb or beef
3 cups water

1. Drain the rice and peas and mix them together.
2. Cut a 3-inch circle in the top of the pumpkin to make a lid. Scoop out and discard the seeds and loose strings. The pulp of the pumpkin remains intact. Set aside.
3. Heat the oil in a skillet and stir-fry the onions over low heat

until golden. Add this to the rice and split peas. Add the cumin-seed, raisins, barberries (zereshk), dried lime (limoo), pepper and meat; mix well and fill the pumpkin. Cover with the lid.

4. Place the pumpkin in a metal colander and set this in a large pan, larger than necessary, to ease the removal of the cooked pumpkin. Add the water to the pan, cover, and bring to a boil. Reduce to the lowest heat and cook overnight for serving on the Sabbath.

Serve warm. Serves 8 or more.

DOLME KADOO SABZI HALVOEE

Pumpkin Stuffed with Meat and Herbs

The technique for this recipe is the same as for the Dolme Kadoo Halvoee, which is generally prepared for the Sabbath. The stuffing is different here and a bit more tart. Stuffed pumpkin can be prepared any time of the week for special occasions.

1 pumpkin, 3 to 4 pounds
½ cup yellow split peas, or 1 cup frozen lima beans
1 cup raw rice, well rinsed
1 tablespoon corn oil
1 medium onion, chopped (½ cup)
½ pound ground lamb or beef
½ cup chopped fresh dill
½ cup chopped fresh flat-leaf Italian parsley
3 scallions, chopped
1 tablespoon dried tarragon
½ teaspoon salt
¼ teaspoon ground turmeric
¼ teaspoon pepper
10 pieces Aloo Bukhara (see Glossary)
3 cups water

1. Cut a circle 3 or 4 inches in diameter out of the top of the pumpkin. Scoop out and discard the seeds and fibers. Save the cut-out disc to use as a plug.

2. Put the split peas or lima beans in a pan with 2 cups water. Bring to a boil and cook for 2 minutes. Add the rice and cook over moderate heat for 5 minutes more. Drain and set aside.

3. Heat the oil in a skillet and stir-fry the onion and meat over moderate heat for 3 minutes. Turn out into a large mixing bowl. Add the peas and rice. Mix in the dill, parsley, scallions, tarragon, salt, turmeric, pepper and *Aloo Bukhara*. Stuff the pumpkin and fit in the plug.

4. Put the pumpkin in a metal colander and set this in a pan larger than needed, which will ease removal of the cooked pumpkin. Pour in the water, cover the pan, and bring to a boil. Reduce to low heat and simmer for 2 hours, which should be sufficient to cook the pumpkin and stuffing. If the water evaporates too quickly, add another cup of hot water. Remove the colander. In order to ensure that the pumpkin does not disintegrate, it may be necessary to leave it in the colander and serve from that.

Serve warm. Serves 8 with salad and other dishes.

DOLME
Stuffed Vegetables, Persian Style

Stuffed vegetables of many kinds are prepared by communities all over the world. The Persian method follows their traditional seasonings with the emphasis on herbs and slow cooking. Eggplant, lettuce leaves, grape leaves, yellow summer squash, onion, cucumber, Swiss chard, beet greens and in fact anything that can be folded or hollowed out can be stuffed. And *Dolme* can be made in large quantities for celebrations.

STUFFING

1 cup raw rice, coverd with water with 1 teaspoon salt for ½ hour
2 cups chopped tomatoes, fresh or canned
½ cup yellow split peas, soaked in 1 cup water for 1 hour
4 tablespoons corn oil
2 medium onions, chopped (1 cup)
¼ teaspoon ground turmeric
6 scallions, chopped

1 cup chopped celery leaves

*2 tablespoons dried lime (limoo amoni, see Glossary), crushed
 to powder*

½ cup chopped fresh parsley, or 2 tablespoons dried

2 tablespoons dried dill

1 tablespoon dried tarragon

1 teaspoon dried mint

*1 pound ground beef or lamb mixed with ½ cup fine-chopped
 onion*

1 cup puréed tomatoes

2 tablespoons fresh lemon juice

1. Pour off half the water from the rice, put rice in a pan, and bring to a boil over low heat. Stir in the tomatoes and continue to simmer for 7 minutes, or until most of the liquid has evaporated.

2. Put the yellow split peas in a pan, bring to a simmer, and cook over low heat for 15 minutes, or until nearly all the liquid has evaporated. Set aside.

3. Heat the oil in a large pan, add the onions and turmeric, and stir-fry until the onions are light brown, about 5 minutes over moderate heat. Remove pan from the heat and add the rice mixture, split peas, scallions, celery leaves, lime, parsley, dill, tarragon, mint and meat. Mix everything together and set aside. This is enough stuffing for 6 tomatoes, peppers, zucchini, or 12 to 15 cabbage leaves.

4. Select the 6 vegetables you wish to use. An assortment such as tomato, pepper and squash, or cabbage and tomato, is more interesting than all of one kind. Or use whatever is preferred and seasonally available. Prepare them as follows: For the tomato, cut a 2-inch disc in the top and scoop out the pulp, leaving a firm wall. Reserve the pulp for the sauce. For the pepper, red or green, cut a disc in the top and scoop out the seeds and ribs. Save the disc. For the squash, cut each one lengthwise into halves. Scoop out and discard the pulp from each half, leaving a firm wall. For the cabbage, bring a pan of water to a boil. Drop in 2 green outer leaves and submerge in the water for 2 minutes. They will become quite flexible. Remove them with a slotted spoon and set aside. These are to be used for the pan lining. Do the same with 12 to 15 inner white leaves and set aside.

5. Stuff the tomato, pepper and squash about ¾ full with the prepared stuffing. Cover each tomato and pepper with its own disc.

6. Spread the green cabbage leaves on the bottom of a large enough pan. Fit in whatever assortment of vegetables you are using.

7. Stuff each of the white cabbage leaves with about ⅓ cup of the stuffing and fold the leaf to make a package. Put it into the pan, seam side down. Fill the pan with the stuffed leaves and whatever other vegetables you are using. Pour over all the puréed tomatoes and lemon juice. Cover with a dinner or soup plate and the pan cover. Cook the *dolme* over low heat for about 1 hour, or until much of the liquid which accumulates has evaporated.

Serve warm with bread, white rice and salad. Serves 6 to 8.

VARIATION: Here is another stuffing with an entirely new taste sensation.

1 cup raw rice
½ cup yellow split peas
3 tablespoons corn oil
2 medium onions, chopped (1 cup)
¼ teaspoon ground turmeric
¼ cup pomegranate concentrate
1 cup dark raisins or dried currants
2 tablespoons barberry (zereshk), see Glossary (optional)
1 teaspoon salt
⅛ teaspoon pepper
1 teaspoon toasted cuminseeds
1 pound ground beef or lamb
2 green cabbage leaves, softened in boiling water
½ cup tomato purée, canned or fresh
2 tablespoons lemon juice
½ cup water

1. Prepare all the ingredients as in the basic recipe. Stuff the vegetables. Cover the pan bottom with green cabbage leaves, add the vegetables, and cover with the tomato purée, lemon juice and water. Cook over low heat for 1 hour or until much of the liquid has evaporated.

DOLME
Stuffed Vegetables with Pomegranate

In the Persian manner, the pomegranate juice seasons the stuffing with a moderate fruity flavor. The herbs add a freshness and the tomato and lemon an additional acid seasoning. A classic Persian combination.

> 6 red or green peppers, or 3 of each
> 2 tablespoons corn oil
> 1 medium onion, sliced (½ cup)
> ½ pound ground beef
> 1 teaspoon salt, or to taste
> ⅛ teaspoon ground turmeric
> ⅛ teaspoon pepper
> ¼ cup dark raisins
> ¼ cup dried barberries (zereshk), see Glossary (optional)
> ⅓ cup pomegranate concentrate
> 1 cup chopped Italian flat-leaf parsley
> 2 teaspoons chopped fresh mint or ½ teaspoon dried mint
> ½ cup half-cooked rice, as in Basic Persian Rice (Chelo, see Index)
> 1 cup water
> 2 tablespoons tomato purée
> 1 tablespoon fresh lemon juice

1. Cut out and reserve a 1-inch disc from the stem end of each pepper to make a lid. Discard seeds and ribs. Set aside.

2. Heat the oil in a skillet, add the onion, and stir-fry over moderate heat for 2 minutes. Add the beef, salt, turmeric and pepper and stir-fry for 2 minutes more, or until the meat changes color. Remove skillet from the heat and stir in the raisins, barberries, pomegranate, parsley, mint and rice and mix well.

3. Stuff each pepper about ⅔ full of the mixture and replace the stem lid. Mix the water, tomato purée and lemon juice together. Fit the peppers into an oiled pan just big enough to hold them upright, and pour the liquid around them. It should reach halfway up the peppers. Add more water if necessary.

4. Cook in the covered pan over low heat for 1 hour, or long enough to soften the peppers completely and reduce the sauce by half.

Serve warm, spooning some sauce over the top of the peppers. Makes 8 peppers.

VARIATION: Six small eggplants may be stuffed in the same way as the peppers.

MOST O LABOO
Grated Beet and Yoghurt Salad

Housewives in Teheran often buy cooked beets from vendors who hawk their wares. The beets are purchased in quantity and stored in the refrigerator to be used when wanted in salads, soups or traditional dishes.

1 pound cooked beets, peeled and grated
2 cups yoghurt

1. Mix the beets and yoghurt together. Refrigerate.
Serve cold or at room temperature as a snack or as a salad with dairy dishes. Serves 4.

BORANEE BA MAST
Spinach and Yoghurt Salad

A cool, refreshing salad for hot days. The Persian fashion is apparent in its simplicity of seasonings.

1 pound fresh spinach, well rinsed, coarsely chopped
½ teaspoon salt
⅛ teaspoon pepper
1 cup yoghurt

1. Put the wet spinach in a pan, cover, and cook over low heat for 10 minutes. Let the spinach stand in the pan, covered, for 5 minutes more. Cool somewhat and gently press out the excess liquid. Refrigerate.
2. When ready to dine, mix the spinach, salt, pepper and yoghurt together. Toss the salad.
Serve cold. Serves 4.

SALADA FASLE
Seasonal Salad

Persians are not salad eaters in the European sense but this one in its simplicity is closer to our own tastes and most compatible with rice and meat dishes.

> 3 young cucumbers, peeled, sliced thin
> 1 medium onion, sliced thin (½ cup)
> 3 firm ripe tomatoes (1 pound), sliced thin
> ½ teaspoon salt
> ⅛ teaspoon pepper
> 1 tablespoon olive oil
> 1 tablespoon wine vinegar
> 1 tablespoon lemon juice
> 3 tablespoons chopped Italian flat-leaf parsley
> 1 tablespoon chopped fresh mint

1. Mix everything together and toss the salad well. Serve cold. Serves 6 to 8 with other dishes.

TORSHI ANGOOR
Pickled Grapes

These unusual pickles make a tangy supplement to Persian rice or meat dishes. Made during the grape season, they are then available all year. Some cooks fit an entire bunch of grapes, still on the stem, into the jar.

> 1 pound white or red seedless grapes, rinsed and dried
> 2 cups wine or cider vinegar, or enough to cover grapes
> ¼ teaspoon ground cinnamon
> ¼ teaspoon curry powder
> ½ teaspoon grated fresh gingerroot
> 2 teaspoons salt
> ⅛ teaspoon pepper

1. Remove the grapes from stems and put them in 1 or more large-mouth glass jars. Bring the vinegar to a boil, then cool. Mix in the cinnamon, curry powder, gingerroot, salt and pepper and pour the mixture over the grapes. The vinegar must cover the grapes so if necessary boil an additional amount.

2. Cover the jars and let them stand on the kitchen shelf for a minimum of 2 weeks before serving; 1 month is better. Refrigerate after opening.

Serve with any kind of Persian meat or rice dishes.

Makes 2 pints.

TORSHI LEETE
Mixed Vegetable Pickle

Turnip is the only vegetable not recommended in this table pickle since it develops an unpleasant flavor. Otherwise, one can use an assortment according to personal preference and availability.

> 1 pound cauliflower, cut into 1-inch florets
> 1 pound carrots, cut into ¼-inch cubes
> 1 pound green beans, cut into ½-inch slices
> 3 large celery ribs, cut into ½-inch slices
> 1 pound cabbage, shredded
> 6 garlic cloves, chopped
> ½ cup fresh mint leaves
> 1 tablespoon salt
> ¼ teaspoon pepper
> about 3 cups white or cider vinegar
> grape leaves (optional)

1. Mix the vegetables, garlic and mint together. Toss well. Mix the salt, pepper and vinegar together and bring to a boil. Cool.

2. Put the vegetables in large-mouth glass jars. Pour in the vinegar, making certain that it reaches the top of the vegetables. If not, then add more boiled vinegar. Cover the pickle with grape leaves if used, then cover the jar(s).

Let stand at room temperature for 1 month before using.

Serve with any kind of Persian food.

Makes 2 quarts.

LEETE BAADEMJAN BA SABZI

Eggplant Pickle with Herbs

The chopped eggplant provides only the texture of the pickle—it is the extravagant use of herbs, spices and wine vinegar that gives the pickle its authority. The pickle does not deteriorate even after 1 year; once opened, it must be refrigerated.

6 cups water
2 tablespoons salt
2 pounds eggplant (about 2), cut into 2-inch cubes
2 teaspoons Advieh (mixed spice, see Index)
¼ teaspoon pepper
¼ teaspoon ground ginger
3 tablespoons salt
2 cups dried parsley
1 cup dried dill
1 teaspoon dried tarragon
½ cup dried mint
1 tablespoon coarsely crushed coriander seeds
1 garlic clove, put through a press
2½ cups wine vinegar, brought to a boil and cooled

1. Bring the water and salt to a boil in a large pan. Add the eggplant and cook over moderate heat for about 8 minutes, pushing the cubes into the liquid now and then. This should be enough to soften the eggplant. Turn out into a colander and gently press out the liquid. Cool and chop fine by hand; a wood chopping bowl is ideal.

2. Mix the eggplant, all the herbs, seasonings and vinegar together. Mix well. Let stand for 1 hour, mix again, and pack into a glass jar to the top.

Store on the kitchen shelf for 1 month before using. Then refrigerate. Makes 1 quart.

NOTE: I do not recommend a processor for preparing this recipe as it would turn the eggplant into a mush.

BAADEMJAN TORSHI
Eggplant Pickle

This is a fine tart pickle that is used to spark the Persian rice and meat dishes that are herbal and scented but lack the sharpness of strong spices.

6 to 8 small eggplants (2 pounds), stems removed
3 cups water
1 tablespoon salt
½ cup coarsely chopped Italian flat-leaf parsley
¼ cup chopped celery leaves
⅓ cup coarsely chopped fresh mint
6 garlic cloves, chopped
¼ teaspoon hot red chili flakes
½ teaspoon salt
1 teaspoon dried marjoram
1 to 2 cups white or cider vinegar

1. Cut 3 or 4 incisions into 1 side of each eggplant, 1 inch long and 1 inch deep.
2. Bring the water to a boil in a pan with the salt. Add the eggplant, cover the pan, and cook over moderate heat for 5 minutes. This should be enough to make the eggplant soft but still firm. Drain well and cool. Put the eggplant on a cloth towel and press down with a heavy plate for 15 minutes to squeeze out the excess water. Set aside.
3. Mix the parsley, celery, mint, garlic, chili, salt and marjoram together. Stuff 1 heaping teaspoon of the mixture into each of the incisions in the eggplants. Fit the eggplants into a glass jar and add enough vinegar to cover them. Cover the jar.
Let the pickle stand at room temperature for 15 to 20 days to mature. Refrigerate after opening.
Serve with any kind of Persian food.
Makes 1 quart.

SHIRBERENJ
Rice Pudding for Shavuoth

Rice pudding is a classic preparation as the Persian Jews celebrate Shavuoth, the time when Moses presented the Ten Commandments. No meat is eaten on Shavuoth but this nutritious dish can be served at any time—for lunch, a snack or dessert.

> 2 cups raw long-grain rice, rinsed, soaked in water for ½ hour
> ¼ teaspoon ground cardamom
> ½ cup sugar
> 6 cups milk
> 1 teaspoon ground cinnamon

1. Drain the rice, then add ¾ cup water and simmer over low heat for 10 minutes as the water is absorbed. This will half-cook the rice.

2. Transfer the rice to a larger pan; add the cardamom, sugar and 1 cup milk. Bring to a boil and stir well. Add the milk every few minutes, 1 cup at a time, and simmer over low heat for 20 minutes. Stir frequently so that the rice doesn't burn on the bottom of the pan.

Turn out the rice pudding into a serving dish; sprinkle the cinnamon all over it. Add more cinnamon if you wish; more is better.

Serve cold. Serves 6 to 8.

HALWA BERENG
Rice Flour Custard

Purim is a holiday especially dear to Persian Jews. It is in their very genes—the celebration of the time when their own Queen Esther foiled the tyrant Haman and saved the Jews. This is the time of year that Halwa is prepared for family and friends who visit one another. There are several variations of the *halwa* but all have the smooth custard texture, flavored with rosewater and garnished with nuts or dates.

1 cup rice flour
¼ cup corn oil
3 cups water
½ cup sugar
¼ teaspoon ground cardamom
¼ teaspoon whole saffron, ground together with ½ teaspoon
    sugar
2 to 3 tablespoons rosewater to taste
1 tablespoon toasted almond slivers
1 tablespoon toasted pistachio nuts

1. Toast the rice flour in a dry skillet over low heat, stirring continuously, for 2 or 3 minutes or until it turns a beige color. Put the oil in a pan and stir in the toasted rice flour until well mixed. Now add the water and bring to a boil over low heat. Mix in the sugar and simmer over low heat for 10 minutes.

2. Add the cardamom, saffron and rosewater, mix well, and remove pan from the heat. Spread the custard in a heatproof glass dish or bowl so that it is about 1 inch deep. Scatter the nuts over the surface. Cool and refrigerate.

Serve cool. Serves 4 to 5.

VARIATION: Substitute toasted all-purpose flour for the rice flour, using the same method of preparation. In this case, the name of the custard is Halwa Ord.

HALWA ORD TAR (Taralva)
Toasted Custard

2 cups all-purpose flour
3 tablespoons corn oil
⅛ teaspoon ground turmeric
1⅓ cups sugar
6 cups water
¼ teaspoon crushed whole saffron, dissolved in 1 tablespoon
    water
½ teaspoon ground cardamom
1 tablespoon rosewater
¼ cup blanched almond slivers, lightly browned in oil

1. Put the flour in a large pan and toast over low heat for 3 minutes, stirring continuously. Add the oil and turmeric and continue to stir and mash the mixture with a wooden spoon until the color is light brown and all the lumps have been eliminated. Remove from heat and cool well, about 10 minutes.

2. Mix in the sugar while off the heat, add the water, and bring to a boil. Cook over low heat, stirring as the mixture thickens, for about 5 minutes.

3. Stir in the saffron, cardamom and rosewater. Mix well. Pour into 1 or more trays so that the *halwa* has a thickness of about 1 inch. Garnish with the almonds. Cool well, then refrigerate and cut into 2-inch cubes.

Serve cold as a snack or dessert. Serves 8 to 10 persons.

N O T E : Butter is occasionally used instead of oil. Since it can only be eaten after dairy meals its usefulness depends upon whether one is serving meat, in which case oil is used.

NAN BERENJI
Rice Flour Cookies with Poppy Seeds

These little cookies can be served at Pesach or other holidays. Sprinkling cookies with poppy seeds adds to the flavor as well as giving them a festive air. Using margarine rather than butter, makes the cookie *pareve* so that it can be eaten any time.

1 stick, ¼ pound, margarine at room temperature
⅔ cup sugar
2 large eggs, slightly beaten
1 tablespoon water
2 cups rice flour
¼ teaspoon baking powder
¼ teaspoon ground cardamom
2 teaspoons poppy seeds

1. Cream the margarine and sugar together until smooth. Add the eggs and water and mix well. Add the rice flour, baking powder and cardamom and blend together into a dough.

2. Oil a baking sheet lightly. Take 1 heaping teaspoon of the dough for each cookie, roll it into a ball, then press it down to ¼-inch thickness on the baking sheet. Sprinkle with the poppy seeds.

Bake the cookies in a 350° F. oven for 20 minutes.

Cool well; store in a cookie tin or jar. Makes 30 cookies.

HALWA CHOSK
Toasted and Crumbled Sweet

The *halwa chosk* is eaten after Sabbath prayers in the synagogue, especially when the anniversary prayers are said for the dead. Those who come to pray are served this *chosk* to nibble at or to wrap in a paper napkin and take home. It is a sweet, spice-flavored snack to be eaten as is—out of hand.

    1 cup all-purpose flour
    3 tablespoons corn oil
    ⅛ teaspoon ground turmeric
    ¼ teaspoon ground cardamom
    ½ cup sugar, dissolved in 2 cups water
    2 teaspoons ground coriander
    2 tablespoons rosewater

1. Put the flour in a pan and toast over low heat for 3 minutes, stirring with a wooden spoon. Add the oil and continue to stir and mix for about 7 minutes to eliminate all the lumps and until the mixture begins to turn light brown. Add the turmeric and cardamom and continue to stir.

2. Add the sugar water, 2 tablespoons at a time, stirring and smoothing for ½ minute. Add more sugar water as it is integrated into the mixture and begins to take on the consistency of coarse meal.

3. When all the liquid has been added and mixed in, add the coriander and rosewater. Mix well to ensure that at this time the color of the *halwa* is toasted brown and has the texture of bread crumbs.

Serve cool as a snack.

Makes about 2 cups.

SOHAN ASAL
Honey Almond Slivers

The dark brown almond slivers, combined with caramelized sugar, honey and cardamom-flavored saffron are difficult to resist, especially when served for the New Year celebration, Passover or other holidays.

¼ teaspoon whole saffron
¼ teaspoon ground cardamom
½ teaspoon sugar
½ teaspoon water
1 cup blanched almond slivers
2 cups sugar
2 tablespoons honey

1. Grind the saffron, cardamom and sugar to a smooth consistency, using a mortar and pestle. Add the water to dissolve the powder. Set aside.

2. Put the almond slivers in a dry skillet and stir-fry over low heat for about 10 minutes, or until they are deep brown all over. Do not scorch. Set aside.

3. Put the sugar and honey in a heavy skillet and caramelize over low heat for about 15 minutes as the sugar melts. Stir in the saffron mixture quickly when the sugar is completely melted, then stir in the almonds.

4. Very quickly, while the ingredients and the skillet are hot, drop a heaping teaspoon of the mixture onto an oiled cookie sheet. This is easier with 2 teaspoons, one to scoop and the other to push off.

Cool the sweets completely. Remove from the cookie sheet and store in a can or jar with a tight cover. Keep out of the reach of children.

Makes about 2 cups.

BADAM SOUKHTE
Burnt Almonds

These habit-forming sweets are a speciality of the Passover season but they are good at any time. They may be served with tea or coffee or anytime after dining.

    1 cup whole almonds, do not blanch
    1 cup sugar
    ¼ teaspoon ground cardamom
    2 tablespoons fine-chopped pistachio nuts (optional)

1. Put the almonds in a dry skillet and toast over low heat for about 10 minutes, or until the skin changes to a deep brown. Turn the almonds over individually if necessary to toast them uniformly since the flavor is based on the "burning." Set aside.

2. Caramelize the sugar in a skillet over low heat for about 10 minutes, or until it is completely dissolved. Do not overcook. Add the almonds and cardamom to the sugar and rapidly stir them in with a wooden spoon. Keep the skillet over very low heat or place a heat dispersal pad over the gas or electric element.

3. On a flat piece of aluminum foil quickly spoon out a heaping teaspoon of the syrup mixture with 2 almonds. Sprinkle a few fragments of the pistachio over all. This entire procedure must be done quickly so that the caramel does not harden in the skillet. These should be made on dry, cool days.

Cool well. Remove the sweets from the foil and store in a jar or tin with a tight cover.

Makes 2 cups.

HALEK
Fruit and Nut Mix for Passover

Halek is a word also used in Kurdistan and India to denote the ceremonial mixture presented on the table at the Passover Seder. The Ashkenazi haroseth is used for the same purpose, but the combination of ingredients is more complex. There are several types of Persian halek—the combination of nuts, fruits, wine and spices—depending upon the family custom.

¼ cup almonds
¼ cup pistachio nuts
¼ cup walnuts
¼ cup pumpkin seeds
¼ cup hazelnuts
⅛ cup coarsely chopped pitted dates
⅛ cup raisins, light and dark
⅛ cup coarsely chopped dried apricots
⅛ cup coarsely chopped prunes
⅛ cup coarsely chopped aloo bukhara (dried apricots), see Glossary
⅛ cup coarsely chopped dried cherries, seeded
¼ cup red wine
2 teaspoons wine vinegar
¼ teaspoon Advieh (spice mixture), see Index
¼ teaspoon rosewater

1. Coarsely chop the nuts in a processor. Mix the nuts, fruits, wine, vinegar, Advieh and rosewater to achieve a moist, textured consistency.

V A R I A T I O N S : For a fresh fruit *halek*, use apples, pears, pineapple, plums and grapes—as much variety as is available—an equal amount of each when cut into very small pieces. Mix with wine, vinegar, Advieh and rosewater in the proportions noted for the dried fruit and nuts.

Another type:

¾ cup pistachio nuts
¾ cup walnuts
¾ cup almonds
½ cup seedless white raisins
1 cup dark raisins
¾ cup pitted dates
2 apples, peeled and cored
½ teaspoon ground cinnamon
½ cup fresh pomegranate juice, or ½ cup red semisweet wine

1. Grind the nuts coarsely together, then add the fruits and grind together, but not too fine, leaving some texture. Add the cinnamon and pomegranate juice or wine; mix well. The mixture should have a crunchy consistency with a tart/sweet flavor.

MURABO HAVIDGE
Carrot Conserve

Carrot conserve is in reality a jam to be eaten with toast, bread or anything else. The nuts add texture to this relatively smooth concoction.

3 cups sugar
1 cup water
1½ pounds carrots, grated
1 tablespoon shelled pistachio nuts
1 tablespoon blanched almond slivers
½ teaspoon ground cardamom

1. Mix the sugar and water and bring just to a boil in a large pan. Add the carrots and nuts and mix well. Cook over low heat for ½ hour as the mixture reduces to a melange.

2. Stir in the cardamom and remove pan from the heat. Cool. Fill 1 or more pint glass jars to the top.

Store on a kitchen shelf but referigerate once the jar has been opened.

Makes about 2 pints.

MURABO BAY
Quince Jam

Quinces are not as popular in the United States as they are in Europe or among the Persians. This jam, a rarity, is not difficult to prepare and would be a luscious addition to the breakfast table. Quinces become available in the New York markets during October and November.

The quince seeds are sometimes saved and dried. They are then cooked with small amounts of water and taken as a relief for coughing.

1 ripe quince, 1 pound
3 cups sugar
1½ cups water
1 tablespoon dried lime (limoo amoni, see Glossary), broken into
    ¼-inch pieces, or 1 tablespoon lemon juice
¼ teaspoon ground cardamom

1. Do not peel the quince but cut it into slices 2 inches long and ¼ inch thick. Mix the quince, sugar and water together in a large heavy pan and bring to a boil. Reduce the heat to very low and cook for 1 hour. As the slices become translucent, the syrup thickens and darkens.

2. Add the dried lime (*limoo amoni*) or lemon juice, mix, and continue to cook very slowly for 1 hour more. The syrup will develop a deep red or maroon color. It is not necessary to stir except very occasionally. At the end of 2 hours of cooking (some Persians prefer 3 hours or more depending upon the quantity), stir in the cardamom and remove pan from the heat. Cool well. Pack into a glass jar with a tight cover.

Store the jam on a kitchen shelf since it does not have to be refrigerated until it is opened. The jam develops a deeper almost mahogany color as it becomes older. A 1-year-old jam is richly flavorful.

Makes about 2 pints.

SHARBAT SERKANJIBIN
Mint Syrup Concentrate

In Teheran flavored syrup concentrates of several flavors are prepared in large quantities in the home and stored on the kitchen shelves. When guests arrive there is always something on hand with which to prepare a cold drink during the blazing summers.

The syrup is also used, strangely enough, as a dip with lettuce. Not a salad but more of a thirst quencher, the lettuce leaves are broken up and served with a bowl of the mint syrup. Dip and munch.

4 cups sugar
1 cup water
¼ cup white vinegar
7 or 8 sprigs of fresh mint

1. Mix the sugar, water and vinegar together in a pan and bring to a boil. Add the mint and simmer over low heat for 5 minutes. Remove and discard the mint. Cool, bottle, and refrigerate.

Reserve the mint-flavored syrup to prepare summer drinks. Just take 2 tablespoons mint syrup, ¾ cup cold water and ice, and mix everything together.

Makes about 2 pints.

SHARBAT ALBALOO
Cherry Syrup Concentrate

The cherry syrup together with the cherries can be stored in a jar with a tight cover and refrigerated. The cherries themselves are often used as a jam on bread or toast for breakfast.

2 cups sugar
1 cup water
½ pound sour or sweet fresh cherries, preferably pitted
¼ teaspoon ground cardamom

1. Mix the sugar and water together in a pan, bring to a boil, then cook over low heat for 5 minutes. Add the cherries and simmer for 10 minutes. Stir in the cardamom; simmer for another minute. Turn out into a bowl and cool. Store in pint jars.

2. To prepare a cool drink, take ¼ cup of the syrup, add ½ cup cold water and ice, and mix well.

Serve cold.

Caucasus and Central Asia

GEORGIA

UZBEKISTAN

AFGHANISTAN

Seder Meal in a Jewish home in Tblisi, Gruzio, 1924.

GEORGIA

Georgians are a tribal people of an "obstinate" nature, according to early reports, who were settled south of the Caucasus Mountains from ancient times, in what is quite possibly one of the cradles of civilization. Abutting Turkey on the Black Sea, Georgia, a mountainous land of subtropical climate, is a part of the USSR but not Russian in any respect. Famous for its wine, grapes, tea and its cookery, Georgia's vineyards, where the wild grape flourishes, boast a 4,000-year-old history. Grapes are harvested and stomped underfoot, a system as ancient as it is obsolete. Bountiful nature has encouraged the ingenuity of the home cook in establishing a unique regional style.

Like everything else about the country, the language of the 5,250,000 Georgians is unique. In the script of a complex language that is not Indo-European, the medieval epic poem called "vepkistqaosani" (The Knight in the Panthers's Skin) will illustrate its intricacy.

Georgia is a Christian country and was a feudal monarchy from the eighth to the eighteenth century. During this time there were great periods of wars, assassinations, deportations, poverty, disorder, economic disaster, slavery. (It was the homeland of Stalin.)

Many centuries of foreign invasions of this area have contributed to the culture and the cooking. The world trade route went from India to Georgia. The Persian Achaemenid dynasty had a hold over Georgian tribes until 500 B.C. and was a dominant influence. After the conquest of Alexander the Great (331 B.C.) the influence of Persian culture still remained strong in Georgia. By 66 B.C. all of the Caucasus fell within the Roman orbit. The Arabs arrived from Asia Minor in 640 A.D. and the capital, Tiflis (Tbilisi), was held by Muslims for centuries. The Mongols conquered the area in 1236, starting a Mongol period. Great conflicts from a myriad of directions

197

and cultures only contributed to the singularity of the Georgian culture.

There are two separate beliefs about the origins of the Jews of Georgia. One is that they are descendants of the Ten Tribes sent into exile by Shalmaneser, the King of Assyria (858–824 B.C.). Another holds that the Jews were exiled from Judah under Nebuchadnezzar, the ruler of Babylonia (650–562 B.C.). Either of these theories confirms that the Jewish community in Georgia has ancient origins.

The peripatetic traveler, Benjamin of Tudela from Spain, visited Georgia (1160) and spoke of Jewish communities there, as did Marco Polo in 1272. By 1959 there was a population of about 51,000 Jews who were Georgian speaking. There was little anti-Semitism in the large Georgianized Jewish community, which dated farther back than the Middle Ages—until Stalin.

The cuisine of Georgia, common to both Christians and Jews, can be characterized in several ways. Firstly, Georgians are neither rice nor pasta eaters but prefer bread, which replaces both. Secondly, they have devised many dishes, especially those served cold, that have walnut-based sauces, and they are devoted to them. I believe this preoccupation with the walnut comes from the Persians who dominated the country for so many years.

The cultivation of corn was introduced by the Georgian Laz tribesmen in 1670. The Spanish were responsible for distributing corn around the Mediterranean after their conquest of Mexico—and also the hot chili and the tomato, since all of these originated in the Valley of Mexico. The Georgians received these foods via Turkey rather than by any other route, where they filled an important niche in the cooking.

Robust wine vinegar, garlic, spices such as pepper, cuminseed and hot chili are indispensable. Fresh herbs such as parsley, dill, coriander, basil and mint are ubiquitous. Pomegranate juice and seeds contribute mightily to the imaginative preparations.

There is an addiction to sour or pungent tastes. Sugar is not used in the cooking and the sweet-and-sour of China or the Middle East has no place in Georgian food. Imaginative combinations of lamb, which is the most important meat, a myriad of stuffed vegetable dishes, and the internationally known *shashlik*, reveal some of the culinary energy of the cooking.

Living off such a generous land provides an incentive to the enthusiastic cook and being in the path of numerous invaders who left their ideas to be absorbed, has made Georgian cooking probably the most celebrated in the Soviet Union.

PHALI
Young Beet Leaves in Walnut Sauce

Here is an unconventional salad or appetizer from the Georgian repertoire. It utilizes the popular seasonings such as wine vinegar, walnuts, hot chili, dill and garlic, combined in an artful manner both unconventional and robust.

    1 cup boiling water
    1 pound young beet leaves and stem
    1 cup shelled walnuts
    1 teaspoon salt, or to taste
    4 garlic cloves, sliced
    1 or 2 teaspoons jalapeño chili, seeded, to taste
    1 teaspoon ground coriander
    2 medium onions, chopped fine (1 cup)
    ¼ cup chopped fresh dill
    4 tablespoons red-wine vinegar

1. Pour the water over the beet leaves and cook in a covered pan over low heat for ½ hour. Drain, cool, and press out the liquid. Cut into ¼-inch-wide slices.

2. Process together the walnuts, salt, garlic and chili into a paste. Toss with the beet leaves, coriander, onions, dill and vinegar. Mix well.

Serve cold as an appetizer or as a salad course with dinner. Serves 6.

VARIATION: Fresh radish leaves or the tender leaves of cauliflower may be used instead of the beet. The procedure is the same.

LOBIO
Red Bean Appetizer

Lobio is a justly famous appetizer in Georgia and will be just as popular here. The dried red (not kidney) beans provide the substance and all the other seasonings, the fascination.

1 cup dried red beans (not kidney)
6 cups water
1 teaspoon salt
¼ teaspoon black pepper
¼ teaspoon cayenne pepper
2 tablespoons red-wine vinegar
2 garlic cloves, put through a press
2 medium onions, chopped very fine (1 cup)
5 scallions, green and white parts, chopped fine
½ cup walnuts, chopped to very small grains but not to a powder

1. Cover the beans with the water in a pan and bring to a boil. Cook over moderate heat until the beans are soft, about 1 hour. If the water evaporates too quickly, add 1 cup water. At the end of the cooking time there should be about ¾ cup remaining liquid.

2. Coarsely mash some of the beans, leaving half of the softened beans intact. Do this in the pan. Cool the mixture. Add the salt, pepper, cayenne, vinegar, garlic, onions, scallions and walnuts. Mix well. Refrigerate.

Serve cold. Serves 4 to 6.

NOTE: Lobio should be spicy hot, but to taste. You may add or reduce the amount of black and red pepper according to your tolerance. You may also soak the beans overnight in water to cover and then cook them in 3 cups water instead of 6. All other steps are the same.

VARIATION: *Lobio* may also be prepared with fresh green beans. Use 1 pound green beans; trim the ends and cut into 1-inch pieces. Cook them in lightly salted water until they are soft but with some firmness left. Drain, rinse under cold water, and refrigerate. Mix them with the same seasonings and quantities as for the red beans.

Serve cold. Serves 4 to 6.

CAVIAR PATRIJANI
Georgian Caviar

Several different cultures bake, char, boil or broil eggplant in one form or another and prepare an appetizer or salad. The Georgian version, in my opinion, is the most flavorful. It is best eaten cold.

4 cups water
2 large eggplants, 1½ pounds
2 ripe medium tomatoes, quartered (1 cup)
2 red or green sweet peppers, seeded, sliced (1 cup)
2 tablespoons corn oil
2 medium onions, chopped (1 cup)
2 garlic cloves, chopped fine
1 teaspoon salt
¼ teaspoon pepper
1 teaspoon red-wine vinegar

1. Bring 4 cups water to a boil in a large pan, put in the whole eggplants, cover, and cook over moderate heat for 15 minutes, which is enough to soften them. Drain, cool, and peel the eggplants. Press out the liquid gently through a metal sieve.

2. Process the tomatoes and peppers to a purée, then add the eggplant. Heat the oil in a skillet and stir-fry the onions over moderate heat for 2 or 3 minutes, until golden. Add the purée and stir-fry over low heat for 10 minutes.

3. Turn out the mixture into a bowl and briskly stir in the garlic, salt, pepper and wine vinegar. Refrigerate.

Serve cold or at room temperature. Serves 4 to 6.

PCHALI
Herb Fritters

These fritters (*pchali*) use scallions, fresh coriander, parsley and dill, herbs that are typical of the Georgian touch. The Armenians and Azerbaijanis also prepare this fritter in a similar manner—the way of the Caucasus.

4 scallions, sliced thin
1 cup chopped flat-leaf Italian parsley
1 cup chopped fresh coriander
1 cup chopped fresh dill
½ teaspoon salt
¼ teaspoon pepper
3 large eggs, beaten
½ cup flour
¼ cup corn oil for panfrying

1. Toss the herbs, salt and pepper together. Add the eggs and flour and mix well by hand. Do not use a processor.

2. Heat the oil in a skillet. Drop 1 heaping tablespoon of the mixture into the oil, shaping a round fritter. Fry over moderate heat for 2 minutes on each side. Drain briefly on paper towels. Continue with the rest of the mixture.

Serve warm or at room temperature as an appetizer with drinks, or as an additional dish with other Georgian foods.

Makes 20 fritters.

SOKO
Mushroom Barbecue

Under ideal circumstances, walnuts may be gathered in the wild and mushrooms carefully selected in forests—yours for the picking. This was the situation in the early life of the Georgians, and it is evident in their generous use of these ingredients, along with wine vinegar, garlic and enough spice to galvanize the taste buds.

1 pound mushrooms, well rinsed
1 teaspoon salt
½ cup shelled walnuts
2 garlic cloves, sliced
1 tablespoon chopped fresh coriander
¼ cup red-wine vinegar
¼ cup cold water
½ to 1 teaspoon fine-chopped seeded fresh hot red chili

1. Remove the mushroom caps from the stems and sprinkle caps with salt. Reserve the stems for some other recipe. Put the caps over the charcoal barbecue and grill them for 3 or 4 minutes, or until soft. Remove them to a serving dish.

2. Pound the walnuts and garlic to a paste, using mortar and pestle, or in a processor. Remove the paste to a bowl and stir in the coriander, vinegar, water and hot chili. Mix briskly and pour this over the mushrooms.

Serve as an appetizer at room temperature. Serves 4 to 5.

N O T E : Hot chili is variable, and the amount added to the sauce is to taste. It should not overwhelm the other ingredients.

SOKO KWERSTKHI
Mushrooms and Eggs

Familiar ingredients, combined in Georgian style, result in an unusual omelet. Mushrooms in Georgia are collected in the forests and mountain regions. Domestic mushrooms are not grown so one has to wait for good rains to encourage their growth and for the country folk to gather them for the markets.

2 cups water
1½ teaspoons salt
1 pound mushrooms, well rinsed
2 tablespoons butter or margarine
2 medium onions, chopped (1 cup)
3 eggs, beaten
1 tablespoon chopped flat-leaf Italian parsley

1. Bring the water and 1 teaspoon salt to a boil in a pan, add the mushrooms, and cook over moderate heat for 2 minutes. Drain well, cool, and cut the mushrooms into thin slices.

2. Heat 1 tablespoon butter in a skillet, add the mushrooms, and stir-fry over moderate heat for 2 minutes.

3. In a separate skillet, heat 1 tablespoon butter, add the onions, and stir-fry over moderate heat until they are golden, about 3 minutes. Add them to the mushrooms.

4. Beat the eggs well, stir in the parsley with the remaining ½ teaspoon salt, and pour eggs over the mushrooms. Cover the skillet and fry over low heat for 3 minutes to set the eggs and lightly brown the bottom of the omelet. Do not turn it over.

Serve warm. Serves 4 as an appetizer.

KWERSTKHI NIGOZEE SATSABELLY
Egg Salad in Walnut Sauce

H ard-cooked eggs are elevated to a new and robust flavor in Georgian walnut sauce. A small amount of hot chili is included but it can always be increased according to tolerance—though not enough to obliterate the flavor of the sauce.

6 hard-cooked eggs, peeled and halved lengthwise
1 cup shelled walnuts
2 garlic cloves, sliced
1 tablespoon chopped fresh coriander
½ teaspoon salt, or to taste
¼ cup red-wine vinegar
¼ cup cold water
¼ teaspoon ground turmeric
⅛ teaspoon hot red chili flakes

1. Put the egg halves on a serving platter.

2. Prepare the sauce by grinding the walnuts, garlic and coriander together, adding the salt, vinegar, water, turmeric and chili flakes to integrate the mixture. Process to a relatively smooth consistency. Taste and adjust the salt if you find it necessary.

Pour the sauce over the egg halves.

Serve cold or at room temperature. Serves 6 as an appetizer.

SOKO NOGOZEE
Mushrooms in Walnut Sauce

Georgian backyards often have a walnut tree yielding a ready supply of nuts, or the Georgians collect them from the wild. Such is the reason for the frequency in which they can be found in the cooking. Here are warm mushroom dishes infused with herbs and wine vinegar.

  2 tablespoons corn oil (in Georgia as in Turkey sunflower oil is
      used)
  1 pound mushrooms, cut into thin slices
  ½ teaspoon salt, or to taste
  ½ cup shelled walnuts
  3 garlic cloves
  1 tablespoon chopped fresh coriander
  1 tablespoon chopped fresh flat-leaf Italian parsley
  ¼ cup red-wine vinegar
  1 tablespoon chopped fresh dill

1. Heat the oil in a pan, add the mushrooms and salt, and sauté over low heat for 3 minutes.

2. Chop the walnuts and garlic together rather fine. Mix this with the coriander, parsley and vinegar. Add to the mushrooms and simmer over low heat for 5 minutes.

Serve warm, garnished with the dill. Serves 4 as an appetizer.

N O T E : The Georgian pestle is a stone that fits into the hand and the mortar is a wood vessel. These two implements are always in use grinding walnuts and garlic, which frequently go together.

V A R I A T I O N : In this combination, the mushrooms are chopped and combined with walnut paste and herbs. The only oil is provided by the walnuts themselves as they simmer in the mushroom liquid.

  3 tablespoons chopped walnuts
  2 garlic cloves, sliced
  1 teaspoon salt
  1 pound mushrooms, well rinsed and coarsely chopped
  2 medium onions, chopped (1 cup)
  ¼ teaspoon ground turmeric
  2 teaspoons chopped fresh dill

2 teaspoons chopped flat-leaf Italian parsley
2 teaspoons chopped fresh coriander

1. Pound walnuts, garlic and salt together to make a paste, using a mortar and pestle or a processor.

2. Put the mushrooms in a pan and add water almost to the level of the mushrooms. Simmer over low heat for 5 minutes. Remove the mushrooms with a slotted spoon and set aside. Strain and reserve ½ cup of the liquid.

3. Put the onions, turmeric, dill, parsley, coriander, mushrooms and the reserved liquid into a pan. Bring to a boil, then simmer over low heat for 3 minutes. Add the walnut/garlic paste, stir well, and cook for 5 minutes more.

Serve warm with cornmeal mush (Romee, see Index).

Serves 4.

ASPARAGUS SOUP

Simply prepared asparagus and herbs are the principal flavors in this vegetarian soup. It is thickened with beaten eggs.

1 pound fresh asparagus
6 cups hot water
1 tablespoon butter or margarine
2 medium onions, chopped fine (1 cup)
1 teaspoon salt
⅛ teaspoon pepper
¼ cup fine-chopped fresh dill
¼ cup fine-chopped flat-leaf Italian parsley
3 eggs, beaten

1. Peel the asparagus stalks but do not break the tips. Cut each stalk into 1-inch pieces. Soak in cold water for 10 minutes and drain. Put the water in a pan with the asparagus and bring to a boil.

2. In the meantime, melt the butter in a skillet, add the onions, and stir-fry until they are golden, about 3 minutes over moderate heat. Add this to the soup with the salt, pepper, dill and parsley. Cook the soup until the asparagus is tender, about 15 minutes.

3. Remove pan from the heat. Beat the eggs well and add ½ cup of the cooled soup to them, stirring briskly. Return the mixture to the soup pan. Warm the soup gently for 5 minutes but do not boil.
Serve warm. Serves 6 to 8.

LOBIO SOUP
Red Bean Soup

This vegetarian soup is enriched with dried red (not kidney) beans and walnuts, an unlikely combination that Georgian cooking delights in assembling. It is traditional.

¾ pound dried red beans, soaked in water overnight, drained
8 cups hot water
½ cup shelled walnuts, processed to a paste
2 teaspoons salt, or to taste
¼ teaspoon pepper
1 cup chopped celery
2 medium onions, chopped (1 cup)
1 tablespoon chopped fresh mint
1 tablespoon chopped fresh flat-leaf Italian parsley
1 tablespoon chopped fresh dill
2 tablespoons chopped fresh coriander

1. Put the beans and water in a pan, bring to a boil, and cook over moderate heat until soft, about 1 hour. Mash the beans with 1 cup liquid to a purée and return to the pan.
2. Add the walnuts, salt, pepper, celery and onions to the pan and simmer over low heat for 10 minutes. Add the herbs and simmer for 10 minutes more.
Serve hot with bread. Serves 6 to 8.

BOZBASHY

Lamb, Eggplant and
Green-Bean Soup

Georgian soups are thick with a variety of vegetables, especially onion. The bozbashy is a grand soup, filling and nourishing for chilly autumn and winter days.

> 1 pound lamb shank or shoulder chops, cut into 2-inch pieces,
>   bone included
> 8 cups water
> 1 tablespoon corn oil
> 3 medium onions, chopped (1½ cups)
> 1 pound eggplants (2), cut into 1-inch cubes
> ½ pound green beans, cut into 1-inch pieces
> 2 medium sweet red peppers, seeded, cut into 1-inch cubes
> 1 cup chopped peeled tomatoes, or equal amount canned
> ¼ cup chopped fresh coriander
> 3 garlic cloves, put through a press
> 1 teaspoon salt, or to taste

1. Put the lamb and water in a pan, bring to a boil, cook for 3 minutes, and remove the foam. Reduce heat to low and cook, covered, for about 30 minutes or until the lamb is tender but firm. Remove lamb pieces with a slotted spoon and strain the soup.

2. Heat the oil in a skillet and brown the lamb over moderate heat for 3 minutes. Set aside.

3. Bring the lamb broth to a boil over moderate heat. Add the onions, eggplants, green beans, red peppers and tomatoes and cook, covered, for 15 minutes. Add the lamb, coriander, garlic and salt and cook for 10 minutes more.

Serve hot. Serves 8.

MYASNOYA KHARCHO
Lamb, Herbs and Rice Soup

This is a lamb-flavored thick, substantial soup with emphasis on the herbs.

1 pound lamb shank, cut into 2-inch pieces, bone included
3 medium onions, chopped (1½ cups)
9 cups water
1 cup raw rice, well rinsed
¼ teaspoon black pepper
1 whole fresh jalapeño or serrano chili
3 tablespoons tomato paste
3 garlic cloves, put through a press or mashed in a mortar
1 teaspoon salt, or to taste
¼ cup chopped fresh coriander
¼ cup chopped flat-leaf parsley
¼ cup chopped fresh dill

1. Put the lamb in a dry soup pan and stir-fry over low heat for 10 minutes. Add the onions, stir-fry for 1 minute, cover the pan, and cook for 15 minutes. Add the water and bring to a boil over moderate heat. Reduce heat to low and cook for 45 minutes, or until lamb is tender.

2. Add the rice and cook for 10 minutes. Add the pepper, hot chili, tomato paste, garlic and salt and cook for 15 minutes. Lastly add the herbs and cook for 2 minutes more.

Serve hot. Serves 8 to 10.

VARIATION: One pound beef chuck or rib ends of beef with bone can be substituted for the lamb. Follow the same directions.

RIBNOYE KHARCHO
Salmon and Walnut Soup

Traditionally, this remarkable soup is prepared with fresh sturgeon. Salmon is more easily available and is a good substitute. However, should you find sturgeon, a not impossible task, then by all means use it.

8 cups water
1 carrot, halved
2 bay leaves
8 peppercorns
2 sprigs of flat-leaf parsley
1 teaspoon salt, or to taste
1 pound fresh salmon with bone, in one piece
3 medium onions, chopped (1½ cups)
2 tablespoons flour
1 tablespoon corn oil
1½ cups shelled walnuts, processed to a smooth paste
1 tablespoon ground coriander
¼ teaspoon dried oregano
1 whole hot fresh green chili
¼ cup chopped fresh dill, plus 1 tablespoon for garnish
¼ cup chopped flat-leaf parsley
½ cup chopped celery
3 tablespoons tomato paste

1. Bring the water to a boil in a large pan with the carrot, bay leaves, peppercorns, parsley and salt and cook over moderate heat for 5 minutes. Add the salmon and cook for 10 minutes. Remove the salmon and cut it into 1-inch cubes. Discard the bones. Strain the broth and discard the flavorings.

2. Mix onions and flour together. Heat the oil in a pan, add the onion mixture, and stir for 1 minute. Cover the pan and cook over low heat for 5 minutes. Add the fish broth, walnuts, coriander, oregano, hot chili, dill, parsley, celery and tomato paste. Mix and cook over low heat for 15 minutes. Add the fish cubes and cook for 5 minutes more.

Serve hot, garnished with a little chopped dill in each of the soup plates. Serves 8 to 10.

CHIKHIRTMA
Coriander-Flavored Onion Soup

The Georgians have no fear of strong flavors, especially in this vegetarian soup, which relies on spices, herbs and onions for its impact.

2 tablespoons butter or margarine
3 medium onions, chopped (1½ cups)
6 cups hot water
1 bunch of fresh coriander, about 10 sprigs, tied together
1 tablespoon flour
1 tablespoon wine vinegar
¼ teaspoon ground cinnamon
1 teaspoon salt, or to taste
¼ teaspoon pepper
2 eggs, beaten
2 tablespoons chopped fresh dill
2 tablespoons chopped fresh flat-leaf Italian parsley
1 teaspoon lemon juice

1. Melt 1 tablespoon butter in a pan, add the onions, and stir-fry over moderate heat until golden, about 3 minutes. Add the water and the bunch of coriander and bring to a boil. Cook for 10 minutes.

2. Mix the flour with ¼ cup hot broth and the vinegar. Add this to the soup. Add the cinnamon, salt and pepper and simmer over low heat for 15 minutes. Remove pan from the heat. Remove and discard the coriander.

3. Mix the eggs with ½ cup slightly cooled broth and return it to the soup pan with the remaining 1 tablespoon butter. Stir in the dill, parsley and lemon juice.

Serve immediately. Serves 6.

KUPATY
Georgian Beef and Lamb Sausages

These plump, spiced sausages are prepared in the autumn when the pomegranates are ripe and the evenings are cool. Then the sausages are made, blanched in boiling water and left to dry, hanging from a stick on the veranda. Cool air wafting between the sausages assists in the ripening and drying. Some people air-dry the sausages in 2 weeks, others use them after 24 hours. A memorable sight when walking along the shady streets in Georgia is to see the sausages drying on the verandas—a sure sign that autumn has arrived.

1½ pounds boneless beef, cut into ½-inch pieces
½ pound boneless lamb, cut into ½-inch pieces
¼ pound lamb fat, cut into ½-inch pieces
2 medium onions, chopped (1 cup)
1 garlic clove, chopped
2 teaspoons salt
½ teaspoon pepper
¼ teaspoon ground cinnamon
¼ cup water
2 tablespoons barberries, or ½ cup fresh pomegranate seeds (optional)
about 48 inches of veal or cow small intestine, cleaned and prepared for stuffing (see Note)

1. Grind both meats, the fat, onions and garlic together. Mix in by hand the salt, pepper, cinnamon and water. Mix well, then carefully stir in the barberries or pomegranate seeds if used.

2. Cut the intestine into 12-inch pieces and sew up one end of each piece. Stuff with the meat mix—not too tightly, leaving some space for expansion. Sew up the other end of the sausage. Curl the 2 ends together and tie them into a circle. Immerse the sausage into boiling water for 1 minute. (The Georgians would remove them from the water, slip them onto a long stick, and hang them in a cool and shady spot to dry for a day or two. For us, refrigeration is safer.)

3. To cook, panfry the *kupaty* in several tablespoons corn oil until brown on each side, about 5 minutes over moderate heat.

Serve warm. Makes 4 or 5 sausages.

N O T E : Kosher butchers generally stock the intestines for stuffing (*kishke*).

SOLYANKA
Beef, Herbs and Pickles in Tomato Sauce

Fresh flat-leaf parsley, dill and coriander are old standbys that are the usual herbal flavors to combine with beef—but Kosher dill pickles give new flavor to this Georgian mix. A new twist to pique modern tastes.

2 tablespoons corn or olive oil
1¼ pounds boneless beef chuck, cut into 1-inch cubes
1 pound onions (about 3), chopped fine
¼ cup tomato paste
2 pickled cucumbers, cut into ¼-inch dice (1 cup)
2 garlic cloves, chopped fine
2 bay leaves
½ teaspoon salt, or to taste
¼ teaspoon pepper
1½ cups water
2 tablespoons each of chopped fresh flat-leaf parsley, dill and
    coriander

1. Heat the oil in a pan, add the beef and onion, and stir-fry over moderate heat for 3 minutes as the onions change color.

2. Add the tomato paste, cucumber pickles, garlic, bay leaves, salt, pepper and water. Cover and simmer over low heat for 45 minutes, or until the beef is tender. Should the liquid evaporate too quickly, add another ½ cup water.

3. Add the parsley, dill and coriander, stir it into the beef, and cook for 5 minutes.

Serve warm with bread. Serves 4.

CHANAKHY I
Lamb and Assorted Vegetables in a Clay Pot

A chanakhy always has lamb and eggplant with other vegetables, and especially 3 herbs. It is prepared and served in a covered clay pot and is baked slowly in the oven. (Any casserole will do.) All the recipes of *chanakhy* are variations on the same theme, but each is different enough to warrant inclusion.

4 medium eggplants, about 2 pounds
¼ cup chopped fresh coriander
¼ cup chopped fresh dill
¼ cup chopped fresh flat-leaf parsley
1 teaspoon salt
½ teaspoon pepper

1 teaspoon minced lamb fat (optional)
1 pound boneless lamb, cut into 1-inch pieces
1 pound potatoes (about 4), peeled, quartered
5 medium onions, sliced (2 cups)
1 pound fresh tomatoes (about 4), halved
1 cup tomato juice
2 teaspoons minced fresh hot red or green chili

1. Cut an incision 3 inches long and 1 inch deep lengthwise into each eggplant. Scoop out several tablespoons of the seed pulp.

2. Mix together half of the coriander, dill, parsley, salt and pepper and all the lamb fat. Stuff each eggplant with an equal amount.

3. Lightly oil a clay pot or heatproof glass dish that has a cover. Put the lamb on the bottom, potatoes over that, cover with the eggplants, and scatter the onions between the layers. Put the tomatoes cut side down over the onions, pour in the tomato juice, and sprinkle over all the remaining half of the herbs, salt and pepper and the hot chili.

Cover the clay pot or dish and bake at 325° F. for 2 hours. Should the liquid evaporate too quickly, add ½ cup water and continue to bake.

Serve warm in the baking pot or dish. Serves 8.

CHANAKHY II
Lamb, Eggplant and Rice

This version of chana-khy includes rice, which is baked along with the vegetables and herbs.

4 eggplants, 2 pounds
¼ cup chopped fresh coriander
¼ cup chopped fresh dill
¼ cup chopped fresh flat-leaf parsley
1 teaspoon salt
¼ teaspoon black pepper
¼ teaspoon cayenne pepper
1 pound boneless lamb, cut into 1-inch pieces
3 medium onions, sliced into rings (1½ cups)

1½ cups water
1 pound potatoes (about 4), peeled, quartered
1¼ pounds tomatoes (about 4), halved
¾ cup raw rice, well rinsed

1. Cut an incision 3 inches long and 1 inch deep lengthwise into each eggplant. Scoop out several tablespoons of the seed pulp.

2. Mix together half of the coriander, dill, parsley, salt, pepper and cayenne and stuff each eggplant with an equal amount.

3. Lightly oil a clay pot or heatproof glass dish that has a cover. First put the lamb on the bottom, scatter one third of the onions over the lamb, and add the water. Cover the dish and bake in a 325° F. oven for 30 minutes.

4. Add the potatoes, eggplant and more onion rings and the tomato halves, cut side down. Push the ingredients slightly to the sides making a space in the center. Pour in the rice, the balance of the onion rings, and remaining herbs and seasonings. Cover the dish and bake for 1 hour more. Should the liquid evaporate too quickly, add ½ cup water and continue to bake.

Serve warm in the pot or dish. Serves 8.

CHANAKHY III

Lamb, Assorted Vegetables and Garlic

Georgians love vegetables above all else and meat is only an adjunct to the preparation at hand. The emphasis here is on an assortment of vegetables, herbs, seeds but especially a head of garlic, which will be eaten clove by clove. The easy method of preparation is a plus.

1 pound boneless lamb, cut into 1-inch pieces
1 pound potatoes (about 4), peeled, cut into 1-inch pieces
1 pound tomatoes (about 3), cut into 1-inch pieces
2 medium eggplants, 1 pound, cut into 1-inch pieces
1 pound green beans, cut into 1-inch pieces
3 medium onions, chopped (1½ cups)
¼ cup chopped fresh coriander
¼ cup chopped fresh dill

¼ cup chopped fresh flat-leaf parsley
1 whole head garlic, 6 to 8 cloves, not peeled
2 teaspoons dill seed
1 teaspoon coriander seed
¼ teaspoon cayenne pepper
2 teaspoons salt
2 cups water

1. Put everything into a large pan or clay pot and shake it briskly back and forth, clockwise, then counter clockwise. This will mix everything together without stirring. Cover the pan and bake in a 325° F. oven for 2½ hours. There is sufficient liquid in this provided by the water and vegetables, but should it evaporate too quickly, add ¼ cup water.

Serve hot. Serves 8.

SHASHLIK
Georgian Lamb Barbecue

Shashlik is probably the principal Georgian dish that is prepared all over the Soviet Union and is also internationally known. It consists of 8 to 10 cubes of boneless lamb marinated in wine vinegar and barbecued on a skewer over the hot coals after the flames have died down—this is important. Long metal skewers, known as *shampuri*, are used. It is as simple as that.

1 pound boneless lamb with a small amount of fat, cut into 2-inch
    domino-shaped pieces
1 medium onion, sliced (½ cup)
¼ cup red-wine vinegar
2 garlic cloves, sliced
½ teaspoon salt
¼ teaspoon black pepper
2 bay leaves

1. Mix everything together and store in a glass or enamel bowl (no metal). Marinate, covered, in a cool place (or refrigerate) for 1 to 3 days. Some say a week but this is not really essential.

2. Drain off the marinade, put 5 or 6 lamb pieces on a skewer, and grill over hot charcoals after the flames have died down. Grill for 15 to 20 minutes according to your taste, medium or well done.

Serve warm with bread and an assortment of salads.

Serves 4.

N O T E : A modern apartment is no place to grill over charcoal. I have broiled the marinated *shashlik* in a hot gas broiler, which is acceptable but not quite as good as if charcoal broiled.

V A R I A T I O N : A predictable variation of an all-lamb *shashlik* is to add ½ small onion and 1 small tomato alternating with the cubes of lamb. The lamb is marinated but the vegetables are not.

Another variation to accompany the all-lamb *shashlik* is prepared with small eggplants, as follows.

4 or 5 small eggplants, 1 pound
½ teaspoon salt
¼ teaspoon black pepper
1 tablespoon fine-chopped fresh coriander
1 or 2 teaspoons minced lamb fat (optional)

1. Cut an incision ½ inch deep and 1 inch long into the side of each eggplant.

2. Mix the salt, pepper, coriander and lamb fat together. Stuff each eggplant with part of the mixture.

3. Put a metal skewer through the upper part, the thick end, of each eggplant and broil over charcoal for 15 to 20 minutes, or until quite soft.

Serve together with the all-lamb *shashlik* on the same platter. Garnish the platter with sliced onions and several whole long scallions.

Serves 4.

CHAKAPULI
Lamb and Plums in Herb Sauce

All of the ingredients except the fresh plums are very reminiscent of Persian cooking. My theory is that the Persians, over the centuries, had a considerable amount of influence on Georgian cooking. I believe this recipe will also find favor in the American kitchen.

3 pounds lamb, shank or boneless, cut into 2-inch pieces
5 bunches of fresh scallions, about 20, chopped fine
3 cups water
2 tablespoons dried tarragon
1 teaspoon salt, or to taste
¼ teaspoon pepper
¼ cup chopped fresh mint leaves or 2 tablespoons dried mint
1½ pounds fresh plums, 10 to 12
½ cup chopped fresh coriander
3 tablespoons fresh lemon juice

1. Put the lamb in a dry pan, cover, and cook over low heat for 15 minutes, stirring now and then. Add the scallions and water, and bring to a boil.

2. Add the tarragon, salt, pepper, mint and plums. Simmer over low heat for 20 minutes. Add the coriander and lemon juice and cook until tender. Total time will be about 1 hour.

Serve hot with white rice. Serves 8 to 10 with bread and salads.

NOTE: The *chakapuli* may be frozen for future dining. Simply thaw out for several hours and then briefly warm up.

SETSAMANDI (KHARCHO)
Lamb, Rice and Herb Gruel

The *setsamandi* is not thick enough to be called a stew nor thin enough to be considered a soup. It is a strongly seasoned gruel thickened by cooking the rice until it nearly dissolves. The flavor, to me, seems Indian, since turmeric and the surprising tamarind paste are included, along with cayenne. In spite of all these conflicting seasonings and textures, it is Georgian.

1½ pounds lamb shank or breast, cut into 3-inch pieces,
  including the bone
11 cups water
¾ cup raw rice, well rinsed
3 medium onions, chopped fine (1½ cups)
4 garlic cloves, chopped fine
3 celery ribs, cut into ¼-inch cubes (1½ cups)
½ cup chopped flat-leaf Italian parsley
½ cup chopped fresh coriander
1 tablespoon ground coriander
1 teaspoon ground turmeric
1 tablespoon thick tamarind concentrate (see Glossary)
⅛ teaspoon hot red chili flakes
2 teaspoons salt, or to taste

1. Put the meat and water into a large pan and bring to a boil over moderate heat. Remove the foam with a slotted spoon.

2. Add the rice, onions and garlic and simmer in the covered pan over low heat for 1 hour. Stir every now and then to keep the rice from sticking.

3. Add all the other ingredients at once and continue to simmer for ½ hour.

Serve hot with bread, Mchadi (Cornmeal Pancake) and Romee (Cornmeal Mush), see Index

Serves 8.

NOTE: Lamb is fat and it would be prudent to prepare the *setsamandi* or *kharcho* (the Russian word) the day before, refrigerate it, and then scoop off and discard the congealed fat. Rewarm briefly.

TOLMA CHORZI
Beef-Stuffed Cabbage

In this version, the beef is cooked and ground as a basis for the stuffing—a different method from that used in other stuffings.

1 pound boneless beef chuck, cut into 2-inch pieces
3 cups water
3 tablespoons margarine
3 medium onions, chopped fine (1½ cups)
1 teaspoon salt, or to taste
¼ teaspoon pepper
¼ cup chopped fresh coriander
¼ cup chopped fresh dill
22 to 25 cabbage leaves, blanched in boiling water for 3 minutes
   (see Note)
½ cup reserved beef liquid

1. Cook the beef in 3 cups water over low heat for 1 hour, or until tender. Remove, cool, then grind the beef. Reserve ½ cup liquid.

2. Heat 2 tablespoons margarine in a skillet and stir-fry the onions over moderate heat until they are golden. Remove to a bowl, cool, and mix well with the beef, salt, pepper, coriander and dill. Put 1 heaping tablespoon of the stuffing on the end of the cabbage leaf opposite to the stem and roll the leaf over, tuck in the two sides, and roll to the end. Shape a roll 3 inches long and about 1 inch thick. Do this for all of the leaves.

3. Melt the remaining tablespoon of margarine in the same skillet, place the *tolma* (cabbage rolls), seam side down, in a single layer and brown them over moderate heat all around for 10 minutes. Add the beef liquid, cover the pan, and cook for 10 minutes more. There is no sauce.

Serve warm. Serves 6.

NOTE: To remove the cabbage leaves from a head weighing 2 pounds, cut out the core to a depth of 2 or 3 inches. Carefully peel off the leaves one at a time. Dig out more of the core as you go along. Drop the leaves, a few at a time, into a large pan filled with 8 cups boiling water. Leave them for 5 minutes, remove with a slotted spoon, and cool. Trim off a thin slice of the heavy spine of each leaf to make them more flexible for stuffing.

TOLMA
Stuffed Cabbage with Lamb

The Georgians have their personal preferences as to the best stuffing to use in this universally popular stuffed vegetable. This combination, cabbage with lamb stuffing, is the preferred one, although ground beef may also be used.

1 pound ground lamb
2 medium onions, chopped fine (1 cup)
1 egg, beaten
½ cup raw rice, well rinsed
¼ teaspoon black pepper
1 teaspoon salt, or to taste
2 tablespoons chopped fresh coriander
1 tablespoon chopped fresh mint
20 to 25 cabbage leaves prepared as in Tolma Chorzi
2 cups fresh tomatoes, peeled, chopped and puréed, or canned
    tomatoes

1. Mix everything except the cabbage leaves and tomato purée together and set aside.

2. Place 1 cabbage leaf with the spine end away from yourself. Put 1 heaping tablespoon of the stuffing on the end of the leaf nearest you and roll it over, then tuck in the two sides to shape a cylinder 3 inches long and about 1 inch thick. Roll up the leaf but not too tightly. Prepare all the leaves this way to make the *tolmas*.

3. Fit the *tolmas* neatly in a pan in several layers. Pour the tomato purée over the rolls. Cover with a dinner plate and press the leaves down gently. Cover the pan and cook over low heat for 1½ hours. Should the liquid evaporate too soon, add ½ cup water. There should be very little sauce.

Serve the warm *tolmas* with bread. Serves 6.

TOLMA

Stuffed Cabbage Leaves with Pomegranate Seeds

The Georgians have assembled this extravagant stuffing for humble cabbage leaves. The pomegranate seeds provide flavor and an interesting crunch that adds an unexpected texture.

1 pound ground lamb
4 medium onions (one is chopped to make ½ cup for the stuffing
    and 3 are sliced for onion rings)
2 teaspoons ground coriander
2 tablespoons chopped fresh coriander
2 tablespoons chopped fresh dill
2 celery ribs, chopped (⅔ cup)
2 garlic cloves, chopped fine
¼ teaspoon ground turmeric
¼ teaspoon hot red chili flakes
¾ cup raw rice, well rinsed
20 to 25 cabbage leaves
½ cup fresh pomegranate seeds (see Glossary)
1 cup tomato juice
1 cup water

1. Prepare the stuffing: Mix together the lamb, chopped onion, ground coriander, 1 tablespoon of the fresh coriander, 1 tablespoon of the fresh dill, the celery, garlic, turmeric, chili flakes and rice. Set aside.

2. Trim 20 to 25 cabbage leaves as described in the Stuffed Cabbage with Lamb (previous recipe). Stuff each leaf as described to make rolls 3 inches long and 1½ inches thick.

3. Put one layer of the stuffed cabbage in a pan, fitting the rolls closely together. Scatter half of the onion rings on top, then half of the remaining coriander and dill and the pomegranate seeds. Cover this with another layer of the stuffed cabbage and repeat the garnishes. Carefully pour the tomato juice and water over all. Cover with a dinner plate to hold down the leaves. Bring the liquid to a boil, then reduce heat to low, cover the pan, and cook for 1½ hours. Check to see that the liquid does not evaporate too quickly, in which case add another ½ cup water. There should be very little sauce.

Serve warm. Serves 8 with other dishes.

KISHMISH VASHLI TOLMA
Raisin, Apple and Lamb Stuffed Cabbage

Fruit and meat with herbs makes another unfamiliar combination for stuffing cabbage leaves. Rice always provides filler and tomato juice the medium of cooking the *tolma*. Another premier example of Georgian culinary ingenuity.

1 pound ground lamb
⅓ cup raisins, dark or light
1 tablespoon chopped fresh coriander
1 tablespoon chopped fresh dill
1 teaspoon salt, or to taste
½ cup raw rice, well rinsed
20 to 25 cabbage leaves, blanched in boiling water for 3 minutes
    (as in Beef-Stuffed Cabbage)
3 large apples, 1 pound, peeled and sliced, core discarded
2 medium onions, cut into rings (1 cup)
3 cups tomato juice

1. Mix the lamb with raisins and herbs and process to a smooth consistency. Mix this with salt and rice. Stuff the cabbage leaves.

2. Put the stuffed cabbage in one layer in a large pan or skillet and scatter over it half of the apple slices and onion slices. Add another layer of cabbage and the balance of apples and onions. Pour the tomato juice over all and bring to a boil. Cover the pan and cook over low heat for 1 hour.

Serve warm with bread. Serves 6.

NOTE: Leftover stuffing can be used to prepare meatballs 1 inch in diameter. Place them in the pan where there is space and cook with the stuffed cabbage.

ZAPHULIS TOLMA
Summer Vegetables, Stuffed

There is no shortage of vegetables and herbs in the semitropical climate of Georgia. In the other regions of the Soviet Union, Georgia is considered synonymous with a bountiful nature of great variety and quality. Vegetables that appear in the summer are stuffed with lamb, the principal meat of the Georgians.

STUFFING

1½ pounds ground lamb, with some fat
½ cup raw rice, well rinsed
3 medium onions, chopped (1½ cups)
¼ cup chopped fresh coriander
¼ cup chopped flat-leaf parsley
¼ cup chopped fresh basil
¼ teaspoon black pepper
2 teaspoons salt, or to taste

VEGETABLES

5 eggplants, 2 pounds
6 red or green peppers or both, 1¼ pounds
6 ripe but firm tomatoes, 2 pounds
3 tart green apples such as Granny Smith or McIntosh, peeled and cored
2 cups fresh or canned tomatoes, puréed

1. Mix all the stuffing ingredients together and set aside.

2. Cut off ½ inch of the tops of peppers. Scoop out and discard the seeds and ribs. Put the peppers in a bowl and pour boiling water over them to tenderize somewhat. Let stand for 2 minutes, then drain. Save the tops.

Cut into the eggplants 1 inch deep, lengthwise; pry open and scoop out the seeds to provide a pocket big enough to hold about ½ cup of stuffing.

Cut off ½ inch of the tomatoes and scoop out the loose seeds and liquid, leaving a thick firm wall. Save the tops. Core the apples and cut into thin slices. Set aside.

3. Stuff the vegetables about ¾ full and cover them with their tops. Arrange in layers in a large pan as follows: First the eggplants, then one third of the apple slices, the peppers, another third of the apple slices, the tomatoes and the balance of the apples. Pour the tomato purée over all. Cover the pan, bring to a boil, then reduce heat to low and cook for 1½ hours. There is very little sauce, enough to cook the vegetables and stuffing. Should it dry out too quickly, add about ½ cup water.

Serve warm with bread. Serves 8 to 10.

BIYA VASHLEE TOLMA
Stuffed Apples and Quinces

Fruit with a meat stuffing is a rare culinary bird. The first time I encountered this was in Georgian cookery, which does not lack for unconventional combinations. Several nearby cultures also cook quinces with meat as in Bukhara and Persia.

STUFFING

1 pound ground lamb with a small amount of fat
⅓ cup raw rice, well rinsed
2 medium onions, chopped (1 cup)
¼ cup chopped fresh coriander
1 teaspoon salt, or to taste
¼ teaspoon hot red chili flakes

BROTH

½ pound lamb bones
3 cups water

FRUITS

6 small quinces, about 1½ pounds
6 small tart apples, about 1½ pounds
½ pound (3) firm sour plums, pitted and sliced
1 tablespoon chopped flat-leaf parsley or fresh coriander for garnish

1. Mix stuffing ingredients together well and set aside.

2. Put the bones and water in a pan, bring to a boil, and skim off the accumulating foam. Cover the pan and cook over moderate heat for ½ hour. Strain and reserve 2 cups broth. Discard the bones.

3. Cut off about ½ inch of the tops of the quinces and apples and discard them. Core both fruits but leave about ½ inch of the bottom intact to hold the contents. Stuff each one with about 2 tablespoons of the stuffing.

4. Put the stuffed fruits in a pan, preferably in a single layer, and scatter the plum slices over all. Pour over the reserved lamb broth, cover the pan, and cook over low heat for 1½ hours. Should the liquid evaporate too quickly, add ¼ cup water.

Serve warm, garnished with the chopped herb of choice.

Serves 6.

NOTE: An imperfect substitute, but one that is acceptable and traditional, is to use 2 tablespoons red-wine vinegar instead of the sour plums.

VARYA TABAKA
Crisp-Fried Cornish Game Hen

Strangely enough, these "baby" chickens, as they are called, are eaten out of hand without any embellishment. Cooked until crisp, with only the hidden slices of garlic to leave an impact, the *tabaka* is easily prepared.

2 Cornish game hens, about 1 pound each
6 garlic cloves, sliced lengthwise
1 teaspoon salt
½ teaspoon paprika
¼ teaspoon pepper
2 tablespoons corn oil

1. Butterfly the hens and spread them out flat. Push the slices of garlic under the skin wherever possible.

2. Mix the salt, paprika and pepper together and rub the mixture all over the hens.

3. Heat a dry skillet or two over moderate heat for 1 minute. Add the oil, then place the hens skin side up in the oil. Cover with a plate and put a heavy weight, perhaps a stone or metal mortar, on the plate. Fry for 10 minutes. Turn the hens over and fry with plate and weight for 10 minutes more, or until the skin is crisp and brown.

Serve warm with anything you wish such as bread, salads, pickles. Serves 4.

SATSABELI BAZHA
Poultry in Walnut Sauce

This is one of the best known and most flavorful Georgian dishes, combining the characteristic flavorings of the cuisine to make a traditional sauce. Walnuts are paramount to the dish and the slightly acid fruit flavor of pomegranate juice is the basis of the dressing. A unique dish that displays the Georgian genius for adventurous dining.

POULTRY

3½ to 4 pounds chicken, turkey or duck
4 cups water
1 medium onion, halved
1 carrot, halved lengthwise
2 sprigs of flat-leaf parsley
2 teaspoons salt

SAUCE

¾ cup shelled walnuts
5 garlic cloves, peeled, sliced
1 to 2 teaspoons minced fresh hot red chili
2 teaspoons ground coriander
¼ teaspoon ground turmeric
¼ cup chopped fresh coriander
¼ cup pomegranate juice, or 2 tablespoons pomegranate
      concentrate (see Glossary) dissolved in 2 tablespoons water,
      or 2 tablespoons red-wine vinegar
2 tablespoons fresh pomegranate seeds for garnish (optional)

1. Discard the loose skin and fat of whatever poultry you decide to use. Disjoint the chicken or duck into about 8 pieces. Turkey should be cut into 3- or 4-inch pieces, with the breast and thighs the most desirable parts.

2. Put the poultry, water, onion, carrot, parsley and salt into a pan, bring to a boil, reduce heat to low, and cook for about 40 minutes, or until tender. Remove poultry pieces, discard the seasonings, and reserve 2 cups broth.

3. For the sauce, make a paste in a processor with first the walnuts, then adding the garlic, chili, ground coriander, turmeric, fresh coriander and pomegranate juice. Dilute this paste with enough of the reserved broth to provide a smooth but not too liquid dressing.

4. Put the poultry pieces on a serving platter and pour the sauce over all. Garnish with the pomegranate seeds.

Serve cold or at room temperature as an appetizer, salad or main summer dish. Serves 6 to 8 with bread and other dishes.

KATAMI CHAHOHBILI
Chicken in Onion and Tomato Sauce

The chahohbili, in whatever variation, is a popular Georgian method of cooking meat and poultry. Also, cooking in a covered pan over low heat for a longer time means that all the flavor is retained. Meat and poultry are very lean in Georgia and so oil or chicken fat is often added to the cooking. However, since American meat is fat, very little additional oil need be added.

1 pound onions (4), chopped
2 tablespoons fresh chicken fat or corn oil
1 chicken, 3½ pounds, cut into 12 pieces, loose skin and fat
    discarded
¼ teaspoon pepper
1 teaspoon salt, or to taste
¼ cup chopped fresh basil

¼ cup chopped fresh coriander
2 pounds ripe tomatoes, chopped fine, or 2 cups canned
    tomatoes, chopped

1. Put the onions and fat or oil in a pan and stir-fry over moderate heat until onions are golden, about 5 minutes. Add the chicken, pepper, salt, basil, coriander and tomatoes. Mix well, cover the pan, and cook over low heat for 1 hour, or until the chicken is tender and the sauce has formed and thickened.

Serve hot. Serves 6 with other dishes.

VARIATION:

1 chicken, 3½ pounds, cut into 12 pieces, loose skin and fat
    discarded; include giblets except liver
½ cup water
1 pound onions (4), chopped fine
1 pound potatoes (3), peeled, cut into 1-inch cubes
2 pounds ripe tomatoes, chopped, or 2 cups canned tomatoes,
    chopped
1 teaspoon salt, or to taste
¼ teaspoon pepper
4 garlic cloves, chopped fine
1 tablespoon chopped fresh coriander

1. Put the chicken in a dry pan and stir-fry over low heat, adding 1 or 2 tablespoons water every now and then. Continue for 10 minutes, using all the water; cover the pan.

2. Add the onions and potatoes and cook over low heat for 10 minutes more.

3. Separately, put the tomatoes, salt, pepper, garlic and coriander in a skillet and cook, covered, over low heat for 15 minutes, to reduce the sauce to a thick melange. Add this to the chicken, cover the pan, and cook over low heat for 20 minutes more. Should the sauce evaporate too quickly, add ½ cup water and cook 10 minutes longer.

Serve hot. Serves 6 with other dishes.

KATAMI NIGOZEE
SATSABELI

Chicken in Spiced Vinegar
Walnut Sauce

Satsabeli is a salad spiced with hot chili in a walnut paste, intensified with wine vinegar and garlic, standbys in Georgian cookery. The salad is traditionally eaten with Cornmeal Mush (Romee) or Corn Bread (Mchadi), see Index. Both the hot chili and corn originated in the Valley of Mexico and were taken to Europe by the Spanish in the sixteenth century.

Georgians only use wine vinegar, which is usually made at home since almost everyone grows grapes for wine.

> 1 chicken, 3½ pounds, cut into 8 pieces, loose skin and fat
>   discarded
> 4 cups water
> 1 small onion, whole
> 1 large carrot, halved
> 2 parsley sprigs
> 1 teaspoon salt
> 2 cups shelled walnuts
> ¼ cup chopped fresh coriander
> 4 garlic cloves, put through a press
> 1 to 2 teaspoons minced seeded fresh jalapeño chili
> 3 tablespoons wine vinegar or ½ cup fresh pomegranate juice (see
>   Glossary)

1. Cook the chicken in the water with onion, carrot, parsley and salt over low heat for 30 minutes, or until tender. Remove the chicken, strain the broth, and reserve 1 cup.

2. Grind the walnuts to a paste, using some of the broth to facilitate the grinding. Put the paste in a large mixing bowl with the coriander, garlic, chili and vinegar or pomegranate juice and enough of the broth to create a salad dressing. Mix well.

3. Put the chicken on a serving platter and pour the sauce over. Garnish with pomegranate seed when available.

Serve at room temperature. Serves 6 to 8.

VARIATION: The *satsabeli* can be made with 2 whole boneless chicken breasts. Follow the same directions as for the whole chicken. Cook the whole breasts until tender, cut into 2-inch cubes, and pour the sauce over the chicken.

KATAMI SATSABELI BAGA
Duck in Georgian Walnut Sauce

The Georgians like an acid flavor in their food unlike, for example, the Chinese who add sugar now and then. Wine vinegar is not the only flavoring in the Georgian sauce. A traditional and easily available substitute for the vinegar is ½ cup white grape juice, made from unripe and slightly acid grapes. Another traditional seasoning in the sauce is ½ cup of blackberry juice.

> 1 duck, 4½ pounds, whole
> 5 cups water
> 1 large carrot, halved
> 1 medium onion, halved
> 2 sprigs of flat-leaf Italian parsley
> 1 teaspoon salt, or to taste
> 2 cups shelled walnuts
> ¼ cup chopped fresh coriander
> 1 teaspoon ground coriander
> ½ teaspoon ground turmeric
> 3 to 4 tablespoons red-wine vinegar, to taste

1. Cook the duck in the water with carrot, onion, parsley and salt in a covered pan over low heat for 1 hour, or until the duck is tender. Turn the duck over once during this process.

2. Remove the duck, cool it, and cut into 14 pieces; discard loose skin and fat. Put the duck on a serving platter. Skim off all the fat from the broth, or refrigerate for several hours and remove the congealed fat. Reserve 3 cups of warm broth.

3. Process the walnuts to a paste, adding some broth to help the process. Add the fresh and ground coriander, turmeric and vinegar and process until well mixed. Stir this into the fat-free broth and mix well. Adjust the salt at this time. Pour the sauce over the duck.

Serve at room temperature. Serves 8 with other dishes.

NACHINYONAYA FOREL
Stuffed Trout

This is a dish for special occasions, with elegant and unusual flavorings. Note that the heat intensity of chili is variable and you should add just enough to suit your personal preference.

1 whole trout (about 1 pound)
1 teaspoon salt
½ cup shelled walnuts, chopped fine
1 or 2 teaspoons minced seeded hot green chili
1 medium onion, chopped fine (½ cup)
¼ cup fresh pomegranate seeds (see Glossary)
¼ teaspoon ground cinnamon
⅛ teaspoon ground cloves
flour
3 tablespoons corn oil

1. Rinse the trout in cold water and dry. Rub with salt inside and outside. Let stand for ½ hour.
2. Mix the walnuts, chili, onion, pomegranate seeds, cinnamon and cloves together. Do not squeeze the pomegranate seeds, they should remain whole and firm.
3. Stuff the trout. Roll it in flour. Heat the oil in a skillet and fry the trout over moderate heat for 3 minutes on each side. Drain briefly on paper towels.

Serve warm or room temperature. Serves 4 with other dishes.

KHACHAPURI
Cheese Pie

The Georgian/English dictionary translates khachapuri as a Georgian pie. The stuffing of this pie can be either cheese or dry red-bean purée. Georgians justifiably swoon over their khachapuri, of which there are variations based on the type of dough and the filling. This pie is made with paper-thin layers of unleavened dough that produce a flaky pastry folded together, stuffed and baked in moderate heat. It is eaten warm.

DOUGH

> 4 cups flour
> 1 teaspoon salt
> 1 egg, beaten
> 7 tablespoons corn oil
> 1 cup water

CHEESE FILLING (KHWELI)

> 1 pound feta cheese (Georgian brindza)
> ½ pound farmer cheese
> 1 egg, beaten

1. Prepare the dough by mixing together all of its ingredients except for 5 tablespoons oil. Knead for 5 minutes, dusting the dough liberally with flour so that it can be handled easily. Divide the dough into 6 equal parts. Knead them for several moments, roll each part into a ball, and flatten slightly to give a bun shape. Set aside in a warm spot, covered with a plastic bag, for ½ hour.

2. Cover the feta cheese with cold water for 15 minutes, then drain well to remove excess salt. This step is only necessary if you object to the salt. Process both cheeses and the egg into a smooth purée. Set aside.

3. Roll out one of the dough buns on a floured board to a thin pancake of about 12 inches in diameter. Lift the pancake in the air and stretch it out by lifting and turning; the weight of the dough will stretch it out to a paper-thin sheet. It can also be stretched thin in strudel style by pulling it out over the backs of your hands. The soft dough will stretch to about 30 inches in diameter. It does not matter that there may be a few small tears in the sheet.

4. Lay the thin dough sheet on the board and sprinkle about 2 teaspoons of the remaining oil over the entire surface, splashing it on with your finger tips, Georgian style. Fold over the nearest and farthest sides toward the center to shape a rectangle 6 × 8 inches. Once again fold over the left and right sides to the center. Sprinkle this surface with a few drops of oil.

5. Place about ⅔ cup of the cheese mixture in the center of the dough rectangle and spread it out to within 2 inches of the edges all around. Fold over the rectangle, envelope-style, by taking each of the four ends and firmly pushing them one by one into the center of the pie. Pinch together the open spaces so that the cheese is sealed inside. Very lightly brush the pie surface with oil. Continue with the remaining pastry sheets and cheese filling.

6. Bake in a preheated 350° F. oven for 40 minutes, or until the top is light brown. Remove and serve warm for breakfast, snack time or lunch. Makes 6 pies.

NOTE: The stuffed pies can be refrigerated before baking for 3 days and taken out when wanted. Cover each pie with a plastic bag to retain freshness before baking.

VARIATIONS : 1. For a variation of the cheese filling, use 1 pound mozzarella and ½ pound farmer cheese. Process to a smooth purée with 1 egg. The purpose in the selection of cheeses is to duplicate the authentic Georgian cheese known as "*suluguny.*" It is not available in the United States although one Georgian cook told me that it resembles Middle East string cheese. 2. Another traditional stuffing of this typically Jewish-style stuffed *khachapuri* is prepared with dried red beans (*lobio*).

1 pound dried red beans
1 bay leaf
½ teaspoon black pepper
⅛ teaspoon hot chili flakes
1 teaspoon salt

1. Cover the beans with cold water and soak them overnight. The next day cook them with the bay leaf until soft, about 1 hour over low heat. At the end of cooking, the water should be completely evaporated. Remove the bay leaf and stir in the chili flakes and salt.
2. Process the beans to a smooth purée. (My teacher mashed the beans with an old fashioned potato masher, then completed the chore by squeezing and stirring with her hand.)
Stuff the pie with about ⅔ cup of the bean purée, using the same system as for the cheese filling. Bake as directed.

NOTE: Mashed red bean purée is also prepared as a Georgian breakfast. Soaking, cooking, seasoning are carried out just as for the *khachapuri* stuffing.

KHACHAPURI

Puffed Dough, Cheese Pie

The dough in this mixture ultimately becomes puff pastry. This leads me to believe that it would be for special occasions rather than for every day. Strongly flavored feta cheese is used in this case.

STUFFING

¾ pound feta cheese, grated
1 egg, beaten
⅛ teaspoon pepper
1 tablespoon fine-chopped fresh dill
1 scallion, green part only, chopped

DOUGH

3 cups flour
2 eggs, beaten
1 cup buttermilk, kept at room temperature overnight
½ pound margarine

1. Mix everything together and divide it into 8 equal parts. Set aside

2. Mix the flour, eggs and buttermilk together to develop a moist but easily handled dough. Knead for several minutes; sprinkle with flour if necessary. Let it rest, covered, for 15 minutes.

3. Divide the dough into 8 parts and divide the margarine (do not use butter) into 8 parts—1 for each piece of dough.

4. Roll out each part of dough on a well-floured board into a rectangle 4 × 6 inches. Spread over each rectangle one third of its share of margarine.

Fold both sides of the rectangle toward the center; pinch the ends together firmly. Roll the rectangle back to its former size, 4 × 6 inches. Do this with all the pieces of dough; put them on a tray and into the freezer for 20 minutes.

5. Remove the rectangles and repeat this procedure a total of three times.

6. Preheat the oven to 500° F. Remove all the sheets of dough from the freezer. Place 1 part of the cheese mixture along the center of each, leaving a 1-inch space on each end. Fold over both sides to the center and press the ends gently to seal them.

Bake in the hot oven for about 20 minutes, or until golden brown. The pies will puff up.

They are eaten hot from the oven. Makes 8 puff pies.

N O T E : You may freeze the baked pies. Cool them first, then store in plastic bags and freeze for future use. Thaw them at room temperature for 1 hour and reheat in a 350° F. oven for 10 minutes.

ADJAPSANDALI
Mixed Vegetable Sauté

Adjapsandali is a popular salad or condiment, depending upon the preparation and what is available in the kitchen at the moment. For example, you may omit the potatoes and add 2 medium sweet red peppers, cut into ½-inch cubes—or use unpeeled tomatoes coarsely cut up.

> 1 pound eggplants (2), cut into 1-inch cubes
> 2 teaspoons salt
> 3 tablespoons corn oil
> 2 medium onions, chopped (1 cup)
> 1 pound potatoes, peeled, cut into ½-inch cubes
> 1 pound ripe tomatoes, peeled, cut into ½-inch cubes
> 2 carrots, grated (1 cup)
> ¼ cup chopped fresh coriander
> 4 garlic cloves, chopped fine
> ¼ teaspoon pepper

1. Mix the eggplant cubes with 1 teaspoon salt and let stand for ½ hour. Rinse the pieces under cold water and press out the liquid gently. Set aside.

2. Heat the oil in a pan, add the onions, and mix for a moment. Cover the pan and cook over low heat for 5 minutes. Add the eggplants, potatoes, tomatoes and carrots. Mix well and cover; continue to cook over low heat for 20 minutes. Add the coriander, garlic, the remaining 1 teaspoon salt (or to taste) and the pepper. Cover and cook for 10 minutes more.

Serve hot or at room temperature, or refrigerate and serve cold. Serves 6 with other dishes.

STUFFED EGGPLANT SLICES

Another method of combining walnuts and eggplant, enriched with herbs and the light crunch of pomegranate seeds, when available.

1 large eggplant, about 1 pound
2 tablespoons corn oil
1 small onion, chopped fine (¼ cup)
¼ cup shelled walnuts, chopped fine
1 teaspoon salt
1 tablespoon each of chopped fresh coriander, dill, flat-leaf
     parsley
1 heaping teaspoon fresh pomegranate seeds (optional, see
     Glossary)
1 tablespoon red-wine vinegar

1. Trim both ends of the eggplant. Cut it lengthwise into ½-inch-thick slices. Heat the oil in a skillet, put the eggplant slices in, cover the pan, and fry over moderate heat until soft, about 4 minutes. Turn the slices over once. The purpose of this is to cook the eggplant but also make the slices flexible so they can be rolled up.
2. Prepare a stuffing. Mix the onion, walnuts, salt, herbs, pomegranate seeds if you have them, and vinegar. Spread a heaping tablespoon of the stuffing over each slab of eggplant and roll it up the long way. Hold the roll together with a toothpick.
Refrigerate and serve cold or at room temperature.
Makes 4 or 5 rolls.

PATRIJANI
Stuffed Fried Eggplant

Walnuts and garlic are combined with many Georgian dishes. Where one is listed the other is sure to follow. These stuffed baby eggplants can be prepared several days in advance of a party and refrigerated since they are eaten cold. All the ingredients listed in this recipe are characteristic of Georgian cooking.

2 pounds small Italian-type eggplants (about 8)
2½ teaspoons salt
2 medium onions, chopped (¾ cup)
¾ cup shelled walnuts
3 garlic cloves, sliced
3 teaspoons ground coriander
¼ to ½ teaspoon hot red chili flakes, to taste
3 tablespoons red-wine vinegar
¼ cup corn oil

1. Cut each eggplant lengthwise almost into halves so that they can be opened like a book, with the two halves still connected. Sprinkle the insides lightly with 2 teaspoons of the salt, put them in a large pan and cover. Let stand for 1 hour. Rinse with cold water. Close each eggplant and press them gently to remove the accumulated liquid. Open them again and dry on a kitchen towel.

2. Toss the onions with the remaining ½ teaspoon salt and let stand for ½ hour. Put them in a kitchen towel and firmly squeeze out the liquid.

3. Prepare the stuffing. Put the walnuts, onions, garlic, coriander and chili flakes in a processor and process to a smooth paste. Add the vinegar and process for a few seconds more to mix well. Set aside.

4. Heat the oil in a skillet, place the eggplants cut sides down in it and fry over moderate heat, covered, for 5 minutes. Turn them over and fry for another 2 minutes to brown the skin side. Remove and cool. Do not separate the eggplant halves.

5. Spread 1 tablespoon of the stuffing over the cut surface of half of the eggplant. Close, and tie together with white thread if you wish. Return eggplants to the skillet and fry them over low heat on both sides for 5 minutes. Cool and remove the thread. Refrigerate.

Serve cold as an appetizer or side dish. Makes 8.

VARIATION: Instead of frying and stuffing, cook the eggplant in water to soften, dry them on a kitchen towel, then stuff them.

2 pounds small Italian-type eggplants (about 8)
1 teaspoon salt
8 sprigs of Chinese celery (see Note) or 8 sprigs of flat-leaf Italian
    parsley
1 recipe for walnut stuffing, as in the basic recipe.

1. Cut each eggplant lengthwise almost into halves so that they can be opened like a book, with the two halves still connected. Put them in a large pan and add 6 cups hot water and the salt. Bring to a boil, cover the pan, and cook for 10 minutes. At the end of 8 minutes, add the celery or parsley, whichever one is used. Cook for 2 minutes more and drain well. Reserve the herbs.

2. Put the eggplants, cut side down, on a kitchen towel, cover with 1 or 2 large plates to weigh them down, and let stand for 1 hour to absorb the liquid.

3. Spread 1 tablespoon of the stuffing on half of each eggplant; close them up. Tie up each one with the celery or parsley, which has been softened by the cooking.

Refrigerate, then serve cold. Makes 8.

NOTE: The celery in Georgia grows in long, thin stalks; it does not have the thick ribs of the California style. The flavor is also more intense. This same celery is found in New York's Chinatown and, if available, can be used to tie up the eggplant. If not, then use the Italian parsley.

PICKLED BEETS

2 pounds fresh small beets (8 to 10)
2 cups red-wine vinegar
2 cups water
1 teaspoon salt
2 teaspoons sugar
10 whole allspice
6 whole cloves
3 bay leaves

1. Put the unpeeled beets in a pan, cover with water and cook, covered, over moderate heat until tender, about 45 minutes. Cool in the water. Peel, slice, and put into a glass jar. Discard the cooking liquid.

2. Prepare the marinade: Put the vinegar, water, salt, sugar, allspice, cloves and bay leaves in a pan, bring to a boil, and simmer over moderate heat for 5 minutes. Cool and pour it over the beets.

Cover the jar with a cloth towel tied around the top and refrigerate. Hold for 1 week before serving.

Serve at room temperature with any kind of Georgian food.

N O T E : The large round allspice berries are known in many countries, including Georgia, as "English spice." The English first encountered this aromatic spice in Central America, Jamaica and Mexico and were the first to use it—thus the name.

BEETS IN WALNUT SAUCE

This fine salad uses picked beets as a base then in the Georgian style, adds the garnishes as indicated.

1 pound Pickled Beets, cut into ½-inch cubes
½ cup shelled walnuts, chopped very fine
1 medium onion, chopped fine (½ cup)
1 teaspoon ground coriander
2 garlic cloves, put through a press
¼ cup liquid from the pickled beets

1. Mix everything together, toss the salad well, and refrigerate. Serve cold or at room temperature. Serves 4 to 6.
Makes about 1 pint.

BEETS IN SPICED BRINE

Beets are popular in Georgia—especially as pickles. Most Georgians have large, cool cellars in their houses, where the pickles are stored during winter months and are always available to supplement the diet.

2 pounds whole fresh young beets (8 to 10), stems and leaves removed and kept for other dishes

2½ cups water
1 tablespoon salt
4 celery ribs and leaves, halved horizontally
6 sprigs of fresh dill
1 large sprig of fresh flat-leaf parsley
2 bay leaves
1 hot red or green chili, seeded, quartered
1 head of garlic, 6 to 8 cloves, peeled and halved lengthwise

1. Put the whole beets, not peeled, into boiling water to cover and cook, covered, for 20 minutes. Cool and peel the beets. Discard the cooking liquid.

2. Put 2½ cups water and the salt into a pan and bring to a boil. Add the celery, dill, parsley, bay leaves and chili and cook over moderate heat for 2 minutes. Remove and cool the seasonings, herbs and liquid.

3. Put 1 layer of the whole beets in a jar, cover with some of the herbs—the garlic, chili, bay leaf. Add the balance of the beets and the herbs and garlic. Pour the seasoned cooking water into the jar, cover it, and refrigerate for 3 days or more before tasting.

Serve at room temperature as a side dish or pickle.

Makes about 1 quart.

CHARKHALI
Beet and Coriander Pickle

Fresh coriander is one of the important Georgian herbs and the flavor dominates this table pickle.

1 pound fresh beets, cooked, peeled, cut into ½-inch cubes, or use
    1 pound canned beets
⅛ teaspoon cayenne pepper
½ teaspoon salt
4 garlic cloves, put through a press
½ cup loosely packed, fine-chopped fresh coriander
3 tablespoons red-wine vinegar

1. Mix everything together well. Store in a jar with a tight cover and refrigerate for up to 2 weeks.

Serve cold or at room temperature with any kind of dairy or meat dishes.

Makes about 1 pint.

GUREESKAYA CAPUSTA
Pink Pickled Cabbage

The pickle has a beautiful reddish-pink color since the beets act as a dye. This popular if not indispensable pickle is prepared at the advent of cold weather, when fermentation is not too rapid. It is never prepared in summer.

10 pounds cabbage
1 pound celery
2 large carrots
8 to 10 garlic cloves
1½ pounds fresh beets
2 sweet red peppers
1 or 2 fresh jalapeño chilies
1 tablespoon coarse salt for each quart of water (use 4 or 5 quarts)

1. Shred the cabbage coarsely, discarding the core; cut the celery into 4-inch sticks, including the leaves; and cut the carrots lengthwise into 8 long sticks. Cut each garlic clove into 3 long slices; peel the beets and cut them into thin slices; cut each seeded sweet pepper into 8 lengthwise slices, and cut each seeded chili lengthwise into halves.

2. Using either a gallon glass jar or an enamel pail (do not use metal) fill the container as follows: Put 2 layers of beets on the bottom. Add 2 inches of cabbage over that, a few slices of garlic, slices of celery, carrot, 2 pieces of hot chili and 2 slices of sweet red pepper. Repeat the layering, ending with the beets and chili on the top.

3. Bring to a boil 4 quarts of water and 4 tablespoons salt. Cool and carefully pour it over the vegetables. If the liquid does not completely cover the vegetables, then add another quart of boiled water and salt. Weight the vegetables with a plate and a rock on top to keep everything under the liquid. Keep the pickle at room temperature for 2 days, then store it in a cool or cold cellar for 2 weeks before using. Refrigerate if you do not have a cold corner. The cabbage will develop a rich, pink color.

Serve with any kind of Georgian food. All vegetables are eaten. Makes about 1 gallon.

DHAZMARULI BADRIJANI
Baby Eggplant Pickle

The Georgians enjoy this pickle for breakfast with home-made bread. These pickled eggplants may also be considered a chutney in Indian style or they can be served as a rather tart salad.

3 tablespoons corn oil
1 pound small Italian-style eggplants (5 or 6), trimmed and cut
   lengthwise into halves
1 medium onion, cut into rings (½ cup)
1 cup water
3 to 4 tablespoons red-wine vinegar, to taste
1 bay leaf
4 whole allspice
¼ teaspoon hot red chili flakes
1 teaspoon salt

1. Heat the oil in a skillet. Fry the eggplant halves for 5 minutes on both sides to brown lightly. Remove to a glass bowl or jar and intersperse the eggplant with the sliced onion.
2. Put the water, vinegar, bay leaf, allspice, chili flakes and salt in a pan; bring to a boil. Boil over moderate heat for 3 minutes to integrate the seasonings. Cool.
3. Pour the liquid over the eggplant. Cover the jar and refrigerate for 24 hours before serving.

Serve cold or at room temperature with any kind of food.

TQEMALI
Sour Plum Sauce

I prefer to think of this sauce as a rather liquid chutney that can be served with meat dishes. It has a sour intensity seasoned with coriander and heightened with garlic and hot chili, an Asian flavor.

Sour plums are not difficult to find during the spring and early summer months. They are the supermarket variety green or red plums, which invariably are picked unripe for marketing. I suggest for off-season preparation of the *tqemali* that you prepare the plum purée and freeze it. Then whenever wanted it can be defrosted and mixed with the other ingredients. The *tqemali* (sour plum) is used exclusively by the Georgians or their imitators.

    1 pound fresh sour or unripened plums
    4 cups water
    ½ cup fine-chopped fresh coriander
    3 garlic cloves, put through a press or crushed with a mortar and
        pestle
    ⅛ teaspoon hot red chili flakes
    1 teaspoon salt, or to taste

1. Put the plums and water in a pan, cover, and bring to a boil. Reduce heat to low and cook, covered, for 20 to 25 minutes, enough to soften the plums completely. Discard the plum stones. Press the plum pulp and liquid through a colander or a metal sieve.

2. Mix this tart plum purée with the coriander, garlic, chili flakes and salt. Store in a jar with a tight cover and refrigerate for up to 1 month.

Serve at room temperature with Georgian meat dishes. This is the most popular sauce and can be found on every table during meals or celebrations. Makes 2 to 3 cups.

SATSABELI
Vegetable Sauce

T his is a powerful sauce and I suggest that you prepare a half recipe or less unless you intend to use it daily.

  2 pounds ripe tomatoes
  2 pound sweet red peppers
  ½ pound large garlic cloves, peeled
  2 tablespoons salt

1. Process or grind the tomatoes, peppers and garlic together. Add the salt and mix well.

2. Store in a jar with a tight cover, refrigerated or on the kitchen shelf.

Serve as a condiment with Georgian food and especially cooked dumplings. The *satsabeli* is also added to meat dishes to enhance the existing seasonings.

Makes 2 quarts.

ROMEE
Cornmeal Mush

W hen did corn travel from the Valley of Mexico to Georgia? It had to have been after the Spanish conquest in the sixteenth century, along with tomatoes and peppers. In any event, the Georgians incorporated it into their cooking and the unseasoned mush is eaten with sharply seasoned meat dishes such as the Setsamandi (see Index).

  1 cup instant white or yellow cornmeal
  6 cups cold water

1. Mix the cornmeal and water together in a solid-weight metal pan and bring to a boil. Reduce the heat to low and cook, uncovered, for 40 minutes. Stir the mixture now and then. When ready the meal will have absorbed the water and the mush will be firm enough to slice, yet moist enough to have a smooth consistency.

Serve hot while still in the pan by scooping or slicing out serving portions. Serves 4.

MCHADI
Cornmeal Pancake

Thisplain, unseasoned pancake is eaten with any Georgian dish that has gravy or sauce. It is usually pinched off, used to scoop up the gravy and eaten out of hand.

> 3 cups yellow cornmeal
> 1½ cups cold water

1. Mix the meal and water together well. Form it into a round ball.

2. Heat a skillet over low heat. With wet hands, flatten the cornmeal ball into a large pancake about ½ inch thick. Put this into the hot, dry skillet and cook over moderate heat for 5 minutes or long enough to form a crust. Turn the pancake over with a spatula and cook for 5 minutes more.

Serve warm. Serves 4 to 6.

GOZINAKI
Walnut and Honey Crunch

This relatively simple sweet has, as one would expect, the beloved walnuts of Georgia. Honey, a little sugar and a few minutes of cooking are all it takes. The rest is time and patience

> 2 cups shelled walnuts, medium-coarse chopped, not too large
>   pieces
> ½ cup honey of your choice
> 1 tablespoon sugar

1. I chop the walnuts by hand with a sharp knife rather than put them in a processor since the size can then be controlled. However, either works well if some care is taken in cutting the walnuts not too fine or too large, somewhere in between.

2. Put the honey into a pan and simmer over low heat until bubbles begin to rise. Simmer for 3 minutes, then stir in the sugar and continue for another 2 minutes before testing. Put 1 or 2 drops of the syrup into a half glass of cold water. What is wanted is a firm, round ball. If the drops spread out, cook for another minute or two. Total time should be about 7 minutes.

3. Pour the chopped nuts into the syrup, mix well so that all the pieces are coated, and remove from the heat. Spread the mixture out rapidly on a kitchen board that has been moistened well with cold water. Wet a rolling pin with water and roll out the mass to a thickness of ½ inch, but not more. Let this cool for 15 minutes, then slice into 2-inch diamond-shaped pieces. Turn the pieces over as you cut them so they can dry. Let the *gozinaki* dry for 1 hour, then store the pieces in a metal box and cover. Refrigerate or not as you wish.

Makes 25 pieces.

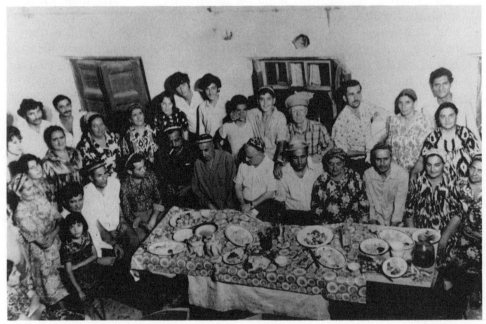

Farewell party for Yona Chaimov before his departure for Israel, Buchara, 1979.

UZBEKISTAN: *BUKHARA AND SAMARKAND*

Bukhara—the name itself conjures up nomadic empires, tribal caravans, magic carpets, silk, spices and trade with the vast hinterland of China. Alexander the Great in 334 B.C., conquering as he went, swept through Uzbekistan in Central Asia—the region of Bukhara, Tashkent and the fabulous city of Samarkand. Central Asia was ruled by a dynasty of Turkish origin, the Muslim Uzbeks whose capital was in Bukhara.

The ancient Silk Route started from the northeast frontier of China and went along the Gobi Desert westward across frightening mountain and desert routes to Samarkand. It was the Bactrian camel aided by caravans of horses that made this possible. Timur, known today as Tamerlane, the conqueror, transformed Samarkand into a city of great architectural monuments not seen before in the Islamic world and they still exist.

It was in the chronicle of the Traveler, Benjamin of Tudela (Spain), in 1170 A.D. that a Jewish community in Samarkand with a population of 50,000 was first mentioned. When the city was destroyed in the sixteenth century by the Muslims, the Jews moved to Bukhara where they found an already established community.

The Venetian Marco Polo reported in 1272 that there were Jews in Samarkand. In his memoirs he related that Samarkand is a "noble" city surrounded by a plain which produces "all the fruits that man can desire." What he also found were the inhabitants of the city making pasta and creating unusual dishes that were foreign to European eyes but not, of course, to Chinese.

In my unsubstantiated opinion (lest I be accused of whimsy), since Samarkand was the beginning of the silk route to China and since there was a historic connection and interchange with that country through trade and conquest, I believe it was from Samarkand that pasta made its first entry into the cookery of Italy and then Europe.

In the sixteenth century the Emir of Bukhara invited Jewish poets and musicians to come from the Persian court to Bukhara, and the community started on aesthetic lines. A form of Judeo-Persian poetry was written. Generations of Jewish court musicians shaped *shashmaqam*, the music of the Uzbeks. Jews wore the traditional costumes of the Uzbeks, brocaded and embroidered silk coats. Some were engaged in the silk trade of which Samarkand was a focal point. The Jews speak a Tajiki-Jewish dialect of the region.

Jewish communities in Central Asia prospered in this crossroads linking Asia, Europe and the Middle East. Culinary influences arrived from all directions, were welcomed and became established.

I was impressed with the orderly fashion in which my Samarkand lady worked. Her recipes were precise and she prepared her bread and pasta dishes, step-by-step, with neatness and dispatch. Yeast was proofed, dough was made, stuffings mixed, sauces made, until everything was ready to be combined into the final composition.

The Jews of Uzbekistan do not rely on sharp, robust spicing like the Georgians or Indians. Flavors are developed low key with herbs, onion, garlic and the natural taste of vegetables. Meat and poultry are used with a light hand to enrich a dish rather than to become the principal ingredient. Pasta is eaten more frequently than rice although the Plov (chicken and rice) made in Bukhara is celebrated.

Cuminseed, coriander, turmeric and pepper are the principal spices used, with a light touch of hot chili now and then. Seasoning is filled with flavor but subtle. No single spice is thrust into the predominant position but is blended into the overall taste impression.

Inventive juxtaposition of ingredients by a people without a great deal of money has produced wonderful dishes within the framework of Judaic dietary laws. They can be easily integrated into the American kitchen, providing a touch of the exotic with recognizable ingredients.

SALATEE BOYIMJAN
Smoked Eggplant Salad

Easily prepared with all natural ingredients and without oil, the salad has considerable flavor, an attractive consistency and is especially appropriate as an appetizer.

2 pounds eggplant (3 or 4)
5 garlic cloves, crushed in a mortar or put through a press
1 teaspoon salt, or to taste

1. Roast the eggplant in a gas or electric broiler until the skin is well charred, which imparts a smoked flavor to the tender inner pulp. This may take about 20 minutes. There are those who char the eggplant directly over a gas flame or, if available, over charcoal. Peel and discard the skins. Let eggplants cool in a tilted bowl for 15 minutes so that the liquid that usually accumulates can run off and be discarded.

2. Chop the eggplant in a wood chopping bowl or by hand with a sharp knife. Add the garlic and salt. Mix well. Refrigerate.

Serve at room temperature as a side dish or salad, or as an appetizer with bread, matzoh or crackers. Makes 3 cups.

KIFTE
Meatballs

The *kifte* are sometimes served with any simple tomato sauce and boiled potatoes.

> 1 pound ground beef, veal, lamb or chicken
> 2 eggs, beaten
> ½ teaspoon salt
> 1 small onion, grated (⅓ cup)
> ⅛ teaspoon pepper
> ⅛ teaspoon baking soda
> 2 tablespoons bread crumbs or soaked bread
> flour for dusting
> oil for panfrying

1. Mix everything except the flour and oil together; stir briskly. Refrigerate for 2 hours.

2. Prepare meatballs 1½ inches in diameter. Dust them with flour. Heat the oil in a skillet and brown the meatballs on all sides over moderate heat for about 3 minutes. Drain briefly on paper towels.

Serve warm as an appetizer or with other main dishes.

Makes 12.

PICHONKA
Chopped Veal Liver

A most unusual yet straightforward recipe of chopped liver with several textures and flavors.

> 1 pound veal (calf's) liver
> ¾ cup corn oil
> 1 pound onions, sliced
> 4 hard-cooked eggs, peeled
> 2 medium potatoes, cut for french fries (2 cups)
> 1 teaspoon salt
> ½ teaspoon pepper
> 2 tablespoons chopped fresh coriander

1. Char the liver on an open flame to kosher. Cool and cut into 1-inch cubes.

2. Heat the oil in a wok or skillet and fry the onions over moderate heat until golden. Remove to a processor bowl. Add the liver cubes to the oil and fry for 2 minutes. Remove to the bowl with the onions. Put the eggs in the pan and fry on all sides for 2 minutes until golden. Add to the bowl.

3. Fry the potatoes until crisp brown. Add the potatoes and the salt and pepper to the bowl and process the whole briefly to an almost smooth consistency. Do not purée. Serve by shaping into a loaf on a serving platter; decorate with crisscross lines. Garnish with 1 tablespoon of the frying oil (optional) and the coriander.

Serve at room temperature. Serves 6.

OSHEE DUIYOZA LAV LAVU

Red Beet and Turnip Melange

This colorful soup is not a borsht but a flavorful pink soup that emphasizes beets, turnips and carrots. It is always made with chicken (you should also try turkey), providing the ever popular poultry with yet another method of preparation.

4 cooked beets (1 pound), peeled, sliced
2 white turnips (½ pound), peeled, sliced
2 carrots, sliced diagonally (1 cup)
1 medium onion, chopped (½ cup)
1½ pounds boneless chicken or turkey, cut into 1-inch pieces,
    plus 2 chicken wings
1 teaspoon salt, or to taste
¼ teaspoon pepper
½ teaspoon ground cuminseed
5 cups water
pieces of flat bread (Noni Tokee, see Index)
2 tablespoons chopped fresh mint

1. Put everything except the flat bread and mint into a large enough pan and bring to a boil. Reduce heat to low, cover the pan, and cook for about 1½ hours to integrate the flavors and soften the meat and beets.

2. Put 1 or 2 squares of the flat bread into each individual soup dish. Pour a generous ladle of this soup/stew over. Garnish with mint to taste. Serves 5 of 6.

NOTE: There is broth to the Lav Lavu but not enough to qualify as a soup or thick enough to be a stew. Bukharans like this culinary oddity. In addition, a few teaspoons of hot oil are dribbled over each serving, a step that I do not find rewarding.

OOROW
Beef, Vegetable and Noodle Soup

This thick, nourishing soup from Samarkand is eaten during the week but not on the Sabbath. It is not prepared for special days but is a regular filling family-style preparation.

In old Bukhara the egg noodles were (and still are in some families) made by hand with eggs, flour and very little water.

> 3 tablespoons corn oil
> 1 large onion, sliced (1 cup)
> 1 large sweet pepper, cut into 1-inch cubes
> 1 garlic clove, chopped
> 1 pound boneless beef chuck, cut into ½-inch cubes
> ½ pound beef bones
> 1 large carrot, cut diagonally into ¼-inch-thick slices (1 cup)
> 8 cups water
> 2 large potatoes (1 pound), peeled cut into 1-inch cubes
> 1 teaspoon salt, or to taste
> ⅛ teaspoon black pepper
> 1 cup coarsely cut cabbage
> ½ pound thin dry egg noodles

1. Heat the oil in a large pan, add the onion, sweet pepper, garlic, beef, beef bones and carrot and stir-fry over low heat for 20 minutes.

2. Add the water, bring to a boil, then reduce heat to low, cover the pan, and simmer for 45 minutes. Add the potatoes, salt, pepper and cabbage and cook, covered for 10 minutes more.

Add the noodles and simmer for 5 minutes more, to *al dente* firmness.

Serve warm. Serves 6 to 8.

PASSOVER SOUP

Beef stock, vegetables and ample seasonings make this a very special soup for the Passover holiday. The addition of crumbled matzoh gives substance to a flavorful soup.

1 tablespoon corn oil
2 medium onions, chopped (1 cup)
1 pound boneless beef chuck, cut into 1-inch cubes
½ pound beef bones
1 small carrot, cut into ½-inch cubes
8 cups water
1 ripe tomato, cut into cubes (½ cup), or an equal amount canned
½ cup chopped fresh coriander
1 teaspoon salt
¼ teaspoon pepper
1 medium potato, cut into ½-inch cubes (1 cup)
4 eggs, beaten
matzoh

1. Heat the oil in a large pan and stir-fry the onions, beef, beef bones and carrot over moderate heat for 3 minutes. Add the water, tomato, coriander, salt and pepper and bring to a boil. Cook, covered, over moderately low heat for 1 hour.

2. Add the potato; cook for 15 minutes. At the last moment, just prior to serving, add the eggs in a steady stream to the simmering soup, stirring them in.

Serve hot, breaking as much matzoh as wanted into each soup plate. Serves 8.

MASTO JUSHAK
Chicken and Vegetable Soup

A favorite soup to be eaten at the Passover Seders or at anytime. Serve and enjoy with matzoh.

3 tablespoons corn oil
1 large onion, chopped (1 cup)
1 large carrot, cut into ¼-inch dice (1 cup)
½ chicken, about 2 pounds, cut into 3-inch pieces
5 cups water
1 teaspoon salt, or to taste
⅛ teaspoon pepper
2 potatoes (½ pound), peeled, cut into ½-inch cubes
3 eggs, beaten
⅓ cup chopped fresh coriander

1. Heat the oil in a pan, add the onion, carrot and chicken, and stir-fry over moderate heat until the color changes, about 5 minutes. Add the water, bring to a boil, and skim off the foam that accumulates. Reduce heat to low, cover the pan, and simmer for ½ hour.
2. Add the salt, pepper and potatoes and continue to cook for 15 minutes.
3. Pour the eggs into the soup in a steady stream, stirring all the time. Remove pan from the heat and sprinkle the coriander over all.
Serve hot with matzoh. Serves 6.

LAGMAN
Mixed Vegetables in Broth with Spaghetti

The *lagman* is another example of the soup (stew) concoction the Bukharans favor. Pasta is the filling ingredient; it was made by hand in Bukharan homes. *Lagman* is a family dish that can be made in large quantities to feed hungry mouths. The emphasis is on the vegetables with small bits of meat for substance. The fresh mint garnish is used to taste—each diner adds as much as he likes. Mint is alleged to have blood-cleansing properties so the Bukharans consider it more than just a flavoring.

8 cups water
½ pound beef bones
1 pound boneless beef chuck, cut into ½-inch pieces
1 zucchini (½ pound), cut into ½-inch cubes
1 carrot, sliced (1 cup)
1 white turnip, peeled, cut into ½-inch cubes
1 large onion, chopped (1 cup)
1 green pepper, cut into ½-inch cubes
2 potatoes (½ pound), peeled, cut into ½-inch cubes
¼ cup cooked chick-peas, peeled and skins discarded
4 whole garlic cloves, peeled
½ cup tomato juice or tomato cubes
1 teaspoon salt, or to taste
1 teaspoon ground cuminseed
1 pound thin spaghetti, cooked al dente according to package directions
3 scallions, sliced thin
¼ cup chopped fresh coriander
3 tablespoons chopped fresh mint

1. Put everything into a large pan except the spaghetti, scallions, coriander and mint. Bring to a boil, then reduce heat to low, cover the pan, and cook for 1 hour or a little more. Meanwhile cook the spaghetti until *al dente*, drain under cold water, and set aside. The broth has reduced and the flavor is intensified.

2. To serve, each diner puts as much spaghetti as wanted into a soup plate and 1 ladleful of meat, vegetables and broth is poured over. Scallion, coriander and mint are added as a garnish according to taste.

Serve hot. Serves 6 generously.

OSHEE SHULA MOSH

*Beef Stew with Rice, Mung Beans
and Vegetables*

Bukharans have many dishes that reveal a Chinese connection. Both trade and conquest influence the dispersal of culinary techniques and the very dishes themselves from one region to another. Here, we assume the Silk Route connecting Peking to Samarkand was also the route by which this preparation came to Bukhara. Mung beans are those that the Chinese use to make bean sprouts.

1 pound mung beans (2 cups), well rinsed
2 cups raw rice, well rinsed
1 large onion, sliced (1 cup)
3 small white turnips, sliced
¼ pound cabbage, sliced into coarse shreds
1 pound boneless beef chuck, cut into ¼-inch cubes (do not grind)
½ pound beef bones
2 carrots, sliced (1½ cups)
¼ cup corn oil
1 teaspoon ground cuminseed
2 teaspoons salt, or to taste
10 cups water

1. Put all the ingredients into a large pan, bring to a boil, and cook over moderate heat for 20 minutes. Cover the pan, reduce heat to low, and simmer for 1½ hours, until you have a thick rice and bean mush.

Serve warm. Serves 8.

HALESA

Beef and Whole-Wheat Berry Gruel

Winter in Bukhara sweeps in across Central Asia, reminding one and all that it is the season to prepare this wonderful thick gruel that is both filling and satisfying. The whole-wheat berries (kernels) are broken into small pieces and provide a thickening agency as well as their fine wheat flavor.

1 pound whole-wheat berries
12 cups water
3 large onions (1 pound), chopped
1½ pounds brisket of beef, cut into 1-inch cubes
½ pound beef bones
2 teaspoons salt
12 cups water

1. Break the wheat berries into small fragments in a processor that grinds spices—a mini processor. Do not powder, there must be some texture. Cover with 4 cups of the water and soak overnight.

2. Put the wheat and its liquid plus 8 cups more water and all the other ingredients into a large well-constructed pan that has a cover. Bring to a boil, reduce heat to very low, cover the pan, and simmer for 8 to 10 hours. Stir occasionally during this long, slow process. Should the liquid evaporate too quickly, add another cup of water.

The mixture will reduce to a thick gruel. The beef bones will enrich the broth, the meat will fall apart, and the onions disappear into this simple and wonderful concoction.

Serve warm with bread. Serves 6 to 8.

KISHKE
Stuffed Derma

This is a grand production and a rarity today since hardly anyone wants to be bothered with finding an intestine at the kosher butcher as well as going through all the other steps involved. Many years ago, when we were children, my mother and grandmother prepared kishke. Then the practice fell out of favor due to the time involved. Now, nostalgia encourages us to try this Bukharan style once more—it is well worth all the effort.

½ pound beef liver
½ pound lung, if available (optional)
¼ pound ground beef
2 cups raw rice, rinsed, drained
1 cup chopped fresh coriander
2 teaspoons salt
1 teaspoon pepper, or to taste
½ to 1 yard large intestine of beef, well cleaned, prepared for
    stuffing
4 celery ribs, halved horizontally
1 small onion, sliced (⅓ cup)
3 bay leaves
1 teaspoon peppercorns
4 quarts clear beef stock

1. Char the liver over flame in a broiler to kosher. Cut into ¼-inch cubes. Boil the lung in water for ½ hour, cool, and cut into ¼-inch cubes.

2. Mix the liver, lung, ground beef, rice, coriander, salt and pepper well together. Sew up one end of the derma and stuff—not too tightly since the rice will expand. Sew up the opening.

3. On the bottom of a large pan put the celery, onion, bay leaves and peppercorns. Pour in the stock. Bring to a boil over moderate heat and add the stuffed casing. Half-cover the pan, reduce to low heat, and cook for about 45 minutes or more, until the skin is tender.

Serve warm, sliced. Serve the clear soup separately.

Serves 10 to 12.

BACHSH
Rice, Beef and Chicken-Liver Mix

This recipe illustrates an unusual technique for preparing a rice and meat mixture. *Bachsh* is a purely Bukharan method in which the rice mix can be cooked in a bag and served either hot or cold. The size and shape of the bag and its filling determine how it will be served.

 2 cups raw rice, rinsed, drained
 1 cup beef steak, cut into ¼-inch dice
 1 cup chicken livers, grilled under flame to make kosher, then cut
     into 1-inch pieces
 1 teaspoon salt
 ½ teaspoon pepper
 2 cups fresh coriander leaves, chopped
 1 medium onion, chopped (½ cup)
 ¼ cup chicken fat, cut into small dice
 4 egg yolks, cooked (optional)

1. Mix everything together and set aside.

2. Fill the bag of your choice almost full and tie it tightly. If you want to serve it cold, use the salami-shaped bag (about 12 inches long and 3 inches in diameter). If you want to serve it hot, use a bag about 5 by 6 inches in size.

3. Put the bag of your choice in a large pan with lightly salted water, bring to a boil over moderate heat, and cook, uncovered, for 2 hours, turning the bags over now and then. If the water evaporates too quickly, add another cup or two.

To serve cold, cool the salami bag well, remove the rice loaf and cut into generous slices.

To serve hot, remove the large bag and shake out the contents to a serving platter.

VARIATION: *Bachsh* may be cooked in a more conventional manner without the bags. This is the way to do it:

1. Using 2 tablespoons corn oil, stir-fry the onion, meat, chicken fat, salt, pepper and coriander leaves in a pan over moderate heat for 3 minutes. Add the liver, stir-fry for 1 minute, then add the rice and stir-fry for 5 minutes.

2. Add 3 cups water, bring to a boil, then reduce heat to low. Cover the pan and cook for 20 minutes. Stir once or twice toward the end of the cooking time. Let the mixture rest, covered, for 15 minutes before serving. This will steam the rice until tender.

Serve warm. Serves 6 to 8 with other dishes.

SIRKANIZ

Rice, Beef, Carrot Cooked in a Bag

Cooking in a sturdy cloth bag is an exclusively Jewish method of preparing seasoned rice, meat and vegetables in Bukhara. It is a cleverly arranged system of cooking a family-style dish that does not require constant attention. While the ladies were tending their rather large families, the *sirkaniz* was simmering away. Note that caraway seed, a potent seasoning, is also referred to (incorrectly) as black cuminseed.

2½ *cups raw rice, well rinsed*
¾ *pound boneless chuck, cut into ¼-inch dice*
½ *pound carrots, cut into pieces ½ inch long, ⅛ inch thick*
2 *teaspoons caraway seeds*
2 *teaspoons salt*
½ *cup dried chick-peas, soaked overnight in water, drained, peeled, skins discarded*

1. Use a cloth bag known as a *soofeechom*, 6 inches wide and 12 inches long. Mix all the ingredients together and pack them into the *soofeechom* firmly but loosely enough to allow the rice to expand. Tie the top of the bag with a string.

2. Put the bag in a large pan and cover it completely with water. Bring it to a boil over moderate heat, then reduce to low, cover the pan, and simmer for 2 hours. Remove the bag and pour off the liquid. Turn the contents of the bag into the same cooking pan and stir in the Garlic Sauce (following recipe).

Serve warm. Serves 8.

GARLIC SAUCE

3 garlic cloves, crushed in a mortar or put through a press
1 teaspoon salt
2 tablespoons water
¼ cup corn oil

1. Mix the garlic, salt and water together. Heat the oil in a small pan over low heat for 1 minute. Dump the garlic mixture into the pan, cover immediately, and let it fry for 1 minute.
   Stir it into the *sirkaniz.*

SHOLA
Rice with Beef and Carrot

The shola is an every-day dish that emphasizes the natural flavors of meat, onion and carrot. The lack of pungent spices is a characteristic of Bukharan cooking.

3 tablespoons corn oil
1 large onion, chopped (1 cup)
¾ pound boneless beef chuck, cut into ½-inch cubes
4 cups water
1 teaspoon salt, or to taste
1 carrot, cut into ¼-inch cubes (½ cup)
2 cups raw rice, well rinsed

1. Heat the oil in a pan, add the onion and beef, and stir-fry over moderate heat for 10 minutes. Cover the pan half of the time.
2. Add the water, salt, carrot and rice and bring to a boil. Reduce heat to very low and stir the mixture for a moment. Cover the pan and cook for 40 minutes, which should be enough to tenderize the beef and evaporate some of the liquid.
   Serve warm with bread. Serves 6.

OSH PLOV
Lamb and Rice

Another family-style dish of lamb and rice, richly embellished with garlic, raisins and carrots.

There is only one spice in this classic Bukharan dish—pepper. All the flavor is provided by the natural taste of the ingredients.

6 tablespoons corn oil
2 pounds lamb chops with the bone, shoulder or rib, trimmed
2 medium onions, chopped (1 cup)
1 pound carrots, sliced julienne
1 teaspoon salt
½ teaspoon pepper
4 cups water
2 small heads of garlic, about 12 cloves, whole
¼ cup dark raisins
2 cups raw rice

1. Heat 3 tablespoons of the oil in a skillet and lightly brown the lamb chops over moderate heat for 1 minute on each side. Remove the lamb and discard the oil, which also removes the strong aroma of lamb.

2. Heat the balance of the oil, 3 tablespoons, in a pan large enough to hold all ingredients and lightly fry the onions over moderate heat for 2 minutes. Add the lamb in one or two layers and cover with 1 cup carrots. Sprinkle the salt and pepper over. Add 1 cup of the water, cover the pan, and cook over low heat for ½ hour.

3. Spread the balance of the carrots over the lamb mixture. Place the garlic heads on top and sprinkle the raisins over all.

4. In the meantime, soak the rice in the remaining 3 cups hot water for ½ hour. Pour off but reserve the water, about 3 cups. Spread the rice over the carrots and carefully pour in the water. Cover the pan, bring to a simmer over moderate heat, then reduce to low heat.

5. After 15 minutes, remove the cover of the pan and with the handle of a wooden mixing spoon push in 5 holes to the bottom of the pan (a Bukharan rice technique). Cover the pan with a cloth towel or paper kitchen towels, cover that with the pan cover, and cook over low heat for 15 minutes more. Let the pan rest off the heat for 10 minutes more to steam through.

Serve warm by placing the rice on the bottom of a serving platter. Cover with the lamb mixture and put the liquefied garlic heads in the center.

Serves 8.

MURGH MAYEE
Chicken Wings in Aspic for the Sabbath

The chicken wings are an ideal dish to prepare on Friday and serve on the Sabbath when no cooking is permitted in religious households. The wings are cooked and provide a fine concentrated stock which, when refrigerated, converts to a natural gelatin aspic.

6 chicken wings, divided into their 3 sections
3 cups water
1 teaspoon salt, or to taste
⅛ teaspoon pepper
2 carrots, cut across into ¼-inch thick slices (1 cup)
1 medium onion, chopped (½ cup)
3 garlic cloves, crushed in a mortar or put through a garlic press
1 tablespoon fine-chopped fresh coriander

1. Put the wings, water, salt, pepper, carrots and onion in a pan. Bring to a boil, then simmer, covered, over low heat for 40 minutes. This is sufficient to tenderize the wings and reduce the liquid.

2. Cool in the pan for 15 minutes, then stir in the garlic and coriander. Turn out into a serving bowl and refrigerate.

Serve wings and aspic cold. Serves 4 with other Sabbath dishes.

KABOB ROCHAN
Quick Chicken Mix

This *kabob* is quick, simple, well seasoned. The fried potatoes folded in give the dish an extra textural interest.

    1 young chicken, about 1½ pounds, or Cornish game hens, cut
        into 8 serving pieces, plus the giblets
    3 ripe tomatoes (¾ pound), sliced
    1 tablespoon corn oil
    2 bay leaves
    4 whole allspice
    1 dried hot red chili, whole
    ½ teaspoon salt
    2 medium potatoes (½ pound), crisp french fried

1. Cook everything except the potatoes in a covered pan over moderate heat for ½ hour, or until the chicken is tender and the tomatoes have cooked down into a sauce.

2. Fold in the potatoes and serve immediately.

Serve warm. Serves 4 as a side dish with rice and salads.

BUKHARAN PLOV
Chicken and Rice, Bukhara Style

The Bukharans combine chicken, rice and carrots in a masterful arrangement that lends itself to large family gatherings. The dried hot chili provides a mild amount of heat, which makes up for the lack of spices in this preparation.

    2 cups raw rice
    2¼ cups water
    2 teaspoons salt
    ¼ cup corn oil
    3 medium onions, sliced (1½ cups)
    1 chicken, 3 pounds, cut into 8 serving pieces, loose skin and fat
        discarded
    1 pound carrots, cut into julienne
    2 dried hot red chilies, whole

1. Cover the rice in a bowl with 1 cup of the hot water, add 1 teaspoon of the salt, mix, and let stand 2 hours.

2. Heat the oil in a pan, add the onions, and stir-fry them over low heat until golden, about 10 minutes. Add the chicken pieces and lightly brown them for 5 minutes. Remove the chicken and onions to a bowl.

3. Put 1 cup of carrots in the oil remaining in the pan. Return the chicken and onion to the pan and cover with the balance of the carrots.

4. Drain the rice. Heat the chicken and carrot mixture over moderate heat, then add the drained rice and chilies to the top of the mixture over the carrots. Add the other 1¼ cups water and 1 teaspoon salt, cover the pan, and cook for 10 minutes. Cover the pan with a kitchen towel with the pan cover over that, reduce heat to low, and cook for ½ hour more.

Let the *plov* rest in the covered pan for about 15 minutes more to steam through. Serve warm. Serves 6 to 8.

KOWO RUGAN
Duck and Potatoes with Cuminseed

Cuminseed is the principal flavor with the duck. The fried potatoes provide substance and filler to stretch the duck meat a little further than nature provided. American ducks are excessively fat so it is necessary to trim and discard much of the loose skin and fat before cooking.

1 duck, 4½ pounds, cut into 3-inch pieces
2 teaspoons salt, or to taste
½ teaspoon pepper
1 teaspoon ground cuminseed
1 medium onion, chopped (½ cup)
2 cups water
2 pounds potatoes, peeled, cut into generous-size french fries
⅓ cup corn oil for panfrying
2 tablespoons tomato paste

1. Put the duck in a large enough pan with the salt, pepper, cuminseed, onion and water. Bring to a boil, cover the pan, and simmer over low heat for 1 hour, or until the duck is tender. If too much fat has accumulated, skim it off at this time.

2. Fry the potato slices in the oil until brown and crisp. Add them to the duck and fold in the tomato paste. Simmer all together over low heat for 10 minutes.

Serve warm with bread and any kind of table pickle. Serves 8.

KEEMA CHOWJA
Stuffed Pigeon, Pan-Roasted

Cooking on top of the stove is a traditional style of Bukharan cooking where home ovens are not always available. Pigeons are everywhere and are killed in the kosher manner by the *shokhet* and stuffed in this delectable manner.

STUFFING

> 1 medium onion, chopped (½ cup)
> ½ cup raw rice, well rinsed
> ½ teaspoon salt
> ¼ teaspoon ground turmeric
> ¼ teaspoon pepper
> ½ teaspoon ground cuminseed
> ½ chopped zucchini
> 1 small carrot, grated (½ cup)
> 1 tablespoon corn oil

PAN-ROASTING

> 2 pigeons, 1 pound each
> ½ pound zucchini, sliced
> 2 cups water
> ½ teaspoon salt
> ¼ teaspoon paprika

1. Mix stuffing ingredients together and stuff each pigeon nearly full. You may or may not sew up the aperture.

2. Put the sliced zucchini, water, salt and paprika into the pan and mix them together. Rest the 2 stuffed pigeons over the vegetables. Bring the mixture to a boil, reduce heat to low, cover the pan tightly, and cook for 1 hour or a bit more to ensure that the pigeons are tender. If the water evaporates too quickly, add another ¼ cup.

Serve warm. Serves 4 with other dishes.

VARIATION: You may use small Cornish game hens of about 1 pound each. The 1-pound size is comparable to a pigeon and the end result is similar. With slow cooking, it will take 1½ hours.

ZAGORA
Carp in Garlic and
Coriander Sauce

Bukharans like their sauces loaded with garlic, salt and coriander. Simply cooked dishes without robust spicing are enhanced by absorbing the sauce as in this case. Carp are plentiful in the many rivers of Uzbekistan.

> 1½ pounds fresh carp, cut into 1-inch wide slices
> 1 teaspoon salt, dissolved in ½ cup water
> ¼ cup corn oil
> 2 large garlic cloves, crushed in a mortar with 1 teaspoon salt
> 3 tablespoons chopped fresh coriander
> ½ cup water

1. Drench the carp with the salt and water and let stand for ½ hour. Drain well and dry the slices on paper towels.

2. Heat the oil in a skillet, add the fish, and fry on both sides over moderate heat for about 4 minutes, which should brown-crisp the slices. Put the fish on a serving platter and keep it warm.

3. Prepare the sauce by mixing together the garlic, salt, coriander and ½ cup water. Stir this briskly and pour it over the fish, turning the slices over once so that they can absorb the sauce.

Serve immediately at room temperature. Serves 4 with salad.

VARIATION: Most kinds of fish can be used for the *zagora*. Usually the whole fish is cut into slices with the bone, whether it be from fresh or salt water. I like fillet of flounder or salmon, which are not Samarkand fish but which respond extremely well to this treatment.

BANDOORA
Fresh Tomato and Basil Salad

A simple salad such as this one is available and welcome at any Bukharan meal.

1 pound ripe tomatoes, sliced
¼ cup chopped fresh basil
2 scallions, sliced thin
½ teaspoon salt
¼ teaspoon pepper
1 tablespoon lemon juice, or to taste
3 tablespoons olive oil

1. Toss everything together. Refrigerate. Serve cool.
Serves 6.

EEKRA
Chopped Vegetable Side Dish

A simply seasoned assortment of vegetables, chopped coarsely and cooked slowly, makes an attractive side dish for dairy or meat dining among the Bukharans.

1 pound eggplants (2), peeled, chopped into ½-inch pieces
2 carrots, chopped (1 cup)
1 large onion, chopped (½ cup)
2 or 3 sweet green peppers (½ pound), chopped
½ pound zucchini, chopped
¼ cup corn oil
½ teaspoon salt

⅛ teaspoon pepper
¼ teaspoon hot dry red chili flakes
¼ teaspoon ground cuminseed

1. Put everything into a large enough pan without water. Cook over moderate heat for 3 minutes, stirring constantly. Reduce heat to very low, cover the pan, and cook for 1 hour. The vegetables will reduce to a moist melange.

Serve warm or at room temperature as a side dish with other food. Serves 6.

MOSH OWAEE JOOR-RAWTEE
Mung Bean and Rice Melange

Yoghurt dishes are much appreciated in Samarkand during the hot Central Asian summers, and this melange becomes even more appealing when served with their homemade Yoghurt Sauce (see Index).

1 cup dried green mung beans
¾ cup raw rice, well rinsed
4 cups water
½ teaspoon salt

1. Mix everything together in a pan and bring to a boil. Cover the pan and simmer over low heat for 1 to 1½ hours, which reduces the mixture to a soft, delicately flavored mush.

Serve at room temperature, mixing in as much of the yoghurt sauce as wanted. To my taste ½ cup mosh to 2 tablespoons of the sauce is a tasty mix.

Serves 4.

KIHRCHIREE
Mung Bean and Rice Medley

Mung beans are a Chinese import in Central Asia, brought along the ancient Silk Route. We see another foreign connection in the title—the kihrchiree of Samarkand is related linguistically to the kitchree of India.

BEANS

    1 cup dried green mung beans
    1 cup raw rice, well rinsed
    4 cups water
    ½ teaspoon salt

SAUCE

    2 garlic cloves, crushed in a mortar or put through a press
    2 tablespoons water
    2 tablespoons corn or olive oil

1. Mix the beans, rice, water and salt in a pan and bring to a boil. Cover the pan and simmer over very low heat for about 1½ hours to reduce the mixture to a thick and somewhat dry mush.

2. Mix the garlic and water together. Heat the oil in a small pan or skillet that has a cover. Over moderate heat, pour the garlic/water mix into the oil and cover the pan immediately to avoid splattering. Remove the pan from the heat. Serve the sauce, as much as wanted, to be spooned over a serving of the kihrchiree.

Serves 4 at room temperature.

OSHEE PYOZEE
Stuffed Onion Shells

This delicious preparation is a Bukharan specialty for the Friday evening dinner, ushering in the Sabbath. Quite simple and flavorful.

4 or 5 medium onions
1 carrot, sliced (½ cup)
2 tablespoons raw rice, well rinsed
½ teaspoon salt
½ teaspoon ground cuminseed
¼ teaspoon pepper
½ pound ground beef or lamb
3 tablespoons corn oil
1 tablespoon lemon juice, or to taste
1 tablespoon tomato paste
1½ cups liquid reserved from the onions
¼ pound chicken leg, wing or breast (optional but recommended)
½ cup cooked but still firm chick-peas
1 small zucchini, sliced, or 1 cup ¼-inch dice of pumpkin

1. Make a 1-inch-deep slit into the side of each onion. Bring 4 cups of water to a boil in a pan. Drop the onions in and cook over moderate heat for 2 minutes. Remove onions with a slotted spoon and reserve 1½ cups of the liquid. Cool the onions somewhat and peel off about 4 layers from each onion. Save the onion heart.

2. Mix together in a processor the carrot, rice, salt, cuminseed and pepper and reduce it to small pieces. Add the meat and mix for a few seconds. Stuff each onion shell with 1 tablespoon of the meat mixture and set aside.

3. Put the oil, lemon juice, tomato paste, reserved onion liquid and chicken leg in a pan. Add half of the stuffed onions, half of the chick-peas over that, the reserved onion hearts and all of the zucchini or pumpkin. Cover this with the balance of the stuffed onions. Cover the pan, bring to a boil, then simmer over low heat for 1 hour. Much of the liquid will evaporate.

Serve warm. Serves 6 with other Sabbath dishes.

NOTE: The small piece of chicken added to the stuffed onions serves to strengthen the sauce and provide extra flavor to the dish. It is not an indispensable addition but one that will enhance the seasonings in the Bukharan manner.

OSHEE POMEEDOR
Stuffed Tomatoes in a
Vegetable Sauce

Every ethnic culture that I know of has its own individual touch with stuffed vegetables. Large ripe but firm tomatoes are popular, filled with natural flavor and predictably delicious when served. Here is the Bukharan version.

STUFFING

6 medium tomatoes (1½ pounds)
1 small onion, chopped (¼ cup)
2 tablespoons raw rice, well rinsed
1 teaspoon salt
⅛ teaspoon black pepper
¼ teaspoon ground turmeric
½ teaspoon ground cuminseed
¼ cup chopped zucchini
1 pound ground lamb or beef

SAUCE

corn oil
1 whole zucchini, ½ pound, sliced
1 small onion, sliced (⅓ cup)
½ teaspoon salt
2 tablespoons tomato paste
½ cup water

1. Scoop out the center of the tomatoes and discard the inner seeds and liquid.

2. Mix the stuffing ingredients together well and stuff each tomato to the top.

3. Oil the inside of a pan large enough to contain the 6 tomatoes. Mix the sliced zucchini and onion, salt and tomato paste dissolved in the water, and pour it into the bottom of the pan. Rest the stuffed tomatoes on this. Bring to a boil, cover the pan, and reduce heat to low. Simmer for 1 hour, which will reduce most of the liquid (tomatoes have a lot of their own) and soften the vegetables.

Serves warm with the sauce. Serves 6 with other dishes.

OSHEE TOS KADOO
Stuffed Pumpkin

It is as logical to stuff a pumpkin as a green pepper, eggplant or grape leaf. Select a pumpkin that weighs from 2 to 3 pounds, which is easy to handle. The pumpkins of Samarkand are huge, sometimes 20 to 30 inches in diameter. These would make an enormous impression but are not practical for stuffing. The *oshee tos* is prepared for special occasions or a family celebration and is very festive.

1 pumpkin, 2½ to 3 pounds
⅓ cup raw rice, well rinsed
¼ pound ground lamb
1 small onion, chopped (¼ cup)
¼ teaspoon ground cuminseed
1 teaspoon salt
¼ teaspoon pepper
¼ cup fine-chopped fresh coriander
¼ teaspoon ground turmeric
1 or 2 cabbage or lettuce leaves
1 cup water mixed with 2 tablespoons chopped onion

1. Cut out a 3-inch-diameter disc from the stem end of the pumpkin and save it. Scoop out and discard the seeds and loose strings from the interior.
2. Combine all the other ingredients except the leaves and water. Stuff the pumpkin and put the stem disc back in place.
3. Put the leaves on the bottom of a deep pan to protect the pumpkin from burning. Add the water and set the pumpkin inside the pan. Bring to a boil, then reduce to very low heat, and cook slowly for 2 hours, or even 2½ to make certain the pumpkin and stuffing are soft. Should the water evaporate too quickly, add another ¼ cup.

Serve warm by scooping out the stuffing and pulp. Serves 4 to 6.

PASHTIDA
Zucchini Pie

This fine appetizer or first course at dinner was taught me by a Bukharan lady in Haifa. She indicated that the dish could be of Balkan origin, but was a tradition in her home.

1 pound zucchini, grated
1½ teaspoon coarse salt
¼ teaspoon pepper
1 garlic clove, put through a press
2 tablespoons bread crumbs
2 or 3 eggs, beaten
2 tablespoon corn oil

1. Mix the zucchini and salt together and let stand for ½ hour to release the liquid. Drain and press out the excess liquid.

2. Add pepper, garlic, bread crumbs and eggs to the zucchini to prepare a batter.

3. Heat the oil in a skillet over moderate heat for 1 minute. The oil should be hot. Add the entire batter and fry for 5 minutes. Turn the pie over and fry for 3 minutes more.

Serve warm, at room temperature or cold, cut into 2-inch cubes. Serves 4 to 6.

VARIATION: The pie may also be baked in the oven. Simply separate the whites and yolks of the eggs. Beat the whites until stiff and fold them into the zucchini mixture with the yolks. Turn out into a well-oiled baking dish, 13 × 9 × 2 inches and bake at 375° F. for 20 minutes or until brown. Serve at any temperature you wish, cut like a pie or into cubes.

GREBE
Pickled Mushrooms

Pickled mushrooms are often heavy with garlic. I prefer using 4 to 6 cloves according to size, but the original recipe cooked in a Samarkand home added an entire head of garlic!

4 cups water
1 pound fresh mushrooms, well rinsed, stems lightly trimmed
½ cup white vinegar
4 to 6 garlic cloves, to taste, peeled, halved lengthwise
1 teaspoon salt, or to taste
2 or 3 whole dried hot red chilies
1 teaspoon corn oil
2 tablespoons chopped fresh coriander

1. Bring 3 cups water to a boil in a large pan, add the mushrooms, cover the pan, and cook over moderate heat for 3 minutes. Drain well,

2. Return the mushrooms to the pan and add just enough water to reach the top of the mushrooms, about 1 cup. Bring to a boil and simmer over low heat for 3 minutes. Drain off only half of the water. Cool the mushrooms and liquid.

3. Put the mushrooms into a glass jar with a tight cover. Mix the remaining liquid, ½ cup vinegar (or a bit more since it should equal the amount of liquid), garlic, salt, chilies, oil and coriander together. Pour it over the mushrooms. Cover the jar and let stand at room temperature for 2 or 3 days before using. Then refrigerate.

Serve with any kind of Central Asian food.

Makes 1 quart.

OCHOR
Marinated Eggplant

This is a vinegar-tart condiment that should be available at all times, it is that useful. As in many Bukharan foods there are actually no spices used, only several kinds of herbs and seasonings.

1 pound smallest eggplants, 6 or 7
4 cups boiling water with 2 teaspoons salt
1 small onion, chopped fine
1 small bay leaf for each eggplant, halved
1 head of garlic, 8 cloves, sliced thin horizontally
2 tablespoons chopped basil
1 teaspoon salt
2 tablespoons chopped parsley
⅔ cup cider vinegar

1. Cut off the stem of each eggplant and cut down to half of its length. Blanch the eggplant in the boiling water for 1 minute. Pour off and reserve 1 cup of the water. Cool the eggplants.

2. Mix together the onion, bay leaves, garlic, basil, salt and parsley. Spread open each eggplant and stuff with 1 tablespoon of the mixture. Fit the eggplants in a glass jar.

3. Mix the vinegar with the 1 cup of reserved blanching water and pour it over the eggplants to cover. Put a plate over the surface of the contents and a weight (a stone) to hold it down so that the eggplants are immersed. Cover the jar and keep it at room temperature for 2 weeks before using.

Ochor is a condiment and can be served with pilau or other Bukharan foods. To serve, cut the eggplants into slices.

Makes 1 quart.

PICKLED EGGPLANT

Sharply seasoned and long-lasting, these eggplant pickles are a typical Uzbek dish. They will go well with any Middle Eastern or Indian food. (Note the use of allspice, which my cook called "English pepper.)

2 pounds eggplants, 3 inches long or smaller
1 head of garlic, 6 to 8 cloves, chopped fine
1 cup chopped fresh basil
1 teaspoon salt
½ teaspoon whole allspice
½ teaspoon peppercorns
5 bay leaves, halved
1 cup water
4 cups red-wine vinegar

1. Cut off the stem end of each eggplant. Cut the eggplants almost into halves from the bulb end to within 1 inch of the stem.

2. Mix together the garlic, basil, salt, allspice, peppercorns and bay leaves. Spread open the eggplant and deposit 1 tablespoon of the spice mix between the halves. Close firmly.

3. Bring the water to a boil in a large pan, add the vinegar and simmer together over moderate heat for 10 minutes. Arrange the stuffed eggplants in a large glass or pottery jar in layers horizontally. Pour the hot vinegar over the eggplants, enough to cover. Put a weight, or a plate with a stone, over all to keep them submerged. Cover the jar.

Let stand at room temperature to marinate for 2 days, then refrigerate for another week before using. In fact the longer, the better.

Makes 1 quart.

MANTU
Steamed Bukharan Beef Pie

These pies or dumplings have a Mongolian parent somewhere since their counterpart is a staple of the Mongolian cuisine. The pies may be made even more Mongolian by cutting the dough squares into 5-inch circles. Add the meat filling and pinch the pie dough together down the center, twisting the top firmly as you move along. Steam for ½ hour.

DOUGH

4 cups flour
1 cup water
1 egg, beaten
1 teaspoon salt

FILLING

1 pound onions, chopped
2 pounds beef chuck, ground
1 teaspoon pepper

1. Mix all the dough ingredients together into a firm ball. Dust with more flour if needed. Cover the dough ball and let it rest for ½ hour. Divide it into 3 equal portions. Shape them into 3 balls and set aside.

2. Mix filling ingredients together.

3. Roll out each dough ball into a thin strip about 4 inches wide and 1 yard long. Cut the strips into 4-inch squares.

4. Put about ¼ cup of the meat filling in the center of each square. Fold two opposite corners into the center, then fold over the other two corners to form an envelope enclosing the stuffing. Twist the dough corners together to seal.

5. Use a Chinese-style steamer with 2 trays; oil the trays generously. Put the pies on the trays and steam over hot water over moderate heat for ½ hour.

Serve warm. Makes about 16 pies.

SAMOOSA
Baked Meat Pies

The *samoosa* were traditionally baked in a tandoor, the oven that is so widely associated with the preparation of the Moghul foods of India. Many Asian cultures used this oven—the Jews to bake their matzoh for Passover and to bake the *samoosa* at any season.

Samoosa may be frozen after baking. Allow 1 hour at room temperature to thaw and reheat in a 375° F. oven for 10 minutes.

DOUGH

> 4 cups flour
> 1½ cups water
> ½ teaspoon salt
> 1 tablespoon baking powder
> 2 eggs, beaten

FILLING

> 2 pounds onions, chopped (4 cups)
> 2 pounds beef steak, cut into ¼-inch cubes
> 1 teaspoon pepper
> 1½ teaspoons salt, or to taste

1. Put the flour in a large bowl. Make a well in the center, add 1 cup of the water, the salt, baking powder and half the beaten eggs. Mix well and incorporate the flour into the liquid. Add more water as you need it to prepare a firm dough. Knead to smoothness and ease of handling. Cover the bowl and keep it in a warm spot for 2 hours.

2. Mix the filling ingredients together briskly with a wooden spoon since this will separate and distribute the onion pieces.

3. Dust the working board or surface with flour. Divide the dough into halves and roll out each half into a loaf shape. Pull off 2 ounces of dough (about ⅓ cup) and press it onto the floured board. Roll it out with a rolling pin to a round disc 5 inches in diameter. An Italian pasta hand machine does this effectively if you wish. Put ½ cup of the meat filling into the center. Fold the top of the disc a third of the way down. Then fold over the right side and the left side to make a triangle. Squeeze the dough together to seal. Paint the top of each *samoosa* with the remaining egg and place them on an oiled baking sheet. Bake in a 375° F. oven for 25 minutes.

Serve warm or at room temperature. Makes 20.

VARIATIONS: The beef and onion mixture is the traditonal combination for the *samoosa*. The potato and spinach that follow are modern innovations.

POTATO

Cook ½ pound potatoes in their skins. Peel and cut into ¼-inch cubes and add equal amounts each of beef and onion.

SPINACH

Coarsely chop 1 pound of spinach or Swiss chard. Cook it with ½ cup water in a covered pan for 5 minutes to soften. Cool and press out the liquid. Combine it with an equal amount of beef and onion.

YAZOZEE
Scallion Pancakes

Here again, one could easily attribute these pancakes to China rather than Bukhara. When I told my teacher, who is Jewish, that she looked Chinese, she replied, "Why not, we are close."

The pancakes are eaten for breakfast and are served with a typically Chinese white radish, which has a green skin near the stem and white skin on the root end. These are found in Chinatowns everywhere. Also served with the pancakes are the all-white daikon and the red garden radish.

1 egg, beaten
3 tablespoons water

¼ cup flour
¼ cup chopped scallion, green part only
½ teaspoon salt, or to taste
⅛ teaspoon pepper
3 to 4 tablespoons corn oil for panfrying

1. Prepare the batter by mixing everything together except the oil.

2. Heat the oil in a skillet and prepare individual pancakes with about ¼ cup of the batter. Brown the pancakes on both sides over moderate heat, about 3 minutes.

Serve warm. Serves 2.

CHALPAKEE JOOR-RAWTEE
Fried Yeast Pancake

The summers are hot in Samarkand and appetites are whimsical, fluctuating with the change in temperature. Dairy dishes at this time of year are popular to revive flagging spirits. So these *chalpakees* are prepared and eaten with Yoghurt Sauce, heavily loaded with garlic. I noticed when learning this dish that the word *chalpakee* is so similar to the Indian *chapatti* that I am convinced these ethnic breads may have had a common origin.

PANCAKE

2 cups flour
1 package (7 grams) dry yeast, or 20 grams fresh yeast
1 cup warm water
2 teaspoons salt
1 egg, beaten
1 tablespoon corn or olive oil, plus 1 cup for frying

1. Pour the flour into a large bowl or dish. Mix the yeast with ½ cup of the water. Sprinkle the salt over the flour. Make a well in the flour and add the yeast mixture, the egg and 1 tablespoon oil. Stir a few times with a fork or your hands, then add the balance of the water to prepare a soft, moist dough that can still be easily handled. Knead on a floured board for 5 minutes.

2. Return the dough ball to a bowl, cover with a kitchen towel, and let it rise for about 45 minutes, long enough to double in size. Punch it down and divide the ball into halves.

3. Roll out one of the balls on a lightly floured board to a thin pancake about 14 inches in diameter. Cut it into 7 or 8 more or less equal pieces—both squares and rectangles.

4. Heat the 1 cup of corn oil in a skillet over moderate heat and fry 1 piece at a time for about ½ minute on each side. The strips will puff up slightly. Remove and drain on a paper towel for a minute. Serve with the Yoghurt Sauce that follows.

Serve at room temperature. Makes enough pieces as an appetizer for 4.

YOGHURT SAUCE

2 cups yoghurt
3 garlic cloves, crushed in a mortar with 1 teaspoon salt
1 tablespoon chopped fresh basil or coriander

1. Mix everything together and serve with the Fried Yeast Pancake. Spoon the sauce on the pancake pieces, as much as wanted.

KADOO BICHAK
Baked Pumpkin and Onion Dumplings

Pumpkin and onion make a popular combination in Bukharan cooking and using them together as a stuffing is imaginative and traditional.

DOUGH

1 package (7 grams) dry yeast, or 20 ounces fresh yeast
1 cup warm water
4 cups flour
1 teaspoon salt
1 egg yolk mixed with 1 tablespoon water (egg glaze)

STUFFING

2 pounds pumpkin or calabasa, cut into ½-inch cubes
1 pound onions, chopped
½ teaspoon hot red chili flakes

1. Dissolve the yeast in ½ cup warm water and let it proof for 10 minutes.

2. Put the flour into a large bowl. Mix in the salt and yeast mixture and gradually add ½ cup water, or enough to prepare a soft moist dough. Knead the dough for 5 minutes, sprinkling with flour if necessary to ease handling. Return the dough to the bowl, cover with a kitchen towel, and let rise for 1 hour. Punch down the dough, which is now ready to prepare the dumplings.

3. Mix the pumpkin and onions together in a pan. Cover and cook over low heat for ½ hour or more to reduce the bulk and soften the vegetables. Considerable liquid may accumulate. Uncover the pan and cook for 10 minutes more. Drain the mixture through a metal sieve to pour off all the liquid. Turn out into a bowl and stir in the chili flakes. Cool.

4. Roll out the dough into a long sausage shape about 3 inches in diameter. Pull off ⅓ cup of dough, about 2 ounces, and roll this out into a pancake 4 inches in diameter and ¼ inch thick. Put 1 generous tablespoon of the stuffing into the center and fold over the top toward the center. Then fold the left and right sides over toward the center to shape a closed triangle. Pinch the folds together to seal. Paint the top of the dumpling with the egg glaze and put on an oiled baking sheet.

Bake in a 375° F. oven for 20 minutes to brown the top.

Serve warm. Makes 20 dumplings.

NOTE: The dumplings may be frozen in plastic bags after baking and cooling. To serve, allow them to thaw out at room temperature for 1 hour. Reheat in a 350° F. oven for 10 minutes.

SAMOOSA PUROEE
Stuffed Fried Dumplings for Purim

These dumplings are a specialty for Purim to celebrate the time when the Persian villain, Haman, was foiled by Queen Esther. The Bukharans feel this has a special significance for them since their origin was ancient Persia.

DOUGH

    4 cups flour
    ½ teaspoon salt

⅛ teaspoon pepper
1 cup water (about)
2 cups corn oil for deep-frying

STUFFING

2 pounds onions, chopped
1 pound ground beef
1 teaspoon salt
¼ teaspoon pepper

1. Mix the flour, salt, pepper, and enough water together to make a soft dough. Knead well for several minutes. Pull off about ⅓ cup of the dough and roll it out into a thin 8-inch pancake. There should be enough dough for 10 thin pancakes.

2. Put the onions in a large pan, cover, and let them soften over very lowest heat for about 1 hour. Stir briskly toward the end of this time to break down the texture. Add the beef, salt and pepper and stir well. Let simmer for 5 minutes to cook the beef. Cool well.

3. Put a pancake down on a lightly floured board. Take 5 heaping teaspoons of the filling and arrange them, one at a time, an equal distance apart, on the lower half of the pancake. Moisten your finger with cold water and wet the lower edge. Fold the top half over and press it down firmly. Using a round pizza cutter, cut the folded pancake into 5 pieces like a pie. The edges will be sealed by the cutter.

4. Heat the oil in a wok or skillet and fry the dumplings over moderate heat until brown and crisp, for about 5 minutes all around. Drain them briefly on paper towels.

Serve warm. Makes about 30 dumplings.

DUSHPERA
Kreplach

The kreplach (dumplings) are folded together in the same way as the Chinese won ton. I believe that in the centuries of trade and exchange of ideas, Central Asia undoubtedly absorbed culinary customs as well. This is one of them.

DOUGH

2 cups flour
about ¾ cup water
¼ teaspoon salt
1 small egg, beaten

FILLING

1 pound ground beef
1 small onion, chopped fine (⅓ cup)
½ teaspoon salt
¼ teaspoon pepper

SAUCE

1 tablespoon corn oil
1 small onion, chopped fine (⅓ cup)
½ cup ¼-inch cubes of beefsteak
1 small garlic clove, chopped fine
2 cups homemade chicken soup
2 tablespoons tomato paste

1. Mix flour, water, salt and egg together into a firm dough; knead well. Let the dough rest, covered, for ½ hour before using.

2. Mix beef, onion, salt and pepper together. Set aside.

3. Take half of the dough and shape it into a cylinder. Roll it out into a strip about 2½ inches wide and as long as it will go. Cut off 2½-inch squares from the entire strip.

4. Put 1 teaspoon of stuffing on the bottom half of each square. Fold the top half over and press firmly. Fold back ¼ inch of the bottom. Twist the two ends away from you outward and seal them together, using a dab of water on the finger. This is the shape of a nurses cap and is the same system used by the Chinese to make won ton. Prepare all the *kreplach* this way.

5. Bring 8 cups water to a boil over moderate heat and cook the *kreplach*, uncovered, for 10 minutes. Do not crowd the pan; add a few at a time. Drain and set aside for the sauce.

6. Heat the oil in a pan and stir-fry the onion over moderate heat for 2 minutes. Add the beef and garlic and stir-fry for another 2 minutes. Add the soup and tomato paste, bring to a boil, reduce heat to low, and simmer for 15 minutes to thicken the sauce.

Mix the *kreplach* and sauce and serve them together.

Serves 6.

DUSHPERA (SAMARKAND)
Meat Ravioli from Samarkand

The Bukharans are expert in "constructions," my word that indicates putting things together like this ravioli—or bread, cooking in a cloth bag, steaming the giant won ton. The *dushpera* has a Chinese ancestor, not surprising for an ancient city that was one of the anchors of the famous Silk Route. For this recipe, you will need a hand-cranked pasta machine (see Note).

DOUGH

> 2 cups flour
> 2 eggs, beaten
> 2 teaspoons salt dissolved in ½ to ¾ cup water

MEAT STUFFING

> 1 pound boneless beef chuck or lamb, ground
> 1 large onion, chopped fine (1 cup)
> 1 teaspoon salt, or to taste
> 1 teaspoon pepper

1. Mix dough ingredients together, using only as much water as needed to develop a firm, dry dough that can be easily handled. Knead the dough, dusting with flour if too sticky, and put it in a plastic bag and to rest in a warm spot for ½ hour. Then knead again for 1 minute. Set aside in the plastic bag.

2. Mix the meat, onion, salt and pepper together. Set aside.

3. Cut the dough ball into 4 equal pieces. Knead them on a floured board for a few moments.

4. Roll out 1 ball of dough to the width of the pasta machine. Put this into the machine and roll it out to a long thin strip, then do it again so that the dough is about ⅛ inch thick and about 24 inches long. Cut the long strip into 2½-inch squares to prepare them for stuffing. Dust the strip and squares with flour if necessary to prevent sticking.

5. Put about 1 teaspoon of the stuffing into the center of each square. Fold it over from the top side to the bottom, pressing the edge firmly to seal together. Turn the thick end of the ravioli toward yourself and make another ¼-inch-wide fold with sealed end.

6. Hold the ravioli upright by its two ends, thick part downward, and turn the 2 ends downward, crossing each other, so that the pointed ends jut out "like a nurse's cap." The ravioli has a rounded shape.

7. Bring 10 cups water to a boil in a large pan and add the ravioli, a few at a time. Cook over moderate heat for 10 minutes. Remove them with a slotted spoon. Continue cooking in this manner until you have the required number. The remainder may be frozen for use later.

Serve warm, about 8 to a person. The *dushpera* may be served plain or with a sauce. Makes about 100.

N O T E : Ethnic cooking changes from the simple uncomplicated methods to the more modern, resulting from interest in mechanical contrivances. A rolling pin may be used to roll out the thin strips of dough and the folding method to stuff, seal and shape them. Or one can purchase two very convenient pieces of equipment:

The first is the small table model of a hand-cranked pasta machine. Dough strips are put into the machine and rolled out in long thin strips, an extremely efficient method of preparing pasta.

The other labor-saving device is a ravioli frame, which is a flat rectangular metal frame about 10 × 12 inches with 45 round holes 1½ inches in diameter. One or 2 thin strips of dough that have been run through the pasta machine are spread over the surface of the frame. Each of the 45 depressions is filled with 1 teaspoon of the *dushpera* meat stuffing. One or 2 more thin pasta strips are laid over the top. Then a rolling pin is firmly rolled over the frame, forcing the dough strips and filling into the holes, shaping perfect *dushpera*. These are separated and cooked according to the recipe directions.

PULONI SIRI

Pasta Squares in Light Tomato Sauce

Here is a meatless pasta dish in the Bukharan style for hot summer days. The basic egg pasta dough is prepared as for Dushpera (Samarkand) here as well as in many other dishes.

2 tablespoons corn oil
2 garlic cloves, put through a press
½ teaspoon salt, or to taste
¼ teaspoon pepper
¼ cup tomato paste
¼ cup water
1 recipe Dushpera (Samarkand) dough (preceding recipe)

1. Heat the oil over moderate heat for 1 minute. Add the garlic, salt and pepper all at once and stir-fry for ½ minute. Stir in the tomato paste and water and simmer over low heat for 2 minutes more.

2. Roll out the egg dough in long strips with a hand-turned pasta machine until it is about ⅛ inch thick. Cut the strips into 3-inch squares. Prepare about 30 squares, or as much as wanted. Bring 8 cups water to a boil in a large pan over moderate heat. Add the pasta squares and cook for 2 to 3 minutes, until *al dente*. Drain well.

3. Arrange the pasta on a serving platter and distribute the tomato sauce over all.

Serve warm. Serves 4 to 6.

KULCHATOY

Cumin-Flavored Chicken with Pasta Squares

This is another traditional pasta recipe from Bukhara and Samarkand. The egg dough as prepared for the Dushpera (Samarkand) can be wrapped in plastic and frozen. Let it thaw out at room temperature for 1 hour to prepare the *kulchatoy*.

3 tablespoons corn oil
2 medium onions, chopped (1 cup)
1 pound boneless chicken or turkey breast, cut into ¼-inch cubes
3 tablespoons water
½ teaspoon salt, or to taste
1 teaspoon ground cuminseed
½ teaspoon pepper
2 tablespoons tomato paste
1 recipe Dushpera (Samarkand) dough (see Index)

1. Heat the oil in a pan. Add the onions and stir-fry over moderate heat for 2 minutes. Add the chicken and stir-fry for another minute. Add the water, salt, cuminseed and pepper, cover the pan, and cook over low heat for 10 minutes. Stir in the tomato paste and cook for 2 minutes more. Set aside and keep warm.

2. Roll out the dough in a hand-turned pasta machine in long strips until they are about ⅛ inch thick. Cut the strips into 3-inch squares. Bring 8 cups water to a boil in a large pan. Cook the pasta squares in the water for 2 to 3 minutes, until *al dente*. Drain well.

Arrange 5 or 6 squares per serving in individual plates. Put ½ cup or more of the cumin-flavored chicken in the center of the pasta.

Serve warm. Serves 6.

KHANOOM
Steamed Vegetable Pasta Roll

Pasta sheets, chopped vegetables and seasonings are assembled and steamed in a Chinese-style steamer (although when I made it the steamer was of Uzbek construction and the cook was from Samarkand). The Jews of Bukhara prepare homemade pasta in sheets, squares and thin noodles. The *khanoom* uses the same pasta recipe as for the Dushpera (Samarkand) and is a specialty of the city of Tashkent.

> 1 recipe Dushpera (Samarkand) dough (see Index)
> 5 potatoes (1½ pounds), peeled, cut into ¼-inch cubes
> 5 onions (1 pound), peeled, chopped
> ½ cup chopped zucchini
> 1 small green pepper, chopped (⅔ cup)
> ½ teaspoon pepper
> 1 tablespoon ground cuminseed
> 2 teaspoons salt
> ½ teaspoon ground turmeric
> ¼ cup corn oil

1. Prepare the dough recipe as directed but use enough water to make a soft, moist dough that can be easily handled. Proceed as directed, then set the dough aside.

2. Mix the vegetables and seasonings together well. Set aside.

3. On a well-floured board, roll out the 4 dough balls into pancakes about 8 inches in diameter. Cut them into halves.

4. Roll out one of the dough halves in the pasta machine to a long thin strip 30 inches long and about 5 inches wide. Generously rub oil on the strip with a pastry brush. Spread about 1 cup of the vegetable stuffing over 10 inches of the surface of the pasta sheet about 12 inches from one end of the sheet. Fold over part of the sheet to cover. Oil the top and add another cup of the stuffing over the sheet. Cover this with pasta, cut off enough to cover the second layer, and press down the edges all around to seal in the stuffing. You now have a rectangle with 2 layers of stuffing ready to be steamed. (Another style of the pasta roll is to take one of the stuffed rectangles and roll it over lengthwise like a jelly roll, about 3 inches in diameter.)

5. Oil the inner platforms of the steamer (mine has 2 platforms with holes to allow the steam to circulate) and place either the rectangle or roll on them. Steam over hot water at moderate heat for 1 hour.

6. Serve warm in slices with chopped bits of red or green hot chili on the side. Tomato ketchup may also be served, or a Bukhara vinegar dip with or without garlic. Or no dip at all.

Makes 4 rolls to be eaten as a snack or a lunch.

Serves 6 to 8.

BUKHARI NON
Bukharan Bread

The Bukharans like to prepare several varieties of bread with peasant textures. Decorated with a surface design made with the fingertips or a hand puncture known as a *parakh*, the breads are not high risers but about 2 to 3 inches high when baked and with a crisp crust top and bottom.

1½ ounces fresh yeast cake (45 grams)
4 cups warm water
5 pounds all-purpose flour (20 cups)
1 tablespoon salt
⅓ cup corn oil
1 egg white
1 egg yolk mixed with 1 tablespoon water (egg glaze)

1. Dissolve the yeast in 1 cup water. Prepare a well in the center of the flour, add the yeast mixture, the salt, oil and egg white. Mix dough together with a fork (my Bukharan teacher used her hands for the entire process), then incorporate the flour. Add the balance of the water, 3 cups, a small amount at a time and mix this into the dough. Dust with flour if necessary to form a soft, moist dough that nevertheless can be handled. Knead for 5 minutes. Cover with a plastic sheet or towel and let rise in a warm spot for 45 minutes to double in size.

2. Prepare the two styles of bread. (At this stage my teacher blessed the risen dough, which "came from the soil.") Punch down the dough ball. Cut it into halves to be made into the *randa* style. Divide the other half into 3 equal pieces to be made into the *parakh* style. Dust with flour to enhance easy handling.

3. Lightly oil a rectangular metal tray (a jelly-roll tray will do) about 12 × 20 inches. Place the larger ball in the center of the tray and press it down to the 4 corners with your fingers to prepare the *randa* style. Push a design into the dough with 4 fingertips by making a border 1½ inches in from the edge of the tray and ½ inch deep. Press this border in all around the entire dough sheet.

Press an indentation in a straight line in 3 places the length of the tray from border to border, so that the design will consist of a border all around and three lines down the center of the flattened dough sheet. Let rise for 15 minutes.

4. Paint the top of the loaf completely and generously with the egg-yolk glaze. Bake on a rack in the center of a preheated 500° F. oven for 20 minutes. Remove the bread and turn out on a rack to cool.

5. To prepare the *parakh* style: Oil a round cake or pie tin 8 to 10 inches in diameter. Take the 3 dough pieces indicated in step 2 and push them down to the edges of the 3 round tins. Take the *parakh* (a hand puncture 3 inches in diameter made of several concentric rings of dull-tipped pins held together in a wood handle) and press it firmly into the center of the dough almost to the bottom to shape a rosette design. It also prevents the dough from rising high at the center.

In the absence of the *parakh*, make a design by puncturing the dough with the tines of a fork in a 3-inch-round circle, about 12 times. Paint the *parakh* generously with the egg glaze and bake in a 500° F. oven for 20 minutes (as for the *randa* style). Remove and cool.

Note that the *parakh* may also be made with a large dough ball equal in quantity to the *randa* loaf. Use a large round pan of 12 to 14 inches in diameter. In this case the rosette design is made 6 times, once in the center and 5 times in satellite rosettes around it. Bake as directed for all styles.

NOTE: My teacher indicated that only fresh yeast was used in Samarkand, that the dry yeast found in American supermarkets was unknown. But for our purposes, compressed or fresh yeast and dry yeast are interchangeable depending upon personal preference.

Uzbek proverb: "If your neighbor is hungry, you should not go to bed with a full stomach."

NONI TOKEE
Baked Crisp Flat Bread

A large, thin, rounded crispy sheet, seasoned with cuminseed and salt. This is an unusual bread that was baked in a tandoor in Bukhara but is quite possible to bake in a home oven. Here is how it is done.

4 cups flour
1 tablespoon ground cuminseed
2 teaspoons salt
about 1 cup water

1. Mix the flour, cuminseed and salt together. Make a well in the flour and stir in the water to prepare a moist but easily handled dough. Dust with flour, if sticky, to achieve this. Knead for 2 or 3 minutes. Shape the dough into a salami-shaped roll, cover with a plastic sheet or kitchen towel, and let rest for ½ hour.

2. Divide the dough into 8 pieces, about 2 ounces per piece.

3. On a well-floured board, knead each piece of dough for a few moments. Roll out each piece to a very thin round disc about 18 inches in diameter and ⅛ inch thick. Place this on a kitchen towel and dust with flour to prevent sticking to the next disc. Roll out all the dough pieces this way into thin sheets dusted with flour.

4. Remove all the racks except one from the oven. Place this rack in the center. Put a wok, round side up, on the rack and preheat oven to 400° F. for 15 minutes. Put 1 dough sheet over the top of the ungreased wok and bake for 2 minutes, which should be enough to brown one side of the sheet lightly. Do not turn it over but remove the sheet and add another to the wok.

The baked flat bread is crisp and can be eaten with both dairy or meat dishes. Makes 8 cumin-flavored rounds.

NONI SEYAW
Whole-Wheat Bread

This dark, firm bread has plenty of substance and suits the Central Asian taste. It is prepared in the *randa* style, using the simplest and most basic ingredients, and baked in a hot oven to develop the crust.

> 2 pounds whole-wheat flour (8 cups)
> 1 package (7 grams) dry yeast, or 20 grams fresh yeast
> 2½ cups warm water
> 2 teaspoons salt

1. Pour the flour into a large bowl and make a well in the center. Dissolve the yeast in 1 cup warm water. Pour it into the well with the salt and gradually incorporate the flour into the mixture. Add the balance of the water, 1½ cups, or enough to prepare a soft moist dough. Knead thoroughly for 5 minutes. Cover the bowl with a plastic wrap or put the dough into a plastic bag and set aside in a warm spot. (My teacher put the plastic dough bag on the sofa and covered it with a pillow!) This will take about 1 hour to double in size. Punch it down.

2. Oil a jelly-roll tray about 12 × 20 inches. Push the dough into the tray, spreading it out to the 4 corners, or in an oval shape if the tray is larger than needed. Push in the *randa* design with your fingertips as noted in the Bukhari Non recipe (see Index). Let rise again for ½ hour.

3. Bake on the center rack of a 500° F. oven for 20 minutes. Remove and cool.

BUKHARAN COMPOTE
Dried Fruit Compote

Bukhara is famous for the variety of fruits grown there and when the season is over the dried fruits are obtainable. Here is a compote to be served at any season. The dried peaches that I obtained from Samarkand were whole and dried with the stones. The raisins were of a delectable flavor and a dark royal blue quite unlike our own.

A chronicle relates that in the seventh century golden peaches were sent to the Chinese of the T'ang dynasty from the kingdom of Samarkand. Are they the same now? Did the trees thrive and become one of the common fruits of China? This writer hopes that the dried peaches recently received from Samarkand are ancestors of those sent to the T'ang emperor.

1 cup dried peaches
1 cup dried prunes
1 cup white raisins
1 cup dried apricots
1 cup dried apple slices
2 cups water
¼ cup sugar, or more to taste

1. Cover all the dried fruits together with water and soak overnight. The next day, add 2 cups water and bring to a boil over moderate heat. Cook for 15 minutes.

2. Add the sugar, reduce heat to low, and simmer for 15 minutes more, which is enough to soften the fruits and create a thickened dark syrup.

Refrigerate and serve cold. Especially useful to serve after dining on meat dishes. The compote is *pareve*.

Serves 6 to 8.

HAROSETH FOR PASSOVER

E very Jewish community has its own version of Haroseth, that indispensable ritual food for the Passover Seder table. Here is the Bukharan version.

1 cup walnuts
1 cup raisins
1 large apple, peeled and cored
½ cup red Passover wine

1. Grind everything together to mix thoroughly but leaving some texture. Do not grind too smoothly.

Makes about 3 cups.

LAWVES
Walnut Fudge

T his remarkable candy is a Bukharan specialty in a cuisine that does not have many sweets. It is prepared for holidays and ceremonial occasions.

3 cups sugar
3 cups water
½ teaspoon lemon juice
2 pounds shelled walnuts, ground not too fine but with some
    texture

1. Mix the sugar and water together in a pan and bring to a boil. Reduce heat to low and simmer for 1 hour to develop a thread when a spoon is lifted from the syrup. (This is the old-fashioned, traditional method of testing the readiness of the syrup. Today, we simmer until the soft-ball stage is reached or 234° to 240° F. on a candy thermometer.)

2. Add the lemon juice, let simmer for a few seconds, then add the walnuts, all except ¼ cup, which is reserved for a garnish. Stir quickly to mix.

3. Turn out the fudge mix immediately onto an oiled cookie tray. Moisten hands with cold water and press down the warm mixture into a round disc 1 inch thick and about 12 inches in diameter. The fudge will be quite warm and this must be done quickly and carefully. Sprinkle the reserved walnuts over the surface and press them down lightly.

4. While still warm, slice the fudge into 2-inch squares or diamond shapes. Cool well and store in a tin with a tight cover.

Makes about 35 pieces.

VARIATION: One pound of shelled pistachio nuts and 1 pound of walnuts ground together and mixed with the sugar syrup is an ever popular combination for the *lawves*.

NOTE: Lemon juice is added not for flavor but because it is a solvent that gives smoothness to the sugar syrup.

HALVA
Oriental Sesame Candy

It seems as though all the Oriental communities make one kind of halva or another. This type of halva will be familiar to Americans, who can buy it by the pound.

1 pound sesame seeds, plain (not toasted)
1 whole clove, broken up
⅛ teaspoon ground cinnamon
2 cups sugar
⅓ cup water

1. Grind the sesame seeds, clove and cinnamon to a paste in a processor.

2. Prepare a syrup with the sugar and water. Simmer over low heat for about 10 minutes. It is ready when you can draw a thin, candied hair by touching the syrup with a fork. Pour this syrup into the sesame paste and process until smooth.

Turn out into a heatproof glass tray or dish and press flat. Cool and cut into cubes.

Makes 1½ pounds.

CHAI CHAYMOKEE

Traditional Bukharan
Buttered Tea

Reminiscent of the buttered Tibetan tea, lightly salted, the preparation of Bukharan traditional tea reinforces my theory of the Chinese and Mongolian influence, subtle though it may be to Western eyes, on the cooking of Central Asia. *Chai*, of course, is tea and the word is used throughout Pakistan, India, Afghanistan and by the Bukharans.

½ cup water
1 tablespoon loose tea, or 1 teabag of black or green tea
½ teaspoon salt
1 teaspoon butter
¾ cup milk
1 tablespoon crushed walnuts (optional)

1. Boil the water and tea together in a pan for 3 or 4 minutes to extract a strong brew.

2. Add the salt, butter, milk, and walnuts if used. Heat over low heat for a few minutes. Stir several times.

Serve hot and strain into serving cups. Serves 2.

AFGHANISTAN

I went to Kabul in 1967 to search for Jews during my work project in Pakistan, but I was too late since they had left for Israel and other destinations. Next my search continued in Israel, and that, too, was a failure since a government official told me, "We have no record of Afghan Jews residing in Israel." After many other false starts, I was rewarded by finding a vital Afghan Jewess and an excellent cook in her tradition here in New York. The Afghanistan Jewish community was of ancient origin and consisted of about 5,000 members living there in 1948. But from then on emigration took its toll and by 1967 almost no one remained of the community.

Afghanistan commentators have traced certain Afghan non-Jewish tribes to Hebrew origins. Early Biblical commentators regarded Khorasan (Afghanistan) as the location of the Ten Lost Tribes. Afghan Jews are adamant in their conviction that the origin of certain Afghan Muslim tribes was Jewish and that the Ten Tribes ultimately disappeared into the autochthonous, or earliest aborigine, population.

Medieval and even earlier sources mention Jewish centers in the city of Ghazni, but my own visit there failed to reveal a community. Arab geographers also attested to Jewish settlements in Afghanistan, but Mongol invasions, epidemics and other tragic occurrences that have afflicted Jewish communities everywhere obliterated the evidence.

There are large gaps in the historical information regarding the Afghan Jews that jumps from one century to another. It was a small society isolated by ranges of mountains, confined to medieval status by the rulers of the country so that from the sixteenth to the nineteenth century there is a blank in the knowledge about them.

Then in the nineteenth century British travelers revealed

299

Bakery in the Old Town, Herat, Afghanistan, 1978. *(Photo © Bohumil "Bob" Krčil)*

that Jewish communities in Afghanistan were largely composed of Jews who came from Meshed in Persia and settled in Herat (the largest Afghan community) and in Balkh and Kabul. They were traders dealing in skins, carpets and antiquities. We must remember that Alexander the Great went to Afghanistan around 325 B.C. and from that visit originated the Gandhara style of Graeco-Buddhist art. (I have a Gandhara Buddha in my collection.)

Afghan Jews speak Tajiki, the Judeo-Persian dialect (not the Pushtu or Dari of the Muslims) and have produced fine religious poetry. Tajiki is also spoken by the Jews of Uzbekistan in Asiatic Russia, that is to say, Bukhara, Tashkent and Samarkand, just across the border from Afghanistan.

It is remarkable that the small and isolated community of Afghan Jews developed their own style of cooking. Kashruth and Jewish dietary practices were closely followed. A religious and simple if not primitive people, Jews clung to their religion as an identity and way of life distinct from their Muslim neighbors. The food they ate was their identification as Jews as well as their sustenance.

Afghan Jews combined the flavors brought from their Persian origins with those of Uzbekistan, north of the border, plus the cooking of the indigenous population. These components, homogenized, made the kebabs, noodle dishes, soups, meat and vegetable stews into honest, nutritious home cooking. The herbal seasonings do not have the extravagant variety of fresh herbs found in Persian cooking nor do the meat dishes contain sufficient hot chili and intense seasonings to compete with the Pakistanis south of the border.

Yoghurt is ubiquitous especially since dietary practices separate dairy foods from meat dishes. Bread is the principal food in the Afghan diet. Rice polo, luxuriously decorated with aromatic spices, raisins, almonds and lamb, are ceremonial foods served to enhance the prestige of the host. Lamb and poultry are the most populat meats for those who can afford it, remembering that meat is money and those with money dine on the most meat. Ground lamb in the form of a variety of kebabs and koftas were, in my opinion, developed in many ethnic cultures because the meat is tough and grinding resolves the problem. Then good taste takes over.

Now, nothing exists of the Afghan Jewish community, small to begin with, living a precarious existence in a hostile, primitive country. Yet, they developed their own customs within the framework of Judaic behavior and then moved on to another life elsewhere.

Only the food reminds them of their original homeland.

MATZO JOSHAWK
Passover Soup

Here is an everyday meat soup to be served with the inevitable homemade matzoh during the days of Passover.

¼ cup corn oil
2 large onions, chopped (1½ cups)
4 cups water
1 pound boneless beef or lamb, cut into 1-inch pieces,
    or 2 chicken legs and thighs with bone, halved.
1 medium potato, peeled, cut into 1-inch cubes
½ teaspoon salt, or to taste
¼ teaspoon pepper
1 egg, beaten

1. Heat the oil in a soup pan, add the onions, and stir-fry over moderate heat for 1 minute, just long enough to change the color. Add the water and bring to a boil. Add the meat or chicken pieces, potato, salt and pepper. Cover the pan and cook for 1 hour, or until tender.

2. Just before serving, dribble the egg in a circle into the simmering soup.

Serve hot with matzoh. Serves 6.

SHORBA YAVRON
Assorted Vegetable Soup

There are many occasions in Jewish cooking when a *pareve* or neutral soup is wanted for dairy occasions or for very hot days. This simple soup, full of flavor, is ideal for summer dining or for vegetarians any time.

    3 tablespoons corn oil
    2 large onions, chopped (1½ cups)
    ½ teaspoon salt, or to taste
    4 cups water
    2 medium potatoes, peeled, cut into 1-inch cubes
    2 large carrots, cut into ¼-inch cubes
    2 celery ribs with leaves, sliced
    ¼ teaspoon pepper
    ¼ teaspoon ground cinnamom
    1 egg, beaten
    2 tablespoons chopped fresh flat-leaf parsley

1. Heat the oil in a soup pan, add the onions and ¼ teaspoon salt, and stir-fry over moderate heat for 2 minutes. (My Afghan cook believes the salt will hasten the frying as the onions change color.) Add the water, potatoes, carrots, celery, remaining salt, pepper and cinnamon and bring to a boil.

2. Simmer the soup, covered, for 30 minutes. When ready to serve, dribble the egg into the pan of soup in a circular motion. Sprinkle with the parsley.

Serve hot. Serves 4 to 6.

CHELO NACHODO
Chicken and Chick-Pea Stew with Rice

Here is a family-style dish to be served any time of the year. It is a substantial soup stew, well seasoned in Afghan style and combined with a crisp-bottomed rice that provides contrasting texture to the stew. The stew and rice are served separately.

STEW

5 cups water
4 chicken legs and 4 thighs, loose skin discarded
1 cup dried chick-peas, soaked in water overnight, drained
2 medium onions, chopped (1 cup)
1 celery rib and leaves, sliced
1 large carrot, sliced diagonally
1 zucchini (½ pound), sliced
1 teaspoon salt, or to taste
¼ teaspoon pepper
¼ teaspoon ground cuminseed
¼ cup chopped fresh coriander
¼ cup chopped fresh dill
¼ cup lemon juice

RICE

4 cups water
1 teaspoon salt
2 cups raw rice, well rinsed
¼ cup corn oil

1. Prepare the stew. Bring the water to a boil, add the chicken pieces, and remove the foam as it cooks. Add the chick-peas, onions, celery, carrot, zucchini, salt, pepper and cuminseed. Cover the pan and cook over moderate heat for 45 minutes. Add the coriander, dill and lemon juice and simmer over low heat for 15 minutes more. This is sufficient to tenderize the chicken and integrate all the seasonings.

2. Bring the 4 cups water and the salt to a boil in a pan. Add the rice and cook over moderate heat for 5 minutes. Drain the rice in a colander and rinse with cold water. Return rice to the pan and pour the oil over all. Cover the pan and cook over low heat for ½ hour. No other water is added and the rice cooks only in the moisture that clings to it after rinsing. The rice will develop a crisp bottom layer.

Serve the rice and stew separately. Each diner takes his own portion of rice and covers it with as much stew as he wishes.

Serve warm. Serves 6.

VARIATION: Two pounds of boneless beef chuck cut into 6 equal pieces may be used in place of the chicken, but cooking it will take longer. Cook the beef stew over moderate heat for 1 hour. Add the coriander, dill and lemon juice, reduce heat to low, and simmer, covered, for ½ hour more, or until the beef is tender.

KOFTA NAKHOD
Meatballs and Chick-Peas

Chick-peas provide bulk in these well-seasoned *kofta*, the name for various types of meatballs in Afghanistan, Pakistan and India. Unlike the custom in other countries, they are boiled in soup or water and served separately from the soup. Chick-peas are one of the forbidden foods for Passover in Afghanistan, so the Kofta Nakhod must wait for another time.

    1 cup dried chick-peas, covered with hot water and soaked
        overnight, or at least 8 to 10 hours
    1½ pounds ground beef
    1 large onion, grated
    ¼ teaspoon pepper
    1 teaspoon salt, or to taste
    ¼ teaspoon ground cinnamon
    1 tablespoon crushed dried mint
    1 tablespoon bread crumbs, matzoh meal or plain flour
    4 cups boiling water

1. Drain the chick-peas in a colander, then grind them rather fine in a processor. Mix everything together except the water.

2. Prepare the meatballs. Moisten the hands with cold water and prepare meat and chick-pea balls 1½ inches in diameter. Put them into the boiling water, one at a time, and simmer over moderate heat for 45 minutes. Remember that the chick-peas are ground but uncooked.

The meatballs may also be cooked in a light chicken broth.

Serve the meatballs and soup separately with bread, rice and pickles. Serves 8. Makes about 18 balls.

POLO SHABATI
Pilau for the Sabbath

Afghans, like families in all other Jewish communities, serve their Sabbath day lunch about midday on their return from the synagogue. The food is baked very slowly from Friday evening before sundown until Saturday. Slow baking in a light oil bath creates potatoes and rice with a crisp bottom crust. Aromatically seasoned with cinnamon, raisins and pepper, the entire meal is cooked in one pan. As an alternate choice to meat, eggs in the shell may be added to the pan and baked, resulting in brown eggs with a delicious roasted flavor.

> 5 cups water with 1 tablespoon salt
> 2 pounds boneless beef chuck, cut into 3-inch pieces
> 3 cups raw rice, well rinsed
> 2 large potatoes, about ¾ pound, peeled, cut into ¼-inch-thick
>   slices
> ½ to 1 teaspoon pepper, to taste
> 1 tablespoon ground cinnamon
> ½ cup light or dark raisins, rinsed under cold water
> 1 cup hot water
> ½ cup corn oil

1. Bring the 5 cups water with salt to a boil in a pan, add the meat, and cook over moderate heat for 5 minutes. Remove the foam that rises during this time. Remove the meat from the liquid and set aside.

2. Add the rice to the same liquid and cook over moderate heat for 5 minutes. Drain the rice through a colander, rinse under cold water, and set aside.

3. Put the sliced potatoes on the bottom of the pan, arranged in an orderly fashion. Spread over this half of the rice and sprinkle with the pepper and cinnamon. Spread the raisins in the center of the rice. Add all the meat over this and the balance of the rice over all. Pour in the cup of hot water and dribble the oil over the surface and around the edges of the pan.

4. Cover the pan and cook over low heat for ½ hour. Reduce heat to very low and cook, tightly covered, for 5 hours to produce the crisp potatoes and rice.

Serve warm. Serves 6.

VARIATION: One hard-cooked egg for each person may be added to the rice and meat pan. Cook the eggs in water with ½ teaspoon salt for 5 minutes. Salt is added to prevent the egg shell breaking. Rinse the eggs in cold water and place them on top of the rice in the pan after adding the hot water and oil. Cover the pan and cook as directed.

NOTE: Rice is not a prohibited food and is eaten during Passover as well as the rest of the year. It is the Basmati rice, found in Pakistan and Afghanistan, and is cleaned by hand three times to remove broken kernels, dirt and other impurities. This, in a general way, prepares the rice for the holiday.

SHAHEE POLO
King's Rice

The extravagantly seasoned and adorned King's Rice is so-called because, according to Afghan Jews, it is fit for a king. It is a very expensive preparation, served only on ceremonial occasions such as Bar Mitzvahs, holidays and for special guests. It is not an everyday kind of rice. Nor is the lamb an ordinary baby lamb! The sheep most often seen in Middle Eastern or North African countries are a special breed (I call them the fat-tail sheep) with such a fat tail that it may drag on the ground. The tail is a prized source of cooking fat. (The lambs are usually fattened at home.)

> ½ cup corn oil
> 5 medium onions, chopped (4 cups)
> 4 pounds baby lamb, cut into 3-inch pieces, including bone
> 2 pounds carrots, cut into thin julienne slices 2 inchs long
> 1 cup dark or light raisins
> 1 cup shelled pistachio nuts (optional but recommended)
> 3 heads of garlic, cloves separated but not peeled, rinsed in water
> 4 cups raw rice, well rinsed
> 3½ cups warm water
> 2 teaspoons salt, or to taste
> 1 teaspoon pepper

1. Heat the oil in a pan large enough to contain all the ingredients. Add the onions and stir-fry over moderate heat for 2 minutes. Add the meat and brown for about 15 minutes. Remove the meat and onions to a platter or bowl. The balance of the oil will remain in the pan.

2. Cover the bottom of the pan with half of the carrots to protect the meat from scorching. Over this, arrange the meat and onions. Cover with the balance of the carrots. Sprinkle the raisins, pistachios and garlic cloves over all.

3. Add the rice to cover the other ingredients and carefully pour in the water, salt and pepper. Bring the liquid to a boil and simmer for about 10 minutes, or until the liquid is absorbed by the rice. Stir the top of the rice lightly to mix but do not disturb the other ingredients. Turn heat to low, cover the pan, and cook for about 1 hour without stirring.

Serve the *Polo* with salads, pickles and Afghan Bread (Noni Afghani, see Index).

Serves 10.

VARIATION: The *polo* can also be prepared with chicken and boneless beef chuck or ribs of beef. Stir-fry 15 pieces of chicken (legs, thighs and breast) or 4 pounds beef, with the onions as in the basic recipe; all other steps are the same. The beef will take longer to tenderize and it is suggested that it be cooked with the onions in a covered pan for 20 minutes before moving on to the next steps.

KEBAB MARINOVAT
Marinated Lamb Kebab

2 pounds boneless lamb steak, cut into 1-inch cubes
3 medium onions, quartered
1 teaspoon salt
1 teaspoon ground cuminseed
¼ teaspoon pepper
¼ cup Cognac or arak or dry red wine

1. Mix everything together and marinate for 1 to 1½ hours. This distributes the flavors and tenderizes the meat.

2. Put 4 pieces of lamb alternating with the onion quarters on each metal skewer. Broil over charcoal, the traditional method, for about 10 minutes, or to taste: rare, medium or well-done. In modern homes a gas or electric broiler will do very well.

Serve warm with other Afghan foods. Serves 6.

MURGH KEBAB
Chicken Kebab

Kebabs of all types, sizes and shapes are standard in Afghan cooking for both Jews and Muslims. They are easily assembled and probably the most basic recipe of all cooking, stretching back to the earliest, primitive times. I saw two workmen barbecuing their lamb kebabs over a few twigs in an open field, resting the skewers on a thick branch cut from a nearby tree, and turning them around every now and then. They then wrapped a piece of Afghan bread around the skewer and pulled off the crisp brown meat.

2 whole breasts of chicken, cut into 1-inch cubes
1 medium onion, sliced thick
1 tablespoon Cognac or arak
½ teaspoon pepper
½ teaspoon ground cinnamon
¼ teaspoon ground turmeric
1 teaspoon salt

1. Mix everything together and marinate at room temperature for a minimum of 1 hour or preferably in the refrigerator overnight.

2. Put 4 or 5 cubes of chicken, without the onion, on each metal skewer and broil over charcoal for 10 to 15 minutes or in a gas or electric broiler.

Serve hot with Afghan Bread (Noni Afghani, see Index), salad and pickles. Serves 4 or 5.

NOTE: My Afghan mentor related that turmeric was much used in Afghanistan in many ways and had a great reputation for its health-giving properties. It is reputed to cleanse the blood, and a little turmeric in one's morning milk would assure a day of good health.

POLONI

Miniature Pasta Squares with
Dairy Sauce

Tish-Ah B'Av and Shavuoth are two holidays when dairy foods are preeminent and meat dishes temporarily set aside. These pasta squares are covered with a well-seasoned, rich dairy sauce. *Poloni* would also be welcome during hot summer days when cooking meat would increase the temperature in the kitchen and eating it create a heaviness not conducive to comfort. Tish-Ah B'Av indicates that this fast day is celebrated on the ninth day of the month of Av. This tragic holiday commemorates the destruction of the First and Second Temples of Jerusalem.

PASTA

2 cups flour
1 egg, beaten
¼ teaspoon salt
½ cup water (about)

DAIRY SAUCE

½ cup cottage cheese
½ cup yoghurt
¼ teaspoon salt
2 garlic cloves, put through a press
1 teaspoon chopped fresh mint
1 tablespoon chopped fresh dill
4 to 5 cups water, lightly salted

1. Mix the flour, egg and salt and add just enough water to prepare a dough firm enough to be handled. Dust with flour to reach the desirable consistency. Put the dough ball into a plastic bag and let it rest at room temperatue for 1 hour.

2. Cut the dough into halves and roll each piece into a very thin pancake. (I do this with my hand-cranked pasta machine.) Then cut the pancakes into ½-inch squares. Set aside.

3. Mix sauce ingredients together and set aside.

4. Bring 4 to 5 cups lightly salted water to a boil in a large pan, drop in pasta, and cook over moderate heat for about 10 minutes, or until tender but still *al dente*. Drain well.

Serve the pasta and dairy sauce separately. Each diner fills his plate with the pasta and spoons over as much sauce as wanted.

Serves 6.

OSHI JOOR-RAWTEE
Rice and Mung Beans, Afghani

An odd combination but a popular one when planning dairy meals. Mung beans are those from which bean sprouts are grown. A similar dairy combination is prepared in Bukhara indicating, through a study of their food, the probable community connections.

1 cup mung beans
3½ cups water
1 cup raw rice, well rinsed
½ teaspoon salt, or to taste
1½ teaspoons ground cuminseed
¼ teaspoon pepper

1. Cook the beans in the water over moderate heat for ½ hour. As the green bean skins rise to the surface during the cooking process, they should be skimmed off with a slotted spoon or a small sieve and discarded.

2. Add the rice, salt, cuminseed and pepper and continue to simmer the mixture over low heat for ½ hour more. It should remain moist.

Serve warm with the same dairy sauce as is used with the Poloni (preceding recipe).

Serves 4 to 6.

OSH PYOZEE
Stuffed Onions

The Bukharan and Calcutta Jews stuff onions each with his own preferred and native seasonings. The Afghan has a stuffing sweetened with prunes and cooked slowly—quite different from the others. The Afghans believe that onions are effective for strengthening the teeth. I cannot dispute this, but the stuffed onions in that case will provide two reasons for preparation, the excellence of the flavor and as a health inducement.

ONIONS

> 2 large onions, about ¼ pound each, peeled
> 4 cups water
> 1 teaspoon salt

STUFFING

> ½ pound ground beef
> 3 tablespoons raw rice, rinsed, cooked until very soft, drained and mashed
> 1 teaspoon salt
> ¼ teaspoon pepper
> ¼ teaspoon ground cuminseed
> 10 medium pitted prunes, cut lengthwise into halves
> 2 tablespoons corn oil

1. Make a ½-inch-deep incision into the side of each onion. Bring the water and salt to a boil over moderate heat and drop in the onions. Cook for 2 minutes, turning them with a slotted spoon during that time. Remove the onions and peel off each layer until you reach the center. Set aside the onion layers and the centers.

2. Put the beef into a bowl with the rice, salt, pepper and cuminseed and mix well. Take 1 heaping teaspoon of the beef mixture and half of 1 prune. Stuff 1 cooked onion layer and roll it up. Do this with all of the stuffing and onion layers.

3. Oil a skillet and lay the stuffed onions and centers in it, cover, and cook over very low heat for 2 hours. The onions will become quite dark but not, of course, burned. This is top-of-the-stove cooking.

Another method is to put the stuffed onions into a baking dish, cover tightly, and bake in a 250° F. oven for 2 hours.

Serve warm. Serves 6 with other dishes.

N O T E : It is also possible to accelerate the cooking time. Add ½ cup water to the skillet and cook, covered, over moderate heat for 1 hour. All the liquid will evaporate and the onions will be browned.

MINIATURE POTATO CUTLETS

P otatoes are often the filler needed during Passover when bread is abolished for the holiday. These small "footballs" of simple but satisfying ingredients can be served during a meal, although I have also served them with drinks as appetizers.

6 potatoes, about 2 pounds
2 eggs, beaten
1 cup fine matzoh meal
1 teaspoon salt, or to taste
¼ teaspoon pepper
½ teaspoon ground cuminseed
½ cup corn oil

1. Cover the potatoes with water in a pan and cook them in their skins, covered, until tender. Cool and peel the potatoes and purée them in a processor. Add the eggs, matzoh meal, salt, pepper and cuminseed and mix well.

2. Prepare small football-shaped cutlets 1 inch long and ½ inch wide. Heat the oil in a skillet and brown the cutlets, a few at a time, over moderate heat. Drain them on paper towels.

Serve warm. Serves 6.

KARTOFF MUMULAY
Stuffed Potato Fritters

Passover is a time when the Afghan Jews must be inventive and thrifty in their cooking. In Afghanistan matzoh meal was prepared at home by pounding sheets of home-made matzoh, using a heavy brass mortar and pestle. In the United States, it is purchased in well-sealed cartons—but my Afghan cook assured me that nothing was lost in the transfer.

STUFFING

¼ cup corn oil
3 medium onions, chopped (1½ cups)
1 pound ground beef
1 teaspoon salt
½ teaspoon pepper

POTATO FRITTERS

3 pounds potatoes, cooked in their jackets until soft
1 egg, beaten
1 teaspoon salt, or to taste
½ teaspoon ground cinnamon
½ teaspoon pepper
1 cup matzoh meal
oil for panfrying

1. Heat the oil in a skillet and stir-fry the onions over moderate heat until golden. Add the beef, salt and pepper, and stir-fry until the mixture is dry and all the liquid has evaporated. Cool.

2. Peel the potatoes and mash them well. Mix together all the fritter ingredients to prepare the dough.

3. Shape ½ cup potato dough into a circle in the palm of your hand. Place 1 generous tablespoon of the stuffing in the center and fold dough over into a slightly flattened sausage shape 3 inches long, 1 inch wide and 1 inch thick. Panfry in oil over moderate heat until brown on both sides. Drain on paper towels and serve warm.

Makes about 25 fritters.

NOTE: Afghan Jews believe that if an egg has a strong aroma, beating it removes the odor. Was this aroma due to lack of refrigeration?

BONJAN SALAT
Spicy Eggplant Salad

The heat in this salad dressing can be increased or reduced to your own taste. My own inclination is to go for it, chili- and pepper-hot, since Afghan food has few highly spiced dishes and this is one that does stimulate the taste buds.

3 medium eggplants, about 1½ pounds in all
2½ teaspoons coarse (kosher) salt
¼ cup corn oil
1½ cups canned tomato sauce or equal amount of homemade
    (the practice in Afghanistan)
¼ teaspoon pepper
1 teaspoon hot red chili flakes, or minced fresh green or red chili
2 teaspoons ground cinnamon
1 tablespoon crushed dried mint

1. Slice the eggplants crosswise into 1½-inch-thick pieces. Sprinkle them with 2 teaspoons coarse salt and let stand for 15 minutes. Rinse eggplants under cold water, which removes the bitter taste, and dry well on a towel.
2. Heat the oil in a skillet and lightly brown eggplant slices over moderate heat for 3 minutes. Remove and put into a serving bowl or dish. Cool.
3. Put the tomato sauce, pepper, chili flakes, cinnamon, mint and ½ teaspoon salt, if wanted, in a pan. Simmer over low heat for 10 minutes, which is long enough to integrate the flavors. Pour this over the eggplant; refrigerate until ready to use. The salad can remain in the refrigerator for several days.
    Serve cold with Afghan food. Serves 8.

TURSHI BONJAN
Pickled Stuffed Eggplant

Small finger-size eggplants are best to use in this pickle, but the smallest Italian variety will do well. The pickle will keep preserved for several months but should be refrigerated after it matures and once it is served.

1 pound smallest eggplants, 8 to 10
4 cups water
1 head of garlic, peeled, about 8 cloves
¼ cup dried mint
2 to 3 tablespoons hot red chili flakes, to taste
1 tablespoon ground cinnamon
1 tablespoon salt
1 to 2 cups white or red vinegar

1. Remove the stem from each eggplant and make 2 cuts down crosswise, to within 1 inch of the bottom. Bring 4 cups water to a boil, add the eggplants, and cook over moderate heat for 5 minutes. Drain and cool in a colander for ½ hour. Set aside.

2. Grind the garlic, mint, chili flakes, cinnamon and salt together to a medium but not too fine consistency. There should be some texture. Push apart the 4 prongs of each eggplant and stuff with 1 teaspoon of the spice mixture. Fit the eggplants into a glass jar and pour in enough vinegar to cover them. If there is any leftover spice mix, put that into the jar with the eggplants.

Let the pickle mature for 5 days before serving, then refrigerate.

SAMOOSI YIRAKOT
Stuffed Vegetable Turnovers

Passover is a time when the ingenuity of the Jewish cook is stretched to the limit to provide dishes to replace bread and at the same time denote a celebration. Several cultures of the Middle East make samoosi (sometimes called samoosas or sumboosuck), turnovers that are stuffed with vegetables, meat or cheese, providing possibilities for pareve, meat or dairy occasions.

DOUGH

1 cup fine matzoh meal
1 egg, beaten
¼ teaspoon salt
½ cup cold water, about

VEGETABLES

1 tablespoon corn oil
1 medium onion, chopped (½ cup)
1 garlic clove, chopped
1 potato, peeled, chopped or cut into very small pieces (½ cup)
½ cup chopped cauliflower
1 carrot, chopped (½ cup)
½ cup green peas, fresh or frozen
½ cup thin-sliced green beans
¼ teaspoon salt
¼ teaspoon pepper
1 cup corn oil, for deep-frying

1. Mix the meal, egg and salt together, adding just enough water to make a moist dough that holds together. Set aside.

2. Heat the oil in a skillet, add the onion and garlic, and stir-fry over moderate heat until light brown, about 3 minutes. Set aside.

3. Take the potato and ½ cup each of any other 3 vegetables and blanch in boiling water for 5 minutes. Drain well. Add these to the pan with the onion and garlic and stir-fry over moderate heat for 3 minutes, to mix well. Add salt and pepper. Cool.

4. Take 1 heaping tablespoon of the dough and press it out on a flat surface into a 2½-inch square. Put 1 tablespoon of the vegetable mixture on the bottom half of the square and fold it over into a triangle. Prepare all the *samoosi* this way.

5. Heat the oil in a wok or skillet and brown the turnovers over moderate heat for about 3 minutes. Drain on paper towels.

Or, you may bake the turnovers on an oiled baking sheet, in a 350° F. oven for 20 minutes, or until brown. In this case, the turnovers are brushed with 1 beaten egg mixed with 1 tablespoon water, before baking.

Serve warm. Makes about 20 turnovers.

BICHAK
Stuffed Baked Tricorners

Bichak are the popular appetizers for the tea or coffee hour. The pumpkin and jam stuffings are on the sweet side while the meat and cheese are savory and could be eaten for lunches with a salad and a dish of yoghurt. An added attraction is that they may be prepared in large quantities, cooled and frozen for the future.

DOUGH

> 1½ cups warm water, about
> 1 teaspoon sugar
> 1 package dry yeast (¼ ounce, 7 grams)
> 3½ cups flour
> 3 tablespoons corn oil
> 1 egg, separated

STUFFINGS:

SQUASH, CALABASA OR PUMPKIN

> ¼ cup corn oil
> 3 medium onions, chopped (2 cups)
> 1 cup hot water
> ¼ teaspoon salt
> 2 tablespoons sugar
> 1 pound butternut squash, calabasa or pumpkin, peeled and cut
>   into ½-inch pieces

Heat the oil in a pan, add the onions, and sauté over moderate heat until the onions turn golden. Add the water, salt, sugar and pumpkin and bring to a boil. Cover the pan and cook over low heat for about 20 minutes as the pumpkin becomes soft and disintegrates. Stir now and then, which in effect mashes the contents. Continue the last minutes of cooking, uncovered, to evaporate all the liquid and create a thick jam. The mash is still moist. Cool.

MEAT

> 2 tablespoons corn oil
> 3 medium onions, chopped (2 cups)
> 1 pound ground beef or lamb
> ½ teaspoon salt, or to taste
> ¼ teaspoon pepper

Heat the oil in a skillet and brown the onions lightly over moderate heat. Add the meat, salt and pepper and stir-fry for 5 minutes, making certain the liquid has evaporated and the mixture is dry. Cool.

CHEESE

> 1 pound farmer cheese
> 1 egg yolk, beaten
> 3 tablespoons sugar
> ½ teaspoon ground cinnamon

Mix everything together. Set aside.

JAM

> 1 cup strawberry or grape jam or prune jam (lekach)
> 2 tablespoons bread crumbs

Mix the jam and crumbs together. Set aside.

PREPARE THE TRICORNERS

> 1 egg yolk, beaten with ½ teaspoon corn oil

1. Mix ½ cup water, the sugar and yeast together and proof in a warm place until the mixture foams, about 10 minutes.

2. Make a well in the flour, add the yeast mixture, oil and 1 egg white, and stir them into the flour. Add the balance of the water, or enough to prepare a soft dough. Knead for several minutes and roll into a ball. Oil the top lightly and leave the dough in the mixing bowl. Cover with foil or a towel and let rise for 45 minutes to 1 hour.

3. Punch down the dough ball. Pull off about ½ cup of the dough and roll into a slightly flattened ball. Prepare 6 balls.

4. On a well-floured board roll out each ball, one at a time, to a 12-inch pancake. Using an empty can or cookie cutter 3 inches in diameter, cut out circles in the pancake. Put 1 tablespoon of whatever stuffing you are using, or a variety of stuffings, in the center of the circle. Fold over the right and left side of the circle to meet in the center and bring up the bottom to cover the stuffing. Pinch the ends together to form a tricorner pastry. Seal in the contents. Paint the tops of the bichak with the egg yolk.

5. Line a baking pan or cookie sheet with lightly oiled aluminum foil. Place the tricorners on the foil and bake in a preheated 350° F. oven for about 40 minutes, or until brown.

Serve warm. Makes 48 to 50 bichak.

N O T E : Cool the bichak, store in plastic bags, and freeze. To serve, thaw out the frozen bichak for ½ hour and heat in a 350° F. oven for 5 to 10 minutes.

MATZOH

The Afghan community prepared the matzoh for Passover in their homes. Muslim growers (my Afghani cook spoke of them as "a good people"!) provided clean wheat kernels from their farms. The rabbi and people of the Jewish community cleaned the stone wheat grinder as part of the Passover ritual and the flour was ground. Each family takes the quantity of flour they will require to their homes. The dough is prepared, with flour and water only, and the round matzoh are baked in a tandoor.

Jewish ladies go from one home to another (with their faces covered in the street, a Muslim custom) helping each other to prepare the Seders. The neighbors congregate in the home of one family and cook as well as celebrate the Seders together.

It is a coincidence that I saw these matzoh being baked in a tandoor in Calcutta by the Baghdadi Jewish ladies preparing for their traditional Seder.

NONI AFGHANI
Afghan Bread

These small oval breads are baked in a tandoor, the stove of the region—sometimes buried in the ground as it is in India. The Afghan oven is above ground and is of rounded bricks, which are heated. Matzoh and the *noni* are shaped and slapped and stuck on the hot bricks for fast baking.

1½ cups warm water
1 package dry yeast (7 grams)
1 tablespoon sugar
4 cups flour
1 teaspoon salt
¼ cup corn oil
1 egg yolk mixed with 1 tablespoon water
1 tablespoon black cuminseeds (see Glossary) or caraway

1. Mix ½ cup warm water, the yeast and sugar together and let it proof for about 10 minutes. When the froth appears, sprinkle ½ teaspoon flour on top and let it continue to proof for 5 minutes more. The froth will rise quickly.

2. Put the flour in a large mixing bowl and sprinkle the salt over it. Make a well in the middle of the flour and add the oil and the yeast mixture. Stir this in and add small amounts of water until you have produced a soft, moist dough that can be handled. Knead well for 5 minutes. Put the dough ball back into the bowl, cover with a towel, and let rise for 1½ hours. Punch down the dough.

3. Divide the dough into 8 equal parts and roll each part into a ball. Roll each ball out into an oval shape 6 to 7 inches long and ½ inch thick. Draw the tines of a fork in 3 lines along the length of each *noni* for a decorative design. Paint each *noni* with the egg mix and sprinkle over all ½ teaspoon black cuminseeds. (This is the traditional seed to use, but caraway seeds may be substituted if the black cuminseed is unobtainable.)

Put the *noni* on an ungreased cookie sheet and bake in a preheated 350° F. oven for 20 to 25 minutes. The brown top will glisten.

Makes 8 *noni*.

HAROSETH
Haroseth, Afghani Style

This recipe is enough for 10 persons, who will use it at the Seders and lather it on the homemade matzoh.

> 1 cup shelled almonds, coarsely ground
> 1 cup shelled walnuts, coarsely ground
> 1 cup black raisins, coarsely ground
> 2 apples, peeled, coarsely chopped
> 2 ripe bananas, coarsely chopped (optional)
> 2 cups red wine

1. Mix everything together and serve at the Seders.

India

CALCUTTA
BOMBAY
COCHIN

THE JEWS OF INDIA

India is an Asian Earth Mother of great cultural and culinary diversity. Harbored among its millions for many centuries were three unusual Jewish communities, located in different regions of the country. I refer to the Baghdadi Jews of Calcutta; the Bene Israel of Bombay on the Konkan peninsula, and the so-called Black Jews of Cochin in southwest India. These three groups developed their cuisines within the framework of Judaic laws in an essentially Sephardic system, independently of each other.

In early times, there was little knowledge of the existence of the Bene Israel and the Jews of Cochin throughout the rest of the world. Only later, during the eighteenth century, after the Jews of Bombay and Calcutta became established in their communities, was the word out that there were other Jews somewhere in India—isolated and even racially different but indisputably Jewish.

Now all the communities have dwindled through emigration to Israel and to countries in the West.

It may be that only through their style of cookery, unique to each community, can the separate identities of the communities be retained.

CALCUTTA—THE BAGHDADI

JEWS
A remarkable Jewish community considered their home to be Calcutta from the seventeenth through the twentieth century. They are the Baghdadi Jews, a community that was essentially transplanted from Baghdad, Iraq, the home of the Babylonian Jews. By about 1800, the Jews had established a vibrant community in Calcutta. Within the vast sea of humanity that made up this city on the Hoogly River, they maintained their Judaic identity.

Calcutta, that always mysterious and sometimes sinister city, was a most unlikely spot to find the Jews. It was here that stupefying heat lay like a blanket over the city, that diseases endemic to the region (bubonic plague, typhoid, typhus, cholera and other abominations) proliferated, and overpowering all was the Hindu mystique. Yet, the Jews prospered! This was at the time that Rudyard Kipling wrote about Calcutta: "Where the cholera, the cyclone, and the Crow come and go."

In about 1800, the universal pull of trade started the movement from Baghdad, in trickles then in concert, to Calcutta. From then on, all the establishments of a Jewish community were organized there: educational, cultural and civic—from schools to synagogues and the cemetery.

The Jews brought with them from Baghdad their preferences such as *hameen*, combinations with vegetables and meat, and the famous *koobe* (stuffed dumpling). What they discovered in India was an almost entirely new group of spices and herbs that the local population were using, such as turmeric, cuminseed, coriander, hot chili, fenugreek (*hilbeh*), cardamom, mustard seed and fresh ginger. In addition, tropical vegetables of the pumpkin family; *loobia*, the long bean; the coconut; bitter melon; and many more growing in the luxurious soil and tropical climate. These were incorporated

325

Interior of the Maghen David Synagogue in Calcutta, India. The author is at right, holding one of the antique torah scrolls.

into their dishes from the "old country" and the gradual evolution of a new style of cooking began.

I was fortunate to have worked in Calcutta during the mid-twentieth century when there was still a substantial number of the Baghdadi Jews living there. By the time I arrived, the Calcutta Jews had their own cuisine firmly stabilized and familiar to the entire community. Some recipes were completely new inventions, while others were Jewish by adoption but came from Baghdad to India. What gave it continuity was its use of the Judaic rules of "kashruth" and its identity with their way of life in a new home.

An estimate of the size of the Jewish population during the twentieth century was about 6,000 souls, a number that has now dwindled to 50 or less at the time of writing this book. Most have left for England, Australia and the United States.

Some families on the new continents still cling to these popular Jewish dishes that are relatively easy to prepare. But, alas, the twentieth century has taken its toll. More modern members of the Calcutta community have altered their eating habits and no longer cook Baghdadi food.

Let's hope the recipes in this volume will remind Indian Jews of their origins, and then nostalgia impel them to revive this marvelous cuisine.

MARAG
Spiced Chicken Soup with Vegetables

The *marag* is more than a soup and not quite a stew. It is a complete light meal in the Calcutta style to serve when heavier food is not wanted. It may include as many vegetables as you wish.

1 medium onion, chopped (½ cup)
¼ teaspoon minced fresh ginger

1 garlic clove, chopped fine
¼ teaspoon ground turmeric
1 teaspoon salt, or to taste
4 cups water
1 chicken, 3 pounds, cut into 8 serving pieces, loose skin and fat
    discarded
½ cup chopped ripe tomato, fresh or canned
1 cup 1-inch pieces of cauliflower
½ cup 1-inch pieces of green beans, or ½ cup green peas
1 carrot, sliced thin
1 medium potato, cut into ½-inch cubes
2 tablespoons chopped fresh coriander

1. Cook the onion, ginger, garlic, turmeric, salt, water and chicken in a covered large pan over moderate heat for 25 minutes.

2. Add the tomato, cauliflower, green beans, carrot and potato, and simmer over low heat for 20 minutes, or until chicken and vegetables are tender. Sprinkle with the coriander and cook for 5 minutes more. Total cooking time is about 45 minutes.

Serve warm with white rice. Serves 6.

BEETROOT KHUTA
Sweet-and-Sour Beef and Beets

This is my favorite Calcutta stew. The grand flavor of the khuta depends on an assortment of natural seasonings instead of a variety of spices, as in a curry.

2 tablespoons corn or peanut oil
1 small onion, chopped (¼ cup)
½ teaspoon chopped fresh ginger
1 garlic clove, put through a press
½ teaspoon thin-sliced fresh hot red chili
1 pound boneless beef chuck, cut in 1-inch cubes
1½ cups water
½ cup chopped ripe tomato, fresh or canned
1 cup sliced cooked beets with ¾ cup reserved liquid from fresh
    or canned beets
1 tablespoon lemon juice

1 tablespoon brown sugar
½ cup fresh mint, chopped
½ teaspoon salt or to taste

1. Heat the oil in a pan and brown the onion over moderate heat for 2 minutes. Add the ginger, garlic and chili and stir-fry for 2 minutes more. Add the beef and water, bring to a boil, cover the pan, and cook for 45 minutes.

2. Add the tomato, beets and beet liquid. Add lemon juice and brown sugar and continue to cook over low heat for 20 minutes, or until beef is tender and the sauce has thickened a little

3. Finally, add the mint, stir well, and simmer for 5 minutes more. Add salt to taste.

Serve warm with rice. Serves 6 with other dishes.

VARIATION: One pound lamb cubes, or one 3-pound chicken, cut into serving pieces, with loose skin and fat discarded, are popular substitutes for the beef. A 4½-pound duck and its giblets may also be cooked in this way. American ducks are fat and so must be well trimmed.

SHOOFTA
Ground Meat Barbecue

Beef is the most popular of the *shoofta* that frequently turn up as an adjunct to a traditional meal, along with dishes that have sauce and rice. *Shoofta* may also be broiled on metal skewers over charcoal or baked in an oiled dish, at 350° F. for 15 to 20 minutes.

1 pound ground beef, lamb or chicken
1 tablespoon chopped fresh coriander
1 medium onion, chopped (½ cup)
½ teaspoon chopped fresh ginger
1 garlic clove, chopped fine
½ teaspoon chopped fresh hot chili
½ teaspoon salt
½ teaspoon ground turmeric
3 tablespoons corn oil

1. Mix the meat, coriander, onion, ginger, garlic, chili, salt and turmeric together well. Use 2 tablespoons of the mixture to shape a cylinder 3 inches long and 1 inch thick. Shape all the mixture in this way.

2. Heat the oil in a skillet and over moderate heat fry the *shooftas* for 3 minutes for medium rare or 2 minutes more for well done.

Serve warm as an appetizer with drinks, or with other dishes for lunch or dinner.

Makes 10 *shooftas*.

GADJAR MURGHI MEETHA
Chicken and Carrot Stew

Another Calcutta classic, a popular, rather sweet combination of chicken and carrots.

> 2 cups shredded carrots
> 2 tablespoons plus 2 teaspoons corn or peanut oil
> 1 garlic clove, put through a press
> 1 teaspoon minced fresh ginger
> 1 medium onion, sliced (½ cup)
> ¼ teaspoon ground turmeric
> 1 teaspoon salt, or to taste
> ⅛ teaspoon pepper
> 1 chicken, 3 pounds, cut into serving pieces, giblets included,
>   loose skin and fat discarded
> 1½ cups water
> 2 bay leaves
> 4 cardamom pods
> 3 tablespoons lemon juice
> 1 tablespoon brown sugar

1. Stir-fry the carrots in 2 teaspoons oil in a skillet over moderate heat for 3 minutes. Remove and set aside.

2. Heat 2 tablespoons oil in a large pan over moderate heat. Add the garlic, ginger, onion, turmeric, salt and pepper. Stir-fry for 2 minutes. Add the chicken and brown the pieces for 3 minutes.

3. Add the water, bay leaves and cardamom pods, bring to a boil, and cover the pan. Cook the chicken until nearly tender, about 25 minutes. Add the carrots, lemon juice and brown sugar. Stir the mixture and continue to cook over low heat for 20 minutes more to combine the flavorings and almost completely evaporate the liquid. This stew is moist but does not have a sauce.

Serve warm. Serves 6 with other dishes such as rice, salads, chutneys.

MURGI CUTLET
Calcutta Chicken Cutlets

These popular Jewish cutlets can be eaten warm or cold, at home or on picnics. Garlic, ginger, turmeric are common seasonings in the cuisine and using them to marinate the chicken produces a fine flavor in a relatively bland meat. Boneless chicken thighs may also be prepared this way.

1 medium onion, sliced (½ cup)
2 teaspoons chopped fresh ginger
2 garlic cloves, sliced
½ teaspoon ground turmeric
½ teaspoon salt
¼ teaspoon pepper
2 whole chicken breasts, halved (4 pieces), skinned and boned
¼ cup flour
2 eggs, beaten
1 cup dried bread crumbs
½ cup corn or peanut oil

1. Process the onion, ginger, garlic, turmeric, salt and pepper to a purée. Marinate the chicken pieces in the mixture for 2 to 3 hours.

2. Dip the breasts into the flour, then into the eggs, then into the bread crumbs.

3. Heat the oil in a skillet and fry the cutlets over moderately low heat for about 4 minutes on each side. The cutlets should cook slowly. Drain briefly on paper towels.

Serve warm. Serves 4.

MUKMURA
Chicken and Almonds in a Lemon Sauce

Mukmura was the first recipe I learned from a Jewish family in Calcutta, and to this day it remains one of my favorites. It is easy to prepare and characteristic of the style of cooking with all ingredients easily available to the American cook.

> 1 chicken, 3 pounds, cut into serving pieces, loose skin and fat discarded
> 1 garlic clove, chopped fine
> 1 teaspoon minced fresh ginger
> 1 medium onion, chopped fine (½ cup)
> ¼ teaspoon ground turmeric
> 1 teaspoon salt, or to taste
> 1 tablespoon raisins, light or dark
> 12 almonds, blanched in boiling water, skinned and halved lengthwise
> 1½ cups water
> 3 tablespoons lemon juice, or to taste

1. Put all the ingredients except the lemon juice into a pan. Bring to a boil over moderate heat, cover, and cook for 20 minutes.

2. Uncover the pan, tilt it slightly and briskly stir the sauce with a wooden spoon to break up the onion pieces. Continue to cook for 15 minutes. Add the lemon juice and cook for 10 minutes more, or until chicken is tender and the sauce has thickened.

Serve warm. Serves 6 with rice and other dishes.

ALOO-M-KALLA MURGI
Pot-Roast Chicken

This aromatic chicken and Golden Deep-Fried Potatoes (Aloo-M-Kalla, see Index) are traditionally served together at the Friday evening dinner. The ritual is part of the Calcutta communities' folklore and one which I experienced many times during my residence there. I now often serve the chicken without the potatoes but with an assortment of Calcutta Jewish dishes, including salads and chutneys.

    1 tablespoon corn or peanut oil
    1 chicken, 3 pounds, cut into frying pieces, including giblets,
        loose skin and fat discarded
    1 medium onion, quartered
    ½-inch fresh ginger, sliced
    1 garlic clove, chopped fine
    ¼ teaspoon ground turmeric
    1 teaspoon salt, or to taste
    ⅛ teaspoon pepper
    3 whole cloves
    1 cinnamon stick (1 inch), broken up
    2 bay leaves
    3 cardamom pods, cracked
    1 cup water

1. Put the oil in a pan or large skillet. Place the chicken pieces in the oil, preferably in a single layer. Brown over moderate heat for 5 minutes.

2. In a bowl, mix the onion, ginger, garlic, turmeric, salt, pepper, cloves, cinnamon, bay leaves, cardamom and water together. Pour this over the chicken. Cover the pan and simmer over low heat for 20 minutes.

3. Turn the chicken pieces over and cook, covered, for 20 minutes more, until almost all the liquid evaporates and the chicken browns a bit more.

Serve warm. Serves 6 with the Golden Deep-Fried Potatoes (Aloo-M-Kalla, see Index).

HARI KABOB
Spiced Chicken and Potatoes

    12 small potatoes, about 2 pounds, peeled
    3 cups water
    1 teaspoon salt
    1 teaspoon minced fresh ginger

1 garlic clove, put through a press
½ teaspoon ground turmeric
1 teaspoon chopped fresh hot red chili
1 chicken, 3 pounds, cut into 8 serving pieces, loose skin and fat
    discarded
½ teaspoon garam masala (see Glossary)
2 bay leaves
2 cardamom pods, cracked
¼ cup corn or peanut oil

1. Soak the potatoes in the water and salt for 1 hour. Add the ginger, garlic, turmeric and chili to the potatoes, and bring to a boil over moderate heat. Cook for 15 minutes, or until potatoes are nearly soft but still firm.

2. Remove potatoes and set aside. Add the chicken to the spice broth with the garam masala, bay leaves and cardamom and cook, covered, over moderate heat for 15 minutes.

3. Meanwhile, heat the oil in a wok or skillet and brown the potatoes over moderate heat until they have formed a crisp coating. Remove them from the oil and add to the chicken pan. Continue to cook everything until both chicken and potatoes are done, about 20 minutes. Remove the cover during this process so that all the liquid evaporates. This is a dry curry.

Serve warm with rice, salad and chutneys. Serves 6

BAMIA KHUTA
Sweet-and-Sour Chicken and Okra

S weet-and-sour fla-vors are characteristic of many of the Calcutta Jewish dishes. Okra is a popular vegetable much in demand throughout India and especially flavorful in this dish.

1 chicken, 3 pounds, cut into 8 pieces, loose skin and fat
    discarded
2 medium onions, sliced (1 cup)
1 teaspoon minced fresh ginger
1 garlic clove, put through a press
1 teaspoon salt, or to taste

½ teaspoon ground turmeric
2 cups water
½ pound fresh okra
2 tablespoons corn or peanut oil
½ cup chopped ripe tomato, fresh or canned
2 tablespoons tamarind paste, soaked in ½ cup water for ½ hour
1 small whole red chili (optional)
1 teaspoon sugar
2 tablespoons chopped fresh mint

1. Put the chicken, onion, ginger, garlic, salt, turmeric and water into a pan. Bring to a boil over moderate heat and simmer, covered, over low heat for 30 minutes.

2. In the meantime, trim the stem ends of the okra and cut a 1-inch slit into the side of each pod. Heat the oil in a skillet and stir-fry the okra over moderate heat for 3 minutes. Remove and set aside.

3. Add the tomato to the chicken and stir firmly to help reduce the sauce to a thick paste. Rub the tamarind paste and water with your fingers, and strain the liquid through a metal sieve. Discard seeds and pulp; add the liquid to the chicken. Add the okra, chili and sugar and simmer over low heat for 10 minutes. Add the mint. Adjust the sugar to balance the sweet-sour flavor.

Serve warm. Serves 6 with rice and other dishes.

BHUNA HAAS
Baked Stuffed Duck

In the tropical climate of Calcutta, with water everywhere and the countryside well stocked with wild greens, ducks are plentiful. Therefore in most of the recipes here that call for chicken, it would be well within the tradition to use duck, if that is your preference (as it is mine). This baked stuffed duck is Jewish and Indian at the same time.

1 small potato, peeled and diced
1 small carrot, peeled and diced
¼ pound green beans, diced

½ cup fresh or frozen green peas
1 duck liver, sliced thin
½ teaspoon garam masala (see Glossary)
½ inch of fresh gingerroot, chopped fine
1 garlic clove, chopped
¼ teaspoon ground turmeric
1 teaspoon salt, or to taste
1 duck, 4½ pounds, loose skin and fat discarded

1. Cook the potato, carrot and green beans in water for 2 minutes. Drain and set aside.

2. Mix together the cooked vegetables and all the other ingredients except the duck to make the stuffing. Stuff the duck and sew up the opening. Prick the duck all over with a fork to allow the fat to cook out.

3. Put the duck in a roasting pan with no exterior seasoning and roast, uncovered, in a 350° F. oven for about 2 hours, basting now and then. Pour off the accumulated fat every half hour. When the duck has become tender, increase the oven heat to 400° F. for 15 minutes to complete the roasting and crisp brown the skin.

Slice and disjoint the duck and serve warm with stuffing.

Serves 6 with other dishes.

AROOK
Chicken and Rice Ball

Arook can be made a day or two in advance of a celebration. The balls can be frozen but should be thawed at room temperature for 1 hour, then warmed in a 375° F. oven for 10 minutes before serving.

½ cup raw rice
2 cups water
2 teaspoons salt
½ pound boneless chicken, chopped fine
¼ teaspoon ground turmeric
½ teaspoon minced fresh ginger
1 garlic clove, chopped fine
¼ teaspoon garam masala

1 tablespoon chopped fresh coriander or celery leaves
1 egg, beaten
2 tablespoons plus 2 teaspoons corn or peanut oil

1. Rinse the rice well. Bring 2 cups water to a boil with 1 teaspoon salt, add the rice, and cook over moderate heat for 5 minutes. Drain the rice and set aside.

2. Mix the rice with chicken, the remaining teaspoon of salt, the turmeric, ginger, garlic, *garam masala*, coriander, egg and 2 teaspoons oil.

3. With moist hands, scoop up 2 tablespoons of the chicken mixture and shape it into a ball about 2½ inches in diameter. Place the rice balls in a baking dish coated with 2 tablespoons oil. Bake in a 375° F. oven for about 30 minutes, or until the balls have turned light brown. Do not turn them.

Serve warm. Makes 8 balls.

BOONA KALEGI
Fried Chicken Liver

I have had these chicken livers threaded on a skewer and grilled over charcoal until brown and sizzling. If you prefer that method of cooking, simply marinate as directed, then put 4 or 5 lobes on individual metal skewers and grill.

1 pound fresh chicken livers, divided into lobes
½ teaspoon minced fresh ginger
1 garlic clove, chopped fine
½ teaspoon salt, or to taste
½ teaspoon garam masala
3 tablespoons corn or peanut oil

1. Mix everything together except the oil and let stand for 15 minutes.

2. Heat the oil in a wok or skillet and add the liver mixture. Stir-fry over moderate heat for about 4 minutes, or until the livers are cooked through but not overdone.

Serve warm. Serves 4.

ANJULI
Fish Salad with Coconut Milk

Anjuli is an unusual sort of salad that is sometimes mixed with coconut milk and lemon juice and served over hot rice. I prefer it served more conventionally as a salad.

3 tablespoons corn or peanut oil
1 pound fillet of flounder, sole, haddock or similar fish, cut into
    2-inch cubes
1 pound small eggplants (about 3), cut into ¼-inch-thick slices
2 cups rich coconut milk
¼ cup lemon juice, or to taste
1 teaspoon salt
1 teaspoon thin-sliced fresh hot green chili
1 medium potato, cooked in its skin until soft, peeled, cut into
    ½-inch cubes
2 small onions, sliced very thin (½ cup)
4 scallions, cut into ¼-inch-thick slices

1. Heat the oil in a skillet and brown the fish cubes over moderate heat for 5 minutes. Remove with a slotted spoon and set aside.

2. Fry the eggplant slices, covered, in the same oil until soft, about 3 minutes; drain on paper towels.

3. Put the coconut milk into a serving bowl with the lemon juice, salt and chili. Mix well. Add the other ingredients by layers, starting first with the potato cubes, then the onion rings, scallions, fish cubes and the eggplant on top.

Chill briefly in the refrigerator or serve at room temperature.

Serves 4 to 6.

MUCHLI KA KARI
Fish Curry

Fish is the cheapest and most easily available food in Bengal, the Indian state of which Calcutta is the capital. This is a traditional fish curry eaten by all of the communities.

2 or 3 medium onions, chopped (2 cups)
¼ cup corn oil

½ inch of fresh gingerroot, chopped fine or crushed
3 garlic cloves, chopped fine or crushed
1 teaspoon, or more to taste, minced fresh hot red chili
1 teaspoon salt
½ teaspoon ground turmeric
1 cup chopped ripe tomatoes
½ cup water
1½ pounds whole fish—sea bass, red snapper, flounder
2 bay leaves

1. Fry the onions in the oil in a pan over moderate heat until the color is golden. Add the ginger, garlic, chili, salt and turmeric. Stir-fry the mixture for about 5 minutes to develop a thick paste.

2. Add the tomatoes and water and continue to stir the mixture briskly.

3. Cut the fish into 1-inch-wide slices, including head, and add to the curry with the bay leaves. Cover the pan and cook over low heat for 15 minutes. The curry will have a thick, ample sauce.

Serve warm. Serves 6 with white rice and chutney.

MUGAZ
Brain Curry

1 pound brain of beef, veal or lamb
2 tablespoons corn or peanut oil
1 small onion, ground to a paste (¼ cup)
½ teaspoon minced fresh ginger
1 garlic clove, chopped fine
1 teaspoon ground coriander
½ teaspoon ground cuminseed
1 teaspoon minced fresh hot red chili
¼ teaspoon ground turmeric
½ teaspoon salt, or to taste
¼ cup chopped ripe tomato, fresh or canned

1. Soak the brain in cold water for ½ hour. Drain and remove the loose membranes.

2. Heat the oil in a skillet or saucepan and stir-fry the onion over low heat for 2 minutes. Add the ginger, garlic, coriander, cuminseed, chili, turmeric and salt. Continue to stir-fry until the mixture becomes red/brown, about 4 minutes. Add the tomato and continue to cook.

3. Add the whole brain and cook, covered, for 10 minutes. Turn the brain over and cook until the curry is dry, about 5 minutes more. Remove the pan from the heat. Cut the brain into generous portions while still in the pan.

Serve warm with rice, salad, chutney.

Serves 4 or 5 with other dishes.

BHAJI
Curried Vegetables

A bhaji may be prepared with any number of vegetables depending upon availability in the bazaar or supermarket and personal preference. Most bhajis start with potatoes and then other vegetables are added such as cauliflower, loobia (Chinese long beans), green beans (called French beans in Calcutta), eggplant and several kinds of squash. The vegetables are cut into pieces and fried with the local flavorings.

Flavorings such as onion, gingerroot and garlic are intensified by adding fresh or dried hot chili, turmeric, cardamom (one of the most expensive of all spices) and tomato for color.

Bhajis supplement meat, fish and rice dishes, but can stand alone for the vegetarian purist.

1 medium onion, sliced thin
2 tablespoons corn oil
1 teaspoon minced gingerroot
1 garlic clove, chopped fine
½ teaspoon minced fresh hot chili, green or red
½ teaspoon ground turmeric
1 teaspoon salt, or to taste
2 whole cardamom pods
1 pound small potatoes, peeled, cut into ½-inch cubes
1 cup water
2 cups 1-inch cauliflowerets
1 cup 1-inch pieces of green beans
½ cup chopped ripe tomato

1. Fry the onion in the oil in a large enough pan over moderate heat for 3 minutes until it begins to turn brown. Add the ginger, garlic, chili, turmeric, salt and cardamom. Stir-fry for 2 minutes.

2. Add the potatoes and water and cook over moderate to low heat for 15 minutes to soften the potatoes. Add the cauliflower, beans and tomato. Stir a bit, cover the pan, and cook until all or most of the liquid has evaporated and the vegetables are soft. *Bhaji* is a dry curry.

Serve warm. Serves 6.

PILAU MATABAK
Old-Fashioned Rice Mix

This is a real Jewish rice, cooked by the Orthodox Jews of Calcutta. It is a complete meal of fish, rice, potatoes and onions, artfully combined and seasoned. Any gala occasion would be a good time to serve this pilau.

POTATOES

4 small potatoes, cut into ¼-inch-thick slices
1 cup sliced onions (about 2)
¼ teaspoon ground turmeric
½ teaspoon salt
1 tablespoon corn or peanut oil
½ cup water

RICE

1 tablespoon corn or peanut oil
2 cups raw rice, rinsed and well drained
¼ teaspoon ground turmeric
¼ teaspoon salt
½ teaspoon garam masala
3 cups water

FISH

½ pound fillet of sole, flounder or similar fish, cut into 2-inch
    cubes
¼ teaspoon salt
¼ teaspoon ground turmeric
1 tablespoon corn or peanut oil

1. Mix the potatoes, onions, turmeric and salt together.

2. Put 1 tablespoon oil in a pan, place the onions on the bottom of the pan, and cover them with the potato slices. Fry the mixture slowly over low heat for 5 minutes. Do not stir. Add the water, cover the pan, and continue to steam/fry for 15 minutes, or until the water has been completely absorbed. Set aside.

3. Heat 1 tablespoon oil in a pan, add the rice, and brown lightly over moderate heat for 2 minutes. Add the turmeric, salt and *garam masala* during the process. Add the water, stir the mixture, bring to a boil, cover, and turn heat to low. Cook for 10 minutes. Set aside.

4. Rub the fish with salt and turmeric. Heat remaining oil in a skillet and lightly fry the fish over moderate heat for 2 minutes. Remove fish and spread the cubes over the potatoes and onions in that pan. Cover completely with the rice. Cover the pan and cook the pilau slowly over low heat for 15 minutes. This may also be done in a 350° F. oven for 20 minutes.

Serve warm. Serves 6 to 8 with other dishes.

PILAU
Spiced Rice with Green Peas

This is a standard preparation of pilau for the Sabbath evening dinner or any other time. Any kind of long-grain rice may be used although the aromatic Basmati rice is traditional.

1 teaspoon whole cuminseeds
2 tablespoons corn or peanut oil
¼ cup chopped onion
2 cups Basmati rice, well rinsed, soaked in water for ½ hour, drained
¼ teaspoon ground turmeric
½ teaspoon salt, or to taste
1 cup green peas, fresh or frozen
1 cardamom pod
1 whole clove
1 cinnamon stick (1 inch)
3¼ cups water, or more if needed

1. Toast the cuminseeds in a dry skillet over low heat for 2 minutes. Set aside.

2. Heat the oil in a pan and fry the onion over moderate heat for 2 minutes, or until it turns golden. Add the rice and stir well. Add the turmeric, salt and cuminseeds and continue to stir-fry for 2 minutes.

3. Add the peas, cardamom and cinnamon; stir well and add the water. Bring to a boil, turn heat to low, cover the pan, and cook for 12 to 15 minutes. Stir once toward the end of that time. If the rice appears too firm, add another tablespoon or two of water. Cook for another minute, turn off the heat, and allow the rice to rest in the covered pan for 15 minutes before dining.

Serve warm. The rice may be lightly reheated just before dining. Serves 6.

BRINJAL MAHASHA
Stuffed Eggplant and Other Vegetables

Mahashas prepared from an assortment of vegetables were a common sight on Calcutta tables. They were then and are now one of my favorite Asian dishes for buffet dining with large groups of people.

½ pound ground beef or chicken
1 cup raw rice, well rinsed, soaked in water for ½ hour, drained
½ teaspoon ground turmeric
¼ cup chopped mint leaves
1 teaspoon minced fresh gingerroot
1 garlic clove, put through a press
1 teaspoon salt, or to taste
2 tablespoons tamarind paste
¾ cup water
2 teaspoons brown sugar
6 small eggplants (about 2 pounds)
1 tablespoon corn or peanut oil

1. Mix the beef, rice, turmeric, mint, ginger, garlic and salt together. Set aside.

2. Soak the tamarind in the water for ½ hour, stirring with your fingers until it dissolves. Strain the liquid through a metal sieve and mix in the brown sugar. Reserve. Discard tamarind pulp and seeds.

3. Roll the eggplants back and forth several times to soften the inside pulp. Cut off the top of each one ½ inch below the stem and save the top. Scoop out and discard the interior pulp, leaving a firm shell about ¼ inch thick.

4. Fill the eggplants about ¾ full of stuffing and fit the stem end back into the opening. Rub the oil on the bottom of a pan; fit the stuffed eggplants into it. Cover the pan and fry over moderate heat for 5 minutes. Do not turn them.

5. Pour the tamarind and sugar mixture over the eggplants. Cover the pan and cook over low heat without turning the eggplant for about 40 minutes, which is enough to cook the stuffing. Should the liquid evaporate too quickly, add ¼ cup water. The *mahashas* are dry and do not have a sauce.

Serve warm. Serves 6 with other Calcutta dishes.

VARIATIONS: Several vegetables are also traditional and lend themselves to stuffing.

TOMATO

Use 6 medium tomatoes, ripe but still firm. Cut off the top about ½ inch below the stem. Scoop out and discard the pulp but leave a firm wall about ¼ inch thick. Stuff the tomatoes with the stuffing described, replace the tops, and cook in the same manner.

RED OR GREEN SWEET PEPPERS

Use 6 medium peppers. Cut out the stem in a circle. Scoop out and discard the seeds and ribs. Fill the peppers with the stuffing, push the stem top back into place, and cook the same as the other vegetables.

ONION

The onion requires a more intricate method of preparation but is an extraordinary production. Use a large Spanish onion, peeled. Cut a 1-inch-deep incision into the onion from the stem to the root end. Drop the entire onion in a pan of boiling water for 1 minute. Remove it with a slotted spoon and carefully peel off the first layer. Do this as many times as you can, about 8, until you reach the center core.

Chop the onion core and add it to the rice/beef mixture. Stuff each onion layer with 1 heaping tablespoon of the mixture and fold the 2 ends around to an egg shape. Put them in the oiled pan and continue as for the other vegetables.

CUCUMBER

Select 6 to 8 Kirby or other young cucumbers. Do not peel them. Cut off one end and scoop out as much of the center pulp as possible leaving a firm wall. Stuff and cook the cucumbers like the other vegetables.

MAHMOOSA
Scrambled Egg and Potato Fry

There are several variations of this popular breakfast or lunch melange. Every cook seems to have special kitchen tricks that result in great enthusiasm for it at table. The potato and egg combination is perhaps the most popular although the spinach/egg and the eggplant/egg combinations have many admirers. In any event, this idea of small vegetable cubes, lightly seasoned and cooked with eggs, is a Calcutta winner.

¼ cup corn or peanut oil
1 large onion, chopped (¾ cup)
1 teaspoon ground turmeric
1 pound potatoes (about 4), peeled, cut into ¼-inch cubes
4 eggs, beaten
½ teaspoon salt, or to taste
¼ teaspoon pepper, or more to taste
10 fresh coriander leaves for garnish

1. Heat the oil in a large skillet, add the onion, and stir-fry over moderate heat until golden. Add the turmeric, stir in for 1 minute, then add the potato cubes and stir continuously for 5 minutes to brown them. Cover the pan for 1 minute to ensure the potatoes are softened, and uncover.
2. Push the potatoes to one edge of the pan. Pour the eggs into the open space and let them set for ½ minute. Then incorporate the potatoes into the eggs, add salt and pepper, and scramble the mixture over *low* heat for another 5 minutes so that both potatoes and eggs are light brown.
Serve warm, garnished with the coriander leaves. Serves 6.

VARIATIONS:

CHICKEN

¼ cup corn or peanut oil
1 medium onion, chopped (½ cup)
1 teaspoon ground turmeric
1 pound potatoes, peeled, cut into ¼-inch cubes
1 cup ¼-inch cubes of cooked chicken
4 eggs, beaten
½ teaspoon salt, or to taste
¼ teaspoon pepper
10 fresh coriander leaves for garnish.

1. Heat the oil in a large skillet and prepare the onion, turmeric, potatoes as in the basic recipe, then stir in the chicken. Complete the recipe as described.

NOTE: Chicken *Mahmoosa* is usually made with leftover chicken that has been either roasted or boiled.

SPINACH

¼ cup corn or peanut oil
1 medium onion, chopped (½ cup)
½ teaspoon ground turmeric
½ pound fresh spinach leaves, well rinsed, coarsely chopped
4 eggs, beaten
½ teaspoon salt, or to taste
¼ teaspoon pepper
10 fresh coriander leaves for garnish

1. Heat the oil in a large skillet, add the onion, and stir-fry until golden, about 2 minutes. Add the turmeric and fry for ½ minute. Add the spinach and stir-fry over low heat for 5 minutes to wilt it.
2. Push the mixture to one side, add the eggs, salt and pepper, and continue as in the basic recipe to completion, with garnish.

EGGPLANT

¼ cup corn or peanut oil
1 medium onion, chopped (½ cup)
½ teaspoon ground turmeric

1 eggplant (½ pound), ends trimmed and cut into ½-inch cubes
4 eggs, beaten
½ teaspoon salt, or to taste
¼ teaspoon pepper
10 fresh coriander leaves for garnish

1. Heat the oil in a large skillet and continue the steps as out-lined in the basic recipe. It is suggested that the eggplant should be stir-fried over low heat for 5 minutes, then the skillet covered for 5 minutes more to steam through the mixture. Uncover, add the eggs, and continue to completion.

ALOO-M-KALLA
Golden Deep-Fried Potatoes

Calcutta cooks have their own method of preparing the perfect potatoes. Their reputation is at stake. The potatoes are served with the Pot-Roast Chicken (Aloo-M-Kalla, see Index) and are consid-ered one dish. However, each can be prepared separately for a different menu.

4 pounds firm small potatoes, about 24
2 teaspoons salt
½ teaspoon ground turmeric
4 cups corn or peanut oil for deep-frying

1. Peel the whole potatoes evenly. Put enough water to cover the potatoes into a large saucepan. Bring the water to a boil with the salt and turmeric. Add the potatoes, and cook over moderate heat for 5 minutes. Drain and cool. Take a sharp metal prong or toothpick and poke 3 or 4 holes into the potatoes about ½ inch deep.
2. Arrange the potatoes in a large flat pot or wok. Cover them (or almost) with the oil and bring this to a boil over moderate heat. Then immediately turn heat to low. Simmer/fry for about 45 min-utes or more, until the potatoes have formed a golden crust. Shake the pan several times during this process to ensure that the frying is uniform.
3. Turn up the heat and crisp-brown the potatoes for 5 minutes. Remove them with a slotted spoon and drain in a metal sieve or basket.

Serve immediately. The potatoes should have a crisp, firm exterior and a soft, melting interior. Serves 8 with the Pot-Roast Chicken and other dishes.

SALATA
Cucumber Salad

The large supermarket cucumbers should be peeled and seeded before slicing since they contain much water and seeds. They do not compare with young cucumbers or those that are sold in Calcutta's central market, the New Market. The salad may be prepared one day in advance of serving to allow it to develop a pickled intensity.

1 pound young Kirby cucumbers, not peeled
2 teaspoons salt
½ cup cider or malt vinegar
2 teaspoons sugar
½ inch of fresh ginger root, chopped fine
1 garlic clove, put through a press
2 tablespoons chopped mint
3 scallions, sliced thin
½ teaspoon chopped fresh hot chili (optional)

1. Slice the cucumbers thin and toss them with the salt. Let stand for 20 minutes. Put them in a kitchen towel and squeeze firmly; considerable water will be released.

2. Bring the vinegar and sugar just to a boil. Cool for a few minutes, then pour it over the cucumbers. Add the ginger, garlic, mint, scallions and chili. Mix well and refrigerate.

Serve cold with any kind of Indian food. Serves 6 to 8.

BRINJAL BHURTA
Smoked Eggplant Salad

This smoke-flavored salad can also double as an appetizer with toast, crackers or pappadums.

> 1 pound eggplants (about 2)
> ¼ cup grated onion
> ½ teaspoon minced fresh hot chili
> ½ teaspoon salt, or to taste
> 1 teaspoon corn or peanut oil
> 1 tablespoon lemon juice.

1. Broil the eggplants in an oven broiler or over charcoal for about 15 minutes, turning them for even cooking. Test for tenderness. Let the eggplants rest in the broiler with the heat off for 10 minutes more to complete the cooking. Remove and cool. Peel off the skin and discard the liquid that accumulates. Chop the pulp into small pieces by hand, not in a processor.

2. Mix the eggplant pulp with the onion, chili, salt, oil and lemon juice. Whip well with a fork to mix. Refrigerate.

Serve cool or at room temperature. Serves 4.

SAMBUSAK
Cheese Turnovers

It seemed that almost the entire community of Calcutta knew how to make the cheese *sambusak*, the most popular of all the tea and coffee snacks. The cheese was the handmade plaited cheese, preserved in a lightly salted brine. Several families made the cheese for sale; it was not usually prepared in individual homes. The same cheese, called string cheese, is available in New York in Middle East groceries and many supermarkets.

The turnovers freeze well but should be thawed out at room temperature for 1 hour before serving, or you may reheat them in the oven, 350° F. for 10 minutes.

PASTRY

> 2 cups flour
> ¼ teaspoon salt
> ¼ teaspoon sugar
> 1 teaspoon baking powder
> 3 ounces margarine or butter, sliced
> about ½ cup cold water

CHEESE FILLING

> 4 ounces Cheddar, kashkaval or mozzarella
> 4 ounces feta cheese
> 1 large egg
> ¼ teaspoon pepper

1. Mix the flour, salt, sugar and baking powder together. Add the margarine or butter and cut it into the flour, then rub it into the flour with your fingers. Add the water, a little bit at a time, mixing to create a moist, workable dough. Knead it for 2 minutes, wrap in plastic paper, and refrigerate for 1 hour or more until ready to use.

2. Grate the cheeses together in a processor, add the egg and pepper, and mix to a smooth consistency but not overly so. Refrigerate for 1 or more hours until ready to use.

3. When ready to bake the turnovers, divide the dough into walnut-size pieces; roll each into a round ball. Then roll out into a 4-inch pancake. Put 1 heaping teaspoon of cheese filling on the bottom half, moisten the bottom edge with a little water, and fold the top edge over to make a half-moon shape. Press the edges firmly with the tines of a fork. Put the turnovers on an ungreased cookie sheet and bake in a 375° F. oven for ½ hour, or until light brown.

Serve warm or at room temperature. Makes 20.

HALBA (HILBEH)
Fenugreek Chutney

This unique chutney, known as Jewish paste, has a slightly bitter and viscous consistency but nevertheless an appealing taste. It may be refrigerated for 2 or 3 days and used when wanted with any kind of Indian food.

2 tablespoons ground fenugreek
2¼ cups cold water
¼ cup chopped fresh coriander
1 teaspoon minced fresh ginger
1 garlic clove
3 tablespoons lemon juice
½ teaspoon salt, or to taste

1. Mix the fenugreek and 1 cup water. Let the mixture stand for 15 minutes. The water will rise to the top. Pour it off carefully, add another cup of water, and let stand for another 15 minutes and again pour off.

2. Process the coriander, ginger, garlic, lemon juice and salt together. Add this purée to the fenugreek with ¼ cup water; mix well. The fenugreek will swell to several times its original bulk and become firm. Add a few teaspoons cold water, should this happen and mix to dilute the thickness.

Serve with any kind of Indian food.

Makes ½ cup.

PUDEENA
Sweet-and-Sour Mint Chutney

1 tablespoon tamarind paste
¼ cup water
1 cup loose fresh mint leaves, no stems
1 cup fresh coriander leaves, no stems
1 teaspoon chopped fresh gingerroot
1 garlic clove, sliced
½ teaspoon sugar
¼ teaspoon salt
1 teaspoon sliced fresh hot chili, green or red

1. Soak the tamarind in the water for ½ hour. Mix it together with your fingers, strain, reserve the liquid, and discard the pulp and seeds.

2. Place all the ingredients including the tamarind liquid in a processor and process to a smooth paste. Refrigerate this green chutney.

Serve at room temperature. Makes about 1 cup.

Oil press in the village of Cheul in the Konkan, India. Oil pressing was the main occupation of the Konkan Jews until the 19th century, but today this is the only family still doing so in the village. *(Photo by Carmel Berkson)*

BENE ISRAEL—THE JEWS OF BOMBAY

The western coast of India, influenced by the monsoons and bathed in the warm waters of the Arabian Sea, is home to the Bene Israel, a unique Jewish community.

The Bene Israel claim their ancestors left Galilee (Palestine) in 175 B.C. Their ship was wrecked in the Indian Ocean. Seven men and seven women were cast ashore on the Konkan peninsula, a spit of land south of what is now Bombay—and survived. Isolated for centuries, their descendants adopted the customs, names, dress and foods of their Hindu neighbors. Their language then and now is Marathi.

They were oil pressers and agriculturalists in their villages. Their presence and origins were not known to the outside world and for many years they apparently remained unaware of other groups of Jews in India. But by the middle of the eighteenth century they had contact with the Cochin Jews in the southwest and the Baghdadis who had come from Iraq and settled in Bombay.

All during their history, starting with the shipwreck, they clung to some fundamentals of Jewish tradition: the dietary laws, the Sabbath and holidays such as Rosh Hashanah, Yom Kippur and Simhat Torah among others.

Another theory of their origin is that they were an offshoot of the Yemenites, and we know they had been in touch with Jewish settlements in Yemen. The Yemenites themselves have documented the information that their men were familiar with the Jews of India (Bene Israel and Cochin) and traveled there to obtain Jewish wives.

Bombay, the Indian metropolis in western India, was acquired by the British East India Company in 1661 and was a magnet for trade. The Bene Israel moved from their villages in

353

the Konkan region and established a permanent Jewish settlement in Bombay about 1750. It was at that time that they were able to return to traditional Judaism and fill in the gaps lost in their isolation. In addition to established educational and cultural institutions, they erected six synagogues.

In 1947, at the height of the community's existence in Bombay, there were about 24,000 souls. Reduced to about 13,000 in 1969, the population has now declined to a small fraction of that number due to their emigration to Israel and England.

The cookery is characterized by the cooking of the Maharashtra people around them, the use of spices, the system of assembling the curries, the dietary laws and customs of the original shipwrecked Bene Israel, who adopted the world around them and fitted it into a Judaic mold.

Coconut milk, hot chili, cardamom, cinnamon, turmeric, ginger, cumin, coriander and garam masala are standard flavorings that are a hallmark of the cooking. They are, in fact, India's.

Preparing for Passover, condiments are freshly ground in a general house cleaning. Matzoh is baked for prayer rather than as a substitute for bread. Rice is not forbidden as it is in the Ashkenazi tradition. Familiar Judaic rituals and activities are no different from those of other Jewish communities of India. One year I celebrated Passover with a family who were reading the Haggadah translated into Marathi while others at the Seder table read passages in Hebrew and English.

Now the Bene Israel are dispersed to many lands; the aroma of spices cooking in a Bombay home is only a memory of a now vanished world.

PEJH
Rice Porridge for Breakfast

This very plain cereal is served for breakfast on Passover. My teacher pointed out that she did not really like it as a child since she could not have sugar during Passover—it was not considered kosher. A type of plump rice, known as Rangoon, was used to prepare the porridge in those days.

> 1 cup raw rice, well rinsed
> 1 teaspoon margarine
> 1 cup milk or coconut milk
> about 2 cups water
> pinch of salt

1. Brown the rice in the margarine over low heat for 2 minutes. Add the milk, bring to a boil, then add ½ cup water at a time, as the mixture thickens and develops into a cereal. Continue to cook over low heat for about ½ hour, stirring now and then. Make certain that the rice is tender and that the cereal has the consistency of a loose gruel.

Serve warm for breakfast on Passover. Serves 2 or 3.

COCONUT CURRY SOUP

This delicious soup could be, according to American tastes, served as a first course like any other soup. But there is something in the hand of the Bene Israel housewife that pulls me to dine traditionally and have the soup with the curries and rice. It is a lubricant when dining.

Cocum (see Glossary), the dried mangosteen skin, was the original flavoring, providing the unique pungent flavor (see Glossary). Tamarind or lemon juice are the legitimate substitutes, with my preference for the first.

> 2 cups coconut milk, canned or prepared from ½ fresh coconut
> 1 teaspoon Basic Green Masala (see Index)

½ teaspoon ground cuminseed
¼ teaspoon ground turmeric
½ teaspoon salt
4 cocum, or 1 tablespoon tamarind liquid or lemon juice
1 tablespoon cornstarch or fine rice flour, dissolved in 3
      tablespoons cold coconut milk or water

Mix everything together except the tamarind liquid (or sub-stitute). Simmer over low heat, stirring continuously, until the soup comes to a boil, about 10 minutes. Add the tamarind liquid and cornstarch and bring to a boil again. Do not cover the pan.

Serve warm with Bene Israel foods. The soup is eaten along with the other foods.

ALBARAS
Baked Layered Beef

The *albaras* is easily assembled and has all the virtues of well-seasoned Indian food. It makes an ideal family-style dish. When quantities are doubled, it becomes the star at a buffet party, when the air is warm and appetites vigorous.

2 pounds boneless beef chuck, cut into pieces 3 inches long and
    ½ inch thick
1 tablespoon Basic Green Masala (see Index)
1 teaspoon garam masala
1 teaspoon Dry Masala for Meat (see Index)
3 medium onions, sliced (1½ cups)
3 ripe tomatoes, sliced, or an equal amount canned
1 tablespoon cider vinegar
2 cups green peas, fresh or frozen

1. Combine the beef with the three *masalas*, mix well, and marinate in a covered dish at room temperature for 2 to 4 hours.

2. Using a well-oiled oven casserole, put half of the onions on the bottom, cover with half of the tomatoes and half of the beef. Repeat the onion, tomato and meat. Sprinkle all the vinegar over this mixture.

3. Bake, covered, in a 350° F. oven for 1½ to 2 hours, or long enough to tenderize the meat and produce a rich, thick sauce. For the last 10 minutes of the baking add the green peas.

Serve hot. Serves 6 with rice.

VARIATION: Two pounds of shoulder lamb chops, well trimmed of fat, are a substitute for the beef. Follow the same steps and timing.

CHICKEN ROAST

Here again the Bene Israel use their own combinations of spices and seasonings, which differ from the communities around them. This dry roast is full of flavor, which the potato also absorbs.

3 tablespoons corn or peanut oil
1 pound onions, chopped (about 2½ cups)
1 tablespoon minced fresh gingerroot
2 teaspoons garam masala
½ teaspoon ground turmeric
2 teaspoons salt, or to taste
2 chickens, each 3 pounds, and giblets, cut into 10 pieces each, loose skin and fat discarded
1 pound small potatoes (about 6), peeled, halved
1 tablespoon Dry Masala for Meat (see Index)
½ cup water

1. Heat the oil in a pan and stir-fry the onions over moderate heat until light brown, about 6 minutes. Add the ginger, garam masala, turmeric and salt and stir-fry for 2 minutes.

2. Add the chickens and giblets, cover the pan, and cook over low heat for ½ hour. Add the potatoes, Dry Masala and water. Mix, cover the pan, and cook for 20 minutes more, which should be sufficient to tenderize the chicken and potatoes. The dry roast, as it is called, has little or no sauce.

Serve warm. Serves 8 with other dishes.

CURRIED CHICKEN

The seasonings in this curry are not timid, but they do reveal the particular hand of the Bene Israel community. You may care to reduce the *masalas* somewhat (by 25%) when you first try it but it is meant to be quite intense. Some like it hot!

3 tablespoons corn or peanut oil
2 medium onions, chopped (1 cup)
1 pound ripe tomatoes, chopped, or an equal amount canned
    (3 cups)
1 tablespoon Basic Green Masala (see Index)
1 teaspoon garam masala
1 teaspoon Dry Masala for Meat (see Index)
½ teaspoon minced fresh gingerroot
½ teaspoon ground turmeric
1 teaspoon salt, or to taste
1 chicken, 3½ pounds, cut into 10 pieces, plus the giblets, loose
    skin and fat discarded
½ cup water
2 medium potatoes (½ pound), peeled, cut into 1-inch cubes

1. Heat the oil in a pan and stir-fry the onions over moderate heat until brown—dark but not charred. Add the tomatoes and stir briskly for 2 minutes; cover the pan and cook for 10 minutes.

2. Add the Basic Green Masala, *garam masala*, Dry Masala, ginger, turmeric and salt. Cook for 5 minutes, stirring constantly.

3. Add the chicken and water, cover, and cook over low heat until approaching tenderness, ½ hour. Should the sauce evaporate too quickly, add another ½ cup water. Add the potatoes and simmer until the chicken and potatoes are tender, another 15 minutes.

Serve warm. Serves 6 with other dishes.

VARIATION: Either beef or lamb may be used in place of the chicken. Use 2 pounds of boneless beef chuck or lamb and follow the same steps as for chicken. The meat will take longer to tenderize and so one should add 1½ cups water and cook for ½ hour longer.

CHICKEN WITH FRESH SPICES

A spicy curry does not necessarily mean that the amount of incendiary chili is the paramount seasoning. The Bene Israel use garlic, ginger, cardamom, clove, cinnamon and turmeric to produce the intensity. Coconut milk also is important to mellow and blend the whole.

3 tablespoons corn oil
3 medium onions, sliced thin (1½ cups)
3 garlic cloves, put through a press
1 inch of fresh gingerroot, grated
3 or 4 fresh hot red chilies to taste, seeded but whole
2 cardamom pods
2 whole cloves
2 peppercorns
1 cinnamon stick (1 inch)
1 teaspoon salt, or to taste
2 ripe tomatoes, sliced thin, or an equal amount canned (1 cup)
¼ teaspoon ground turmeric
1 chicken, 3 pounds, cut into 8 serving pieces, loose skin and fat
    discarded
¼ cup chopped fresh coriander
3 cups coconut milk
juice of 1 lemon, 2 to 3 tablespoons

1. Heat the oil in a pan, add the onions, and stir-fry over moderate heat until they are golden brown. Add the garlic, ginger, chilies, cardamom, cloves, peppercorns, cinnamon and salt. Continue to stir-fry for 3 minutes more. Add the tomatoes and turmeric and mix well for 2 minutes.

2. Add the chicken and fresh coriander and stir for 3 minutes until the chicken changes color. Pour in the coconut milk and bring to a boil. Reduce heat to low, cover the pan, and simmer for 40 minutes, stirring occasionally, until the chicken is tender and the sauce has thickened. Stir in the lemon juice.

This curry does have ample sauce.

Serve hot with rice, salad and cooked vegetables. Serves 6.

KANGI
Fish Curry

This delicious curry has many flavors locked up in the *masalas*. This modern recipe of a classic uses tomato paste in the sauce. The old, traditional method is described in the Variation.

2 tablespoons corn oil
¼ cup tomato paste
1 tablespoon Basic Green Masala (see Index)
2 teaspoons Dry Masala for Fish (see Index)
¼ teaspoon ground turmeric
½ teaspoon salt
½ teaspoon ground cuminseed
¾ cup water
2 pounds whole fish—sea bass, porgy, red snapper—cut into 2-inch thick slices
2 tablespoons lemon juice or tamarind liquid

1. Heat the oil in a skillet, add the tomato paste, and stir-fry over moderate heat for 1 minute.

2. Add the Green Masala, Masala for Fish, turmeric, salt and cuminseed and stir-fry for 2 minutes. Add the water and fish. Turn the fish slices over to coat them with the sauce. Cover the skillet and reduce heat to low.

3. Add the lemon juice or tamarind and simmer for 15 minutes. Turn the fish pieces over once during this time.

Serve warm with rice or chapatti. Serves 6.

VARIATION: The old-style fish curry omits tomato and water. In its place, add 1 cup of coconut milk, canned or homemade. Bring to a boil, add the fish slices and lemon juice or tamarind liquid or *cocum* (see Glossary). Use the same *masalas* and timing.

FISH MOLEE

Fish *molee* can be as chili-hot as you wish but the chili should not completely obliterate the taste of the fish. One should take this into account when adding fresh green chili.

3 tablespoons corn oil
1 medium onion, sliced thin (½ cup)
1 inch of fresh gingerroot, chopped fine
2 garlic cloves, chopped fine
¼ teaspoon ground turmeric
1 teaspoon ground cuminseed
1 teaspoon salt, or to taste
1 small ripe tomato, sliced thin (¼ cup), or an equal amount
    canned
1 pound saltwater fish such as porgy, red snapper, sea bass, with
    the bone, cut into 1-inch-thick slices
4 to 6 small hot green chilies, to taste, seeds removed through a
    cut in the side
3 pieces of cocum (optional) (see Glossary)
2 cups thick coconut milk
1 tablespoon lemon juice, or 2 tablespoons if cocum is not
    available

1. Heat the oil in a pan, add the onion, and stir-fry over moderate heat for 3 minutes. Add the ginger and garlic and stir-fry for 2 minutes. Add the turmeric, cuminseed and salt and stir briskly.
2. Add the tomato and continue stir-frying for 2 minutes. Add the fish slices and the chilies and *cocum*, turning the fish in the sauce. Add the coconut milk, bring to a boil, and simmer for 15 minutes more, which is enough to cook the fish. Baste now and then. Sprinkle the lemon juice over all.
Serve hot with rice and side dishes of vegetables.
Serves 4 to 6 with other dishes.

GREEN MANGO SALAD

T art green mangoes are popular in India as well as in several other cultures where mangoes are grown, such as Mexico and Guatemala. Mango is often eaten chilled with a pinch of salt.

    1 medium green mango, peeled, cut and chopped coarsely
    2 young Kirby cucumbers, peeled, seeded and chopped
    1 medium onion, chopped (½ cup)
    1 tablespoon grated fresh coconut
    ¼ teaspoon sugar
    ½ teaspoon salt

Mix everything together and serve immediately. The salad is especially welcome in the heat of Bombay. Serve with meat and fish dishes.
Serves 4.

POTATO CHOP

S everal communities in India such as the Calcutta Jews and Anglo-Indians make potato chops. This is an old Bene Israel recipe with their typical seasonings. It is hearty, full of flavor, and satisfying for lunch or a big party buffet.

STUFFING

    2 tablespoons corn oil
    1 medium onion, chopped (½ cup)
    1 pound ground beef
    1 teaspoon Basic Green Masala (see Index)
    ½ teaspoon garam masala
    ½ teaspoon Dry Masala for Meat (see Index)
    ¼ teaspoon ground turmeric
    ½ teaspoon salt
    2 cups green peas, fresh or frozen

POTATO CHOP

2 pounds potatoes, cooked in their skins until soft but firm,
    peeled
¼ cup corn or peanut oil for panfrying
1 egg, beaten with ¼ teaspoon oil
dry bread crumbs

1. Heat 2 tablespoons oil in a skillet, add the onion and beef, and stir-fry over moderate heat for 2 minutes. Add the three *masalas*, the turmeric and salt, and continue to stir-fry for 5 minutes to evaporate all the liquid. Add the peas and stir-fry for 2 minutes more. The mixture should be dry. Cool.

2. Grate the potatoes, not too fine, by hand or in a processor. Oil your hands lightly and shape about ½ cup potatoes into a ball. Press your thumb into the ball to open a cup shape. Fill this with a heaping tablespoon of the meat stuffing. Pinch all the edges together and make a round, flattened chop 1½ inches thick and 2½ to 3 inches in diameter.

3. Heat ¼ cup oil in a skillet. Dip the chops into beaten egg, then into bread crumbs on both sides. Brown on all sides over moderately low heat for about 5 minutes.

Drain briefly on paper towels.

Serve warm or at room temperature. Makes about 12 chops.

VARIATION: An admirable vegetarian stuffing may be made by omitting the meat and substituting 1 pound of vegetables cut into ¼-inch dice. Use green beans, carrots and green peas. Cauliflower, cabbage and other soft vegetables are too watery and will not work. Fry the vegetables until they are almost cooked, about 5 minutes; cool. Use the vegetables in place of the meat with the same seasonings and follow the same cooking steps.

CHAPATTI
Sweet Whole-Wheat Chapatti

The sweet *chapatti* is unique to the Bene Israel community. The addition of sugar adds an attractive dimension to this national bread. Brown sugar is known as jaggery in India; it is darker and more flavorful than ours. Nevertheless, we can use our regular dark brown sugar to sweeten the dough.

> 3 cups fine whole-wheat flour (atta)
> 2 tablespoons hot corn oil
> ¼ cup brown sugar
> about 1 cup water
> oil for deep-frying

1. Put the flour in a bowl or processor. Add the hot oil and mix well. Dissolve the sugar in the water and add it to the flour, stirring continuously. Mix into a firm dough. Knead until smooth, cover the dough with a cloth, or put it in a plastic bag, and let it rest for 2 hours.

2. Break off a walnut-size piece of dough. Roll it into a ball. Lightly oil this ball (do not use flour) and roll it out into a pancake 5 inches in diameter.

3. Heat the oil in a skillet or wok over moderate heat. Put the pancake into the hot oil and baste it rapidly. The *chapatti* will puff up into a ball. Turn it over and fry on the other side for a minute. Remove and drain in a sieve.

Serve hot immediately after frying.

Makes 16 to 18.

PURAN POLI
Stuffed Chapatti

The Hindu celebration of Holi and the Jewish Purim fall on the same evening since both are regulated by the lunar year. This was pointed out to me when learning this recipe since this native Indian dish—sweet Stuffed Chapatti—is served to celebrants of both holidays. (There is no way that I can equate the two disparate holidays, but there it is anyway.)

You may adjust the amount of sugar, but the Bene Israel prefer their chapatti sweet.

FILLING

1 cup dried chick-peas, soaked in water overnight, drained
1 tablespoon margarine or butter
¼ to ½ cup sugar, to taste
⅛ teaspoon salt
⅛ teaspoon ground cinnamon
⅛ teaspoon ground cardamom

PANCAKE

2 cups white flour
½ cup water, about
melted margarine, oil or ghee

1. Cover the chick-peas with water again and cook over moderate heat until soft, about ½ hour. Drain and cool. Pull off as much of the loose skins as you are able. Purée the chick-peas until fairly smooth.

2. Heat the margarine in a skillet, add the purée, and stir-fry for 1 minute. Add the sugar, salt, cinnamon and cardamom and stir-fry over low heat until the mixture is dry, about 10 minutes. Set aside.

3. Mix the flour and water together into a firm dough. Knead well, then cover and set aside for 1½ hours.

4. Roll a heaping tablespoon of the dough into a ball. Roll the ball out into a pancake 5 inches in diameter. Put into the center 1 tablespoon of the filling, then role the pancake into a ball again. Roll it out again into a pancake 8 inches in diameter.

5. Heat a large dry skillet over moderate heat. Put the outer side of the pancake, the side that you have rolled, face down into the skillet. After 10 seconds turn it over and cook for 2 minutes. As you turn it over, slip in ½ teaspoon melted margarine, oil or ghee.

Serve warm with a vegetable curry (bhaji). Makes 12 pancakes.

V A R I A T I O N : *Channa ka dal,* which is the split yellow lentil, may be used instead of the chick-peas; both of them can be found in Indian groceries.

BASIC GREEN MASALA

4 ounces fresh coriander, leaves only
1 head of garlic, medium, about 8 cloves
4 to 6 ounces semihot green chili
½ teaspoon salt

1.Blend everything together in a processor to a more or less smooth paste.

Store in a jar with a tight cover. Refrigerate for up to 1 week. Can be used in both meat and fish curries.

Makes 1 cup.

N O T E : There was considerable influence on the Bene Israel style of cooking from the Muslim servants and later on, during the colonial period, from the British. The Muslims concentrated on the meat dishes and, like the Jewish households, abhorred pork.

The indoor servants were the Muslim women, while the outdoor servants, such as gardener and laundryman, were men.

DRY MASALA FOR MEAT

1 tablespoon hot red chili flakes
1 tablespoon ground coriander
¼ teaspoon garlic powder
1 teaspoon ground aniseed
¼ teaspoon ground ginger
¼ teaspoon ground turmeric

1. Mix everything together and store in a jar with a tight cover. Use in meat curries.

DRY MASALA FOR FISH

1 tablespoon hot red chili flakes or powder
1 tablespoon ground cuminseed
1 tablespoon ground coriander
¼ teaspoon ground turmeric
¼ teaspoon mustard powder
1 cardamom pod, broken up

1. Mix everything together and store in a jar with a tight cover. Use in fish curries.

MINT CHUTNEY

¾ cup fresh coriander leaves
½ cup fresh mint leaves
1 head of garlic, about 10 cloves
¼ pound semihot green chilies, seeded, sliced
1 tablespoon sugar
juice of 1 lemon, about 3 tablespoons
¼ teaspoon salt
¼ cup grated green mango during the season, or ¼ cup whole
     seedless grapes
1 cup fresh grated coconut

1. Process everything together to a smooth consistency except the coconut, and grapes if used instead of the mango. Add the coconut and the whole grapes and stir them into the chutney.
Store in a jar with a tight cover up to 1 week.
Serve with any kind of Bene Israel food.

Family portrait of the Daniel family in traditional Hindu dress, Cochin, India. *(Photo courtesy the Dan Kala Collection)*

COCHIN—THE BLACK JEWS

The Black Jews of Cochin are one of the three Jewish groups in that southwest city of India on the Arabian Sea. The other two are the so-called White Jews and the manumitted or freed slaves. The Black and White Jews worshiped in different synagogues, the Whites in their famed old Paradesi synagogue. But it is the Black Jews that we are concerned with here.

Legend, hearsay and community stories form an historical background to the origin of the Black Jews. Benjamin of Tudela, that peripatetic Spanish traveler (1170 A.D.), indicated that there were about 1,000 Jews in Cochin in his time. Other references attest to the antiquity of the Black Jews' presence there.

The Portuguese and Dutch rule of the region from the sixteenth to the eighteenth century contributed to the establishment of Mattancheri, the Jewish quarter in Cochin, known today as it was then as Jew Town. This was not a ghetto but the part of town where the Jews gathered. There was no disparagement attached to the name.

The Jews of Cochin speak Malayalam, the Indian language of the region, and are engaged in trade and crafts. For instance, some years ago during one of my trips to Cochin, I met a Black Jewess called Zipporah, who sold bananas and eggs for a living.

The Jews of Cochin lived in a joint family system. It was conceived for the protection of the very young and very old as in conservative Hindu families. There is a feeling of the caste system in their manner of doing this. My host said that his large family lived in one compound. The old grandmother held the money and distributed funds to family members when it was needed. There was no secrecy nor was advantage

369

taken by any one member to obtain more money than was genuinely needed.

The dark skin and general physiognomy of the South Indians are also characteristic of the Jews of the region. "We are not bothered about our color," one of the Jews said to me, since they identify with the Judaic way of life—not their appearance.

The cookery of the Black Jews (and that of the White Jews) is that of the Indians around them, except that the rules of meat and dairy dishes are observed and family differences and customs influence the seasonings.

The cooking is spicy with the emphasis on ginger, coriander, mustard seed, fresh and dry hot chili, fenugreek, cardamom and the ever-present curry leaves (see Glossary). Since little meat or poultry is eaten in the intense heat and humidity of the climate, the food could almost be considered vegetarian. Yoghurt is a popular and common food.

Diets change when people move from one ambience to another so one must assume that the eating habits of the Black Jews, as they settle down in other countries, has also changed. For that reason, recording their cookery as it once was in Cochin is more than a formality but an obligation.

Now the community has been reduced to a few families. Several thousand left for Israel in 1970 and afterward, due to their strong commitment to the State of Israel. The life known before in this small, unique Jewish community has been irrevocably changed.

KIDDUSH WINE

1 cup large raisins
2 cups water

1. Put the raisins and water in a bottle on Thursday evening before the Sabbath. Soak the mixture at room temperature for 24 hours. Shake the bottle several times during this time.

You now have the kiddush wine.

RAISIN VINEGAR

1 cup raisins taken from the wine bottle
2 cups water

1. Use the same raisins that were in the wine. Mix them with the water and store in a glass or pottery crock. Let it stand at room temperature for 2 months. The mixture will convert naturally to vinegar of a fine fruity quality.

ARAK, A LIQUOR

The cashew has a pear-shaped fruit from which the "nut" dangles; it grows outside of the fruit. The juice is squeezed from the cashew apple, as it is called, and fermented to produce arak, the liquor of Cochin.

The only other country where I have eaten the fresh ripe cashew apple is Guatemala, during the month of February when it is in season. The nut is pulled off the apple and processed, and the fruit are sold fresh or converted to wine.

KOLI SOUP

Aromatic Chicken and
Vegetable Soup

Meat is not the most important ingredient in this essentially vegetable soup. An entire gamut of spices is added to give the soup a full quality, and the chicken itself can be used for another meal.

5 cups water
1 chicken, 3 pounds, quartered, plus giblets and 2 more legs,
    loose skin and fat discarded
1 carrot, cut into ¼-inch cubes
1 medium potato, cut into ½-inch cubes
1 large ripe tomato, chopped
1 medium onion, chopped (½ cup)
1 cup cauliflowerets, cut into ½-inch pieces
¼ cup chopped celery leaves
¼ cup chopped parsley
¼ cup chopped fresh coriander
5 whole cardamom pods
1 cinnamon stick (1 inch)
4 whole cloves
½ teaspoon salt
2 bay leaves
2 whole allspice
5 whole peppercorns

1. Bring the water to a boil in a large pan over moderate heat. Add the chicken and cook, covered, for 20 minutes. Add all the other ingredients and cook over low heat for 45 minutes. Keep the pan covered to retain the aroma of the seasonings.

Serve hot with or without the chicken. Serves 6.

PUZUKKU

Chicken Curry

This is a favorite Passover curry among the Jews of Cochin. It is a quick curry, without complications, but delicious in the Indian way.

3 tablespoons corn oil

2 medium onions, chopped (¾ cup)

1 Cornish game hen, 2 pounds, cut into 8 pieces

*1 large ripe tomato, cut into ½-inch cubes, or equal amount of
    canned tomato (¾ cup)*

1 tablespoon white or cider vinegar

½ teaspoon salt, or to taste

¼ teaspoon white pepper

¼ teaspoon ground turmeric

½ cup water

2 medium potatoes, peeled, cut into ¾-inch cubes

1. Heat 2 tablespoons oil in a pan, add the onions and game hen and stir-fry over moderate heat for 5 minutes. Add the tomato, vinegar, salt, pepper, turmeric and water. Cover the pan and cook over low heat for 20 minutes.

2. Meanwhile, heat the remaining tablespoon of oil in a skillet, add the potato cubes, and stir-fry over moderate heat for 5 minutes or until brown. When the hen is almost tender, add the half-cooked fried potatoes and continue to cook, covered, for 15 minutes more or until everything is tender. Should the liquid evaporate too quickly, add another ¼ cup warm water.

Serve warm with rice or bread. Serves 6 with other dishes.

VAZUNIGA
Fried Eggplant Mixture

A typical vegetarian dish from Cochin will include a mixture of local vegetables and spices, fried until light brown. Deep-frying does not necessarily mean greasy food. The oil in the *karai* (wok) should be hot. When the spices and seasonings are tossed with the vegetables and then plunged into the hot oil, they are immediately sealed and a crisp outcome is assured.

1 eggplant, ½ pound, cut into 1-inch-thin slices

3 small onions, sliced thin (1 cup)

1 semihot green chili, seeded, sliced thin

1 garlic clove, chopped fine

½ teaspoon salt; or to taste
¼ teaspoon chopped fresh gingerroot
¼ teaspoon paprika
¼ teaspoon ground coriander
⅛ teaspoon ground turmeric
⅛ teaspoon pepper
oil for deep-frying, about 1 cup
1 tablespoon white vinegar

1. Mix everything together except the oil and vinegar. Toss well.
2. Heat the oil in a wok or skillet over moderate heat. Add the vegetable mixture immediately and fry until golden and crisp, stirring now and then. Use a slotted spoon to transfer the mixture to a metal sieve or colander and allow the excess oil to drip out for 5 minutes. Turn out into a serving bowl and sprinkle with the vinegar.

Serve warm with rice, bread or any type of Cochin food.

Serves 4.

CHORAKA
Squash and Cauliflower Sauté

No water is added to this sauté since all the moisture needed is found in the vegetables. The result is a more natural-tasting combination for dedicated vegetarians—of which there are many in India.

2 tablespoons corn oil
½ teaspoon mustard seeds, black or white
½ teaspoon hot red chili flakes
1 pound cauliflower, cut into ½-inch florets
1 small green pepper, cut into ½-inch cubes
1 pound zucchini, cut into ½-inch cubes
¼ teaspoon ground turmeric
¼ teaspoon paprika
1 small garlic clove, chopped
1 teaspoon salt, or to taste
½ cup chopped tomato, fresh or canned
6 to 8 curry leaves (see Glossary)

1. Heat the oil in a wok or large skillet, add the mustard seeds and chili flakes, and stir-fry for a few seconds. Add everything else all at once and stir-fry over moderate heat for 2 minutes.

2. Cover the wok or skillet and steam-fry for 3 minutes. Stir for a moment, cover the pan, and cook over low heat for 10 minutes. Do not overcook so as to preserve the fresh texture of the vegetables.

Serve warm with rice and other dishes. Serves 6 to 8.

SAMBAR
Vegetable Curry

This curry contains a large number of vegetables, some of which could be omitted, if desired. The traditional method, however, is to use everything available in the market. The hot chilies, mustard seeds, fenugreek and curry leaves, among other things, are typical in this essentially tart curry.

Christian Goa influenced some of the Cochin foods since Goanese artisans came to Cochin for several centuries to construct or repair the synagogues and restore the artistic embellishments. They left behind something of their cooking style as well as their handicraft.

VEGETABLES

2 tablespoons red lentils, rinsed
1 cup eggplant cubes, about ½-inch pieces
1 medium potato, peeled, cut into ¼-inch cubes
10 small okra, ends trimmed
½ cup ½-inch cubes or red or green sweet pepper
1 cup cauliflowerets, cut into ½-inch pieces
½ cup green peas, fresh or frozen
2 medium onions, chopped (1 cup)
3 garlic cloves, chopped fine
½ cup sliced celery leaves and ribs
1 cup shredded cabbage
1 teaspoon ground turmeric
1 teaspoon salt
½ inch of fresh gingerroot, put through a garlic press

¼ teaspoon hing (asafetida)
1 tablespoon ground coriander
1 cup water

SPICES

2 tablespoons corn oil
½ teaspoons mustard seeds
1 or 2 dried red chilies, whole
1 garlic clove, chopped fine
½ teaspoon fenugreek seeds
15 curry leaves (see Glossary)
1 tablespoon lemon juice

1. Put all vegetable ingredients into a pan, cover, and cook over moderate heat for 15 minutes.

2. Heat the oil in a skillet and add all the spice ingredients except the lemon juice. Stir-fry over moderate heat for 3 minutes. Add the lemon juice and remove from the heat. Add this spice mix to the vegetables at the end of their 15-minute cooking time and mix well.

Serve the curry hot with plain white rice, Rava Idlees (see Index) or bread. Serves 6.

MUTTACHAR
Spiced Eggs with Sauce

Aromatic curry leaves and an assortment of spices and seasonings change poached eggs into an altogether more exotic dish than one usually encounters.

1 tablespoon corn oil
1 small onion, chopped (¼ cup)
2 cups water, or 1 cup water and 1 cup coconut milk
½ teaspoon salt
¼ teaspoon ground turmeric
¼ teaspoon paprika
½ teaspoon ground coriander
1 ripe tomato, cut into 6 slices

¼ cup sliced green mango (optional)
1 semihot green chili, seeded, cut into 8 slices
10 curry leaves (see Glossary)
1 teaspoon lemon juice
4 eggs

1. Heat the oil in a skillet and stir-fry the onion over moderate heat until golden. Add the water (or coconut milk) and bring to a boil. Add the salt, turmeric, paprika and coriander and simmer over low heat for 5 minutes.

2. Add the tomato, mango (if used) and green chili. Crush the curry leaves to release the flavor and add to the skillet with lemon juice. Simmer for 10 minutes.

3. Last, carefully add the whole eggs and poach them for 3 minutes, basting them once or twice.

Serve hot with rice. Serves 4.

PACHUDDY THIER
Spiced Yoghurt Sauce

This delectable sauce is served generously over warm rice. It is a purely vegetarian combination in which the absence of meat or fish is not noticed, one of the basic characteristics of true vegetarianism.

2 cups yoghurt
juice of 1 lemon
¼ teaspoon salt
½ garlic clove, put through a press
½ teaspoon fresh gingerroot, put through a press
½ teaspoon fine-chopped hot green chili
1 teaspoon corn oil
¼ teaspoon black mustard seeds
¼ teaspoon fenugreek seeds
1 dried hot red chili, whole
5 curry leaves (see Glossary)

1. Mix the yoghurt, lemon juice, salt, garlic, ginger and green chili together.

2. Heat the oil in a skillet, add the mustard seeds, fenugreek, whole red chili and curry leaves, and stir-fry over moderate heat for 2 minutes. Add this to the yoghurt mixture and mix well together.
Serve at room temperature, spooned over hot rice.
Serves 4.

VARIATION: To give the sauce additional texture and substance, add 1 cup of unpeeled young cucumber, cut into ¼-inch cubes. Also, add 2 teaspoons chopped fresh coriander to the yoghurt mix.

UPPUMA
Semolina Cereal

Semolina is called cream of wheat in the United States and *sooje* in India. It produces delicious snacks or desserts. Here, in the Cochin style, it is spiced and sweetened, which puts it into a class of its own and is characteristic of this region of India.

1 tablespoon corn oil
¼ teaspoon mustard seeds
5 curry leaves (see Glossary)
⅛ teaspoon fenugreek seeds
1 medium onion, chopped (⅓ cup)
2 whole semihot green chilies
1 cup semolina
1 cup water
¼ teaspoon salt
1 tablespoon grated coconut
1 teaspoon sugar

1. Heat the oil in a pan, add mustard seeds, curry leaves, fenugreek, onion and green chilies, and stir-fry over moderate heat for 2 minutes, or until the onion turns golden.
2. Add the semolina and stir-fry over low heat until it turns light brown. Add the water, salt and coconut and cook for 3 or 4 minutes, stirring continuously. The mixture should be firm and moist but not soupy. Sprinkle with sugar, if wanted.
Serve warm for breakfast or as an evening snack.
Serves 3 or 4.

RAVA IDLEES
Steamed Wheat Cakes

I dlee is the traditional bread of South India. It is made by all of the communities including the Jews of Cochin. *Idlees* are light in texture and at their best when eaten with vegetable curries and yoghurt dishes.

1 teaspoon sugar
1 teaspoon dry yeast
4 cups warm water
2 cups white flour
2 cups semolina (soojee)
2 tablespoons melted margarine
¼ teaspoon salt

1. Mix the sugar, yeast and ½ cup warm water together and let stand, to proof, for ½ hour.
2. Mix both flours, the margarine, salt and yeast mixture with the balance of the water to make a sticky dough. Let stand for 2 hours to ferment.
3. Using the steaming cups especially made for *idlees* (or you may improvise with a multicup egg poacher), put about 2 heaping tablespoons of the dough in each cup. Steam over hot water for 10 minutes. The *idlees* when ready should be about 1 inch thick at the center and 3 inches in diameter.
Serve at room temperature. Makes about 40 cakes.

PARUTHERUM
Jaroseth

A sweet and pungent *jaroseth* is unusual since other cultures do not use vinegar and it therefore lacks pungency. The date paste, for those who cannot find it already prepared, is nothing more than seedless dates ground to a paste with the smallest amount of water. I suggest ½ pound dates and 3 tablespoons water, processed together to smoothness.

½ pound dark raisins
½ pound date paste
¼ cup blanched almonds
2 tablespoons sesame seeds
1 cup sugar
¼ cup wine vinegar
¼ teaspoon salt
1 cup water

1. Process everything together to a smooth paste. Put it in a pan and simmer over very low heat for ½ hour. Cool.

Serve at room temperature with matzoh at the Passover Seders.

NEYYAPPAM
Fried Sweet Cakes

The sweet cakes are usually eaten on Hanukkah or the day before Yom Kippur. Of course, they can be prepared any time during the year and served during the tea or coffee hour.

Several South Indian foods are mixed together and allowed to ferment overnight. In the hot, tropical atmosphere there is a slight fermentation process and a light acid flavor is added to the food to give it additional interest.

2 cups water
½ cup sugar
⅛ teaspoon salt
1 cup white wheat flour
1 cup semolina (soojee)
1 tablespoon sesame seeds
1 tablespoon chopped almonds
1 tablespoon chopped cashew nuts
1 tablespoon chopped raisins
2 dates, chopped
2 apricots, chopped
½ teaspoon baking powder
¼ teaspoon ground cardamom
oil for deep-frying

1. Mix the water, sugar and salt together in a pan and bring to a boil. Remove from the heat and cool until just warm.

2. Add all the other ingredients except the baking powder, cardamom and oil. Mix well and let stand at room temperature, covered, overnight. The next day stir in the baking powder and cardamom.

3. Heat the oil in a skillet or wok over moderate heat. Take 1 heaping tablespoon of the dough and drop it into the oil. Fry it on all sides for about 4 minutes or until well browned. Remove and drain on paper towels. Continue with the batter until all are fried.

Serve warm for breakfast or any other time. Makes 20 cakes.

PAYASAM
Tapioca Sweet

This tasty dessert is served after meals or during the tea or coffee hour. If coconut milk is used, the dessert is *pareve* and may be served after a meat meal. Using dairy milk is extremely flavorful but then can only be served with dairy meals if the law of kashruth is to be followed.

1 tablespoon corn oil or margarine
10 whole cashew nuts
¼ cup raisins
3 tablespoons tapioca beads
2 cups milk or coconut milk or half and half
3 tablespoons sugar
⅛ teaspoon salt

1. Heat the oil or margarine in a pan and stir-fry the cashews and raisins together over low heat for 3 minutes to brown lightly. Remove them from the pan and set aside.

2. Add the tapioca to the same pan and toast the beads over low heat for a few moments. Add the milk you prefer, the sugar and salt. Bring to a boil and simmer until thick, about 10 minutes.

Serve warm or at room temperature, sprinkled with the cashews and raisins. Serves 6.

PARIPU PAYASAM
Split-Pea Sweet with Coconut Milk

Jewish sweets are essentially the sweets of all the Indians of Cochin. Coconut milk is an important ingredient as would be expected in a region where coconuts are so plentiful.

> ½ cup yellow split peas or red Egyptian lentils
> 2 cups water
> ¾ cup brown sugar
> ⅛ teaspoon salt
> 2 cups coconut milk
> ½ teaspoon ground cardamom
> 1 tablespoon coconut slivers, browned in margarine or oil

1. Cook the peas and water together over moderate heat until the water has almost evaporated and the peas (or lentils) are nearly mush, about 20 minutes.

2. Add the sugar, salt, coconut milk and cardamom, mix well, and bring to a boil. Simmer over low heat for about 15 minutes. The result is a sweet, thick, flavorful dessert.

Serve warm, garnished with the coconut slivers.

Serves 4.

ACHAR
Lime Pickle

Homemade lime pickle in the South Indian manner is spicy, chili-hot and dynamic with food. The lime in the vinegar may be held as long as 1 year without deteriorating. The cut-up lime pickle may be prepared with as many limes as you wish, for example half of the recipe. My own inclination is to prepare the entire recipe and store it in the refrigerator for use when wanted.

Note that the small yellow lime (*nimboo*) found in India is the same one found in Central America and the Keys of Florida.

LIME

>10 whole yellow limes
>1 cup vinegar, white or cider
>1 tablespoon salt
>5 to 10 hot green chilies, to taste, sliced

PICKLE

>2 tablespoons corn oil
>10 fenugreek seeds
>½ teaspoon black mustard seeds
>5 whole hot dried red chilies
>10 curry leaves (see Glossary)
>1 teaspoon sugar
>2 garlic cloves, halved lengthwise

1. Mix everything together and store it in a glass jar for 3 months before preparing the pickle.

2. Remove the 10 limes from the vinegar and cut into ½-inch pieces, removing any seeds.

3. Heat the oil in a skillet, add the fenugreek and mustard seeds, red chilies, curry leaves, sugar and garlic. Stir-fry over moderate heat for 3 minutes. Add the lime pieces and stir-fry for 1 minute more, mixing thoroughly.

Cool and store in a glass jar with a tight cover.

Serve with any kind of Indian food. Refrigerate after using.

INDAPAZAM
Date and Tamarind Chutney

After spending many years of my life in India, I am always seeking new dishes from any region of the country. This is one of the best table chutneys in India and probably my favorite. It is a thick paste that may be scooped out like marmalade and served with any kind of Asian or European food. It has a long life in the refrigerator. A full recipe should be prepared to be kept on hand for any culinary situation.

1 tablespoon corn oil

½ teaspoon black mustard seeds

½ teaspoon fenugreek seeds

3 dried hot red chilies, whole

10 curry leaves (see Glossary)

½ teaspoon chopped fresh gingerroot

1 garlic clove, chopped fine

½ pound date paste

½ pound tamarind paste, dissolved in 2 cups water, strained and seeds discarded

2 teaspoons salt

1 tablespoon sugar

2 tablespoons vinegar, white or cider

1 tablespoon hot red chili flakes, toasted in a dry skillet for 2 minutes

1 teaspoon paprika

1. Heat the oil in a skillet, add the mustard and fenugreek seeds, the whole chilies, curry leaves, ginger and garlic. Stir-fry over moderate heat for 2 minutes. Set aside.

2. Mix the date paste in a pan with the tamarind liquid, salt, sugar, vinegar, chili flakes and paprika. Simmer over low heat for 15 minutes, stirring frequently. Add the fried spices and continue to simmer and stir for 20 minutes more.

Cool well; store in a glass jar with a tight cover.

Refrigerate for up to 1 year.

Red Sea

YEMEN

ETHIOPIA

EGYPT

A Jewish Yemenite family celebrating the Sabbath.

YEMEN

Yemen, part hot semidesert terrain along the Red Sea coast and part mountainous interior, is a small, harsh, forbidding country located in the southwest corner of the Arabian peninsula. Yet this country—backward, underdeveloped, medieval as it was—supported several Jewish communities for centuries. Legend has it that the Queen of Sheba (Yemen was also known as the Kingdom of Sheba) held the Jews in high esteem and once visited Jerusalem to investigate the wisdom of King Solomon.

In any event, given the lack of material that could confirm the dates of the arrival of the Jews in Yemen, we believe that Jewish settlements have existed there since perhaps the time of the Second Temple Period.

Merchants, plying the famous and lucrative spice route through Yemen, maintained contact with India, Babylonia (Baghdad), Egypt, North Africa and Ethiopia. As some Jews prospered during the early centuries of the Christian Era, others, less fortunate, decided to migrate to Yemen. They established communities there and became landowners, farmers, silversmiths, carpenters, blacksmiths and specialists in other crafts. Through it all, they followed the Judaic way of life.

But practices during the Ottoman Empire (sixteenth century to 1918), as well as the degrading behavior of the local Yemenite population, brought about a hostile environment. In 1882 the first important wave of emigration to Palestine started, and it continued until 1914, by which time approximately one third of the Jews had left Yemen. In Palestine they made contact with their coreligionists for the first time and ended their insularity.

When Israel was created in 1947–48, it led to an astonishing event—the famous airlift, sometimes known as Operation Magic Carpet. It moved most of the remaining Yemenite com-

387

munity (about 50,000) to Israel during 1949 and 1950. They took with them their traditional way of life, including a limited but appealing style of cooking.

Agriculture is an important factor in establishing a cuisine, and semidesert or mountainous terrain does not produce the quantity and variety of food that is needed to inspire the creation of new combinations, which also conform to dietary laws. But within their limitations, they created food with an exotic appeal, proven today by the popularity of many Yemenite restaurants that have proliferated around Israel.

Both song and story celebrate the admiration that has always been felt by the Jewish men of India for the Yemenite girls. This led to both intermarriage and an interchange of customs, some of which influenced their food, especially the seasonings.

Yemenite cooking can be reduced to a few categories, with the Indian influence quite often apparent. There are unusual and delicious breads for daily and Sabbath use; meat soups and meat stews (chicken is used only in soup—never roasted or fried); a spice mix for seasoning foods, and a hot chili chutney with fenugreek, a spice that is certainly of Indian origin. The Jews did not make cheese, but butter was prepared from the milk and cream of the cattle.

Yemenites have no desserts as such, but substitute fresh fruit in season. The snacks that replace sweets (jala) are the dry green beans, dry fava beans, dates, almonds and other mixed nuts. They make a Jaroseth of sesame seeds, honey, almonds, walnuts and red wine; or with dates, sesame, walnuts, almonds, peanuts, raisins, wine and hot water, cooked together to a paste. The nibbling goes on and on during the Sabbath.

Arak, a colorless alcoholic liquid, is the national drink of the Jews. It is made from grapes, plums, apricots or other seasonal fruits, and the taste differs according to the fruit used. Since there is no wine in Yemen, arak is the Sabbath ritual drink.

On the following pages are just a few recipes—the essential spice mix, some soups and some samples of their bread—to enable you to taste for yourself the flavor of Sephardic cooking in Yemen.

MARAG
Yemenite Bone Soup

This is a most popular soup for daily and Sabbath dining. The pumpkin provides a slightly sweet flavor and the richness and substance of the soup is provided by the bones.

> 8 to 10 cups water
> 2 pounds beef bones, particularly shank, cut into 2-inch pieces
> 3 fresh ripe tomatoes, halved (1½ cups)
> 2 large onions (½ pound), halved
> 1 handful of fresh coriander
> 1 pound pumpkin or calabasa, in one piece, strings and seeds removed
> 1 zucchini, halved
> 2 potatoes (½ pound), peeled and halved
> 1 teaspoon salt, or to taste

1. Put the water and beef bones into a large pan and bring to a boil over moderate heat; skim off the foam as it rises, 2 or 3 times. Add the tomatoes, cover the pan, and cook over low heat for 2 hours.

2. Add the onions, coriander, pumpkin, zucchini, potatoes and salt. Cook for another ½ hour, or until all the vegetables are soft.

Serve the broth warm and serve the vegetables separately, on the side. Serves 6.

NOTE: Add about 1 cup bulghur to this dish and it becomes Bulghur Soup, another Sabbath day dish. The bulghur expands to a thick mush, which is eaten in place of bread during the cold weather.

FATOOT IM HILBEH

Beef Soup with Fenugreek

This soup is pungent, the *hawaish* (spice mix) plus the hot chili guarantees that. The fenugreek is a viscous spice and is therefore also a thickener of sorts to the soup. For Passover, matzoh is added. *Hawaish* is reminiscent of the *garam masala* (hot spice) of India. In my opinion, it was inspired by the cultural and commercial contact with that country.

> 5 cups water
> ½ pound boneless beef chuck, cut into 4 pieces
> 2 tablespoons Hawaish (see Index)
> 4 medium potatoes, peeled (1¼ pounds)
> ½ teaspoon salt
> 3 tablespoons ground fenugreek
> ½ teaspoon hot red chili flakes
> 4 sheets of matzoh, broken into 2-inch pieces
> lemon wedges

1. Put the water, meat, *hawaish*, potatoes and salt in a pan and bring to a boil. Turn heat to low and simmer, covered, for 1 hour, or until meat and potatoes are tender. Remove them and set aside.

2. Add the fenugreek and chili flakes and bring the soup to a boil, stirring continuously to dissolve the seasonings. Add the matzoh, stir into the soup for a moment, and remove the soup from the heat. Cover the pan and let stand for 5 minutes.

Serve hot with lemon wedges. Serve the meat and potato separately.

Serves 4.

CHOUIA

Meat Stew

This simple, uncomplicated dish is full of flavor. Liquid in the vegetables and the slow cooking will tenderize the meat. Traditionally, the *chouia* is cooked over charcoal in clay pots. Lamb or goat may also be used in place of beef.

A prepared jar of Hawaish should be on the kitchen shelf ready to use. Notice that salt has been omitted.

1½ pounds beef chuck, cut into 3-inch cubes
½ cup chopped fresh coriander
½ cup chopped flat-leaf Italian parsley
½ pound (about 2) tomatoes, halved
1 medium onion, halved
4 large garlic clove, sliced
1 tablespoon Hawaish (see Index)

1. Mix everything together, cover the pan, and cook over low heat for 3 hours.

Serve warm. Serves 6 with other dishes.

HARISS TEMANI
Beef and Green-Pea Bake for Passover

This Yemenite dish is a hameen for Passover and, surprisingly, prepared for breakfast. A substantial dish, baked slowly and thoroughly, it is similar to the cholent of Eastern Europe and the hameen of the Oriental communities.

3 cups water
½ pound boneless chuck, cut into 4 pieces
1 pound beef bones
1 cup dried green split peas (vatana)
4 medium potatoes, peeled (1¼ pounds)
2 whole heads of garlic, 8 to 10 cloves, not peeled
1 ripe tomato, quartered
2 tablespoons Hawaish (see Index)
1 small onion, quartered
½ teaspoon salt

1. Put everything into a pan and bring to a boil. Cover tightly and place in a very slow oven, about 225° F., and bake it overnight, about 12 hours.

Serve with matzoh the next morning for an early breakfast. Serves 4.

NOTE: Dry green or garden peas are known as *vatana* in India and are available in supermarkets.

HILBEH MA BEDA
Scrambled Eggs with Fenugreek

Hilbeh is fenugreek, a spice relished in India and connected with Yemen through the interchange of commerce. It is also the name of a condiment made from fenugreek and seasonings; a recipe is included in this chapter.

Meat is not eaten at the evening meal since, according to my Yemenite confidant, it is hard to digest. This egg dish is a traditional substitute.

2 tablespoons corn oil
1 medium onion, chopped fine (½ cup)
¼ cup fresh or canned tomato, chopped fine
4 to 6 tablespoons prepared Hilbeh, to taste (see Index)
1 garlic clove, put through a press
4 eggs, beaten
¼ teaspoon salt

1. Heat the oil in a skillet, add the onion, and stir-fry over low heat until brown. Add the tomato and fry for another minute.

2. Add the *hilbeh* and garlic and simmer for 3 minutes. Add the eggs and salt and scramble the mixture until the eggs are just set.

Serve warm with bread. Serves 4.

SAMAC
Yemenite Fish

2 pounds kingfish, sea bass or similar saltwater fish, cut into
    1-inch-thick slices
2 teaspoons lemon juice
1 teaspoon salt

3 tablespoons corn oil
3 garlic cloves, sliced
2 teaspoons ground cuminseed
½ teaspoon pepper
1 small hot green chili, seeded and chopped
½ cup chopped fresh coriander
½ cup chopped flat-leaf Italian parsley
1½ cups water
¼ cup tomato purée

1. Rub the fish slices with lemon and salt and let stand for 15 minutes.
2. Heat the oil in a pan, and stir-fry the garlic, cuminseed, pepper, chili, coriander and parsley over moderate heat for 2 minutes. Add the water and tomato purée, bring to a boil, and cook for 2 minutes.
3. Add the fish slices and simmer over low heat for 20 minutes, to thicken the sauce and cook the fish until just done.
Serve warm or at room temperature with bread and condiments. Serves 6.

MATZOH

Yemenite matzoh is baked in a clay oven covered with tin. Charcoal is put in the bottom of the oven and burned. When the tin is red hot the oven is ready to receive the dough.

A special flour, kosher for Pesach, is purchased from the Ashkenazi Jews, who grow the grain and prepare it. The purest of water is also obtained and this is put in either new clay or glass containers and covered until the next day when it is to be used.

Three P.M. is the auspicious hour for the preparation of the matzoh (ben hashmasote). The complete time it should take from mixing the dough to baking the matzoh is 18 minutes. One person mixes the dough, another rolls out each matzoh, and another slaps it on the hot clay of the oven. It takes about 5 seconds to bake and is then removed by hand or with a clean towel. The matzoh are prepared by both men and women working together, although it is agreed that the men have more strength to prepare the matzoh than women.

4 cups flour
3 cups water

1. Mix together into a firm dough. Using about ½ cup dough, roll it out into a thin round matzoh, about 14 inches in diameter. Bake according to directions above.

WARDA
Sesame Loaf

In Yemen, the yeast was homemade, a sourdough starter.

1 package dry yeast (7 grams)
2 cups lukewarm water, or more if necessary
1 teaspoon salt
4 cups flour
sesame seeds

1. Dissolve the yeast in the water, then mix well with the salt and flour. Knead into a smooth dough. Let rise in a warm place, covered, for several hours.
2. Form loaves into an oblong shape, 12 inches long, 6 inches across and 1 inch thick. Press 3 lines with your fingers along the length of the loaves. Scatter a teaspoon of sesame seeds over each loaf.
3. Bake in a 375° F. oven for about 20 minutes, or until the top is brown.
Makes 4 or 5 loaves.

AJIN
Bread Dough

Ajin is the basic dough ball from which several types of Yemenite breads are prepared. Notice that there is no leavening, although the Yemenites in their home country made what we might call sourdough starter and used some of that.

4 cups flour
2 tablespoons oil (butter is used in Yemen)
2 tablespoons vinegar
1 teaspoon salt
1 teaspoon sugar
2 cups water, or enough to make a soft dough
¼ pound margarine, at room temperature

1. Mix everything except the margarine together, knead a bit for smoothness. Then rest the dough, covered, for 3 hours.

2. Divide the dough into 8 pieces. Flatten out 1 piece to about 6 inches in diameter. Incorporate about 2 teaspoons of margarine into the dough circle, pushing and kneading it in but maintaining the circle.

3. Cut a line open from the center of the circle to the outside edge. Take one end and roll it around counterclockwise into a ball. This is the ajin. Prepare all pieces of dough in the same way. Bake as directed in individual recipe.

JACHNOON
Baked Bread with Whole Eggs

Jachnoon is Sabbath food since it is prepared ahead. Eggs baked in this fashion turn a rich amber and have a pronounced nutty flavor. To bake eggs is a traditional Jewish method of preparation in both the Middle East and India.

4 Ajin (preceding recipe)
5 eggs in the shell
butter or margarine

1. Take 4 rolled-up *ajin* and place them in a well-buttered pan just big enough to contain them. Push 1 egg between each ajin, plus 1 more in the center.

2. Bake at low heat, 250° F., all night, or about 6 to 8 hours during the daytime—a modern approach.

Remove from the oven and serve at room temperature.

SUBYA
Holiday Bread

This bread (*subya*) is one of those Sabbath dishes that are prepared on Friday before sundown and baked slowly for an entire evening to be ready for the Sabbath. *Subya* is a particularly rich and tasty bread and the black caraway seeds give it an unusual aromatic flavor. The black seed is known in Yemen by its Biblical name of *kezach*.

> 3 Ajin dough balls
> 2 eggs
> butter or margarine
> 1 tablespoon black caraway seeds, or to taste

1. In a well-buttered heatproof glass dish or baking pan measuring about 9 × 5 × 3 inches, flatten out 1 *ajin* to fit the dish. Pour over this one well-beaten egg, then another flattened-out *ajin* and another egg. Continue with the third or even fourth *ajin* and egg, if you wish. Sprinkle the top with the caraway seeds.

2. Bake in a slow oven, 250° F., for 3 or 4 hours, until the top is brown.

Serve at room temperature, sliced.

MALAWACH
Fried Bread Pancake

This pancake *(mal-awach)* is traditionally eaten at breakfast with boiled eggs, tomatoes, sometimes honey and Schug (see Index), the hot chili condiment.

    1 Ajin (see Index)
    2 teaspoons margarine or butter

1. Flatten out the *ajin* to about 10 inches in diameter to make a pancake that is not more than ¼ inch thick.

2. Heat a skillet and melt the margarine over moderate heat. Fry the pancake until brown and crisp, for about 5 minutes on each side.

Serve warm.

HAWAISH
Spice Mix

It is *hawaish*, the spice mix, that gives Yemenite cooking its identity. All their spices are mixed proportionately and stored, to be easily measured out for recipes, as required.

    2 tablespoons ground cuminseed
    1 tablespoon pepper
    ½ teaspoon ground coriander
    1 teaspoon ground turmeric
    4 whole cloves, broken up
    seeds from 4 cardamom pods
    ¼ teaspoon grated nutmeg

1. Mix everything together. Store in a glass jar with a tight cover. Keep 2 bay leaves in the mixture to keep the spices dry and clean. Do not include the bay leaves when using the mixture.

Use when needed.

SCHUG
Hot Green Chili Chutney

Yemenites have a great tolerance for the hot chili, which came to them as an immigrant from Central America—even reaching isolated mountain communities of Yemenite Jews.

1 bunch of fresh coriander, leaves only (about 2 cups)
1 small head of garlic (8 cloves), peeled
1 tablespoon salt
6 ounces fresh hot green chili, seeded
¼ teaspoon pepper
2 tablespoons ground cuminseed
4 cardamon pods, seeds only, or ½ teaspoon ground cardamom
4 whole cloves, broken up.

1. Process all the ingredients to a relatively smooth paste. Store in a jar with a tight cover. Refrigerate. Use in cooking as well as for a table condiment.

HILBEH
Fenugreek Condiment

There are the old, traditional Yemenite foods, and then in contemporary times, modifications of the old theme. The first recipe is an old-time and simpler version of the *hilbeh*. The second recipe has several more ingredients, with a distinctive jolt from the hot chili. The addition of tomato is a modern touch.

Hilbeh is also popular with the Jewish community in Calcutta, where it is referred to as "Jewish paste."

¼ cup ground fenugreek
4 cups water
juice of ½ lemon, about 2 tablespoons
1 tablespoon Schug (preceding recipe)

1. Soak the fenugreek in 3½ cups water for 2 hours. Stir well. Drain off the water, which removes the slightly bitter taste.

2. Mix together the fenugreek, ½ cup water, lemon juice and schug, stirring briskly.

Use as a table condiment.

VARIATION:

¼ cup ground fenugreek
4 cups water
½ teaspoon salt
3 tablespoons tomato purée
1 tablespoon chopped fresh coriander
⅛ teaspoon pepper
1 teaspoon fine-chopped fresh hot green chili

1. Soak the fenugreek (hilbeh) in 3½ cups water for 2 hours. Drain; add ½ cup water and salt. Mix.

2. Add the tomato purée, coriander, pepper and chili. Mix well and refrigerate.

Serve with any kind of Yemenite food.

An Ethiopian Jewish woman in the village of Gondar. *(Photo courtesy North American Conference on Ethiopian Jewry)*

ETHIOPIA

Who are the Ethiopian Jews and what is their origin? Pursuing the researches of scholars, we find they are of Hamitic origin and of the Agau family of Ethiopian tribes. They speak Amharic, the official language of Ethiopia, and their outward appearance is that of the non-Jewish Ethiopians. They live in their own small primitive villages, usually near a river in the provinces surrounding Lake Tana and to the north in the mountains. Their homes consisted of round huts with conical straw roofs. They are (or were) poor farmers and craftsmen.

Their religion is based on the Bible that is written in the Ge'ez language. They follow the dietary laws of Judaism and celebrate the important Holy Days and Festivals such as Yom Kippur, Rosh Hashanah, Sukkoth, Hanukkah, Purim, Passover and Shavuoth. The name "Falashas," by which Ethiopian Jews have been known since the Middle Ages, is considered by them to be derogatory. They would now prefer to be known as Beta Israel, translated as the House of Israel. These are the cold unadorned facts as we know them.

There is another side to the coin. Biblical sources and the accumulation of fact and legend, relate that Menelik, the son of King Solomon and the Queen of Sheba, went from Jerusalem to Ethiopia with a group of Israelites and started a community of Jews. In 200 B.C. the Greeks mention the Ethiopian Jews; we know they existed. According to Ethiopian chronicles, Judaism was widespread at that time and the local population followed the Jewish religion. Ethiopian Jews are black like the rest of the population. There was an early period (fifteenth and sixteenth centuries) when they lived in political independence from the rest of Ethiopia.

Ethiopian Jews are perhaps the most extraordinary of all the communities found in the Diaspora. Racially different from all and isolated for 2,500 years, they still were able to cling to their Jewishness and the rituals that were of ancient if not Biblical origin. Exact numbers of the Jewish population are not known but have been estimated from 100,000 in the eighteenth century down to about 25,000 in 1969. Then in 1985, news reached the outer world that the government of Israel had spirited out about 15,000 Falashas. It was a dramatic entry into the modern world for all and traumatic for some. In 1991, Israel flew in thousands more—probably the entire balance of the Ethiopian Jews.

There had been, in the distant past, an historical connection between the Ethiopian, Yemenite and Indian Jews. Trade was the glue that cemented these relationships, especially in ancient times when there was an open world to discover. The cooking of Ethiopian Jews, therefore, characterized by the use of pungent spices, is in my opinion a result of communication with India. Mustard, cardamom, coriander, caraway, turmeric, ginger are spices that I associate with India. The hot chili and tomato arrived later, perhaps as late as the eighteenth century after its introduction from Central America.

The staff of life for Ethiopians is *Injeera*, a large pancake prepared from a fermented batter of *teff*, an African grain of the millet family. A meal without this life-sustaining bread would be unthinkable.

It is heartwarming to remember that a poor people in primitive surroundings developed their own small cuisine. Using local ingredients, living off the land, and cut off from the mainstream of Judaism, they still maintained a Judaic way of life in hostile surroundings. Is this not an admirable characteristic of the Ethiopian Jews?

HOW TO MAKE BUTTER
(KEBE)

In Ethiopia, in preparation for making butter, a container of milk is first put aside for 2 days. It is then put in a churn, made from a large dried calabash, and shaken until the butter is formed. The lumps of butter are removed and the whey is discarded.

The butter is then put in a container (made of clay as is all the kitchen equipment) with *avish*,* turmeric, coriander, ginger, garlic and onion—all well chopped. The mixture is brought to a slow simmer and cooked for about 15 minutes. Then it is cooled and the solid pieces settle to the bottom. The seasoned butter is poured off into another container and the solids are discarded.

The butter can then be stored for long periods without refrigeration and in this respect is similar to *ghee*, the clarified butter of India.

Everything except meat dishes is cooked in the seasoned butter since kashruth laws are followed.

*A spice not available here

TELAH
Barley Beer, the Ethiopian Common Drink

This description of how to make barley beer—mixing, fermenting, adding water, and so forth, is not a real recipe. It is only designed to reveal what simple, almost primitive people can develop without the refinements of yeast and containers for fermentation, and yet come up with a national drink.

½ cup barley, preferably with the husks
5½ cups water
2 tablespoons hops (gesho leaves)
1 cup wheat flour
additional water

1. Soak the barley in a bowl with water to cover for 3 days. Drain the barley and discard the water.

2. Put the barley on a tray, cover with another tray, and leave until the barley sprouts, about 6 days. Then put the sprouted barley on a clean, dry tray and dry it in the sun. Grind the barley to a flour known as "*bickle*."

3. Powder the hops *(gesho)*. Take ½ cup water and mix it with the hops and all the barley flour except 1 teaspoon. Set aside in a jar for 3 days to ferment.

4. Mix the wheat flour with 1 cup water and leave it overnight. Roll it out into a loaf *(dabo)* and bake it. Cool the bread, break it into small pieces, and mix it with the hops and barley flour as noted above. Add 2 more cups water.

Add the remaining teaspoon of barley flour to this mixture and put into a container with a tight cover for 3 to 4 days. Add 2 more cups water, mix well, and strain. This is the beer.

TECH
Honey Beer

This is a fine home beer produced by the Ethiopian Jews. It is reminiscent of the "mead" made by my grandmother for Passover in the early days of my youth in Vermont. No one makes this family drink anymore but it is so easy it would be a shame to ignore it.

> ½ cup honey
> ¼ cup hops *(gesho leaves)*
> 3 cups water

1. Mix everything together. Put the liquid in a glass jar or stone crock with a tight cover at room temperature for 7 days. The liquid will ferment and turn into beer. It can then be refrigerated.

Serve cool.

HOW ETHIOPIANS MAKE COFFEE

They first take green coffee beans and toast them in a dry skillet over moderately low heat for about 3 minutes. During this time the beans will become black and oily, the skins shuck off and blow away. Then the beans start to smoke and turn color. As the smoke thickens, the skillet is passed around the room to the guests who inhale. The smoke apparently provides a stimulant.

The beans, now toasted, are cooled and ground. Traditionally, the beans are pounded, using a large wooden mortar and pestle. I have seen this done on farms in Haiti, also.

The ground coffee is mixed with water to taste and black cardamom seeds, then brewed or prepared Turkish style with sugar.

CHOW
Spice Mixture

These spice mixtures are what give the distinctive Ethiopian flavor to their meats and vegetables—the same as curry paste in India or *hawaish* in Yemen. The paste has considerable power and one can increase the spiciness of any dish by adding more *chow* to what is being cooked.

1 garlic clove, sliced
1 teaspoon grated fresh gingerroot or ground ginger
¼ teaspoon ground caraway
½ teaspoon ground cardamom
¼ teaspoon mustard seeds
¼ teaspoon avish (not available here)
¼ teaspoon ground coriander
½ teaspoon ground turmeric
⅓ cup water
¼ teaspoon fresh hot red chili
¼ teaspoon paprika

1. Process everything together into a smooth mixture that will be as thick as toothpaste. Then refrigerate in a jar with a tight cover, to be used when needed. Makes about ½ cup.

QUEMAM
Dry Spice Mixture

1 garlic clove, sliced
1 teaspoon chopped fresh gingerroot, or ½ teaspoon ground
    ginger
¼ teaspoon ground caraway
½ teaspoon ground cardamom
¼ teaspoon mustard seeds
¼ teaspoon avish (not available here)
¼ teaspoon ground coriander
½ teaspoon ground turmeric

1. Mix everything together and store in a jar with a tight cover. Use when required.

KAE ATAR WOT
Green Pea Stew

A well-seasoned vegetarian dish, high in protein, obviates the necessity of meat. This is one good example in the Ethiopian cooking style.

1 cup dried green split peas
4 cups water
1 medium onion, chopped (½ cup)
1 tablespoon corn oil
1 tablespoon tomato paste
2 teaspoons Chow (see Index)
½ teaspoon salt

1. Cook the peas in 3½ cups water over low heat for about ½ hour, or until peas are soft and water has almost completely evaporated. Set aside.

2. Stir-fry the onion in a dry pan for 2 minutes, add the oil, and stir-fry for 2 minutes more. Add the balance of the water (½ cup), the tomato paste, chow and salt and continue stirring.

3. Add the split peas and mix well over moderate heat for 3 minutes until everything is reduced to a thick, well-seasoned purée.

Serve warm with Ethiopian Pancakes (Injeera, see Index). Serves 4.

VARIATION: Kae Misr Wot is the same as the Kae Atar Wot except that the red Egyptian lentil is substituted for the green split peas. The technique is the same.

Misr and Atar dishes are eaten with a simple salad of shredded lettuce, small cubes of tomato, diced semi hot green chili, salt and a few drops of vegetable oil.

ALEECHA
Mixed Vegetable Stew

Quemam, the spice mixture described a few recipes back, is the principal seasoning in this vegetarian dish. It is used in the same fashion as the *garam masala* of India and the five-spice mixture of China. Note the generous amount of garlic included—an Ethiopian taste.

1 medium onion, sliced (½ cup)
10 garlic cloves, sliced thin
3 large carrots, sliced thin (2 cups)
1 cup water
3 tablespoons corn oil
1 teaspoon ground turmeric
1 to 3 fresh hot green chilies, halved, to taste
1 pound cabbage, coarsely sliced
1 teaspoon Quemam
1 tablespoon tomato paste
1 teaspoon salt, or to taste
4 medium potatoes, 1 pound, cut as for french fries

1. Stir-fry the onion, garlic and carrots in a dry pan over moderately low heat for 2 minutes. Add ½ cup water and cook for 5 minutes. Add the oil and continue to simmer.
2. Add the turmeric, chilies and cabbage. Cover the pan and steam to reduce the bulk for 2 minutes. Stir well and add the quemam, tomato paste, salt and potatoes.
3. Cover the pan and cook for 5 minutes. Add the balance of the

water and simmer for 5 minutes more to soften the potatoes and thicken the sauce somewhat.

Serve at room temperature with Ethiopian Pancakes (Injeera, see Index). Serves 6.

SIGA WOT
Spiced Beef Stew

Ethiopians first make the meat kosher with salt and water before cooking. They are village people, mostly poor farmers. In Gondar, the principal region for the Jews, clay pots, skillets and flat trays are used for cooking over charcoal.

> 3 large onions, chopped (4 cups)
> 3 tablespoons corn oil
> 3 tablespoons Chow (see Index)
> 3 tablespoons tomato paste
> 1 teaspoon salt, or to taste
> 2 cups water
> 1½ pounds beef chuck, cut into ½-inch cubes

1. Stir-fry the onions in a dry pan over moderate heat for 4 minutes to reduce the bulk, stirring constantly. Add the oil and stir-fry for 1 minute more.

2. Add the chow and tomato paste, continue to fry, then add the salt and ¼ cup water. Stir well. Add the beef and the balance of the water. Cook in a covered pan for 45 minutes, or until the beef is tender. There should be a moderate amount of sauce left.

Serve warm with Ethiopian Pancakes (Injeera, see Index).

Serves 4 to 6 with other dishes.

VARIATION: The stew (wot) may be made with chicken (doro wot). Use a 3-pound chicken, cut into serving pieces; discard loose skin and fat. The wot can also be made with lamb or goat replacing the beef.

ALICHA
Beef, Sheep or Goat Curry

I have used the catchall term "curry" since that is what it is, although not so-called by the Ethiopians. But it helps us identify the system of cooking.

2 onions, sliced (1 cup)
2 tablespoons corn oil
2 pounds meat with bone, cut into 3-inch pieces
2 garlic cloves, sliced
1 teaspoon salt, or to taste
1 fresh hot green chili, sliced
¼ teaspoon crushed fresh gingerroot
¼ teaspoon crushed mustard seeds
¼ teaspoon ground caraway
¼ teaspoon ground turmeric
1½ cups water

1. Stir-fry the onions in a dry pan over moderate heat for 2 minutes. Add the oil and stir-fry for 1 minute more. Add the meat and brown for 5 minutes, stirring frequently.

2. Add all the spices and seasonings at one time and stir well. Add the water, bring to a boil, cover the pan, and cook over moderate heat for about 45 minutes, or until the meat is tender. Should the curry dry out too quickly, add another ½ cup water. At the end of cooking time, there should be very little sauce.

Serve warm or at room temperature. Serves 6.

ASA WOT
Spiced Fish

Ethiopian Jews used freshwater fish from the numerous rivers in their region, as well as those from Lake Tana in the Gondar district. The fish are well cleaned and completely skinned before preparing, so as to remove the fish odor. Being without refrigeration, there was good reason for this precaution. In addition, the chow spice would also mask the odor of the fish.

1 pound freshwater fish of your choice, well skinned and eyes
  removed, thoroughly rinsed
3 tablespoons corn oil or butter
3 to 4 tablespoons Chow, to taste (see Index)

1. Heat the oil or butter in a skillet, add the *chow*, and stir-fry over moderate heat for about 3 minutes. Add the fish and fry for 5 minutes on each side.

Serve at room temperature or cold.

SHUROE
Spiced Chick-Pea Flour Mix and Sauce

Shuroe is a mix of chick-pea flour and spices. Chick-pea flour is known as *besan* in India and is available at any Asian grocery dealing with Indian products.

CHICK-PEA AND SPICE MIX

1 cup chick-pea flour
½ teaspoon ground turmeric
½ teaspoon grated fresh gingerroot or ground ginger
¼ teaspoon paprika
¼ teaspoon hot red chili powder
¼ teaspoon ground aniseed

SAUCE

1 cup water
1 teaspoon corn oil
2 tablespoons chick-pea flour mix
½ teaspoon salt

1. Mix together the chick-pea flour, turmeric, ginger, paprika, hot chili and aniseed. Mix well and set aside.

2. To prepare the sauce, bring the water and oil to a boil in a skillet, add 2 tablespoons of the mix and the salt and simmer over low heat for 3 to 4 minutes. The sauce will thicken quickly to a thick purée.

Serve warm with *Injeera* (see Index). Or serve the sauce with any *wot* (stew) as a side dish. Serves 2.

Reserve the balance of the *shuroe* mix for another occasion.

INTATISHA WOT
Wild Mushroom Fry

During the rainy season (the winter months) in the Gondar region, mushrooms spring up and are collected by the peasants. They are prepared in this fashion.

> 1 large onion, sliced (¾ cup)
> 1 tablespoon corn oil
> 2 tablespoons Chow (see Index)
> 1 teaspoon salt, or to taste
> ½ cup water
> 2 pounds fresh mushrooms, in thick slices

1. Stir-fry the onion in a pan over moderate heat for 3 minutes to reduce the bulk. Add the oil and stir-fry for 2 minutes more.

2. Add the *chow*, salt, ¼ cup water and the mushrooms. Stir-fry for 3 minutes. Add the balance of the water and continue to stir-fry until the mushrooms have softened and the sauce has thickened somewhat. The *chow* will provide intensity and may be reduced or increased according to taste.

Serve warm or at room temperature with Ethiopian Pancakes (*Injeera*) (see Index). Serves 6.

ATAR ALLECHA
Spiced Green-Pea Purée

There are two versions of this simple purée, which indicates the lack of available ingredients. In order to develop an ornate cuisine one would necessarily require a wide variety of vegetables, spices, seasonings, fruits, meat and poultry and, above all, equipment. The Ethiopians could rely only on spices.

1 small onion, chopped (⅓ cup)
2 garlic cloves, chopped fine
1 tablespoon corn oil
1 cup green split peas, covered with water for 1 hour, cooked for
      ½ hour, drained and mashed
½ teaspoon ground turmeric
½ teaspoon salt
1 small hot green chili, chopped fine (2 to 3 teaspoons)
1 cup water

1. Stir-fry the onion and garlic in a dry pan over moderately low heat for 2 minutes. Add the oil and stir-fry for 1 minute.

2. Add the mashed peas, turmeric, salt and chili; mix well. Add the water and cook for 3 to 4 minutes to reduce the mixture to a thick, green, well-spiced purée.

Serve warm with Ethiopian Pancakes (*Injeera*, see Index). Serves 4.

VARIATION: If you substitute 1 cup red Egyptian lentils for the green split peas and follow the same instructions, you will have Misr Allecha.

DABO
Special Sabbath Bread

In the Jewish villages of Ethiopia, cooking and baking was done over charcoal fires since ovens did not exist. Of course this simple source of heat in the kitchen was no different from that of hundreds of other cultures at that time.

1 teaspoon dry yeast
2 tablespoons baking powder
3 cups lukewarm water
2 egg yolks
1 teaspoon salt
1 tablespoon sugar
1 tablespoon corn oil
4 cups flour

1. Dissolve the yeast and the baking powder in the water. Mix in the egg yolks, salt, sugar and oil. Add the flour and prepare a smooth dough by kneading for 5 minutes. Let the dough rise in a covered bowl at room temperature for about 6 hours. Punch it down.

2. Put the dough in a lightly oiled large round skillet, and let rise, covered, for 1 hour. Cook it, still covered, over gas or electricity on top of the stove at low heat for 25 to 30 minutes. Turn the loaf over and bake for 5 minutes more.

Serve at room temperature, on the Sabbath.

INJEERA
Ethiopian Pancakes

Although in Ethiopia, the *injeera* are prepared with *teff*, a grain of the millet family, for our purposes, standard white flour is used. Traditionally, Jews in the mountain villages baked the *injeera* on a large clay dish, about 24 inches in diameter, similar to the *comal* of Guatemala in which the tortillas are baked. *Injeera* are prepared in a large skillet with a batter that has been allowed to ferment, giving it a characteristic pleasing flavor. The spongy texture is useful in soaking up gravy as well as in gripping cooked vegetables. The *injeera* serves as both spoon and fork; table utensils are not used.

1 teaspoon dry yeast
2½ cups warm water
4 cups flour
1 teaspoon baking powder
oil

1. Dissolve the yeast in the water, add it to the flour, and mix well. Let the mixture stand at room temperature overnight. (In winter it takes 2 days to allow fermentation.)

2. Stir in the baking powder and let the mixture stand for 10 minutes.

3. Put about ½ teaspoon oil in a large skillet, add about ½ cup of the batter, and fry over low heat for 1 or 2 minutes. When bubbles appear, cover the skillet for 15 seconds. Turn out the pancake to a dish. Prepare all the pancakes this way, frying on one side only.

The *injeera* are served at room temperature with meat and vegetable dishes. Makes about 20 pancakes.

Felix Iskaki, a textile merchant, in his store in Cairo, Egypt, 1979.
(Photo by Micha Bar-Am)

EGYPT

EGYPT The history of the Jews in Egypt is inextricably wedded to the Bible. Moses and the Exodus from Egypt, complete with miracles and divine intervention, dates from the thirteenth century B.C. The remarkable Judaic history in Egypt unravels from one Egyptian Dynasty to another from then into the twentieth century A.D. Myth and reality became entwined, inseparable from Jewish and Christian history.

Egyptian Jewry traces its origin back to the time of the prophet Jeremiah (587 B.C.). At the time of Alexander the Great and his conquest of Egypt in 332 B.C. synagogues had been founded and Alexandria became a great Jewish center—the greatest city in the civilized world after Rome. Elephantine, near the present Aswan dam, boasted an ancient Jewish community. One astonishing Roman report stated that at the beginning of the Christian era there were one million Jews in Egypt, pious and committed to the Torah.

The Arab Moslem conquest in 640 A.D. made many changes in the ancient Egyptian culture. For one thing it brought a period of commercial ties between the Jews of Egypt and Kairouan in present-day Tunisia. There was a high standard of Jewish learning in Egypt with a close relationship to the academies in Babylon.

Moses Maimonides, the celebrated Jew of Cairo (1135–1205), lived there during an era of both feast and famine. When the Ottoman Turks conquered Egypt in 1517, there started an era of tolerance. Then the Spanish Jews, victims of the infamous Inquisition, arrived in the sixteenth century. At that time there were three classes of Jewish communities in Alexandria and Cairo: The first was Arabic speaking, indigent, needy or poor. The second was made up of the Spanish immigrants; and the third the North African settlers from the Maghreb.

415

In the nineteenth century, the opening of the Suez Canal brought prosperity to Egypt and an influx of settlers until the Jewish population grew to 25,200. There were communities of Italian and Eastern European Jews in Alexandria, and Italian and Turkish in Cairo. The Jews of Salonika (Greece) followed. The new Jews from Europe, Africa and the Middle East all added their influence to the cuisine and it developed a Judaic style.

It would be a great culinary coup to report that I had discovered a cache of ancient Jewish recipes from the time of Moses in Egypt. Alas, this is not to be—it is the ordinary foods of everyday life in Egypt, the accumulation of the new foreign communities, that we have.

Onions, garlic and cucumbers have been eaten in Egypt since 3,000 B.C. Slaves building the pyramids, some of them Jews, were fed garlic and onions for strength. Lentils, beans, rice, simply seasoned, are incorporated into Sabbath and daily foods. Hot chili is hardly ever used but pepper and allspice are paramount seasonings. Vegetables and salads, in the hot, desiccating desert air, become life savers when interest is lost in meat and poultry. One cannot find spectacular culinary inventions but rather home cooking with nourishing combinations.

The census of 1947 indicated that 65,000 Jews lived in Egypt and that they received some form of education, more than the other communities around them. After that time it was all down hill. After the State of Israel was established the persecution began with bombs, looting, forced donation of funds, arrest, beatings, the same bag of tricks against Jews as in the Sephardic Diaspora.

The census of 1971 revealed that only 400 Jews remained in Egypt and in 1990 less than 150. It is an ancient community moving toward extinction.

M'LOUKHIA
Green Soup

This is popular in Egypt and especially with the Jews. Fresh *m'loukhia* leaves have a more refreshing flavor and should be used when available. Otherwise dried leaves or powder is acceptable.

> 1 tablespoon corn oil
> 1 small head of garlic (6 cloves), peeled, ground
> 1 tablespoon ground coriander
> 8 cups homemade chicken broth
> 1½ cups powdered m'loukhia, or 1 cup ground fresh leaves
>   (see Glossary)
> 1 teaspoon salt
> 1 whole fresh hot red chili (optional)

1. Heat the oil in a skillet and stir-fry the garlic and coriander over moderate heat for 1 or 2 minutes, or until golden.

2. Put the broth in a pan and bring to a boil over moderate heat. Add the *m'loukhia*, salt, chili (if used) and the stir-fried seasonings. Simmer for 10 minutes, stirring frequently.

Serve hot with white rice, adding as much rice as wanted to the soup bowl. The chicken parts used to prepare the broth are served as a side dish to the soup. Serves 6.

VARIATION: Using a 4½-pound duck, remove as much skin and fat as possible since American ducks are very fat. Prepare a conventional duck broth with the meat. Refrigerate the broth overnight and remove the congealed fat. Prepare the *m'loukhia* in the same way as chicken, with the warm duck pieces as a side dish.

SOUPE DE LENTILLE
Red Lentil Soup

This soup is known as Thursday soup since it was usually prepared on that day by Egyptian Jews. It is really a cream of lentil, well seasoned and thickened with the potato purée. Elsewhere, red lentils are known as Egyptian lentils.

½ pound red lentils, well rinsed and soaked in water for 1 hour,
    drained
5 cups water
1 small onion, left whole
1 small potato, peeled, halved
6 sprigs of fresh coriander
1 tablespoon corn oil
4 garlic cloves, mashed, using mortar and pestle
1 teaspoon salt
¼ teaspoon ground cuminseed
⅛ teaspoon ground turmeric

1. Put the lentils, water, onion, potato and coriander in a pan. Bring to a boil, then reduce heat to low and cook, covered, for ½ hour. Process the mixture to a smooth consistency and return the mixture to the pan.

2. Heat the oil in a skillet and add the garlic, salt, cuminseed and turmeric. Stir-fry over moderate heat for 3 minutes. Add this to the soup. Bring to a boil and simmer over low heat for 15 minutes more.

Serve hot with toasted bread croutons or dry toasted pita.
Serves 6.

BATATA BEL LAMOUN
Golden Potato Soup

Lemon is the predominant flavor in this almost vegetarian soup. It is known as Friday Soup since it is prepared by the Egyptian Jews for Friday evening dinner to usher in the Sabbath. It can be prepared for dairy meals by omitting the kosher chicken consommé cubes used in this modern version of a traditional soup.

1 large carrot, sliced
3 celery ribs and leaves, sliced
6 cups water
1 tablespoon corn oil
2 garlic cloves, chopped fine

2 pounds potatoes (about 6), peeled and sliced
2 teaspoons salt, or to taste
¼ cup lemon juice
2 kosher chicken consommé cubes, crumbled
¼ teaspoon ground turmeric

1. Purée the carrot and celery with 3 cups of the water in a processor. Put this into a large pan and add the balance of the water.

2. Heat the oil in a skillet, add the garlic, and stir-fry over low heat for 2 minutes, just enough to change the color. Add this to the soup pan. Bring to a boil over moderate heat and skim off and discard the foam that accumulates.

3. Add the potatoes and cook over low heat for about 45 minutes. The potatoes will begin to disintegrate. At this point, remove the pan from the heat and mash the potatoes in the pan with a hand masher or ricer. Bring the soup to a boil again, add the salt, lemon juice, consommé cubes and turmeric.

4. Simmer over low heat for ½ hour more, stirring frequently to prevent the potatoes sticking to the pan. The soup will have turned a golden color. Adjust the salt and lemon juice should you wish a more intense flavor.

Serve hot in a soup plate with as much rice as wanted.

Serves 6 to 8.

V A R I A T I O N : Should you prefer, use 6 cups homemade chicken broth instead of water and eliminate the consommé cubes.

FASSOULIA BEDA
White Bean Stew

Here a standard Egyptian formula converts dried large white beans into a vegetarian stew. The beans are not soaked in water overnight (although they could be), but the skins come off during cooking, giving the stew a rougher texture. A lightly spiced tomato sauce adds flavor to the beans.

BEANS

1 pound dried white haricot beans, rinsed
5 cups water

SAUCE

4 tablespoons corn oil
1 medium onion, chopped (1 cup)
½ cup canned tomato sauce or equal amount freshly made
2 garlic cloves, put through a press
1 teaspoon salt, or to taste
½ teaspoon ground cuminseed
¼ teaspoon pepper

1. Put the beans and 3 cups of the water into a large pan and bring to a boil. Turn the heat to low, half-cover the pan, and simmer until the water is almost absorbed. Bring the other 2 cups of water to a boil, add to the beans, and continue to simmer. The total cooking time to soften the beans is about 2 hours. The stew will take on a creamy look and consistency.

2. To make the sauce, heat the oil in a skillet, add the onion, and sauté over low heat until golden. Add this to the bean pan with the tomato sauce, garlic, salt, cuminseed and pepper. Bring to a boil and simmer over low heat, covered, for 15 minutes. If the liquid has evaporated too quickly, add ½ cup more boiling water and simmer for 5 minutes more.

Serve warm with rice. Serves 6.

SOFRITO
Spiced Beef and Vegetable Stew

Allspice seems to have made inroads in the cooking of Egyptian Jews. Sometimes known as the "English spice," it is of North American origin taken, perhaps by the English, to Egypt. This family stew of beef and vegetables is a Friday night dish, containing a few pods of cardamom that give it an exotic twist.

1 tablespoon corn oil
1 large onion, chopped (2 cups)
2 pounds beef chuck, steak or shoulder meat, cut into 1-inch
    cubes
4 cups boiling water
⅛ teaspoon ground allspice
2 garlic cloves, put through a press
¼ teaspoon pepper

2 teaspoons wine vinegar
1 large carrot, sliced
4 medium potatoes (1 pound), cubed
1 pound green beans, halved
1 teaspoon salt, or to taste
4 cardamom pods (habahan)

1. Heat the oil in a large pan, add the onion and beef, and stir-fry over moderate heat for 2 minutes until they change color.

2. Add the water, allspice, garlic, pepper and vinegar and bring to a boil. Reduce heat to low and cook for 1 hour, or until beef is tender.

3. Add the carrot, potatoes, beans, salt and cardamom. Simmer the stew over low heat for ½ hour more. There will be a generous amount of sauce for the stew.

Serve warm with rice and other Sabbath dishes. Serves 6.

BAMIA

Meatball and Okra Sauté in
Tomato Sauce

Okra must be one of the most ubiquitous vegetables in the Middle East. Every culture is mesmerized by this finger-shaped, gummy (when overcooked) member of the cotton family. In India, where I first discovered this botanical exotic, okra was known as lady's-fingers, as well as *bamia*.

MEATBALLS

1 pound ground beef
1 egg, beaten
¼ cup bread crumbs
3 garlic cloves, put through a press

OKRA

¼ cup corn oil
1 large onion, chopped (1 cup)
1½ pounds fresh okra, the smallest size available

2 generous tablespoons tomato paste
2 cups boiling water
¼ teaspoon ground allspice

1. Mix the meatball ingredients together thoroughly and prepare miniature meatballs—¾ inch in diameter. Set aside. You will need only 8 or 10 meatballs for the soup; the rest may be refrigerated or frozen.
2. Heat the oil in a pan, add the onion, and sauté over moderate heat until it turns golden. Add the okra and stir-fry over low heat for 5 minutes. This sometimes brightens the color.
3. Dissolve the tomato paste in the water and add this and the allspice to the okra pan. Bring to a boil and cook for 3 minutes, then add 8 or 10 meatballs and simmer the entire mixture for 10 minutes more. Do not overcook since okra are notoriously mucilaginous.

Serve warm with rice and other dishes for the Sabbath or for daily dining. Serves 6.

MAYEENA
Matzoh and Potato Bake

Passover food is limiting but Egyptian Jews have artfully concocted a mayeena that conforms to the Passover ritual for both dairy and meat occasions.

MATZOH

8 matzohs, broken into 3-inch pieces
2 eggs, beaten
2 tablespoons corn oil
1 pound cooked chicken or beef, cut into small cubes
2 medium onions, chopped (1 cup)
¼ teaspoon ground allspice
¼ teaspoon pepper
1 teaspoon salt
⅛ teaspoon grated nutmeg

POTATOES

3 large potatoes, about 1 pound, peeled
2 eggs, beaten
¼ teaspoon salt
⅛ teaspoon pepper

1. Moisten the matzohs in warm water for a few minutes to soften them and gently press out excess liquid. Oil a heatproof glass or metal baking dish (1½ quarts). Dip the matzoh pieces into the eggs and lay them in the baking dish in an orderly fashion.

2. Heat the oil in a skillet, add the meat, onions, allspice, pepper, salt and nutmeg, and stir-fry over moderate heat for 3 minutes. Spread the mixture over the matzoh in the baking dish.

3. Cut the potatoes into quarters; boil them until soft but still firm. Process to a purée.

4. Spread the purée smoothly over the meat. Poke 8 holes about 1 inch deep into the purée. Beat the eggs with the salt and pepper and pour it over the potatoes. Bake in a 375° F. oven for ½ hour.

Serve hot, cut into generous squares, with wedges of lemon.

Serves 6 to 8.

V A R I A T I O N : *Mayeena* may be prepared as a dairy dish. Simply replace the meat with 2 cups cottage cheese (1 pound) mixed with 1 cup grated yellow Cheddar cheese. Scatter this over the matzoh in the baking dish and cover with potato purée and egg.

Bake in a 375° F. oven for ½ hour.

TAGARINES
Noodle Pancake

This is not the exotic dish that one would associate with ancient Egypt but a more down-to-earth preparation of modern times. It is more European—Greek or Turkish—than North African.

½ pound dry egg noodles, broken into 1-inch pieces
4 tablespoons corn oil
5 medium onions, sliced thin (2 cups)
½ pound ground beef
1 teaspoon salt
¼ teaspoon pepper

1. Cook the noodles in lightly salted water until *al dente*, about 5 minutes. Drain well, set aside.

2. Heat 2 tablespoons oil in a skillet, add the onions, and fry over low heat for 3 minutes until just golden. Add the beef, salt and pepper and stir-fry the mixture for 5 minutes more. Turn out into a bowl and reserve.

3. Add the remaining 2 tablespoons oil and half of the pasta to the same skillet and cover with the meat/onion melange. Cover with the remaining half of the pasta. Fry over moderate heat until the bottom pasta becomes crisp and firm, about 5 minutes. Flip the pancake over on a large dinner plate and slide the other side into the skillet. Brown over moderate heat for 5 minutes more.

Serve this crisp pancake warm with salads. Serves 4.

FOOL ACHDAR
Green Fava Beans

Fava beans, both fresh and dry, are a particular favorite of the Egyptians and one of the most ancient of cultivated plants. The Egyptian bean is smaller, rounder and perhaps more flavorful than the American fava bean. The dry, brown fava beans in Mideastern groceries are about 1 inch long and flat. They require soaking in water overnight.

2 pounds fresh fava beans
1 cup water
2 tablespoons corn oil
¼ teaspoon salt
¼ teaspoon white pepper
¼ cup chopped fresh coriander

1. Shell the beans and put them in a pan with the water, oil, salt and pepper. Bring to a boil over moderate heat and cook, covered, until tender, about 20 minutes. Drain well and remove from the heat.

2. Add the coriander, cover the pan, and let stand for 5 minutes. Mix well.

Serve warm with rice. Serves 6 with other dishes.

NOTE: Canned green fava beans, imported from the Mideast, are often available in groceries that cater to Mediterranean cooks.

KOSHARY
Lentils and Rice

Vegetarian and dairy foods go well together, especially when well seasoned and enriched by the lentil. A completely kosher combination.

There are several botanical varieties of lentil and the one we use here is the greenish-brown type found in supermarkets.

LENTILS

> 1 tablespoon corn oil
> 1 medium onion, chopped (½ cup)
> 1 cup dried lentils, soaked in water for 1 hour, drained
> 1 cup water
> ¼ teaspoon pepper
> ¼ teaspoon ground cuminseed

RICE

> 2 cups water
> 2 cups raw rice, rinsed in cold water
> ½ teaspoon salt, or to taste
> crisp fried onions for garnish

1. Heat the oil in a pan, add the onion, and stir-fry over moderate heat for 2 minutes. Add the lentils, 1 cup water, the pepper and cuminseed. Bring to a boil and cook for 5 minutes.

2. Add the 2 cups water to the lentil mixture and bring to a boil over moderate heat. Add the rice and salt and continue to boil. Then reduce heat to low, and cover the pan with a kitchen towel and the metal pan cover. Cook for 15 minutes; stir once or twice during this procedure. Test the rice for doneness. It may be necessary to add another 5 minutes over low heat to the cooking time, and let the mixture rest, off the heat, for another 10 minutes without opening the cover.

Serve warm, garnished with the crisp fried onions. Serve with a side dish of yoghurt.

Serves 8.

M'RAAD
Eggplant Salad

This delectable salad may be served with any kind of Egyptian or Oriental food. Eggplant is apt to absorb a lot of oil, but salting it reduces this tendency, as does the steam-frying in a covered skillet.

EGGPLANT

2 pounds large eggplants (about 3)
2 tablespoons salt
oil for panfrying, about ¼ cup

SAUCE

5 garlic cloves, put through a press
½ cup water
⅛ teaspoon ground turmeric
¼ teaspoon paprika
¼ teaspoon ground cuminseed
1 tablespoon tomato paste
1 tablespoon white or cider vinegar
¼ cup chopped sweet red pepper for garnish

1. Trim off both ends of the eggplants. Cut them into slices about ½ inch thick. Sprinkle the slices with salt and let stand for ½ hour. Drain off the discolored liquid and wipe the slices dry, pressing them gently.

2. Heat the oil in a large skillet and lightly brown the eggplant slices on both sides over moderate heat for about 4 minutes on each side. Cover the pan since this will steam-fry and reduce the amount of oil needed. Remove eggplant to a large serving platter and keep warm while you make the sauce.

3. Stir-fry the garlic in the same skillet for about 10 seconds. Add the water, turmeric, paprika, cuminseed and tomato paste and simmer the mixture over low heat for 5 minutes. Stir in the vinegar. Pour the sauce over the platter of eggplant and garnish with the chopped red pepper.

Serve at room temperature. Serves 6 to 8 with other dishes.

SALADE EGYPTIENNE
Popular Egyptian Salad

Àll the vegetables, with the exception of cabbage, are cut to the same size and combined with an assortment of fresh herbs. A salad for all seasons.

VEGETABLES

3 firm almost ripe tomatoes, cut into ¼-inch cubes
3 young cucumbers, not peeled, cut into ¼-inch cubes
3 large green sweet peppers, cut into ¼-inch cubes
6 scallions, sliced thin
1 cup shredded cabbage
1 pound small white turnips, peeled, cut into ¼-inch cubes
    (optional)
4 garlic cloves, chopped fine
½ cup chopped parsley
½ cup chopped fresh coriander
½ cup chopped fresh dill
1 teaspoon ground coriander
½ teaspoon ground cuminseed

SAUCE

1 tablespoon corn oil
1 tablespoon white or cider vinegar
juice of 1 lemon
¼ teaspoon hot red chili flakes

1. Mix the vegetables, herbs and spices together and toss several times. Set aside.

2. Just before dining, mix the sauce ingredients thoroughly, and add to the vegetables. Toss well to integrate all the seasonings.

MAHCHI
Stuffed Zucchini

Almost every Sephardic culture prepares stuffed vegetables with some sort of seasoned stuffing. Indians cook their stuffed vegetables in a tamarind sauce; Egyptians use a sauce of tomato and lemon juice. This is enhanced during the cooking process with garlic, allspice and onion. An added bonus for our time is that the mahchi are almost entirely fat free.

ZUCCHINI

    2 pounds small zucchini (about 6), 3 to 4 inches long
    2 tablespoons corn oil
    1 garlic clove, chopped fine or put through a press
    ⅛ teaspoon ground allspice
    ½ teaspoon salt, or to taste

STUFFING

    1 cup raw rice, well rinsed
    ⅓ cup water
    3 tablespoons corn oil
    1 large onion, chopped (2 cups)
    1 pound ground beef
    1 garlic clove, chopped fine or put through a press
    1 teaspoon salt, or to taste
    juice of 1 large lemon (¼ cup)
    ½ cup canned tomato sauce or equal amount of homemade

SAUCE

    2 cups water
    1 tablespoon tomato paste
    ½ teaspoon salt
    2 tablespoons lemon juice
    2 tablespoons corn oil

1. Trim ¼ inch from each end of the zucchini. Cut each one crosswise into halves. Scoop out the pulp with an apple corer, close to the outer skin of each zucchini piece. Reserve 1 cup of the pulp.
    2. Heat the oil in a skillet; add the pulp, garlic, allspice and salt.

Stir-fry over low heat until the pulp has browned and reduced to a mush, about 10 minutes. Set aside.

3. Put the rice and ⅓ cup water into a pan and simmer over low heat for about 2 minutes, or just long enough for all the liquid to be absorbed. Set aside.

4. Heat the oil in a skillet, add the onion, and stir-fry over low heat until it has changed color to a light golden brown. Cool slightly.

5. Mix together the beef, cooked zucchini pulp, cooked rice, garlic, salt, lemon juice and the tomato sauce. Stuff each zucchini half almost to the top. Tap the bottom of the zucchini now and then so that the stuffing is firmly settled in. Fit the stuffed zucchini snugly into a skillet or pan in one or two layers.

6. Put all the sauce ingredients together, stir well to mix, and pour over the zucchini. Bring to a boil, then cover the pan and cook over low heat for 1 hour. At the end of about 45 minutes, turn the zucchini over carefully, and cook, uncovered, for 15 minutes more. Total cooking time is 1 hour. Almost all the liquid will have evaporated from the sauce.

Serve warm. Makes 12 to 14 pieces.

VARIATIONS: To stuff onions, peel 4 medium onions and scoop out the center of each onion from the stem end. Use the same stuffing to fill shells almost to the top. May be cooked with zucchini or separately. The onion centers are cooked in the pan with other vegetables.

To stuff tomatoes, cut out the stem ends of 4 ripe but firm medium tomatoes and scoop out seeds and liquid. Stuff and cook the same way as the other vegetables.

NOTE: These three vegetables—zucchini, onions and tomatoes—are the most popular vegetables for *mahchi*. They are usually made in large numbers for family gatherings at Passover and Rosh Hoshanah.

The Maghreb - North Africa

MOROCCO

TANGIER

TUNISIA

LIBYA

Picnic at the "Diplomats" woods. Tangier, Spanish Morocco, c.1910.

MOROCCO

The early history and ancient legends, as well as inscriptions on Roman tombstones in Morocco, reveal the presence of Jews there before and after the second century A.D. Prior to the Arab conquest in the eighth century, Jewish missionaries, it is told, converted whole Berber tribes. But during the next several centuries political and religious vicissitudes forced the spiritual and intellectual Jews to leave for Christian Spain.

Then, in 1492, the Spanish Inquisition resulted in the movement of Jews back to Morocco. The city of Fez attracted the new immigrants and it became the spiritual center, based on the Judaic Spanish tradition. Exiles from both Spain and Portugal occupied important positions in the courts of the ruling Muslim Sultans. Marranos, Spanish Jews who had accepted Christianity in Spain, reconverted to Judaism.

Many of the Jews of Morocco were engaged in a variety of professions and businesses—farmers, craftsmen in precious metals, traders in beeswax, rubber, ostrich feathers!—as well as the more dignified commercial activities. Some families in the maritime trade were wealthy and influential. Others were court bankers or officials to the sultan and were in privileged positions.

But the majority of the Jewish population suffered in poverty. Droughts, famine, taxes were all responsible. *Dhimmi*, the poll tax imposed on Jews and other non-Muslim communities, was a scheme designed to impoverish and denigrate, and was practiced by the incumbent rulers in some Islamic countries. Many Jews were serfs but nonetheless pious and Judaic. Ultimately Jews moved from mountain villages to urban centers and port cities to escape hostile Muslim residents of the Moroccan interior.

The miseries of the Jews were manifold during the nineteenth century and early twentieth. There was a plague epi-

433

demic and severe overcrowding in the *mellas* (the Jewish quarters) in the cities.

After the Holocaust, the census of 1948 indicated 238,000 Jews lived in Morocco. In 1962 it had shrunk to 130,000, and in 1968 to about 42,000, due to a mass exodus to Israel and also to a large number settling in France and Canada. Illiteracy, poverty, poor health was their lot in spite of there being a few wealthy families. The myth that all Jews are rich was shattered in Morocco. By 1970, only 35,000 lived in Morocco and the numbers have gradually decreased to the present day. So one sees the Jewish community being shifted between Spain and Morocco and finally the gradual dwindling away to be absorbed elsewhere.

The food, however, is a different matter. The Moroccan cuisine is considered the most inventive, flavorful and perhaps ingenious of the cooking styles of the Maghreb; at least the French say this about their former colony. Frequently, it is included in the world's ten greatest cuisines, which is an indication of its reputation in culinary circles. Jewish cooking is an amalgam of traditional local dishes married to Sephardic ideas brought to Morocco at the time of the Inquisition and, importantly, guided by kashruth. From these various influences, a universal Jewish style emerged and was polished over the centuries.

The hallmark of Moroccan cooking is the use of aromatic spices such as cinnamon, coriander, ginger, saffron, turmeric and paprika for color. Dried fruits—figs, apricots, prunes, raisins—are included in meat dishes and complement the spices that emphasize the sweet fruits. Almonds, walnuts and olives, the produce of a rich agriculture, are lavishly incorporated in many dishes. To top if off there is the famous *harissa*, a chili-hot condiment, available for a sharp contrasting impact.

Salads in their numbers, both fresh and cooked, are some of the most popular concoctions in a semidesert atmosphere. From the Jewish point of view they are *pareve* and can be served with both dairy and meat dishes. Cous cous is the single preparation most closely identified with Morocco and other Maghreb countries.

The Sabbath and its admonishment to pray and rest has also produced an assortment of scheena, those all-inclusive one-dish meals that are prepared late on Friday, cooked all night over smoldering coals, and are ready for dining after synagogue at noontime on the Sabbath. They are generally meat, potatoes, chick-peas and seasonings, very slowly baked and melting in flavor and aroma.

It is apt to be familiar foods that bring about nostalgia in people who have been forced to flee their homeland. So it is with the Moroccan Jews; though living now in alien lands, they find comfort in cooking and eating Pastiya, a variety of Scheena, and the familiar fresh salads.

Of about 300,000 Jews in Morocco in past centuries, only 15,000 remain at the time of writing this book.

FOOLIM
Crisp-Fried Fava Beans

A traditional street-corner appetizer, easy to prepare as nibbles or to serve with drinks.

1 pound dried fava beans
oil for deep-frying
salt (optional)

1. Cover the dried beans with water and refrigerate them for 4 days. Drain and remove the skins, which will peel off easily. Divide the favas into two lobes and dry them on towels.

2. Heat the oil in a wok or deep skillet and fry the favas a few at a time over moderate heat until brown, about 3 minutes. Remove from the oil with a slotted spoon and drain them on paper towels. Sprinkle with salt if you wish.

Store in a glass jar with a tight cover.

MARK DIL GRA IL CHIMRA

Pumpkin and Chick-Pea Soup

This special soup is served on Rosh Hashanah, the New Year.

2 tablespoons corn oil
3 medium onions, chopped (1½ cups)
½ pound dried chick-peas, soaked overnight in water, drained,
    and chopped in a processor
2 pounds pumpkin, chopped
2 tablespoons honey
½ teaspoon salt
¼ teaspoon white pepper
8 cups beef broth or water
2 tablespoons flour dissolved in ¼ cup water

1. Heat the oil in a pan and stir-fry the onions until they turn golden. Add the chick-peas, pumpkin, honey, salt and pepper, and stir-fry the mixture over moderate heat for 5 minutes.

2. Add the beef broth or water, bring to a boil, and cook over moderate heat for ½ hour. Add the flour mixture for thickening and simmer over low heat for 15 minutes more.

Serve hot. Serves 6 to 8.

VARIATION: The law of milk and meat in the kosher ritual prevail for this soup. It is possible to serve this in a dairy meal by eliminating the beef broth entirely and substituting 6 cups water and 2 cups milk.

SOUPE DE PESACH

Vegetable Soup for Passover

This soup, which is special for Passover but may be prepared at any time, utilizes seasonal vegetables. In a general way, it is personal preference that is the guide in the selection. For example, some may not like turnip or beans and they could be omitted without a loss of flavor for the soup.

½ cup dried *fava beans*
½ cup dried *chick-peas*
10 cups light homemade chicken broth
2 cups water
1 teaspoon salt
½ teaspoon white pepper
½ teaspoon paprika
2 pounds chicken pieces—breast, leg, thighs
1 pound potatoes, peeled, cut into ½-inch cubes
2 leeks, both white and tender green parts, trimmed and sliced
¼ pound green beans, cut into 2-inch pieces
2 white turnips, peeled, sliced (1 cup)
1 large onion, sliced (1 cup)
1 cup green peas, fresh or frozen
2 carrots, sliced (1½ cups)
2 celery ribs with leaves, cut into ¼-inch-wide slices

1. Cover the favas and chick-peas separately with water and soak overnight. Drain.

2. Put the chicken broth and water in a large pan, and bring to a boil over moderate heat. Add the salt, pepper, paprika, chicken pieces, favas and chick-peas. Cook, covered, for 20 minutes. Add the potatoes and cook for 5 minutes more.

3. Add all the other vegetables—leeks, green beans, turnips, onion, peas, carrots and celery—and simmer over low heat for ½ hour, or until everything is tender. Adjust the salt and pepper to taste and simmer for 10 minutes more.

Serve hot with matzoh. Serves 8.

SHACKSHOOKA
Eggs and Sauce

This vivid preparation, also prepared in other countries of the Maghreb, makes an ideal lunch along with several kinds of salads. You may prefer to reduce the amount of hot chili but the family-style way is to have a piquant sauce.

2 tablespoons corn oil
1 medium onion, chopped fine (½ cup)

1 garlic clove, chopped fine
¼ teaspoon ground turmeric
1 teaspoon salt
½ to 1 teaspoon hot red chili flakes
1 pound ripe tomatoes, fresh or canned, peeled, chopped
6 eggs

1. Heat the oil in a large skillet; add the onion and garlic and stir-fry over moderate heat for 1 minute. Add the turmeric, salt and chili flakes and stir-fry for 2 minutes.

2. Add the tomatoes, stir well, cover the skillet, and simmer over low heat for 15 minutes.

3. Break the eggs, one at a time, well spaced apart, into the sauce. Cover the pan and simmer for 5 minutes.

Serve warm with bread. Serves 6.

SCHEENA
Sabbath Beef and Potato Roast

Slow cooking over very low heat for many hours is the secret to this famous Sabbath dish. The roasted eggs become brown, and have a delicious flavor unlike any eggs you have eaten.

Cholent is the Eastern European name for a similar preparation for the Sabbath. Middle Easterners from India and Iraq refer to this method of cooking as *hameen*. All of them are designed to honor the Sabbath by not cooking and so the dish is prepared just before the Sabbath falls, on Friday afternoon.

3 pounds small potatoes, about 12, peeled
1 cup dried chick-peas, soaked in water overnight, drained
1 pound beef chuck, cut into 1-inch cubes
2 pounds beef shin bones, cut into 2- or 3-inch pieces
1 pound ground beef mixed with ¼ teaspoon pepper and shaped
     into a loaf
8 raw eggs in the shell
1 teaspoon salt

1. Put the potatoes and chick-peas in a clay or metal pot large enough to contain all the ingredients. Add the beef cubes and bones on top. Place the ground beef loaf on one side, the eggs all around the pot and sprinkle salt over all.

2. Cover the mixture completely with water. Bring to a boil on top of the stove and cook over low heat for 15 minutes. Put the pan in the oven and bake at the lowest heat, about 200° F., for 8 to 10 hours or overnight.

Serve warm on the Sabbath at about noon after returning from the synagogue. Serves 8.

NOTE: It is possible to prepare the *scheena* at any time by assembling all the ingredients in a pan at about 7 A.M. and baking in a 225° F. oven for 8 to 10 hours, dining at 7 P.M. I have done this in a reduced version, half the ingredients, and it works extremely well.

VARIATION: This variation of the *scheena* is made during the winter season with barley, when it is known as *Zerrah*.

1 cup raw barley, well rinsed
2 cups water
½ teaspoon paprika
1 whole dry red chili
1 whole head of garlic, not peeled
½ teaspoon salt
2 tablespoons corn oil
1-inch cube of beef fat (optional)

1. Put all the ingredients in a pan with a tight cover. Simmer very slowly over the lowest heat for 8 to 10 hours.

Serve warm. Serves 4.

HAMEEN

Beef, Chick-Pea and Egg Bake for the Sabbath

This is a hearty, substantial combination for the cold winter season. The slow baking does not require constant supervision. Put the pan in the oven and forget about it for 10 hours, more or less. The pan cover should be tight and can be wrapped in aluminum foil to make it so. For the American kitchen put this in a 225° F. oven at 7 A.M. and dine at 7 P.M. any time of the year.

1½ cups dried chick-peas, soaked in water overnight, drained
2 whole small onions, peeled
8 small potatoes (2 pounds), peeled
1 cup raw rice, well rinsed, drained
¼ teaspoon salt
¼ teaspoon pepper
1 teaspoon corn oil
1 cup water, unseasoned
1 pound beef chuck, cut into 8 pieces
1 pound beef or veal shin bones
8 eggs in the shell
8 cups water in which 1 teaspoon salt, 1 teaspoon pepper have
    been dissolved
¼ teaspoon ground turmeric

1. On the bottom of a large pan put the chick-peas, with the onions and potatoes on top.

2. Seal the rice, salt, pepper, oil and 1 cup unseasoned water in an aluminum foil package or a plastic baking bag; fasten firmly. Arrange this on one side of the pan.

3. Put the meat and bones on the other side of the pan and arrange the eggs in the center. Add the 8 cups water with salt and pepper and the turmeric to the pan. Bring to a boil over moderate heat, cover, then reduce heat to low and cook for 1 hour.

4. Put the pan in a 200° F. oven and bake very slowly from early Friday evening to the following day, Sabbath. About halfway through add 1 cup of water if the evaporation has been too rapid. When finally cooked, the ingredients will be moist but with little sauce.

The hard-cooked eggs are peeled and eaten with the rest of the ingredients.

Serve warm. Serves 8.

BOULETTE DE VIANDE

*Meatballs with Celery and
Green Peas*

Moroccan cooks are orderly and systematic. There is a place for everything and everything is kept in its place—as demonstrated in this casserole.

MEATBALLS

2 pounds ground beef
¼ teaspoon grated nutmeg
½ teaspoon salt
¼ teaspoon pepper
1 tablespoon corn oil
¼ cup chopped parsley
1 medium onion, grated (½ cup)
2 tablespoons water

CASSEROLE

1 pound young celery ribs, cut into 2-inch finger-size sticks
1 pound green peas, fresh or frozen
1 cup water
½ teaspoon salt
½ teaspoon ground turmeric

1. Mix meatball ingredients together thoroughly. Prepare balls 1½ inches in diameter. Set aside. Makes 20 balls.

2. Place the celery on the bottom of a well-oiled pan, with the peas on top. Add the water, salt and turmeric and bring to a boil over low heat. Simmer for 10 minutes.

3. Add the meatballs, one by one, cover the pan, and cook for ½ hour.

Serve warm. Serves 6 to 8 with other dishes.

PASTEL
Stuffed Triangles

Pastel is a Spanish word that means pastry roll or filled pastry. The Jews of Morocco came from Spain and it is conceivable that the origin of the triangles is Spanish. In any event, these excellent appetizers have traveled well. The triangles can be stored in plastic bags and frozen after they have been fried and well cooled. To serve again, allow them to thaw for 1 hour, then reheat in a 350° F. oven for several minutes, until crisp.

2 pounds ground beef
½ teaspoon salt
⅛ teaspoon black pepper
8 cups water
3 bay leaves
2 medium onions, quartered
6 peppercorns
¼ cup chopped parsley, or half and half with fresh coriander
1 teaspoon grated mace
½ teaspoon grated nutmeg
½ pound fresh spinach, chopped fine, or 10 ounces frozen
   chopped spinach, well thawed and squeezed out
½ teaspoon harissa (see Index) or hot red chili flakes
⅛ teaspoon white pepper
3 tablespoons white or cider vinegar
1 package of rectangular spring-roll skins
1 egg, beaten
½ cup water
oil for deep frying

1. Mix the beef, salt and pepper together. Divide it into 3 equal parts and roll each into a ball.

2. Bring the water to a boil with the bay leaves, onions and peppercorns over moderate heat. Add the beef balls and cook for 45 minutes to ensure that the meat is well cooked. Remove the balls, cool them somewhat, and crumble them up.

3. Put the crumbled beef in a large dry skillet. Stir-fry it over low heat for 1 minute, adding parsley, mace, nutmeg, spinach, *harissa*, white pepper and vinegar. Continue to stir-fry until the mixture is dry, 5 to 7 minutes. Cool and set aside.

4. Cut the spring-roll skins into long strips 2½ inches wide. Beat the egg and water together. Paint 1 strip with the egg mixture, using a pastry brush. At the lower left side corner put 2 teaspoons of the beef mixture. Fold it over toward the right side to shape a triangle, then turn it up to the left, always shaping a triangle. The skin will stick together with the painted egg. Complete the length of the skin strip. Set aside. Complete all the skin strips and stuffing this way.

5. Heat the oil in a wok or deep skillet. Fry the triangles over moderate heat until brown and crisp, 2 to 3 minutes. Remove them and drain on paper towels.

Serve warm. Makes 60 triangles.

PASTEL DE BATATA
Stuffed Potato Fritter

This popular Passover dish can be prepared in any quantities. Soup, matzoh, an assortment of salads are the accompaniments to the fritters.

MEAT

> 1 pound ground beef
> ½ cup water
> 1 teaspoon salt
> ¼ teaspoon pepper
> 4 bay leaves
> ¼ cup lemon juice

POTATOES

> 2 pounds potatoes (about 6), cooked in their skins, peeled
> ½ teaspoon ground turmeric
> ½ teaspoon salt
> ⅛ teaspoon pepper

FRITTER

> oil for panfrying
> flour for dusting
> 1 egg, beaten

1. Put the meat ingredients into a pan and cook over low heat, covered, for 15 minutes or until quite dry. Remove the bay leaves, then process the mixture to a fine consistency. Set aside.

2. Mash the potatoes and mix well with the turmeric, salt and pepper.

3. Take about ⅓ cup mashed potato and flatten it out in your palm to 3 inches in diameter and about ½ inch thick. Put into the center 1 heaping tablespoon of the meat; fold over the edges toward the center and shape a round fritter. Prepare all the fritters this way.

4. Heat the oil in a large skillet. Dip each fritter into the flour, then into the egg, and brown over moderate heat for about 3 minutes on each side. Drain briefly on paper towels.

Serve warm. Makes 12 fritters.

TAZEEN
Veal, Nut and Fruit Melange

The tazeen is a pot roast cooked on top of the stove and richly aromatic in the Moroccan style. It is a sweet food to celebrate Rosh Hashanah and guarantee that the New Year will be a sweet one. The meat provides additional richness to the fruit and nuts and is compatible with them.

3 tablespoons corn oil
2 pounds small pickling onions, the smaller the better, peeled
2 pounds boneless veal, cut into 1½-inch cubes
1 pound pitted prunes
1 pound light raisins
1 pound shelled walnuts
1 teaspoon salt
3 to 4 tablespoons sugar, to taste
½ teaspoon ground cinnamon
1½ cups water

1. Heat the oil in a large pan and brown the onions over low heat for 7 to 8 minutes. The onions should become honey-colored. Add the veal and stir-fry for 3 minutes more.

2. Add the prunes, raisins, walnuts, salt, sugar, cinnamon and water. Bring to a simmer, cover the pan, and cook over low heat for 2 hours. The stew should be reduced to a moist consistency with some liquid. Should the mixture dry out too quickly, add another ½ cup water and continue to cook until the desired harmony is produced. Serve warm. Serves 8 with other dishes.

NOTE: I suggest that you try half of the recipe since it is not so intimidating or expensive.

JUDGJA BIL ZEITOUN
Chicken and Olives

Morocco is olive country and the combination with chicken and the other seasonings is inspired. A fine dish that would do well in a contemporary Western dinner.

> 1 pound pitted green North African olives
> 1 chicken, 3½ pounds, cut into 6 pieces, loose skin and fat discarded
> 4 garlic cloves, sliced
> 2 tablespoons corn oil
> ¼ cup chopped parsley
> ½ teaspoon salt
> ½ teaspoon pepper
> ½ teaspoon ground turmeric
> 1 cup chopped ripe tomatoes, fresh or canned
> 1 cup water

1. Blanch the olives in boiling water for 1 minute. Drain.

2. Put the chicken and garlic in a dry pan and stir-fry over moderate heat for 4 to 5 minutes. Add the oil, parsley, salt, pepper, turmeric and tomatoes. Mix well, add water, and bring to a boil.

3. Cook the chicken in the covered pan over low heat for 40 minutes. Add the olives and cook for 15 minutes more to integrate the flavors.

Serve warm with bread and salads. Serves 6.

COUS COUS JUDGJA
Chicken Cous Cous

Cous cous is a pasta beloved by North Africans of the Maghreb. The term is used for the pasta itself and for any dish made with it. There are many combinations that consist of a meat or fish stew, the pasta granules (the *cous cous*) and sometimes a soup, as in this Moroccan presentation.

SOUP

½ cup dried chick-peas, soaked in water overnight, drained
2 medium onions, sliced (1 cup)
½ pound carrots (about 3), cut into finger-size pieces
3 celery ribs without leaves, cut into 2-inch pieces and halved
    vertically
2 tablespoons corn oil
8 cups water
¼ teaspoon salt
¼ teaspoon pepper
⅛ teaspoon ground turmeric
2 tablespoons paprika
½ pound small potatoes (about 4), peeled, halved
½ pound pumpkin, cut into finger-size pieces
1 pound zucchini, cut into finger-size pieces
2 parsley sprigs, whole

CHICKEN

1 tablespoon corn oil
1 small onion, quartered
1 chicken, 3½ pounds, cut into 8 pieces, giblets included, loose
    skin and fat discarded
¼ teaspoon salt
⅛ teaspoon pepper
⅛ teaspoon ground turmeric
1 cup water
1 pound cous cous, or more

1. Put the chick-peas on the bottom of a large pan. Place onions on top, then the carrots, celery and oil. Stir-fry over moderate heat for 3 minutes.

2. Add the water, salt, pepper, turmeric and paprika; bring to a boil, then reduce heat to low. Cover the pan and simmer for 45 minutes. Make certain the chick-peas are soft but not mushy.

3. Add the potatoes, pumpkin, zucchini and parsley and cook for 20 minutes more. Set aside.

4. Heat the oil in a pan, add the onion and chicken, and stir-fry over moderate heat for 5 minutes. Add the salt, pepper, turmeric and water. Bring to a boil and cook over low heat for about 45 minutes, or until chicken is tender. Set aside.

5. Prepare the *cous cous* in water according to directions if purchased ready made. Or prepare homemade *cous cous* and steam it in a *couscousier.*

6. Serve the *cous cous*, the chicken and the soup in separate bowls.

Serve with Salada Madbucha (see Index).

Serves 8.

PASTIYA (also BESTILA)
"Pigeon" Pie

This is probably Morocco's most famous culinary preparation, world class and deservedly so. My Jewish teacher thought that it was a Jewish innovation possibly brought from Spain at the time of the Inquisition, although Muslims also have their version of this aromatically seasoned, slightly sweet pie. The original preparation was made with pigeon, but it is gradually being converted to the more easily available chicken (outside of Morocco), and in the United States the Cornish game hen.

The *pastiya* is a ceremonial dish served at weddings, Bar Mitzvahs and occasions when the company is to be honored. But why wait for such a special time when it can be served at buffet parties or for the sheer pleasure of dining on Morocco's exotic classic?

It should be noted that the Muslim version is served sprinkled with confectioners' sugar and ground cinnamon.

3 pounds onions, peeled and sliced thin
2 tablespoons corn oil
3 teaspoons salt
¼ teaspoon white pepper
¼ teaspoon whole saffron, dissolved in ¼ cup hot water
about 5 pounds chicken parts—legs, thighs, breast, or two
     3-pound chickens, quartered, skin and fat discarded
⅔ cup chopped Italian flat-leaf parsley
5 large eggs, beaten with 1 teaspoon salt
½ pound almonds, blanched and toasted (see Note)
1½ tablespoons sugar
1½ teaspoons ground cinnamon
½ pound margarine, melted
1 pound Greek fillo sheets about 12 × 17 inches
1 egg yolk, plus 1 teaspoon of the white, beaten

1. Put the onions, oil, 2 teaspoons of the salt and the pepper into a large pan and stir-fry over moderate heat for several minutes. Cover the pan, reduce heat to low, and fry for about 15 minutes more to reduce the bulk of the onion.

2. Pour in the saffron water and mix well.

3. Place the chicken pieces on top of the onion, cover the pan, and continue to cook for ½ hour more, or until the chicken is quite tender. No liquid is added since the onions and chicken will provide all the moisture needed.

4. Remove the chicken, cut off all the meat, and discard the bones. Cut the meat into small (about ½-inch) pieces. Set aside.

5. Stir the parsley into the onion. Pour in the eggs and over very low heat stir the mixture until it is slightly cooked, about 5 minutes. Set aside.

6. Grind or chop the almonds medium-fine in a processor, leaving some texture. Mix in the sugar and cinnamon. Set aside.

7. Coat the bottom and sides of a baking pan measuring 10 × 14 × 3 inches with the melted margarine. (A modern note—formerly vegetable oil was used.)

8. Open the package of fillo and spread the sheets out flat. Cover them with a lightly damp kitchen towel to prevent them from drying out. Lay down 2 sheets over the pan bottom and coat the top sheet with the margarine, using a pastry brush. The excess inch or two of fillo around the sides may be cut off with a sharp knife or folded in. Lay down 10 sheets in this manner, coating every other sheet.

9. Spread the boneless chicken pieces over the pastry and smooth out the surface from corner to corner. Lay down 8 more fillo sheets in a similar manner, brushing every other sheet with margarine, and spread the ground almond, sugar, cinnamon mixture over that.

10. Lay down 6 more fillo sheets and over these, spread out the onion/egg mixture. Cover with 8 more fillo sheets, brushing each of the last 3 sheets with margarine. At this point, tuck in the fillo around the inner sides of the pan so that the top presents a smooth surface.

11. Cut the completed pie into 3-inch squares, 4 strips down and 5 strips across, all the way down to the bottom of the pan. Brush the surface of each square with the beaten egg yolk.

Bake in a preheated 350° F. oven for 1 hour. Remove the pan and once again cut through each square to the bottom.

Serve warm. Makes 20 generous pieces, adequate for 20 portions along with Moroccan salads and other dishes.

NOTE: To prepare the almonds, blanch them in boiling water, cool them slightly, and remove the skins. Dry the almonds. Heat oil in a skillet, add the almonds, and fry over low heat for several minutes, until almonds reach a toasted, light tan color. Remove them and toss on paper towels to drain off excess oil. (A Moroccan friend said that she puts the blanched almonds on a cookie tray in a 350° F. oven and toasts them for about 15 minutes.)

VARIATION: Individual pies are often the most convenient method of preparation for appetizers and cocktail parties. They are substantial portions with all the characteristic flavors of the large pie. The disadvantage is that the fragments of filling do have a tendency to fall out. This is not important when served on a plate, but it is inconvenient when standing up with a drink in one hand.

20 fillo sheets
melted margarine
1 egg yolk plus 1 teaspoon of the white, beaten

1. Prepare all the steps taken for the large pie filling and set them aside as done previously. Mix the chicken, onion and almonds together, the complete filling for the individual pies.

2. Butter 1 sheet of fillo and fold it in half lengthwise. Put 2 heaping tablespoons filling at one end of the fillo and fold it over twice. Fold over each side toward the center so that the individual bundle is about 5 inches in width, and continue rolling until you have reached the end of the sheet. You should have a pie 2 inches thick and 5 inches in length. Prepare all the pies this way and place them on a cookie sheet brushed with margarine. Paint the surface of each pie with egg yolk.

Bake in a preheated 350° F. oven for about 45 minutes, somewhat less than the large pie.

Serve warm. Makes 20 individual pigeon pies.

DOUARA
Passover Variety Meat Casserole

This is a special preparation for Passover. The combination of textures and flavors is inviting. Moroccans look forward to serving it for the holiday.

1 pound beef liver
2 beef kidneys
1 beef brain
1 veal tongue, about 1½ pounds
leftover roast beef, cut into 1-inch cubes (optional)
1 teaspoon ground cuminseed
¼ teaspoon white pepper
½ teaspoon salt
½ teaspoon paprika
2 cups light homemade chicken broth

1. Char the liver over a charcoal fire or in a gas or electric broiler as part of the kosher ritual. Cut the liver into 1-inch cubes. Set aside.

2. Trim the kidneys of excess fat, cut them open and remove the inside cartilage. Cut into ¼-inch-thick pieces. Set aside.

3. Soak the brain in hot water with 1 teaspoon vinegar for 15 minutes. Drain, then cover with cold water for 15 minutes. Remove the skin and membranes. Cut into 1-inch cubes. Set aside.

4. Cook the tongue in water with 1 teaspoon salt, covered, over moderate heat for 1 hour or more. When the tongue is tender, drain and peel off the outer skin. Cut into 1-inch cubes.

5. Put the seasonings and broth into a large pan and bring to a boil. Add all the meats, mix well, and cover the pan. Simmer over low heat for 20 minutes to integrate the flavors and complete cooking the meats. There should be some sauce.

Serve warm with white rice or potatoes. Serves 8.

EL SAN
Tongue Sauté with Garnishes

This unusual treatment of tongue exhibits the Moroccan tendency to include sugared nuts and raisins with meats.

1 veal or beef tongue, 2 pounds
2 tablespoons corn oil
¼ teaspoon ground turmeric
¼ teaspoon ground cuminseed
½ teaspoon salt
½ cup water
½ pound blanched almonds
¼ pound dark seedless raisins
1 tablespoon sugar

1. Cook the tongue in sufficient water over moderate heat until it is tender. Drain, and pull off the coarse outer skin. Cut the tongue into ¼-inch-thick slices. Set aside.

2. Heat 1 tablespoon of the oil in a skillet. Add the turmeric, cuminseed, salt, tongue and water. Mix well, cover the skillet, and fry over low heat for about 15 minutes, or until the liquid evaporates. Set aside.

3. To prepare the garnish, heat the remaining tablespoon of oil in a skillet and stir-fry the almonds over low heat until they are light brown. Add the raisins and sugar and continue to stir-fry for 2 minutes more. Turn out the mixture in a dish and serve as a garnish to the tongue. Each person sprinkles as much as he wants on his own portion of tongue.

Serve warm or at room temperature. Serves 4 to 6 with other dishes.

EL LASAN BIL CAPAR
Beef Tongue with Capers

Tongue is one of my favorite foods. Moroccan style is different and compelling, especially when served at a buffet along with other regional dishes.

    2 pounds beef or veal tongue
    10 cups water
    4 garlic cloves, sliced thin
    5 bay leaves
    1 tablespoon corn oil
    ¼ teaspoon ground turmeric
    1 teaspoon salt
    ½ teaspoon pepper
    ¼ cup capers

1. Cook the tongue in the water in a covered pan over moderate heat for 1 hour. Remove the tongue and peel off the skin. Return tongue to the liquid and continue to cook it until tender, about 30 minutes. Remove and set aside. Reserve 1 cup of the liquid. Cut the tongue into ¼-inch-thick slices.

2. Put the reserved liquid in a pan with the garlic, bay leaves, oil, turmeric, salt and pepper. Simmer over low heat for 5 minutes. Add the tongue, cover the pan, and cook for 10 minutes. Add the capers and simmer for 10 minutes more.

Serve warm with bread and salads. Serves 6.

OSBANA
Kishke

To stuff a kishke (osbana) in any culture is not one's everyday activity, but the osbana with all its ramifications is a popular dish for Passover.

    2 pounds beef liver, koshered by charring in a broiler or over
        charcoal
    1½ pounds boneless beef chuck

1 teaspoon salt
¼ teaspoon pepper
1 teaspoon paprika
¾ teaspoon ground cuminseed
¼ teaspoon hot red chili flakes
3 feet of small intestine of beef (kishke), prepared for stuffing, one
    end sewn up

1. Cut the liver into ¼-inch cubes and cut the beef into thin 2-inch squares, more or less.

2. Mix the salt, pepper, paprika, cuminseed and chili flakes together. Mix this with the liver and beef in a large bowl. Take 1 slice of the beef, put 1 tablespoon of liver in the center, and roll it up cylinder shape. Stuff the kishke with all the rolls very tightly. Sew up the end firmly.

3. Bring a large pan of water to a boil and put the kishke into it, curled in concentric circles. Cover the pan and cook over moderate heat for ½ hour. Drain the water and remove the kishke. (At this point it may be cooled and refrigerated for future use.)

Cut the cooked kishke into 3-inch lengths and grill them over charcoal or a gas or electric broiler until crisp brown, about 15 minutes.

Serve warm with or without a sauce. Makes 10 to 12 pieces.

SALSA (Sauce)

1 tablespoon corn oil
1 cup chopped peeled tomatoes, fresh or canned
2 tablespoons tomato paste
¼ teaspoon salt
¼ teaspoon white pepper
1 garlic clove, chopped fine
1 celery rib, tender portion, chopped
2 tablespoons fine-chopped fresh coriander
2 tablespoons fine-chopped parsley
½ cup water

1. Heat the oil in a skillet; add the tomatoes, tomato paste, salt, pepper, garlic, celery, coriander and parsley, and stir-fry over low heat for 5 minutes. Add the water, cover the skillet, and simmer over low heat for 20 minutes. Stir now and then.

Serve hot on the side with the kishke. Makes about 2 cups.

IL KUBT DEBOCH
Liver Sauté

T he liver sauté is a Friday night specialty to usher in the Sabbath.

    1 pound chicken livers
    1 pound beef liver
    3 tablespoons corn oil
    1 large onion, chopped (¾ cup)
    3 garlic cloves, chopped fine
    1 tablespoon ground cuminseed
    ½ teaspoon salt
    1 tablespoon paprika
    1 to 2 teaspoons hot red chili flakes, to taste
    ½ cup water

1. Char the chicken and beef livers under or over flame to make them kosher. Cut the chicken livers into lobes and the beef into little finger slices.
2. Heat the oil in a skillet and stir-fry the onion and garlic over moderate heat until golden. Add the liver, cuminseed, salt, paprika and chili flakes and stir-fry for 2 minutes.
3. Add the water and cook over moderate heat until the water evaporates, shaking the pan frequently.
Serve warm. Serves 6 to 8.

HET BIL FLAFEL HOMAR
Fish and Sweet Red Pepper

T he imaginative combination of fresh fish from the Mediterranean, fresh coriander and sweet pepper is sparked with assertive garlic slices—increased or decreased to taste.

    1 cup water
    ¼ cup corn oil
    4 to 6 garlic cloves to taste, halved lengthwise
    1 teaspoon salt
    ¼ teaspoon pepper
    ⅛ teaspoon ground turmeric

2 pounds sea bass or similar fish, cut into 2-inch-wide slices
1 bunch of fresh coriander, chopped (½ cup)
4 medium sweet red peppers (1 pound), seeded, quartered
1 teaspoon ground cuminseed

1. Put the water, oil, garlic, salt, pepper and turmeric in a pan and bring to a boil over moderate heat. Cook for 3 minutes.

2. Add the fish slices, coriander and red peppers. Cover the pan and cook for 15 to 20 minutes, basting several times. Uncover the pan and sprinkle the cuminseed over all, but do not stir.

Serve hot. Serves 6 with other dishes.

BOULETTES DE POISSON
Fish Balls

The fish balls are an eclectic preparation that may be served as an appetizer with drinks or a main dish with several salads. They can be fried in a small amount of oil or baked in a 350° F. oven for ½ hour, according to personal preference.

1 pound fish fillets—flounder, turbot or similar fish
1 small onion, sliced (¼ cup)
3 garlic cloves, sliced
¼ cup chopped parsley and fresh coriander (equal amounts of each)
1 green pepper, seeded, chopped (½ cup)
¼ teaspoon salt
⅛ teaspoon pepper
½ teaspoon paprika
2 eggs, beaten
2 teaspoons flour
¼ cup corn oil

1. Process all the ingredients except the eggs, flour and oil to a smooth paste. Stir in the eggs and flour.

2. Prepare round balls 1½ inches in diameter. Heat the oil in a skillet and panfry the balls over moderate heat for about 5 minutes on all sides. Drain on paper towels.

Serve warm. Makes 12 balls.

BOULETTES DE POISSON AVEC SAUCE

Fish Balls in Sauce

This traditional Moroccan-style fish recipe uses aromatic seasonings and spices that are far removed from the mild seasonings of the fish balls we are used to. In addition, the fish purée can be used to prepare fritters without a sauce, to be served as an appetizer with drinks.

FISH BALLS

> 2 pounds fillet of whiting, flounder or similar white saltwater
> fish, ground fine
> 1 tablespoon grated orange rind
> 1 teaspoon grated mace
> ½ teaspoon white pepper
> ¼ teaspoon ground turmeric
> ⅛ teaspoon ground ginger
> ¼ teaspoon salt
> 2 tablespoons bread crumbs
> 1 tablespoon chopped fresh coriander
> 1 tablespoon grated onion
> 1 tablespoon corn oil

SAUCE

> 2 pounds ripe tomatoes, canned or fresh, chopped
> 3 tablespoons corn oil
> 6 garlic cloves, put through a press
> 2 whole dried hot red chilies
> 1 teaspoon paprika
> ¼ teaspoon salt

1. Mix together all ingredients for fish balls. Prepare fish balls 1½ inches in diameter. Moisten hands with cold water to facilitate forming the fish balls. Set aside.

2. To make the sauce, put the tomatoes in a saucepan and simmer, covered, over low heat for 10 minutes. Add the oil, garlic, chilies, paprika and salt. Continue to simmer for 5 minutes, stirring now and then.

3. Add the fish balls carefully to the sauce, cover the pan, and simmer over low heat for 1 hour.

Serve warm with salads and bread. Serves 8.

VARIATION: The fish balls may be prepared as appetizers without sauce. Prepare all the balls as described. Deep-fry in corn oil over moderate heat for 3 minutes. Drain on paper towels.

Or, they can also be panfried by slightly flattening the balls and frying for 3 minutes on all sides, using about ¼ cup oil.

CHIZU SALADA
Carrot Salad

A popular, colorful and piquant salad that can be refrigerated for up to 1 week.

1 pound carrots
3 cups water
1 teaspoon salt
1 teaspoon ground cuminseed
1 teaspoon paprika
¼ teaspoon white pepper
¼ teaspoon ground hot red chili flakes (optional)
2 tablespoons olive oil
1 garlic clove, chopped fine
juice of 1 lemon
1 tablespoon chopped flat-leaf parsley for garnish

1. Peel the carrots and cut them into ¼-inch-wide slices. Bring 3 cups water and the salt to a boil in a large pan, add the carrots, and cook over moderate heat until they are soft but with some firmness. Do not overcook. Drain and cool. This step can be done several hours in advance of dining.

2. Mix the rest of the ingredients with the carrots. Toss the salad well. Garnish with a few fragments of the parsley. Refrigerate.

Serve cool or at room temperature.

SALADA MADBUCHA
Cooked Salad

This salad is really a condiment and should be used as such. It can be prepared in moderate or large quantities, has plenty of flavor, and can be served with any kind of food including curries. It may be refrigerated for 2 weeks.

1 tablespoon corn oil
1 medium onion, chopped (½ cup)
8 garlic cloves, smoothly puréed or put through a press
5 green peppers (1¼ pounds), charred in a gas or electric broiler,
    peeled, seeded, quartered
¼ cup chopped celery
½ cup water
½ teaspoon salt
¼ teaspoon pepper
⅛ teaspoon ground turmeric
1 teaspoon paprika
2 pounds ripe tomatoes, blanched in boiling water, peeled, sliced,
    or equal amount of canned tomato
2 tablespoons tomato paste

1. Heat the oil in a large skillet and stir-fry the onion and garlic over moderate heat until golden. Add the green peppers, celery, water, salt, pepper, turmeric and paprika and mix well. Cover the skillet and simmer over low heat for 15 minutes. Stir now and then.

2. Add the tomatoes and simmer for 15 minutes. Adjust the salt and pepper for more intensity if you wish. Add the tomato paste, stir a moment, and remove from the heat.

Cool, refrigerate. Serve with any kind of *cous cous* or Moroccan food.

VARIATION: This is a simpler version of the *salada*, which may appeal to cooks.

2 pounds ripe tomatoes, sliced
1 pound green peppers, seeded, sliced
3 semihot green chilies, seeded, sliced
4 garlic cloves, sliced thin
¼ teaspoon pepper

½ teaspoon paprika
½ teaspoon salt
¼ cup corn oil

1. Put everything in a pan and simmer over low heat, stirring frequently. When all the liquid has evaporated, about 1 hour, the *salada* is finished.

Cool and refrigerate.

OLIVES AVEC SAUCE
Olives in Sauce

This condiment can be served with an assortment of Moroccan foods. Diners will help themselves to as much as they want.

3 tablespoons corn oil
5 garlic cloves, chopped fine
⅛ teaspoon ground turmeric
2 tablespoons tomato paste, dissolved in ½ cup water
2 pounds pitted ripe olives
½ teaspoon salt
¼ teaspoon white pepper

1. Heat the oil in a pan, add the garlic and turmeric, and stir-fry over moderate heat for 1 minute. Add the tomato mixture, olives, salt and pepper and mix. Simmer in the covered pan over low heat for 15 minutes.

Serve warm with rice, meat or fish dishes.

ORANGE ET OLIVE NOIRE
Orange and Black Olive Salad

Another salad with unconventional ingredients and spices in Moroccan style. The black olives are the Moroccan type, small with wrinkled skins.

3 medium oranges
½ pound black olives
3 tablespoons olive oil
1 teaspoon ground cuminseed
2 teaspoons paprika
⅛ teaspoon white pepper
2 garlic cloves, chopped fine

1. Peel the oranges, removing the white membrane. Divide the oranges into sections. Remove the seeds, then cut the sections into 1-inch pieces.

2. Mix the orange pieces and all the other ingredients together. Toss well to mix.

Serve cool or at room temperature.

FLAFEL
Sweet Red Pepper Salad

Passover is salad time and this is typical.

2 pounds sweet red peppers
2 tablespoons corn oil
1 tablespoon wine vinegar
¼ teaspoon salt
3 garlic cloves, put through a press

1. Halve the peppers and seed them. Char the halves over charcoal or in a gas or electric broiler for several minutes on the skin side. Cool and pull off as much of the skin as possible. Cut the peppers into 1-inch cubes or long slender strips.

2. Mix the oil, vinegar, salt and garlic well. Add this to the peppers and toss to integrate the dressing.

Serve at room temperature. Serves 6 to 8.

SALADE SHACKSHOOKA
Smoky Pepper Salad

There are various types of *shackshooka*, which means something "mixed up." Some are salads while others may be cooked appetizers or an entrée such as Shackshooka (Eggs and Sauce). This *shackshooka* is another Passover salad favorite.

    2 pounds sweet green peppers
    2 tablespoons corn oil
    2 garlic cloves, chopped fine
    1 pound ripe tomatoes, peeled, cut into 1-inch cubes
    1 teaspoon paprika
    ½ teaspoon salt

1. Halve the peppers and remove the ribs and seeds. Char the skins and remove. Set aside for 20 minutes, then cut into 1-inch cubes.

2. Heat the oil in a large skillet. Add the garlic and stir-fry over moderate heat for 1 minute. Add the green peppers, tomatoes, paprika and salt; stir well. Simmer the mixture, covered, over low heat for 15 minutes.

Cool; refrigerate until ready to serve. Serves 6 to 8.

SALADE RUSSE
Russian Salad for Passover

I do not know why this attractive salad is called Russian, neither did my teacher. In any event, it is served on Passover, but would be an adornment at any time of the year. Note that canned beets, well drained, are an acceptable substitute for freshly cooked beets.

    2 pounds beets, cooked, peeled, sliced
    1 pound potatoes (about 4), cooked in the skin, peeled, sliced
    6 large hard-cooked eggs, sliced
    1 medium onion, cut into thin rings

½ cup lemon juice
2 teaspoons olive oil
1 teaspoon salt
⅛ teaspoon pepper
½ cup chopped parsley

1. Prepare a large serving platter in this manner: Place single slices of beet to cover the platter. On each slice of beet place 1 slice of potato, a slice of egg on that and a ring of onion over that.

2. Prepare the sauce by briskly mixing together the lemon juice, oil, salt, pepper and parsley. Distribute the sauce over all.

Serve at room temperature. Serves 8.

SLK SALADA
Spinach Salad

Passover salad.

This is a traditional

2 pounds spinach
½ cup water
1 tablespoon corn oil
2 garlic cloves, chopped fine
1 teaspoon ground cuminseed
1 teaspoon paprika
juice of 1 lemon, or more to taste

1. Wash the spinach thoroughly; break off and discard tough stem ends. Put the spinach in a pan with ½ cup water. Cover and cook over low heat for 5 minutes. Remove pan from the heat and let stand for 2 minutes more. Drain well and gently press out excess liquid.

2. Heat the oil in a large skillet, add the garlic, and stir-fry over moderate heat for 1 minute. Add the spinach and stir-fry for another minute. Add the cuminseed, paprika and lemon juice and toss the spinach and seasonings well to integrate the flavors.

Serve warm or at room temperature. Serves 6.

HAROSETH
Date Paste for Passover

Dates are often the principal fruit used when preparing the Passover Haroseth in North Africa and other oriental countries. This is a classic preparation, using enough wine to moisten the paste well.

  1 pound dates, pitted
  ½ pound walnuts, chopped
  1 tablespoon dark raisins
  ½ cup sweet red wine

1. Grind the dates and raisins together in a processor. Add the chopped walnuts and the wine; mix well together. Refrigerate until ready to use at the Seder.

Makes about 4 cups.

HAROSETH
Passover Sweets

Passover is a difficult time for desserts since most sweets are *hamatz* or forbidden. The Moroccans have solved part of the problem with these delectable date and nut balls.

  1 pound shelled hazelnuts
  ½ pound shelled almonds
  ½ pound pitted dates
  ½ pound white raisins

1. Grind the nuts together coarsely, then add the dates and raisins. Continue to grind everything together (or use a processor) until you reach a consistency that is smooth but still has some texture.

2. Prepare balls of the mixture about ¾ inch in diameter. Put each ball on a small square of wax paper.

Serve when wanted during Passover. Makes about 40.

TANGIER

Tangier, during the era of antiquity, was inhabited by Phoenicians, Romans, Carthaginians and Berbers. The existence of a Jewish community at that time has also been corroborated. During the colonial period, this town, situated at the entrance to the Straits of Gibraltar, was a crossroads for the Spanish, Portuguese and English colonists.

Jewish settlers escaping the Inquisition (1492), and from the Netherlands and Morocco, arrived and maintained the continuity from ancient times. But all was not sugar and spice for what was essentially a poor community. The usual petty persecutions from one sultan or another plagued the town until modern times.

In 1923 Tangier was declared an international zone, thereby entering a time of intrigue beloved by mystery writers. There was a population of 10,000 Jews. The Spanish influence was pervasive and the Spanish language was spoken by all.

When the Jews of the prosperous city adjacent to Tangier, Tetuan (Morocco), arrived in the nineteenth century, the community began to flourish with Jewish authors and poets writing in the Spanish language. In 1951 there were 15,000 Jews in the International Zone of Tangier; 2,000 of them were from Spanish Morocco. But a strong movement for emigration had begun in spite of an attempt by some residents to preserve this unique community. Madrid, Geneva, Canada and the United States were the favored destinations, with very few leaving for Israel.

The inhabitants of Tangier are known as Tangerines, an amusing but accurate name.

Pointed toward Spain but politically ruled by the whims of sultans, the town of Tangier lived a life of its own, distinct from both Spain and Morocco but dependent on both. The Jewish community, religious and poor, nevertheless developed a variety of dishes: some to celebrate the Sabbath, some for daily use, and many based on the inevitable *cous cous*.

Fish was the principal food, the logical outcome of living in a port town with such quantity and variety of fish from the Mediterranean. The seasonings were mostly garlic, onion, tomato, herbs and the occasional cayenne pepper to stimulate the taste buds. No dramatic culinary styles were uncovered, but the sweet *cous cous* of the Tangerines is unique. Home-style cooking, leaning toward Spanish taste, is the key to the cooking of Tangier.

When Tangier was annexed by Morocco, the Jewish community started to dwindle and by 1970 there were only 250 Jews remaining. It was the end of an era.

COUS COUS
Tangieran Cous Cous

The Tangerines like their *cous cous* sweet, *really* sweet, with plenty of sugar, sweet pumpkin, cinnamon and prunes. This production is unique in all of the North African countries that make various types of *cous cous*. It is usually served on holidays, when moving into a new house, or at other celebratory activities.

MEATBALLS

1 pound ground lean beef
½ teaspoon salt
2 garlic cloves, put through a press
⅛ teaspoon pepper
1 tablespoon sugar
2 tablespoons bread crumbs
2 tablespoons corn oil
1 small onion, chopped (⅓ cup)

SAUCE

¼ cup corn oil
½ pound shallots, peeled, whole
2 pounds pumpkin or calabasa, cut into 2-inch cubes
1 pound dried medium prunes
2 cups water
¼ teaspoon ground turmeric
1 tablespoon ground cinnamon
1 cup sugar

2 cups prepared cous cous

1. Mix the beef, salt, garlic, pepper, sugar and bread crumbs together and prepare miniature meatballs ½ inch in diameter.

2. Heat the oil in a pan, add the onion, and stir-fry for 1 minute. Add the meatballs, a few at a time, and brown them over moderate heat for 3 minutes, turning them over carefully. Set aside.

3. To make the sauce, heat the oil in a large pan, add the shallots, and brown lightly over moderate heat for 3 minutes. Remove shallots and set aside.

4. Put the pumpkin cubes in the same pan (there will be enough oil left in the pan) in a single layer. Scatter the shallots over that and place the prunes on top. Mix the water, turmeric, cinnamon and sugar together and pour the mixture over the other ingredients. Bring to a boil, cover the pan, and cook over low heat for 35 minutes, long enough to soften the pumpkin and integrate the seasonings.

5. Steam the cous cous over hot water according to directions. Unlike cous cous in Tunisia, for example, the steaming in the couscousier is not done above the meat or fish stew cooking in the bottom of a divided steamer.

Serve the meatballs, pumpkin sauce and cous cous at the same time, but in separate dishes. (Some cooks prefer to mix and serve meatballs and cous cous together.) Garnish with 2 teaspoons ground cinnamon and 1 tablespoon sugar mixed together. Tangerines sprinkle this mixture over the cous cous during dining, but I consider it gilding the lily. Serve warm.

Serves 6.

PESCADO COCHO
(Colorado)
Fish in Red Sauce

B ecause Tangerines live surrounded by water, they love fish and have a large number of fish recipes. This fish stew is served religiously on Friday evenings as an appetizer, the first course before the soup, meat or poultry entrée. The whole garlic cloves absorb the flavors in the sauce and are eaten with the fish. Garlic lovers may add a few more, according to one's tolerance.

¼ cup corn oil
½ teaspoon paprika
⅛ teaspoon hot red chili flakes
½ cup diced green pepper
1 ripe tomato, fresh or canned, chopped (½ cup)
6 to 8 garlic cloves, to taste, whole, not peeled
½ teaspoon salt
1½ pounds fillet of halibut, cod, haddock or similar fish, cut into
    6 pieces
⅓ cup water
1 cup green fava or broad beans, fresh, canned, or frozen

1. Pour the oil into a deep skillet, add the paprika, chili flakes, green pepper, tomato, garlic and salt, and stir-fry over low heat for 4 minutes.
2. Place the pieces of fish on the sauce, add the water, cover the pan, and cook for 10 minutes. Add the fava beans (called *habas* in Spanish) and cook for 20 minutes more. There will be a thick sauce remaining.

Serve warm with bread. Serves 6.

PESCADO EN EL HORNO
Baked Fish

Fish prepared this way is a complete family-style meal. Of course, bread and salads would be an expected accompaniment.

> 1 whole fish, 2 to 2½ pounds, red snapper, sea bass, flounder or similar fish
> 1 lemon, sliced thin
> 2 pounds potatoes, peeled and sliced thin
> 1 medium onion, sliced (½ cup)
> 1 green pepper, cut into long strips
> juice of ½ lemon (1 tablespoon)
> ½ teaspoon salt
> ¼ teaspoon ground turmeric
> ⅛ teaspoon pepper
> 1 tablespoon chopped parsley
> 3 tablespoons corn oil
> ¼ cup water

1. Lightly oil a heatproof glass or metal baking dish. Stuff a few lemon slices in the fish cavity. Put the fish in the dish and cover with the potato slices. Cover with the onion, green pepper and remaining lemon slices. Sprinkle with the lemon juice, salt, turmeric, pepper and parsley. Pour the oil and water over all.

2. Cover the dish and bake in a 350° F. oven for 45 minutes. Uncover the dish and bake for 15 minutes more to brown the potatoes.

Serve warm. Serves 6 with other dishes.

PESCADO EN BLANCO
(o Amarillo)
Fish in White Sauce

The fish is cooked in a simple way, then glorified with the lemon sauce. This preparation is also known as fish in a yellow (amarillo) sauce, which seems more accurate since the turmeric and egg provide the yellow. The language is Spanish, showing its origin.

FISH

¼ cup corn oil
3 garlic cloves, diced
¼ teaspoon ground turmeric
1 teaspoon chopped parsley
¼ teaspoon salt, or to taste
1 pound fillet of haddock, flounder, cod or similar fish, cut into
    4 equal pieces

SAUCE

1 large egg, beaten
juice of ½ lemon, about 1 tablespoon

1. Put the oil, garlic, turmeric, parsley and salt in a skillet and mix. Roll the fish pieces in the mixture and marinate for 4 to 6 hours.
2. Beat the egg and lemon juice together.
3. When ready to dine, cook the fish in the covered skillet over moderate heat for 7 to 8 minutes. Remove skillet from heat and pour sauce over all. Shake the pan briskly and serve immediately.
    Serve warm. Serves 4 with bread and salads.

ALBÓNDIGAS DE PESCADO
Fish Balls in a Simple Sauce

There are no harsh seasonings in this Jewish dish. The taste relies on the vegetables and tomato sauce combined with the flavor of fresh fish.

FISH BALLS

1 pound boneless fish—turbot, cod, haddock or similar fish,
    ground
2 garlic cloves, put through a press
⅛ teaspoon pepper
⅛ teaspoon ground turmeric
1 tablespoon chopped parsley
1 tablespoon bread crumbs
¼ teaspoon salt
1 egg, beaten

SAUCE

1 small onion, chopped (⅓ cup)
1 ripe tomato, chopped (½ cup)
3 tablespoons corn oil
⅛ teaspoon ground turmeric
2 green celery ribs, strings removed, cut into 3-inch sticks
1 tablespoon tomato paste
½ cup water

1. Mix fish ball ingredients together into a smooth paste. Wet hands with cold water and prepare fish balls of 1 inch in diameter. Makes 20 balls. Set aside.

2. To make the sauce, put the onion, tomato, oil and turmeric into a pan and simmer over low heat for 3 minutes. Add the celery, tomato paste and water and continue to simmer for 5 minutes.

3. Add the fish balls, cover the pan, and cook without stirring for 15 minutes.

Serve warm with bread. Serves 6 with other dishes.

TUNISIA

TUNISIA   Jews settled in Tunisia as early as the era of King Solomon, tenth century B.C. It is also possible that Jews lived in ancient Carthage, which was founded in 814 B.C. The cemetery of Carthage, on the outskirts of present-day Tunis, contained epitaphs testifying to the existence of a large number of Jews.

And so the melting pot, which is Tunisia, began with the earliest Phoenician traders, Jews, and succeeding visitors or invaders. The Romans destroyed Carthage and turned Tunisia into the breadbasket of the Roman Empire—growing wheat, olives and grapes. The marvelous regional breads of present-day Tunisia must therefore reach back into Roman times.

In the seventh century, Arabs conquered the area and Tunisia became part of the Arab domain. They brought with them their spices—cumin, coriander, caraway, pepper, cloves, nutmeg—and their culinary customs. A thriving Judaic center arose in Kairouan and for 250 years the Jews flourished there as doctors, traders and craftsmen. In 1057 the city was destroyed by the Arabs, and though it has been completely rebuilt (including impressive Islamic mosques) I was unable to discover one synagogue where once there had been a famous center of Jewish learning.

The most momentous event for the Jews at that time was their expulsion from Spain when the Spanish promulgated their infamous Edict of Expulsion on March 31, 1492. Portugal followed with their expulsion in 1497 and the diaspora from Iberia started.

The Jews crossed into North Africa and filtered into Tunisia, principally Tunis, joining the already-settled community there in the Hara, the Jewish quarter, which had been established in the eleventh century. An additional community from Leghorn (Livorno), Italy, joined the Tunisian

471

Inner courtyard of a Jewish home in the Hara, Tunis, c.1900. *(Photo by Jean-Pierre Allali)*

Jews in the sixteenth and seventeenth centuries, thereby adding the Italian flavors and style of cooking to the existing cuisine. (When the State of Israel was established and Tunisia gained its independence from France in 1956, politics being what it is, the ancient Jewish quarter, including the oldest synagogue in Tunis and the old cemetery, was bulldozed into eternity.)

A brief intrusion occurred in 1535, when the Spanish conquered Tunisia and ruled for about 40 years. They were fresh from their conquest of Mexico and Guatemala and it is logical that they may have brought the hot chili with them as well as other New World botanical discoveries, which profoundly influenced the cuisine. Hot chilies were incorporated into *harissa*, the ubiquitous spicy table condiment beloved by Tunisians.

The Turks conquered Tunisia from the Spanish in 1574 and introduced their celebrated pastries, which are the backbone of Tunisian sweets to this day.

No cuisine develops in isolation. The stage was now set for the assembly and evolution of a cuisine that included disparate but compatible ideas from the Phoenicians, Romans, Arabs, Spanish, Portuguese, Turks, Italians and finally the French, when they established a French Protectorate in 1881. Tunis, the capital city, became an important center of Jewish learning.

It was the French, with their genius for culinary adventures, who pulled all the components of the existing cooking styles together. The presentation of dishes was of special importance in developing a sophisticated culinary environment and the French stressed this facet of food preparation.

A world-wide dissemination of food stuffs resulted in such imports as the tomato from the Valley of Mexico, turmeric from India, the artichoke from the Romans—all for the delectation of the nineteenth-century Tunisians.

Tunisian Jewish cooking in the twentieth century is based on religious dietary laws, married to the existing established style of cooking that the Jews found upon their arrival from Spain, the use of this wealth of ingredients, plus their own intrinsic ingenuity in inventing or modifying local foods. Cooking for the Sabbath resulted in the *t'fina* of many varieties—that exclusively Jewish *pot-au-feu*, which obviates the necessity of cooking on the Sabbath. Then there is the *cous cous*, the national dish of Tunisia, which the Jewish cook glorifies with several modifications, some of them presented here.

Personal preferences in dining are not due to political exhortations but are reflections of a culture, a way of life, sometimes based on one's economic status. The Jewish cooking of Tunisia, as in other countries of the Maghreb, often makes something out of nothing or more frequently places an individual stamp on the country's existing style of cooking.

Now the community has dwindled to 1,000 or 2,000 members, with most of the many thousands leaving for Israel and France. It is the end of an ancient community with perhaps only their cuisine to remind them of things past.

MENU
For Sabbath Eve Dinner

While I was cooking in Tunisia, a friend invited me to join her family for a typical Friday night dinner. Instead of serving one course at a time, as we do, all the food for the whole meal was there on the table from the beginning—the inevitable *cous cous* was accompanied by side dishes and a great display of salads and pickled vegetables. Recipes for the starred dishes are included in this book.

COUS COUS ROYALE*
(A Cous Cous of Chicken, Beef, Boulettes, Chick-Peas,
Vegetables in Soup)

AKOUD*
(Sweetbreads in Red Sauce)

HRAIMI
(Fish in Red Sauce)

ARTICHOKE SALAD
SALADE CUITE*
  (Cooked Salad)
MZOURA* (Carrot Salad)
TOURCHI BATATA*
  (Potato Salad)

LEFT (Turnip Pickle)
AJLOOK* (Yellow
  Squash Pickle)
SELK HAMAR (Beet Pickle)
TOURCHI FARKOUS
  (Cucumber Pickle)

Fruit

CHAKCHOUKA DE MATIN
Breakfast Sauce

This vivid sauce can be used as a flavoring, especially with breakfast eggs. The sauce is prepared for an entire week, but this amount could be used up sooner depending upon the number of diners. It should be refrigerated.

1 can (12 ounces) tomato paste
4 garlic cloves, sliced
⅔ cup water
2 tablespoons harissa (see Glossary)
1 tablespoon ground coriander
1 tablespoon ground caraway
1 teaspoon salt, or to taste
1 tablespoon paprika
⅓ cup corn oil

1. Put the tomato paste, garlic and water in a skillet and simmer, covered, over low heat for ½ hour. Add ½ cup more water if the liquid evaporates too quickly.
2. Add the harissa, coriander, caraway, salt, paprika and oil. Simmer, covered, over very low heat for ½ hour more.
Cool and refrigerate until ready to use. Makes 2 cups.
To use the sauce with breakfast eggs: Measure out ½ cup sauce and add to ¼ cup water; simmer over low heat for 3 minutes. Break

6 eggs carefully into the sauce, cover the skillet for 2 minutes, then uncover and fry until eggs are as firm as wanted.

Serve warm with plenty of bread to sop up the sauce.

SOUPE DE PESACH
Passover Soup

Tunisians like cardoons, the fleshy ribs from a plant of the artichoke family. Along with all the other vegetables and seasonings it makes a fine soup for the holiday.

> 3 cardoon ribs, cut into ½-inch cubes (see Glossary)
> 3 kohlrabies, peeled, cut into ½-inch cubes
> 5 carrots, cut into ¼-inch cubes
> ¼ cup chopped parsley
> ¼ cup chopped fresh coriander
> 1 pound beef chuck, cut into thin 2-inch pieces
> ½ teaspoon pepper
> 1 teaspoon salt, or to taste
> 1 teaspoon paprika
> 5 cups water
> 3 sheets of matzoh, broken into 1-inch square pieces

1. Put everything into a pan except the water and matzoh. Steam over low heat for 10 minutes, shaking the pan vigorously. Add the water, bring to a boil, and simmer over low heat for 1 hour.

2. When the meat is tender, put the matzoh pieces on top of the soup, cover the pan, and simmer for 10 minutes more. Do not stir.

Serve hot, meat and vegetables together. Serves 6.

CHORBA
Soup with Orzo

Orzo is that rice-shaped pasta associated with Greece and other Mediterranean countries. In Tunisia, it is known as "birds' tongues."

> ½ pound boneless beef chuck
> 4 celery ribs and leaves

2 tablespoons corn oil
3 tablespoons tomato paste
1 teaspoon salt, or to taste
¼ teaspoon white pepper
½ teaspoon paprika
4 cups water
½ pound orzo

1. Cut the beef and celery ribs into ¼-inch cubes. Chop the celery leaves.
2. Heat the oil in a pan and stir-fry the beef and celery over moderate heat for 1 minute. Add the tomato paste and stir-fry for 3 minutes. Add the salt, pepper, paprika and water. Bring to a boil. Simmer, covered, over low heat for 20 minutes.
3. Add the orzo and cook for 10 minutes, until *al dente*.
Serve hot. Serves 6.

BISSARA
Fava Soup

This is a poor man's soup, to be made when there is not enough money around to buy meat. Flavorful and substantial, the soup is served with generous quantities of day-old bread and is considered to be the entire meal.

1 pound skinless, dried fava beans
4 cups water
2 tablespoons corn oil
½ teaspoon salt, or to taste
2 teaspoons harissa (see Glossary)
2 teaspoons ground cuminseed
lemon wedges

1. Cook the fava beans in the water in a covered pan over moderate heat for about 1 hour, or until soft. Add more water (½ cup) should the liquid evaporate too quickly. Mash the beans coarsely in the pan. (This is not a purée.)
2. Add the oil, salt, *harissa* and cuminseed and simmer slowly over low heat for 20 minutes.
Serve hot with lemon wedges and an extra plate of *harissa*.
Serves 4.

BSAL BIL LOUBYA
Bean, Onion and Beef Stew

There are no frills in this nourishing, filling, big family stew of straightforward flavors, heavy with onions. The beans should be soft but not disintegrating. My Tunisian informant told me that there were 10 children in the family who had to be fed on a limited budget. The *bsal* could do it.

2 pounds dried white haricot beans
1½ pounds onions, sliced coarse
2 pounds short ribs of beef, cut into 3-inch pieces
2 tablespoons corn oil
2 celery ribs and leaves, cut into 3-inch pieces
1 can (6 ounces) tomato paste
3 ripe tomatoes (1 pound), sliced
3 teaspoons paprika
1 teaspoon pepper
2 teaspoons salt, or to taste
8 cups water

1. Soak the beans in water overnight. Drain.
2. Put the beans on the bottom of a pan large enough to hold all the ingredients. Add all the other ingredients on top. Bring to a boil over moderate heat, reduce heat to low, and cover the pan. Cook slowly over low heat for 2 hours, to produce a thick stew in which the onions have dissolved and the meat is tender.
Serve warm with bread. Serves 10.

RAGOÛT DE PETITS POIS
Beef and Green Pea Ragout

2 pounds beef, shin or chuck, in one piece
4 cups water
1 teaspoon salt
3 tablespoons corn or olive oil
2 medium onions, chopped (1 cup)
1 garlic clove, sliced thin
1 teaspoon paprika

¼ teaspoon pepper
1 ripe tomato, chopped (⅔ cup), or equal amount of canned
2 tablespoons chopped parsley
2 tablespoons chopped dill
2 tablespoons chopped fresh coriander
¼ cup chopped celery, leaves and ribs
1 medium carrot, sliced (½ cup)
½ pound green peas, fresh or frozen

1. Cook the beef in water with the salt in a covered pan over moderate heat for about 1 hour, or until beef is tender. Remove the beef and reserve 1 cup of the cooking liquid.

2. Heat the oil in a pan; stir-fry the onions and garlic over moderate heat for 2 minutes. Add the paprika and pepper and mix well, then add the tomato, parsley, dill, coriander, celery and carrot. Cook for 10 minutes. Add ⅓ cup of the reserved liquid and simmer over low heat for 10 minutes.

3. Add the beef and green peas and the balance of the liquid (⅔ cup). Simmer over low heat for 15 minutes, basting now and then. Do not cover the pan.

Serve the meat, sliced, in the center of a platter, surrounded by the peas and sauce. Serve warm. Serves 6 to 8 with other dishes.

RAGOÛT DE BAMIA
Beef and Okra Ragout

The ragout is served with bread and several salads. Shin beef (ever popular with Chinese) has a gelatinous substance and makes a rich sauce; it is the preferred beef in this recipe.

2 pounds beef, shin or chuck, in one piece
4 cups water
1 teaspoon salt
2 tablespoons corn or olive oil
2 medium onions, sliced (1 cup)
1 garlic clove, sliced thin
2 teaspoons paprika
¼ teaspoon pepper
2 ripe tomatoes, chopped (1 cup), or equal amount canned
1 pound okra, rinsed

1. Cook the beef in water with the salt for 1 hour, or until tender. Remove the beef and reserve 1 cup of the cooking liquid. Slice the beef.

2. To prepare the sauce, heat the oil in a pan and stir-fry the onions and garlic for 2 minutes. Add the paprika, pepper and tomatoes and stir-fry for 2 minutes. Add ½ cup of the reserved liquid and stir briskly to smooth out any lumps.

3. Trim ¼ inch from the stem ends of the okra pods. Add okra to the sauce, then add the beef slices and the balance of the liquid. Cover the pan and simmer over low heat for 15 minutes to cook the okra.

Serve warm, the beef in the center of the platter, with okra and sauce all around. Serves 6 to 8 with other dishes.

MAKOUD
Beef and Potato Pie

The texture of this pie borders on that of a soufflé, but it has more density.

1 pound potatoes (about 3), cooked in their skins until soft,
    cooled and peeled
2 hard-cooked eggs, peeled and mashed
½ pound roasted or boiled beef, cut into ¼-inch cubes
½ cup fine-chopped parsley
1 teaspoon salt, or to taste
¼ teaspoon white pepper
5 raw eggs, beaten
2 tablespoons corn oil

1. Mash the potatoes; add the hard-cooked eggs, beef, parsley, salt and pepper and mix well. Add the beaten eggs and mix.

2. Heat the oil and add it to a heatproof glass or metal baking dish, round or square, and swirl it around. Add the pie mixture, which should be about 2 inches deep. Bake in a 375° F. oven for about 30 minutes, or until the top becomes brown.

Serve warm. Serves 6 with salads and bread.

HHOMSS BIL CAMOUN
Chick-Peas, Calf's Foot and Veal

The *Hhomss* is one of the dishes that can be prepared as a *t'fina*. The same recipe is used except that all the ingredients are placed in a pan and put into an oven at low heat on Friday evening and cooked the entire night for serving midday on the Sabbath.

2 pounds dried chick-peas, soaked in water overnight, drained
1 calf's foot, about 2 pounds, chopped into pieces
2 pounds veal ribs or shoulder, cut into serving pieces
2 tablespoons corn oil
1 teaspoon paprika
1 or 2 teaspoons harissa, to taste (see Glossary)
1 teaspoon ground cuminseed
2 teaspoons salt
1 pound potatoes (about 3)
⅛ teaspoon pepper
2 eggs, beaten

1. Put the chick-peas, calf's foot and veal in a large pan and cover with hot water, about 4 cups. Bring to a boil over moderate heat, then continue to cook, covered, over low heat for about 1½ hours, or until the meats are tender. Add 1 or 2 cups additional hot water if the liquid evaporates too quickly.

2. Heat the oil in a skillet over moderate heat. Add the paprika, *harissa*, cuminseed and salt, all at once, and swirl the mixture around for a few seconds. Add this to the chick-pea mixture.

3. Cook the potatoes in their skins until soft. Cool, peel and grate them. Thoroughly mix in the pepper and eggs to make batter for dumplings. Take 1 heaping tablespoon of the mixture for each dumpling and drop it into the meat pan. Cook, covered, for 15 minutes more.

Serve hot with *cous cous* or bread. Serves 8.

MSOKI

Lamb Ragout and Vegetables for Passover

This grand dish, prepared and served the first evening of Passover, features lamb and an extravagant variety of vegetables. Traditionally, lamb is the meat to be used; however, in modern times either beef or veal can replace the lamb. As many vegetables as are seasonally available are included since it is, in fact, the vegetables that provide the flavors and textures. It does not mean, however, that one cannot reduce the variety somewhat, based on personal preference, without loss of flavor.

In the traditional families of Tunisia, a lamb was purchased and fattened for about 3 months prior to Passover. The fattened lamb was slaughtered and the meat divided according to its uses. Some portions were reserved to be made into merguez, the incomparable spice sausage, others for the msoki; the innards (liver, heart, tongue, tripe, brain) were set aside for their particular recipes. The lambskin was cured and turned into a throw rug. Everything was utilized.

½ cup corn oil
2 tablespoons tomato paste
1 teaspoon pepper
2 teaspoons salt
3 pounds lamb shank or shoulder, cut into serving pieces
18 inches of masran (kishke) of Libya (stuffed intestine), optional
1½ pounds carrots, cut into 1-inch pieces
1½ pounds potatoes, peeled, cut into 1-inch cubes
2 artichoke hearts
1½ pounds white turnips, cut into 1-inch cubes
2 heads of fennel, quartered
1½ pounds green peas
2 medium onions, quartered
6 garlic cloves, chopped fine
1 pound celery ribs (remove leaves and reserve), cut ribs into
    2-inch pieces
3 cardoon ribs, cut into 2-inch pieces (see Glossary)
1½ pounds fresh fava beans

1½ pounds fresh spinach
water to cover, about 4 cups
½ cup 1-inch pieces of fresh dill
½ cup 1-inch pieces of fresh parsley
½ cup 1-inch pieces of fresh coriander
1 head of Romaine lettuce, cut into 2-inch pieces
1 teaspoon quatre épices (see Note)
1 pound matzoh, each sheet broken into 8 pieces

1. Put the oil, tomato paste, pepper and salt in a pan large enough to contain all the ingredients. Stir-fry over moderate heat for 1 minute. Stir with a wooden spoon. Add the meat and kishke and fry for 2 minutes, shaking the pan frequently.

2. Add the vegetables, one by one, with the hard vegetables first—carrots, potatoes, artichokes, white turnips, fennel, peas, onions, garlic, celery, cardoon, fava beans and spinach. Shake the pan in a throwing motion that will turn the vegetables and meat over. Fry and turn for 15 minutes to cook it down.

3. Just cover the mixture with water, about 4 cups, and simmer over low heat for about 1 hour, or until meat is tender.

4. Add the celery leaves, cut into 1-inch pieces, the dill, parsley, coriander and lettuce. Push the mixture aside in the center and add the spice mix, stirring it around slightly. Cook in the covered pan for 10 minutes.

5. Lastly, place the broken matzoh over the top of the ragout. Cover the pan, remove from heat, and let the msoki stand until ready to serve when the family returns from the synagogue for the first Seder.

Serves 8 to 10 persons.

NOTE: In India each cook blends spices to make the seasoning called garam masala, so in Tunisia they blend their own quatre épices. I use equal amounts of cardamom, cinnamon, white pepper and cumin.

AKOUD
Sweetbreads in Red Sauce

The traditional *akoud* was prepared in the old days with the genitalia of beef. It was then, and is now, considered a delicacy when the ingredients are available—not an easy task in the United States. The modern method is to use sweetbreads, tripe, or beef cubes, in that order of popularity.

2 tablespoons corn oil
5 garlic cloves, sliced thin
½ teaspoon salt
¼ cup tomato paste
1½ cups water
1 pound sweetbreads (beef or veal), cut into 1-inch cubes
1 teaspoon paprika
2 teaspoons ground cuminseed
1 teaspoon ground caraway
1 teaspoon harissa, or to taste (see Glossary)

1. Heat the oil in a pan and stir-fry the garlic over moderate heat for 1 minute. Add the salt, tomato paste, water, sweetbreads, paprika, cuminseed, caraway and *harissa*. Reduce heat to low, cover the pan, and cook for about 1 hour, or until sweetbreads are tender and the sauce has thickened considerably.

Serve warm as an appetizer. Serves 4 to 6 with other dishes.

VARIATIONS:

TRIPE

Cook 1 pound of tripe in water with ½ teaspoon salt and 1 large slice of fresh orange until tender, about 1 hour; drain. Cut the tripe into 2-inch cubes. Prepare the *akoud* sauce with all the ingredients except the tripe, and cook over low heat for ½ hour. Add the tripe cubes and simmer for 15 minutes more.

BONELESS BEEF CUBES

Cut the beef into 1-inch cubes and add it to the *akoud* sauce at the same time as the tomato paste and water. Simmer in a covered pan over low heat for 1 hour, or until the beef is tender. Should the liquid evaporate too quickly, add ¼ cup warm water.

GANAOUIA AVEC POULET
Chicken and Okra

For those who like their okra to be firm and flavorful rather than soft and gummy, this aromatic recipe should satisfy. The onions and tomatoes combine into a well-seasoned jamlike sauce.

> 3 tablespoons corn oil
> 2 pounds onions, sliced thin (4 cups)
> 1 pound ripe tomatoes, fresh or canned, sliced (2 cups)
> 5 garlic cloves, sliced thin
> 1 teaspoon salt, or to taste
> ¼ teaspoon pepper
> ¼ teaspoon ground turmeric
> 1 cinnamon stick, 3 inches, halved
> 1 chicken, 3 pounds, plus 1 chicken breast, cut into serving
>   pieces, loose skin and fat discarded
> 2 cups water
> 1½ pounds fresh okra, stem ends trimmed

1. Heat 2 tablespoons oil in a pan, add the onions, and stir-fry over moderate heat until light brown, about 5 minutes. Add the tomatoes, garlic, salt, pepper, turmeric and cinnamon stick and stir-fry the mixture for 3 minutes.

2. Place the chicken on top, add the water, cover the pan, and cook over moderate heat for ½ hour.

3. Put 1 tablespoon oil in a skillet and in it stir-fry the okra over moderate heat for about 5 minutes, or until they turn color slightly. Add okra to the chicken pan, fitting the pods in around the chicken pieces. Cover the pan and simmer over low heat for 15 minutes. The sauce should now be reduced and thick, the chicken tender and the okra crunchy.

Serve warm with bread, rice or orzo (chorba). Serves 6.

VARIATION: Beef may be prepared the same way, replacing the chicken. Cut 2 pounds boneless beef chuck into 1-inch cubes. Continue as for the chicken except that the cooking time is extended to 1 hour before the okra pods are added.

LA MINNINA
Chicken and Brain Soufflé

The *minnina* is a very special dish for a special occasion. It is prepared in substantial quantity (20 eggs!) and is attractive to look at as well as being of fine flavor and texture. You may prepare half of the recipe for fewer people.

I believe that this dish is of Spanish origin and came with the Jews when they fled Spain during the Inquisition. *Minnina* in Spanish means "pussy cat," but the connection, if any, escapes me.

1 cup homemade chicken broth
1 raw chicken breast, skinless
1 beef brain
10 hard-cooked eggs, peeled
juice of 1 lemon
⅛ teaspoon ground turmeric
1 teaspoon salt
¼ teaspoon white pepper
⅛ teaspoon ground cinnamon
10 raw eggs
oil
lemon wedges

1. Simmer the chicken broth in a pan for about 10 minutes or until it is reduced by half. Cool and set aside.

2. Cut the chicken breast into julienne. Cover the brain with hot water for 10 minutes. Drain; remove the membranes and veins. Cut into ½-inch cubes. Set aside.

3. Divide the hard-cooked eggs into yolks and whites. Break up the yolks rather coarsely with your fingers. Slice the whites.

4. Put the chicken, brain, egg yolks and whites, lemon juice, turmeric, salt, pepper and cinnamon in a large bowl. Mix together. Break 10 raw eggs over the mixture and let stand for 5 minutes.

5. Preheat oven to 400° F. Generously oil a deep heatproof glass or other baking dish, 9 × 5 × 3 inches or larger, so that the soufflé does not overflow. At this time, mix the eggs into the chicken/brain combination with your fingers, slowly and not too thoroughly, so that the streaks of yolks and whites will be visible when sliced after baking.

6. Pour the mixture into the baking dish. Bake at 400° F. for 10 minutes. Reduce heat to 350° F. and bake for about 1 hour more, or until the soufflé is dry when tested with a wood skewer.

At this time, pour the chicken broth over the surface of the soufflé and bake for 5 minutes more to let it absorb the liquid.

Remove from the oven and cool.

Serve at room temperature, in slices with lemon wedges.

Serves 10.

POISSON COMPLET
Fish and Chips Complete

The complete fish plate sounds like a dish being served in England rather than Tunisia. Nevertheless, the fish and other ingredients are part of the ritual when serving at home or dining in restaurants, where the *poisson complet* seems to be generally available. Any local saltwater fish can be used as well as one's favorite fillet of flounder, sole or anything else. The Tunisians prefer tuna or mullet from the Mediterranean.

FISH

> 6 slices of fresh tuna (2 pounds), or 6 small sea bass, red
>   snapper or similar fish (2 pounds)
> flour for dusting
> ¼ cup corn oil

SALAD

> ¼ corn oil
> 4 whole sweet green peppers, each poked with a fork in 3
>   different places
> 2 fresh hot red or green chilies
> 3 ripe tomatoes (1 pound)
> 4 garlic cloves, put through a press
> ¼ teaspoon salt
> ½ teaspoon paprika
> 3 tablespoons water

1. Rinse the fish in cold water and dry with towels. Dust with flour and shake off the excess. Heat ¼ cup oil in a skillet and fry the fish over moderate heat for 3 minutes on each side. Drain on paper towels. Reserve in a warm place. Discard the oil.

2. Heat ¼ cup oil in a skillet. Fry the green peppers on all sides over moderate heat for about 3 minutes. Remove and let cool. Fry the hot chilies for 1 minute and remove. Fry the tomatoes for 2 minutes and set aside. Open the hot and sweet peppers; remove and discard the seeds, stems and ribs. Peel off the skins. Do the same for the tomatoes.

3. Chop all the vegetables into ¼-inch pieces. Add the garlic, salt, paprika and water. Stir-fry the mixture in a dry skillet over moderate heat for 3 minutes. Set aside.

Each serving should have a piece of fish and generous serving of salad (at room temperature), with some french fried potatoes and a fried egg alongside.

Serve warm or at room temperature. Serves 6.

ADMA DE R'MEL
Eggs Baked in Sand

Eggs are prepared among the Calcutta Jews in the same manner as here, that is to say, baked overnight for the Sabbath on charcoal stoves. The principal difference is that in Calcutta the eggs are hard-cooked first, prior to baking.

Baking the uncooked eggs in sand has its pitfalls if the eggs are not completely covered. If not, then they burst like hand grenades, with the resulting chaos all over the kitchen.

Eggs, as many as you wish
fine sand in an ovenproof container

1. Cover the eggs completely with the sand and bake them over very low heat overnight as part of the *T'fina*. The eggs and the shell will turn a nutlike brown. This is the old-style method of preparing the eggs in homes where the sand-filled container was part of the standard kitchen equipment.

The modern method for these delicious and unexpectedly interesting eggs is to include them in the shell in a *t'fina* preparation.

COUS COUS ROYALE
Jewish Cous Cous

All cous cous prepa-
rations in Tunisia are not the same—there are modifications
within a certain style based on the region. This Jewish cous
cous consists of the following recipes: Homemade Cous
Cous, Beef and Vegetable Soup, Meat-Stuffed Vegetables
(boullettes) and the Sauce. In my opinion it may be the best
cous cous of the Mahgreb.

STUFFING

> 5-inch celery rib
> 5-inch sprig of fresh dill
> 5-inch sprig of parsley
> 5-inch sprig of coriander
> 1½ teaspoons salt
> 2 medium onions, chopped (1 cup)
> 1 pound ground beef
> 1 slice of day-old French or Italian bread (6 inches), soaked in
>   water, squeezed dry
> ½ teaspoon pepper
> 1 garlic clove, chopped fine
> 2 tablespoons dried mint, crumbled
> 1 egg yolk
> 2 tablespoons chopped fresh dill
> 2 tablespoons chopped fresh parsley

SAUCE

> 1 pound ripe tomatoes, quartered
> ½ teaspoon salt
> 2 teaspoons paprika
> ¼ teaspoon pepper
> 1 garlic clove, sliced thin

VEGETABLES

> 4 of the smallest eggplants, peeled, halved lengthwise from the
>   bottom to within 1 inch of the stem end
> 4 zucchini, halved crosswise, each half cut lengthwise almost to
>   the end

4 potatoes, peeled and divided lengthwise into halves, each half
    cut through almost to the end
4 large canned artichokes, halved almost completely
4 chunks of cabbage, 3-inch pieces that are held together but
    with open leaves
salt
flour for dusting
1 whole egg plus 1 egg white
1 tablespoon tomato paste
3 tablespoons corn oil
oil for deep-frying, about 1 cup

1. Sprinkle the celery and the sprigs of dill, parsley and coriander with ½ teaspoon of the salt and let stand for 10 minutes. Press out liquid very gently in a paper towel. Chop fine and mix with the onions. Mix with the remaining salt and all the other stuffing ingredients and set aside.

2. Mix the sauce ingredients together in a pan and simmer, covered, for 10 minutes. Set aside.

3. To make the boullettes, sprinkle the prepared vegetables with salt and let stand for 15 minutes. Rinse in cold water and dry. Stuff each with about ¼ cup of the beef mixture and dust with flour. Any leftover stuffing can be added to the pan.

4. Beat together the eggs, tomato paste and 2 tablespoons of the oil to make a batter. Dip the stuffed vegetables (boullettes) into the egg batter.

5. Heat the oil for deep-frying and brown the boullettes on all sides for about 5 minutes.

6. Place the boullettes in 1 or 2 large skillets in a single layer. Cover with water, about 1½ cups.

7. Pour the sauce into the skillet, or skillets, with the boullettes and water, and cook over moderate heat until the liquid has almost all evaporated, about ½ hour. Do not cover.

8. Now the complete cous cous is ready. Serve in the following manner: the boullettes on a platter, the broth from the beef and vegetable soup in individual cups, the beef and vegetables from the soup in their own dish, and the cous cous in a bowl.

Serves 10.

SEMOULE
Homemade Cous Cous

> 3 pounds semolina
> 4 tablespoons olive oil
> ½ cup water, about
> 1 tablespoon coarse salt

1. Mix the semolina and 2 tablespoons oil together by tossing it up and down with your hands. Add the water and continue tossing. Push the moistened semolina through a metal sieve with about ¼-inch square holes. (Do not use a fine sieve since the semolina will not pass through.) These granules are the *cous cous.*

2. Mix the sieved semolina with salt and the remaining 2 tablespoons oil, tossing it to ensure that it has been well mixed.

3. Place the mixture in the top section of the *couscousier.* Put 2 cups water in the bottom section and bring to a boil. Cover the top with a kitchen towel and let the *cous cous* steam for ½ hour.

4. Remove the *cous cous* to a large pan, add 3 cups water, mix well, and allow the water to be absorbed for 15 minutes. Return the *cous cous* to the *couscousier* and steam, covered, for ½ hour more.

5. Turn the *cous cous* out into a pan and cover it with a towel. It is ready to be served with the other segments of the Royale.

N O T E : Prepared *cous cous*, imported from France and Tunisia, is available in Middle Eastern groceries and in some supermarkets. You may prefer to use this.

COUS COUS BOUILLON
Beef and Vegetable Soup

The soup, beef and vegetables are part of the complete *Cous Cous Royale.*

> 2 tablespoons corn or olive oil
> 2 pounds boneless beef, cut into 10 pieces
> 6 cups water
> 1 teaspoon salt
> ¼ teaspoon pepper

1 ripe tomato, quartered
1 celery rib, leaves and stem, quartered
3 whole carrots
3 whole zucchini or courgettes
½ pound cabbage in 1 piece, blanched in hot water for 5 minutes,
    drained
½ cup parsley, in sprigs
½ cup dill, in sprigs

1. Put the oil, beef, water, salt and pepper in a large pan or the bottom section of a *couscousier*. Bring to a boil, reduce heat to low, cover, and simmer for 1 hour, or until the beef is almost tender.

2. Add all the other ingredients and simmer for 15 minutes more to integrate the seasoning. Should the liquid evaporate too quickly, add another cup of water.

Serve warm, the beef and vegetables on one platter and individual cups of soup for each diner.

SALADE FRAÎCHE
Fresh Salad

This simplest of salads is served as one of the many dishes on a *cous cous* table. A salad of texture.

2 young cucumbers, peeled and cut into julienne
2 medium carrots, cut into julienne
1 tablespoon thin-sliced celery
½ teaspoon salt
2 tablespoons lemon juice, or to taste

1. Toss everything together.
Serve at room temperature.

MZOURA
Piquant Carrots

The mzoura is a popu-
lar condiment pickle that can be refrigerated and used for 1
week, when it will be time, of course, to make more.

1 pound carrots
1 tablespoon corn oil
1 teaspoon harissa (see Glossary)
1 teaspoon salt, or to taste
½ teaspoon ground caraway
½ teaspoon ground coriander
¼ cup white vinegar

1. Cook the whole carrots in water over moderate heat until
tender but still firm. Drain and cool. Cut them diagonally into ¼-
inch-thick slices.
2. Heat the oil in a skillet, add the harissa, salt, caraway, coriander and vinegar, and stir-fry over low heat for 2 minutes, stirring
constantly with a wooden spoon.
3. Add the carrots and stir-fry for 3 minutes more. Turn out into
a bowl; cool and refrigerate.
Serve with any kind of Tunisian food. Serves 6.

TOURCHI BATATA
Potato Salad with Cumin

Salads are obligatory
in Tunisian dining, and a service without several salads
would be unthinkable. The potato salad is especially taste-
ful combined as it is with cuminseed and harissa.

1 pound potatoes (about 4)
2 tablespoons corn oil
1 teaspoon harissa (see Glossary)
½ teaspoon salt, or to taste
1 teaspoon ground cuminseed
juice of 1 lemon

1. Cook the potatoes in their skins until soft but not overdone.
Cool and peel. Cut them into ½-inch cubes.

2. Heat the oil in a skillet, add the harissa, salt, cuminseed and lemon juice and bring to a boil over moderate heat. Swirl the pan around for a few seconds to make certain that the sauce is well mixed. Then pour it over the potato cubes. Toss lightly. Refrigerate.

Serve cool or at room temperature. Serves 6.

TASTIRA HARRA
Fried Chopped Salad

Tastira in Tunisian language means to chop with two crossed knives, as when combining flour and shortening. This old traditional method has been superseded by the processor.

2 tablespoons corn oil
1 pound green peppers (about 4)
2 ripe tomatoes (½ pound)
2 or 3 semihot chilies, to taste
4 garlic cloves, sliced
½ teaspoon salt
1 tablespoon olive oil
juice of 2 lemons
1 fried egg per person

1. Heat the oil in a skillet and stir-fry the green peppers on all sides to char the skins. Do the same for the tomatoes and chilies. When cool, peel, seed, and quarter all the vegetables.

2. In a processor, chop the garlic first, then lightly chop the peppers, then the chilies and last and lightest the tomatoes. Turn out into a salad bowl. Mix in the salt, olive oil and lemon juice.

Garnish the salad with 1 fried egg for each person.

Serve at room temperature. Serves 4 or 5.

NOTE: Should you prefer to chop the vegetables by hand, which would control the size of the pieces, cut everything into about ¼-inch cubes.

SALADE CUITE
Cooked Salad

This salad is both a table condiment (chutney) and a salad. It can be served anytime and with any sort of Tunisian food.

  4 green peppers (1 pound), seeded and quartered
  4 ripe tomatoes (about 1 pound), quartered
  1 teaspoon salt
  1 teaspoon caraway seeds
  2 dried hot red chilies, whole
  1 tablespoon paprika
  2 tablespoons corn or olive oil

Put everything into a pan, cover, and simmer over low heat for ½ hour. The mixture will reduce to a thick melange. Stir once or twice during this procedure.

Serve at room temperature. May be refrigerated for several days. Serves 6.

AJLOOK
Zucchini Lemon Salad

The *ajlook* is another of those salads that are really chutneys or condiments. This one is particularly useful since one can use it as an appetizer on bread or crackers.

  1 zucchini or courgette (8 to 10 ounces), cooked, whole
  1 teaspoon harissa (see Glossary)
  ½ teaspoon paprika
  ½ teaspoon salt
  ¼ teaspoon caraway seeds
  ¼ teaspoon ground caraway
  1 tablespoon fresh lemon juice

1. Mash the squash with a fork but not too smoothly. Add all the other ingredients. Refrigerate.

Serve cool.

MHAMARS (AUBERGINES FARCIES)

Stuffed Baked Eggplant

A well-seasoned stuffing for eggplant. The advantage is that you may prepare them in advance and bake when almost ready to serve. They are best served warm.

4 medium eggplant (2 pounds)
3 tablespoons corn oil
1 medium onion, chopped fine (½ cup)
½ cup fine-chopped parsley
¼ teaspoon salt
¼ teaspoon white pepper
1/16 teaspoon grated nutmeg, a good pinch
1 pound ground beef or chicken
2 eggs, beaten
2 eggs, separated
1 tablespoon margarine
flour for dusting

1. Cut the eggplants lengthwise into halves. Scoop out the pulp, leaving a wall about ⅜ inch thick. Chop the pulp into ¼-inch pieces.

2. Heat the oil in a large skillet. Add the eggplant pulp, onion, parsley, salt, pepper and nutmeg and stir-fry over moderate heat for 3 minutes. Add the beef or chicken and continue to stir-fry for 5 minutes, to reduce the bulk and evaporate the liquid that accumulates. Cool the mixture for a few minutes.

3. Mix the beaten whole eggs and 2 egg whites together and stir into the meat mixture. Reserve the 2 yolks.

4. Rub a heatproof glass or metal baking dish with margarine (which is pareve) and dust it with flour as though one were baking a cake. Tap out the excess flour.

5. Stuff each of the 8 eggplant halves and smooth over the surface. Beat the egg yolks. Using a pastry brush, spread egg yolk over the top of the eggplants to form a crust. Bake in a 350° F. oven for ½ hour.

Serve warm. Serves 8 with other dishes.

T'FINA CAMOUNIA
Cumin-Flavored Beans and Beef

T'fina is an exclusively Tunisian Jewish method of preparing a major dish for the Sabbath. This is one of the several types of t'fina that usually contain dried white haricot beans, meat and seasonings. T'fina is prepared similarly to the Ashkenazi method of setting up *cholent* for the Sabbath.

The vegetarian method from the first part of the recipe can be prepared anytime at all without reference to the Sabbath. For the American kitchen, the *t'fina* with meat can be assembled early in the morning, cooked over very low heat for 8 hours (using a heat dispersal pad when half through cooking time) and served the evening of the same day.

1 pound dried white beans
4 cups water
5 garlic cloves, put through the press
3 teaspoons ground cuminseed
1¼ teaspoons salt
2 teaspoons paprika
1 tablespoon tomato paste
1 ripe tomato, chopped fine (½ cup)
3 tablespoons corn oil
1 pound potatoes (about 3), cooked in their skins until soft,
	peeled
3 large eggs, beaten
⅛ teaspoon ground turmeric

1. Soak the beans in water to cover overnight, then drain. Add the 4 cups water and beans to a large pan and cook them over low heat until they are soft but not disintegrating, about 45 minutes.

2. Mix together the garlic, cuminseed, 1 teaspoon salt, the paprika, tomato paste and chopped tomato. Heat the oil in a skillet, add the mixture, and stir-fry over moderate heat for 5 minutes. Add to the simmering bean pan and continue to cook slowly for 10 minutes.

3. Mash the potatoes, not too smoothly. Add the beaten eggs, ¼ teaspoon salt and the turmeric and mix. This is the dumpling mixture. For each dumpling, take 1 heaping tablespoon of the mix and drop it into the simmering bean pan. Do this with all the potato purée. Cover the pan and cook at low heat for 15 minutes.

Serve hot. Serves 8 with bread and salads.

VARIATION:

2 pounds boneless beef chuck, cut into 8 pieces
8 eggs in the shell
4 small potatoes, 1 pound, peeled

1. Using the vegetarian bean ingredients in the basic recipe, put the white beans in a large pan. (Do not soak overnight.) Add the 4 cups water, garlic, cuminseed, salt, paprika, tomato paste and ripe tomato to the pan. Place the pieces of beef over that. Arrange the eggs and potatoes around the top of the meat. Cover the pan and bring to a boil over moderate heat. Reduce heat to very low and cook, if using the traditional method, all of Friday evening, to be served warm about midday on Saturday.

Serves 8.

CHAKCHOUKA DE SAIF
Summer Vegetable Melange

Vegetables in Tunisia are more seasonal than in the United States, where supermarkets carry almost everything throughout the year. Thus the *chakchouka* is possible in Tunisia only in the summertime when all the vegetables are available. It is a complete vegetarian meal, aromatically seasoned and with a small amount of sharp spice. My Tunisian cook emphasized that the aniseed, paprika and pepper were added toward the end of the cooking since this also eliminated the possibility of an aftertaste or, shall we say, a "burp."

3 tablespoons corn oil
1 pound onions (about 4), sliced
1 pound ripe tomatoes (about 3), sliced
1 pound green peppers (about 3), seeded, sliced
2 fresh artichoke hearts, sliced

3 carrots (¼ pound), sliced

1 cauliflower (1 pound), cut into florets

2 or 3 semihot green chilies (use whole for moderate flavor or
    seeded and sliced for more intense heat)

4 garlic cloves, sliced

6 ounces tomato paste

3 cups water

1½ pounds potatoes (about 5), peeled, quartered

½ cup sliced fresh dill

2 teaspoons ground aniseed

2 teaspoons paprika

1 teaspoon white pepper

1 teaspoon salt, or to taste

1. Put the oil in a large pan over moderate heat and add the
onions, fresh tomatoes, green peppers, artichokes, carrots, cauliflowerets, chilies and garlic and stir-fry for 10 minutes until softened and reduced in bulk. Add the tomato paste and water, cover
the pan, and bring to a boil.

2. Add the potatoes and dill and cook until the potatoes are soft.
At this stage, stir in the aniseed, paprika, pepper and salt. Cook
slowly over low heat for 15 minutes more. There will be some sauce
with the vegetables.

Serve warm. Serves 6 to 8.

VARIATION: *Chakchouka* often includes eggs or merguez (Tunisian lamb sausage) or both for a more substantial meal. My own
preference is to have both. Add 1 sausage and 1 whole egg per
person during the last minutes of cooking time.

BANATAGE
Stuffed Potato Fritter

Several Jewish com-
munities in India prepare the *banatage*, known locally as
"potato chops." The seasonings are different but the techniques in assembling them are similar.

The *banatage* is a popular Passover dish in Tunisia.

STUFFING

1 tablespoon corn oil
2 medium onions, chopped (1 cup)
¼ cup coarse-chopped parsley
½ pound beefsteak, cut into ¼-inch cubes
⅛ teaspoon white pepper
⅛ teaspoon ground turmeric
½ teaspoon salt

POTATOES

2 pounds potatoes
½ teaspoon salt
⅛ teaspoon white pepper
⅛ teaspoon ground turmeric
1 teaspoon lemon juice
1 egg, beaten

FRITTER

4 hard-cooked eggs, peeled and quartered
1 cup corn oil (about)
½ cup flour
2 eggs, beaten

1. Heat the oil in a pan and stir-fry the onions over moderate heat until light brown. Add the parsley and beef and stir-fry for 5 minutes. Add the pepper, turmeric and salt and fry for another minute. Set aside.

2. Cook the unpeeled potatoes, covered with water, until soft. Cool and peel.

3. Grate the potatoes. Add salt, pepper, turmeric, lemon juice and 1 beaten egg. Mix well.

4. Divide the potato mixture into 12 equal parts. Moisten your hands with cold water. Flatten 1 part of potato into a circle about ½ inch thick. Put 1 heaping tablespoon of the meat filling on it, press in 1 piece of the hard-cooked egg, and close the fritter into an oval shape about 1½ inches thick and 2 inches long. Prepare all the fritters this way.

5. Heat the oil in a skillet. Dip each fritter into the flour then into the beaten eggs. Fry over moderate heat for 5 minutes, or until fritters are golden color. Drain on paper towels.

Serve warm with lemon wedges. Makes 12 fritters.

MAKROUD

Semolina Log Stuffed with
Date Paste

Makroud is one of the most popular Tunisian sweets. Crusty, chewy, sweet and substantial would be a fair way to describe this delicious concoction.

1½ pounds prepared date paste (see Note)
peel of 1 orange, chopped fine
2 teaspoons ground cinnamon
⅓ cup pine nuts
1 cup corn oil
5 cups fine semolina, lightly toasted in a dry skillet until the
    color changes
2 teaspoons baking soda
2 tablespoons flour
about 1 cup cold water
oil for deep-frying
2 cups Honey Dip (see Index)

1. Mix the date paste, orange peel, cinnamon and pine nuts together. Set aside.

2. Heat 1 cup oil until it is hot.

3. Mix the semolina, baking soda and flour together. Add the hot oil and mix well. Cool the mixture. Add the water, little by little, to prepare a moist, soft dough that holds together. Set aside for 15 minutes.

4. Spread 2 cups dough out into a rectangle 5 inches wide, ½ inch thick and 12 inches long. Spread ¾ cup of the date mixture over the dough rectangle, leaving a border of ½ inch all around. Fold over the edges toward the center into a square log 1½ inches wide and deep, covering the date paste completely. Slice the log diagonally into 1½-inch-wide pieces.

5. Heat the oil for deep-frying in a wok or pan and fry the pieces over moderate heat until brown but not too dark, about 2 minutes. Remove and drain in a colander.

6. Heat the honey dip and let it simmer over low heat. Dip the fried *makroud* into the syrup, moistening them all over. Remove to a colander and let them drain and dry.

Serve at room temperature at tea or coffee hour.

Makes 24 pieces.

NOTE: Date paste can be purchased in Israel as well as in some Middle Eastern shops in New York. It can be made at home by using a processor and grinding to a paste 1½ pounds of pitted dates.

YOYO
Tunisian Donuts in Honey Syrup

You can see these *yoyo* in almost every *pâtisserie* in the Tunisian capital city of Tunis. The commercial ones are double the size of those prepared in this recipe for home use.

Yoyo may also be baked on an oiled cookie sheet in a 375° F. oven for 20 minutes. In this case, they are not dipped into the syrup, but become an attractive donut cookie.

The Tunisian homemaker in days gone by prepared *yoyos* by hand, rolling out a piece of dough into a cigar shape and connecting the two ends. A donut cutter is easier and the taste is not altered.

DONUTS

> 2 eggs, beaten
> 2 tablespoons sugar
> 2 tablespoons corn oil
> ½ teaspoon baking powder
> 1 cup flour
> orange peel, a strip 3 inches long, ½ inch wide, chopped fine
> ¼ cup blanched almonds, chopped fine
> ¼ teaspoon orange-flower water (optional)
> oil for deep-frying

HONEY DIP

> 2 cups sugar
> ¼ teaspoon lemon juice
> ¼ teaspoon orange-flower water
> ⅛ teaspoon vanilla extract
> ¼ teaspoon cornstarch, dissolved in 2 tablespoons cold water

1. Mix donut ingredients except the oil together into a firm dough. Add 1 or 2 tablespoons more flour if necessary.

2. Roll out the dough into a ½-inch-thick round flat shape, using a 3-inch donut cutter to cut out the donuts.

3. Heat the oil in a wok or skillet over moderate heat until it is hot, then reduce heat to low. Add the donuts, a few at a time, and fry for 2 to 3 minutes, or until brown on both sides. The donuts will rise to the top when done. Remove from the oil and drain on paper towels.

4. To make the dip, mix the sugar, lemon juice, orange-flower water and vanilla together in a pan and just cover with water. Simmer the mixture over low heat for about 45 minutes to thicken. At the last minute add the cornstarch mixture, which provides a glossy surface to the yoyo. Stir and remove the honey dip from the heat. The honey dip is ready to be used as a dip immediately or can be set aside for a future time.

5. While using it, continue to simmer the dip over very low heat. Using a fork or chopstick to hold the yoyo, dip each one into the syrup all around. Remove it to a colander or strainer to catch the excess. During the dipping process, the honey will thicken and it may be necessary to add 1 or 2 tablespoons warm water to maintain the perfect consistency.

Spread the yoyo on a platter to air-dry. If you wish, to add a festive air, garnish with coarsely chopped pistachios or almonds.

Makes 10 to 12 yoyo.

MANICOTTI (Dabla)
Pastry Roses

Crisp, drenched in honey syrup, these rose-shaped pastries are popular during the coffee hours in Tunis. They can be prepared in the home with a little judicious planning.

10 eggs
2 teaspoons baking soda
5 to 5½ cups flour
cornstarch
corn oil for deep-frying
Honey Dip (preceding recipe)

1. Beat the eggs; add the baking soda and 5 cups flour to prepare a firm dough. If too moist or sticky, add more flour. Sprinkle cornstarch liberally over the board or table where the preparation takes place.

2. Shape the egg dough into a long log and cut it into 10 equal pieces. Roll out each piece paper-thin, 6 inches wide and perhaps 30 inches long. Sprinkle lightly with cornstarch. The rolling out can be done with a rolling pin or a pasta machine.

3. Cut the large strip into 2-inch-wide strips about 12 inches long. Wrap the strips around the fingers of your hand in loose circles, with about ½-inch space between each circle. Moisten the end of each roll with water and press it against the dough to seal the circles.

4. Pour enough oil into a wok or deep pan to reach a depth of 3 inches, and heat the oil. Using the wooden handle of a spoon, or a chopstick, slip the dough circles into the oil and fry over moderate heat for about 2 minutes, until light brown. Turn them over and fry for another minute. Swirl the *dabla* around from the center to bring out the shape of a rose in bloom. Remove from the oil and drain.

5. Heat the prepared syrup. Dip the *dabla* into the syrup all around, lift out, and drain in a colander until the coating is dry.

Serve with tea, or preferably espresso coffee.

Makes 20 *dablas*.

HARISSA
Hot Red Chili Paste

There are many *harissa* recipes from all the regions of the country. This one, from a Jewish home, is a good hot one, flavored with lemon juice and cuminseed.

    1 cup dried hot red chilies
    1 cup garlic cloves
    2 tablespoons salt
    corn oil to cover

1. Break the dry chilies open and shake out and discard the seeds. Soak the husks in cold water for 2 or 3 hours to soften, then drain. Soak the garlic cloves in water for 1 hour. Drain. Crack the cloves lightly with the flat of a cleaver and peel. Drain well.

2. Grind the chilies and garlic cloves together in a processor to produce a fairly coarse texture. Add the salt and mix well. Put the paste in a jar and cover with oil, about 2 tablespoons. Cover the jar tightly and refrigerate until ready to use. Makes about 1½ cups *harissa*.

TO SERVE

> 1 teaspoon olive oil
> 1 tablespoon lemon juice
> a few grains of ground cuminseed

Put about 1 tablespoon of *harissa* in a small plate. Surround the *harissa* with the oil. Sprinkle the lemon juice over, with a pinch of cuminseed over all.

Serve with any kind of Tunsian food.

SALADE AU CITRON
Lemon Salad

A Tunisian *salade* is not a salad at all. It is more like an Indian chutney and in fact also goes well with any Indian or Oriental food. It may be refrigerated for several months and used when wanted.

> 2 large lemons, quartered lengthwise, seeds removed
> 1 teaspoon salt
> 1 tablespoon paprika
> 2 tablespoons corn or olive oil
> 2 garlic cloves, sliced thin
> 2 cups water

Mix everything together in a pan, cover, and simmer over low heat for about 40 minutes, or until the water evaporates and the mixture has reduced to a thick jam. The lemons become glazed.

Cool and store in a jar with a tight cover.

Jewelers in Tripoli, 1926. The Jewish goldsmiths of Tripoli had their own market, called the Goldsmiths' market. *(Photo courtesy the Janet Naim collection).*

LIBYA

LIBYA   Reports of the early history of Jewish settlements in Libya are recorded about 300 B.C. and thereafter. There was a movement of Jews from Egypt under the Ptolemys, during the days when the borders were more fluid than they are today.

When Libya became a province of the Roman Empire, the Jews were involved in agriculture, and they were potters, sailors, perhaps weavers in Cyrenaica, adjacent to the Egyptian border. Libya continued to undergo changes, with the Arab period occurring in the eleventh and twelfth centuries and the Turkish conquest taking place in the fifteenth century. Throughout this time there were periods of feast and famine, so characteristic of Jewish history in Libya.

Jews from Leghorn (Livorno), Italy arrive in Libya in the seventeenth century. They settled in Tripoli, the capital, and the Italian influence on the cuisine began.

From 1911 until World War II Libya was an Italian colony and the Italian influence on the cooking increased. The war also made it possible for Fascists and Arabs to have an open season against the poor, small, undefended, religiously observant Jewish communities around the country. But, I digress!

How would one describe Libyan Jewish cooking? Greatly influenced by Italy, it still relies on the basic practices of the Maghreb (North Africa). *Cous cous*, chick-peas, white beans, lamb, beef, fish, hot chilies, parsley, basil, tomato paste, cuminseed, caraway, turmeric and nutmeg add flavor to foods that are hearty, simply seasoned and imaginatively combined. The kosher dietary laws are paramount to the cookery.

Cous cous, a pasta, is the national food of Libya and of the Jews. It is prepared at home. Arab influence contributed cinnamon and other spices, which are used with meat, especially the use of the cinnamon stick, as being more subtle than the ground cinnamon. Italian influence inspired the use of tomato

507

paste and sauces, which, in turn, came from Central America via the Spanish.

The hot red chilies especially took firm hold in the area and these are used generously although often subdued by lemon juice. Hot and pungent flavors are hallmarks of the cooking.

Libyan cooking is seasonal and depends upon the availability of vegetables and fruits. Jews had an obsession with the freshness of the foods, fish and fowl. Jewish men were the shoppers for the Sabbath and Holidays, buying up the necessary quantity and variety of foods in the bazaar. The women stayed home and cooked.

T'fina, dishes prepared for the Sabbath, can be translated as "buried in the coals"—the way they once cooked the food and kept it warm until the families returned from the synagogue to partake of the Saturday noonday meal. Ashkenazis had their *cholent* and the Jews of Libya (and Tunisia) their t'fina. A grand illustration of this is the Lamb with Kishke and Peas. (Everyone has a word for it—in Morocco it's *scheena* and in Baghdad, *hameen.*)

All that is gone now. After the State of Israel was established, Libya emptied of Jews. An estimated number of 38,000 went to Italy and Israel, the two most logical destinations.

Another chapter of the Diaspora was closed.

BESTIL
Stuffed Potato Fritter

In India, these fritters are called "potato chops." In New York, *knish*. The difference depends on the seasonings since the fillings are all made with beef and the shell of mashed potatoes. Here is the Libyan version. The fritters may be made in advance and then quickly rewarmed in the oven. They can be served as an appetizer with drinks or as one of the dishes at a lunch or dinner.

FILLING

½ cup water
1 pound ground beef
1 medium onion, chopped (½ cup)
¼ teaspoon ground cinnamon
½ teaspoon salt
¼ teaspoon pepper

POTATO DOUGH

2 pounds medium potatoes
2 tablespoons corn oil
½ teaspoon salt

FRITTER

flour for dredging
2 eggs, beaten
oil for panfrying

1. Put all the filling ingredients into a skillet. Mix well and stir-fry over moderate heat until all the liquid has evaporated, about 10 minutes. Turn out on a plate and set aside.

2. Boil the potatoes in their skins until cooked through but still firm. Peel and grate. Mix with the oil and salt to make a dough.

3. Take about ¼ cup potato dough in the palm of your hand for each fritter. Flatten it out to a ½-inch-thick circle. Put in 1 heaping tablespoon of the beef mixture. Fold over and shape a cylinder 3 inches long and 1 inch thick. Dredge the cylinder with flour and then dip into the egg. Heat the oil in a skillet and brown the fritters on all sides over moderate heat. Drain briefly on paper towels.

Serve hot. Makes 12 fritters.

BUREKA
Meat-Filled Turnovers

These turnovers are reminiscent of the Tunisian *brik*. The outer wrapper is the same as that used in Chinese spring rolls, which are also duplicated in Viet Nam, all cultures with which I am acquainted.

1 medium onion, sliced (½ cup)
1 celery heart with leaves, sliced (1 cup)
1 handful of flat-leaf parsley, stems discarded (½ cup)
1 pound lean ground beef
1 tablespoon olive oil
¼ teaspoon pepper
⅛ teaspoon ground turmeric
¼ teaspoon ground cinnamon
1 teaspoon salt
1 cup water
1 small potato, peeled, cut into 6 pieces (½ cup)
2 eggs, beaten
1 package round Chinese spring-roll wrappers (8)
oil for deep-frying

1. Chop the onion, celery and parsley in a processor or by hand. Put them in a pan with the beef, olive oil, pepper, turmeric, cinnamon, salt, water and potato. Cook over moderate heat, covered, for about ½ hour. Stir 2 or 3 times during this process. All the liquid should evaporate. Mix briskly to mash the potato.

2. Remove pan from the heat and beat in the eggs while the mixture is still slightly warm. Mix into a smooth purée in a processor or by hand. Cool.

3. Take 1 spring-roll wrapper and fold in the round edges to make a square. Put 2 tablespoons filling into the lower center of the wrapper, dab the lower edges with cold water, and fold over the wrapper to shape a triangle. The edges should stick together.

4. Heat 1 or 2 cups corn oil for deep-frying in a wok or skillet and fry the triangles over moderate heat until brown on both sides, about 3 minutes. Drain on paper towels.

Serve warm. Makes 8 *burekas*.

TABIKHA BIL HOUMUS
Chicken and Chick-Pea Stew

Before the Yom Kippur fast, a generous lunch is served that does not have seasonings aggressive enough to leave one thirsty. The evening meal, prior to the beginning of the fast, also included this stew as one of the traditional holiday dishes. It was hoped that the chick-peas and potatoes would provide substance enough to ward off hunger on the day of the fast. But of course, it was never enough for the entire day.

¾ pound dried chick-peas (1½ cups)
1 tablespoon corn oil
2 pounds potatoes (5), peeled, quartered
1 large onion, chopped fine (1 cup)
½ cup chopped flat-leaf parsley, rinsed under cold water to
    remove bitterness, drained
1 chicken, 3 pounds, cut into 8 pieces, loose skin and fat
    discarded
2 cinnamon sticks, each 3 inches long
¼ teaspoon pepper
1 teaspoon salt, or to taste
2 cups water
pomegranate seeds for garnish (optional)

1. Soak the chick-peas in water overnight. Drain, peel off and discard the skins.
2. Put all the ingredients except pomegranate seeds in a heavy pan and bring to a boil. Reduce heat to low, cover and cook for 1 hour. This should be enough to tenderize the chicken and chick-peas. Garnish with pomegranate seeds during the season when available.

Serve warm. Serves 6 to 8 with cous cous or white rice.

N O T E : A curious but understandable account of the "feelings" of vegetables when they are cut was recounted to me by a Libyan. The chopped parsley in this recipe, for example, exudes a light bitterness when cut as a self-protection against being eaten or damaged. By oozing bitterness, the animal might be discouraged from eating and destroying the herb. Is this true? Do vegetables have feelings?

TABIKHA BIL KARRATE
Leek, Lamb and Green Pea Stew

Here is another family-style stew with a substantial amount of leek, assembled in the Libyan Jewish style. The leek, that ancient member of the onion family, has been cultivated in Eastern Mediterranean countries for 4,000 years.

4 large fresh leeks
¼ cup olive or corn oil
1 large onion, chopped fine (1 cup)
¼ cup tomato paste, dissolved in ½ cup water
⅛ teaspoon hot red chili flakes
½ teaspoon pepper
1 teaspoon salt, or to taste
3 cups water
3 pounds lean lamb neck, cut into 2-inch pieces, or 6 small lamb
    shanks, cut into 4 pieces each, trimmed of fat
3 cinnamon sticks, each 3 inches long
2 pounds Idaho potatoes, peeled, quartered
1½ pounds fresh or frozen green peas

1. Cut the leeks lengthwise into halves and rinse well in cold water to remove the inevitable sand. Trim off and discard about 3 inches of the top green part and chop the rest fine, by hand or in a processor.

2. Heat the oil in a large pan, add the leeks and onion, and stir-fry over moderate heat until they appear translucent, about 5 minutes. Add the tomato paste, chili flakes, pepper and salt and cook for 3 minutes. Add the 3 cups water and bring to a boil.

3. Arrange the meat and then the cinnamon sticks over the mixture. Cover the pan and simmer over low heat for 45 minutes. Do not stir.

4. Add the potatoes and simmer for another ½ hour. Add the peas and cook for another 15 minutes, or until the meat is tender and separates from the bone.

Serve hot with bread or rice. Serves 8.

MAFRUM
Beef-Stuffed Potatoes

This is a special preparation served on religious holidays and at Friday evening dinner before the Sabbath.

STUFFING

    1 pound ground beef
    1 small potato, peeled, grated (½ cup)
    1 medium onion, grated (½ cup)
    1 tablespoon chopped flat-leaf parsley
    4 garlic cloves, chopped fine
    ¼ teaspoon salt
    ¼ teaspoon pepper
    ⅛ teaspoon ground cinnamon

POTATOES

    3 medium potatoes, peeled (1 pound)
    2 teaspoons salt
    flour for dredging
    2 eggs, beaten
    oil for deep-frying
    2 large ripe tomatoes, sliced
    1 medium onion, sliced thin
    2 cups water in which is dissolved 1 tablespoon tomato paste

1. Mix stuffing ingredients together and set aside.

2. Slice each potato lengthwise into 3 equal parts. Cut each of these slices lengthwise ⅔ of the way through so that it can be opened and stuffed. Sprinkle all of the slices inside and out with the salt. Let stand for 5 minutes. Rinse off with water and dry on a towel.

3. Open the prongs of each potato slice and stuff the inside with about ¼ cup of the stuffing. Roll it in the flour and then in the beaten eggs. Heat the oil in a wok or skillet and fry the stuffed potatoes over moderate heat for 5 minutes.

4. Put the tomato slices on the bottom of a lightly oiled pan. Cover with the onion slices. Place the fried stuffed potatoes on top. Add the water and tomato paste. Bring to a boil, then simmer, covered, over low heat for 20 minutes, or until all the liquid has evaporated.

Serve warm. Makes 9 pieces, serves 4 to 6.

TABIKHA B'SALK

Beef and Beans in
Swiss-Chard Sauce

A tabikha is a one-dish stew, a daily preparation that may also become a *t'fina* for the Sabbath. It is an eclectic stew with several variations depending upon family preference.

2 pounds fresh Swiss chard
¼ cup olive or corn oil
1½ pounds boneless beef chuck, cut into 1-inch cubes
½ pound beef bones
1½ cups dried white haricot beans, soaked in water overnight, drained
2 pounds Idaho-type or new potatoes, peeled and quartered lengthwise
4 whole garlic cloves
1 teaspoon salt, or to taste
¼ teaspoon pepper
3 cups water

1. Cut off and discard the white, coarse ribs of the chard. Blanch the leaves only, in boiling water for 3 minutes. Drain and shake off excess moisture. Cut the leaves into thin slices. Heat the oil in a large pan, add the chard, and stir-fry over low heat, covering the pan now and then, for about 20 minutes or long enough to evaporate all the water. In a processor, purée the chard to a smooth paste and return it to the pan.

2. Spread the meat and bones evenly over the chard purée. Cover with the beans and arrange the potatoes over all. Add the garlic, salt, pepper and water.

3. Bring to a boil, cover the pan, and cook over low heat for 2 hours. Do not stir. Should the liquid evaporate too quickly, add ½ cup more water. At the end of the time there should be very little liquid left and the chard will have converted to a green sauce.

Serve hot with bread, white rice or *cous cous*. Serves 6.

VARIATIONS: Use 2 to 3 pounds oxtail instead of the beef chuck and follow the same directions. Or substitute calf's foot, cut into 6 pieces.

A 3-pound beef tongue cut into 2-inch-wide pieces is also a popular addition. Cook according to the recipe, but add several marrow bones to intensify the stock. When tongue is tender, peel off the skin and serve.

CHROUF BIL KARIS
Lemon Lamb

Using inexpensive cuts of meat wisely and tastefully has both its culinary and economic rewards. Lamb ribs prepared in Libyan style are raised to a special category.

4 pounds well-trimmed breast of lamb or ribs, cut into 3-inch
    lengths
¼ cup olive or corn oil
¼ teaspoon salt
¾ teaspoon pepper
¼ cup fresh lemon juice
2 cinnamon sticks, each 3 inches long
1 cup water

1. Cover the lamb with water in a large pan and bring to a vigorous boil for 1 minute. Drain and rinse under cold water. This first boiling will remove excess fat.

2. Put the oil in the pan, add the lamb, and stir-fry over moderate heat for 5 minutes.

3. Add the salt, pepper, lemon juice, cinnamon sticks and water. Cover the pan and simmer over low heat for 1 hour, or until the lamb is tender and the liquid is reduced to a thick, lemon-flavored sauce.

Serve warm as an appetizer or a side dish with other foods.

Serves 8.

CHAROUF BIL PISSELLI
O CHEDRA

Lamb with Kishke and Peas

This dish is a complete meal served with *cous cous*, white rice or bread. It is a favorite preparation in the spring and especially during Passover.

Traditionally, the dish is known as a *t'fina* since it is prepared on Friday afternoon for the Sabbath midday lunch. The *t'fina* was cooked on a wood stove. When the fire had been reduced to hot coals, the pan with meat, vegetables and Masran (Kishke) was almost buried in the ashes.

Another typical variation for the Sabbath meal was to put any number of eggs in the shell into the stew pan and cook them for the same length of time. More eggs in the shell were placed in the hot ashes and baked. The eggs in the pan absorbed some of the flavor of the richly seasoned stew while those in the ashes developed a brown tinge and a "baked" flavor.

1 cup loosely packed parsley, leaves only
1 cup loosely packed chopped celery and leaves
2 medium onions, sliced
1 stuffed Masran (Kishke) (recipe follows)
6 cups water
2 pounds lamb chops or shanks, with bone, cut into 3-inch pieces
1 pound fresh or frozen green peas
1 teaspoon salt
½ teaspoon pepper
¼ teaspoon ground cinnamon
¼ teaspoon ground turmeric
2 medium potatoes (½ pound), peeled and quartered

1. Chop the parsley, celery and onions together in a processor or by hand.

2. Cook the Masran (already cooked for 1 hour) and all the other ingredients, with just enough water to cover them, in a covered pan over low heat for 1½ hours more.

Serve warm. Serves 8 with other dishes.

NOTE: Lamb was the preferred meat for Passover; many families would buy a lamb that could be ritually slaughtered. Almost everything of the lamb was used including the skin, which was made into a rug.

MASRAN (KISHKE)
Stuffed Large Intestine

The *masran* is to be incorporated into the Charouf bil Pisselli o Chedra (Lamb with Kishke and Peas, preceding recipe).

1 large beef intestine, about 18 inches in length, well rinsed
¾ pound beef liver, grilled over a flame to make kosher, then
    coarsely chopped
½ pound beef heart or lung, chopped (optional)
½ pound coarsely ground beef
¾ cup raw rice, well rinsed
¼ cup chopped flat-leaf parsley
¼ cup chopped fresh coriander
1 medium onion, chopped fine (¾ cup)
1 teaspoon salt
¼ teaspoon pepper
1 pinch of grated nutmeg
⅛ teaspoon ground ginger
⅛ teaspoon ground cinnamon
2 eggs, beaten

1. Sew up one end of the intestine, leaving the other end open to be filled.

2. Mix all the stuffing ingredients together and stuff the intestine loosely to prevent its bursting open when the rice expands. Sew up the other end.

3. Put the *masran* in a pan with 6 cups water and bring to a boil. Cover the pan, reduce heat to low, and simmer for 1 hour to tenderize the intestine and cook the stuffing. The *masran* is now ready to be included in the Charouf bil Pisselli o Chedra.

EL SAN BEL CARES OU CHERCHEF

Tongue in Lemon Sauce with Artichokes

This is a Jewish dish in the Tripoli style of cooking, an imaginative combination of ingredients, simply assembled.

1 fresh veal tongue, 1½ pounds
4 cups water
1 teaspoon salt
juice of 1 lemon (3 tablespoons)
¼ teaspoon pepper
⅛ teaspoon ground turmeric
2 medium potatoes (½ pound), peeled, each cut into 6 slices
2 packages (9 ounces each) frozen artichoke hearts, or the
    equivalent in fresh artichoke hearts
¼ cup olive oil

1. Put the tongue, water and salt in a pan, bring to a boil, cover the pan, and cook over moderate heat for 45 minutes, or long enough to tenderize the tongue. Remove tongue and peel off the skin. Cut into ½-inch-thick slices. Reserve 2 cups of the cooking liquid.

2. Put the lemon juice, pepper, turmeric, potatoes, artichokes and olive oil in the pan. Arrange tongue slices on top. Cover and cook over low heat for 40 minutes. About half of the liquid will evaporate.

Serve warm. Serves 6 with other dishes.

VARIATION: Two pounds boneless beef chuck cut into 3-inch pieces may be used instead of the tongue. Use the same seasonings and ingredients. Cook the beef in 4 cups water for 40 minutes, which will be enough to tenderize the meat. Remove the meat and reserve 2 cups cooking liquid. Put all the ingredients into the pan with the meat on top and cook over low heat for about 40 minutes. About half of the liquid will evaporate, leaving a richer sauce.

Two pounds of lamb shank, cut into 2-inch pieces including the bone, can be prepared in the same manner.

HRIEME
Hot Spiced Fish

Libyan Jews like their fish chili-hot, and prepared this way it is one of the most popular dishes for all who live in the Maghreb. You may care to reduce the amount of chili somewhat, but traditionally hrieme should be hot.

It may be served as an appetizer or first course at a dinner.

3 tablespoons corn oil
1½ cups water
5 garlic cloves, chopped fine
2 to 3 teaspoons fresh hot red chili, seeded and chopped
1 pound red snapper, sea bass or similar fish, the whole fish
    with head
1 teaspoon ground cuminseed
lemon wedges

1. Mix the oil, ½ cup water, the garlic and chili together in a pan. Simmer the mixture over low heat for 10 minutes.

2. Add the fish, the remaining water and the cuminseed. Cover the pan and cook over low heat for 15 minutes. Baste 2 or 3 times during this period.

Serve warm with lemon wedges. Serves 4.

VARIATION: Here is another appealing version of the hrieme— this time with fillet of fish and an assortment of seasonings.

½ cup water
juice of 1 lemon (about 3 tablespoons)
2 tablespoons tomato paste
¼ teaspoon salt
1 to 2 teaspoons hot red chili flakes, to taste
1 garlic clove, chopped fine
1½ teaspoons ground cuminseed
3 tablespoons corn oil
1 small onion, chopped (¼ cup)
2 pounds fish fillet—sea bass, flounder, red snapper or
    similar fish

1. Mix together the water, lemon juice, tomato paste, salt, chili, garlic and cuminseed. Set aside.

2. Heat the oil in a pan, add the onion and stir-fry over moderate heat for 2 minutes.

3. Place the fillets into a pan large enough to hold them all in one layer and pour the sauce over all. Cover the pan and simmer over low heat for 20 minutes. Baste several times during this period.

Serve warm. Serves 6.

N O T E : A Friday evening meal ushering in the Sabbath might start with the indispensable *hrieme* and include Cous Cous, Stuffed Vegetables, Beef-Stuffed Potato, Broth.

KIFTE BIL HAUT
Fish Balls in Basil Sauce

The Italian influence is unmistakable in this summer fish dish. Basil, parsley and tarragon are the herbs used while the chili pepper is a reminder that the Libyans enjoy a piquant touch.

FISH BALLS

2 eggs, beaten
2 slices of bread, soaked in water, squeezed dry (about ½ cup)
¼ cup chopped flat-leaf parsley
¼ teaspoon dried tarragon
½ teaspoon salt
⅛ teaspoon pepper
⅛ teaspoon hot red chili flakes
⅛ teaspoon grated nutmeg
1 medium onion, chopped (½ cup)
1 garlic clove, sliced
1 pound fillet of flounder, red snapper or similar fish, chopped
flour for dredging
¼ cup corn oil

SAUCE

1 pound tomatoes, fresh or canned
8 to 10 fresh basil leaves, or 1 teaspoon crushed dried basil

⅛ teaspoon pepper
⅛ teaspoon hot red chili flakes
1 tablespoon tomato paste

1. Process smoothly all the fish ball ingredients except the fish, flour and oil. Then add the fish and mix in well.

2. Prepare oval fish balls the shape and size of an egg. Dredge them with the flour. Heat the oil in a skillet and brown the fish on all sides for 2 or 3 minutes. Put them in a baking pan or dish.

3. Process the sauce ingredients into a paste. Pour it over the fried fish balls and bake in a 350° F. oven for 35 minutes.

Serve hot, at room temperature or cold. Serves 6.

TIRSHI
Zucchini and Potato Mash in Spice Dressing

This useful side dish, spicy and vegetarian, makes a fine accompaniment to any Libyan or other North African dish or to Middle Eastern cooking.

1 pound zucchini
½ pound potatoes (about 2)
¾ teaspoon ground cuminseed
1 to 2 teaspoons hot red chili flakes, to taste
¾ teaspoon ground caraway
½ teaspoon salt
1 tablespoon lemon juice, or to taste
4 garlic cloves, puréed
2 tablespoons olive oil

1. Cook the whole zucchini in water until they are soft. Drain and mash them coarsely. Cook the whole potatoes, without peeling, in water until soft. Cool, peel, and mash coarsely. Mix with zucchini.

2. Mix the cuminseed, chili flakes, caraway, salt, lemon juice and garlic together into a paste. Stir this briskly into the vegetables. Put the mixture into a serving dish and dribble the olive oil over all.

Serve at room temperature with cous cous and other foods.
Serves 4 to 6.

TIRSHI
Carrot Salad

Cinnamon is an important flavor in Libyan cooking and it is included in many dishes, sometimes ground and sometimes in stick form. Ground cinnamon will permeate a preparation while the stick cinnamon will just add a hint of spice.

2 pounds carrots, sliced
1 teaspoon paprika
3 or 4 garlic cloves, to taste, put through a press
2 tablespoons tomato paste
¼ teaspoon ground cinnamon
2 tablespoons corn oil
¼ cup red-wine vinegar
¼ teaspoon salt

1. Cook the carrots in water until soft but still firm. Drain well and mash coarsely.

2. Mix the paprika, garlic, tomato paste and cinnamon together. Heat the oil in a skillet and stir-fry the mixture over moderate heat for 1 minute.

3. Add the carrots, vinegar and salt and stir-fry for 2 minutes, making certain that the salad is well mixed. Turn out in a serving bowl and refrigerate.

Serve cold or at room temperature with cous cous.

Serves 6.

TIRSHI
Pumpkin Salad

1 pound pumpkin or calabasa, peeled
½ teaspoon paprika
2 garlic cloves, put through a press
¼ teaspoon ground cinnamon
juice of 1 lemon (about 3 tablespoons)
¼ teaspoon salt
1 tablespoon corn oil

1. Cook the pumpkin in water until soft but not mushy. Drain well and mash coarsely with a fork.

2. Mix the paprika, garlic, cinnamon, lemon juice, salt and oil together, then mix with the pumpkin. Refrigerate.

Serve cold with cous cous or any other North African food.

Serves 6.

COUS COUS WITH VEGETABLES, LIBYAN STYLE

Cous cous prepared in this way, without meat or fish, can be eaten with any Libyan foods, vegetarian or not. You may use as many vegetables as you wish according to personal preference. The more you use, the more the broth is enriched.

Returning the cous cous to a processor on two occasions is a modern trick that takes the place of rubbing it through the sieve.

COUS COUS

2½ cups semolina
2 teaspoons salt
⅔ cup water
½ cup olive or corn oil

VEGETABLES

2 large celery ribs, halved
2 medium onions
1 whole carrot
1 zucchini (½ pound)
1 medium potato, not peeled
1 small eggplant (¼ pound)
4 cups water

1. Mix the semolina, salt and water together. Mix with your fingers into a crumblike consistency. Put it into a processor for about 20 seconds, which will fluff up the grains.

2. Mix in the oil by sprinkling it over and rubbing into the grains of semolina with your fingers to eliminate lumps. The *cous cous* is now ready to steam.

3. Put the celery, onions, carrot, zucchini, potato, eggplant and 3 cups water in the bottom of the steamer (*couscousier*) and bring to a boil. Put 1 recipe of the *cous cous* grains in the top of the steamer, cover tightly, and allow it to steam over low heat for ½ hour. Add 1 cup hot water to the *cous cous* in the top of the steamer, mixing it in lightly as it is absorbed. Continue to steam for 20 minutes. The aroma from the vegetables will influence the flavor of the *cous cous*.

4. Remove the top of the steamer and turn out the *cous cous* into a large dish. Pour 1¼ cups of the vegetable broth over the *cous cous*, mixing it in well by stirring and lightly mashing the grains to eliminate any lumps. Cool the *cous cous* completely and return it to the processor for about 10 seconds, which fluffs up the grains.

At this stage the *cous cous* has "grown" in quantity from the original 2½ cups to about 3 times that amount.

Serve the *cous cous* at room temperature, with the vegetables on the side as a complete vegetarian meal. Serves 4.

M'CHAQUB
Stuffed Matzoh

It is not always easy to provide variety at Passover meals but this ingenious dairy sandwich is a winner.

STUFFING

½ pound feta cheese, mashed
1 medium potato, peeled, boiled until soft, mashed
1 egg, beaten
¼ teaspoon pepper

SANDWICH

6 whole matzoh
3 eggs, beaten
¼ cup corn oil for panfrying

1. Mix stuffing ingredients together well. Set aside.

2. Soak the whole matzoh in warm water until soft but with still some firmness and texture. Remove the sheets from the water and press out the liquid gently. Cut each matzoh into 4 equal squares.

3. Put 1 heaping tablespoon of the cheese stuffing over 1 square of matzoh and cover it with another. Dip the sandwich into beaten eggs.

4. Heat the oil in a skillet and brown the sandwich on both sides over moderate heat for about 4 minutes.

Serve warm at any Passover dairy meal. Makes 12 sandwiches.

SAFRA
Semolina and Date Cake with Honey Syrup

This Libyan cake has a spiced date filling and is saturated with an intensely sweet syrup. It is a rich dessert for the coffee hour. The recipe is attributed to King Solomon, like so many other Libyan treasures.

DATE FILLING

3 tablespoons corn oil
1½ pounds pitted dates, chopped
1 teaspoon ground cinnamon
⅛ teaspoon ground cloves

CAKE

2 pounds semolina (cream of wheat), 4 cups
1 pound sugar (2 cups)
2 teaspoons baking powder
1 cup corn oil
¾ cup water
blanched almonds or whole cloves for garnish

SYRUP

1 cup sugar
½ cup water
1 cup honey
juice of 1 lemon (2 to 3 tablespoons)

1. Put the oil and dates in a heavy skillet and cook over low heat, stirring continuously, for about 20 minutes, or until a thick paste has formed. Remove skillet from the heat and stir in the cinnamon and cloves. Cool the paste.

2. Mix cake ingredients except the almonds or cloves together into a thick batter. Put half of the batter into a cake tin 12 × 12 inches, or 12 × 16 inches. Put in the date filling, pressing it into the corners of the tin so that it covers the batter. Pour in the balance of the batter and smooth out the surface. Score the top of the cake, not too deeply, in 2-inch diamond shapes or square pieces. Put 1 blanched almond in the center of each square or press 1 whole clove into each piece, with the stem down.

3. Put the cake tin into the center of the oven so that it bakes evenly, and bake in a 350° F. oven for 45 minutes.

4. Put all syrup ingredients into a pan and simmer over low heat for 10 minutes, stirring frequently.

5. When the cake is removed from the oven, pour the hot syrup over the top and allow it to be absorbed. Let the cake stand at room temperature for ½ day before eating.

Serves 8 to 10 persons.

NOTE: The *safra* is served anytime as a snack with tea or coffee. It is also served to a person recovering from an illness and in need of fast nutrition and energy, or to a hard-working husband who seems to be failing in his conjugal duties.

Bibliography

Benjamin of Tudela, *The Itinerary of Benjamin of Tudela, Travels in the Middle Ages*, Joseph Simon, Malibu, California, 1983.

Coyle, L. Patrick, *The World Encyclopedia of Food*, Facts on File, New York, 1982.

Encyclopaedia Judaica, Keter Publishing House Ltd., Jerusalem, Israel, 1972 (Macmillan).

Hacohen, Dvora, and Hacohen, Menachem, *One People: The Story of the Eastern Jews*, Adama Books, New York, 1986.

Ibn-Khaldūn, *An Arab Philosophy of History, Selections from the Prolegomena of Ibn-Khaldūn of Tunis (1332–1406)*, John Murray, London, 1950.

Johnson, Paul, *A History of the Jews*, Harper & Row, New York, 1987.

Johnson, Paul, *Modern Times, The World from the Twenties to the Eighties*, Harper & Row, New York, 1983.

Katzner, Kenneth, *Languages of the World*, Routledge and Kegan Paul, London, 1977.

Lewis, Bernard, *The Jews of Islam*, Princeton University Press, Princeton, New Jersey, 1984.

The Oxford Book of Food Plants, Oxford University Press, London, 1969.

Polo, Marco, *The Travels of Marco Polo*, J. M. Dent & Sons, Ltd., Everyman's Library, London, 1908.

Schafer, Edward H., *The Golden Peaches of Samarkand: A Study of T'ang Exotics*, University of California Press, Berkeley and Los Angeles, 1963.

Simon & Shuster's International Dictionary, Spanish/English, New York, 1973.

Stavroulakis, Nicholas, *The Cookbook of the Jews of Greece*, Lycabbettus Press, Athens, Greece, 1986. (This is the preeminent cookbook on the ancient Jewish community in Greece.)

Suny, Ronald Grigor, *The Making of the Georgian Nation*, Indiana University Press, Hoover Institution Press, Stanford University, Palo Alto, California, 1988.

Tannahill, Reay, *Food in History*, Stein and Day, New York, 1973.

The Times Atlas of World History, Times Books Ltd., London, 1984.

527

Index

Aash Rechte (Winter Noodle Soup), 108
Abe Gusht Gondhi Nochodi (Veal and Chick-Pea Dumplings in Chicken Soup), 109
Achar (Lime Pickle), 382
Adasee (Lentil Stew), 107
Adas Polo (Lentil Pilau), 157
Adjapsandali (Mixed Vegetable Sauté), 236
Adma de R'Mel (Eggs Baked in Sand), 488
Advieh (Persian Spice Mixture), 105, 107
Ahasueras, 103
Ajin (Bread Dough), 395
Ajlook (Zucchini Lemon Salad), 495
Akoud (Sweetbreads in Red Sauce), 484
Albaloo Polo (Cherry Pilau with Chicken), 158
Albaras (Baked Layered Beef), 356
Albóndigas de Pescado (Fish Balls in Simple Sauce), 469
Albóndigas de Prasa kon Nuez (Leek and Beef Balls with Walnuts), 14
Aleecha (Mixed Vegetable Stew), 407
Ale Gefen (Stuffed Grape Leaves), 83
Alexander the Great, 249, 301, 415
Alicha (Beef, Sheep or Goat Curry), 409
Allspice (English Spice), see Note 240; see Sofrito, 420
Almodrote (Cheese and Eggplant Casserole), 18
Almond, Almonds: Passover Nut Cake in Syrup (Tezpishti), 29; Sweet for Passover (Mustachudo), 34; to blanch and toast, see Note, 449; Turnovers (Borekas de Nuez u de Almendra), 30
Aloo-m-Kalla (Golden Deep-Fried Potatoes), 347
Aloo-m-Kalla Murgi (Pot-Roast Chicken), 332
Anjuli (Fish Salad with Coconut Milk), 338
Appetizers and First Courses: Cheese Triangles (Samsadas de Quezo), 23; Cheese Turnovers (Boerekas), 54; Chick-Pea Turnovers, Stuffed (Sambusak), 96; Eggplant and Zucchini Turnovers (Handrajo), 21; Eggplant Pie (Tapada), 22; Eggplant Snails (Rodanchas), 57; Egg Salad in Walnut Sauce (Kwerstkhi Nigozee Satsabelly), 204; Fava Beans, Crisp-Fried (Foolim), 435; Fish Balls (Boulettes de Poisson), 455; Fish Balls, see Variation, 457; Fish, Hot Spiced (Hrieme), 519; Fish in Red Sauce (Pescado Cocho), 467; Ground Meat Barbecue (Shoofta), 329; Herb Fritters (Pchali), 202; Individual Pastiya, see Variation, 449; Leek and Beef Balls with Walnuts Albóndigas de Prasa kon Nuez), 14; Lemon Lamb (Chrouf bil Karis), 515; Mushroom Barbecue (Soko), 202; Mushrooms and Eggs (Soko Kwerstkhi), 203; Mushrooms in Walnut Sauce (Soko Nogozee), 205; Red Bean (Lobio), 200; Spinach and Feta Cheese Pie (Spanakopeta), 56; Stuffed Grape Leaves (Yaprakes), 11; Sweetbreads in Red Sauce (Akoud), 484; Tricorners, Stuffed, Baked (Bichak), 318; Yeast Pancake (Chalpakee Joor-Rawtee), 282; Yoghurt and Cucumber Salad with Garlic (Tarator), 52
Apples, Stuffed (Biya Vashlee Tolma), 225
Arab Moslem Conquest, 415
Arak, a Liquor, 371, 388
Armeko (Onion and Tomato Stew), 50
Armiko (Lamb Innards for Passover), 45
Arook (Chicken and Rice Ball), 336
Asa Wot (Spiced Fish), 409
Asparagus Soup, 206
Atar Allecha (Spiced Green-Pea Purée), 411

Baademjan Torshi (Eggplant Pickle), 183
Bachsh (Rice, Beef and Chicken Liver Mix), 261
Badam Soukhte (Burnt Almonds), 189
Bamia (Baked Okra with Lemon), 20
Bamia (Meatball and Okra Sauté in Tomato Sauce), 421
Bamia Khuta (Sweet-and-Sour Chicken and Okra), 334
Bamya (Okra with Sauce), 85

529

Bantage (Stuffed Potato Fritter), 499

Bandoora (Fresh Tomato and Basil Salad), 270

Batata bel Lamoun (Golden Potato Soup), 418

Bean, Beans: Fava, Crisp Fried (Foolim) 435; Fava Soup (Bissara), 477; Green Fava Beans (Fool Achdar), 424; Mung Bean and Rice Medley (Kihrchiree), 272; Mung Bean and Rice Melange (Mosh Owaee Joor-Rawtee), 271; Onion and Beef Stew (Bsal bil Loubya), 478; Red Bean Appetizer (Lobio), 200; red bean filling for Khachapuri, see Variation, 234; Red Bean Soup (Lobio Soup), 207; (white) and Beef, Cumin-Flavored (T'fina Camounia), 497, 498; White Bean Soup (Fasolada), 38; White Bean Stew (Fassoulia Beda), 419

Beef: and Beans in Swiss-Chard Sauce (Tabikha b'Salk), 514; and Green-Pea Bake for Passover (Hariss Temani), 391; and Green Pea Ragout (Ragoût de Petits Pois), 478; (and) Herbs and Pickles in Tomato Sauce (Solyanka), 212; and Matzoh Pie for Passover (Quartico), 43; and Okra Ragout (Ragoût de Bamia), 479; and Okra Sauté (Khoresht Bamieh), 113; and Potato Pie (Makoud), 480; and Potato Roast, Sabbath (Scheena), 438, 439; and Quince Stew with Pomegranate Sauce (Khoresht Bay), 114; and Vegetables, Layered (Kwarma), 98; and Vegetable Soup (for Cous Cous), 491; and Vegetable Stew, Spiced (Sofrito), 420; and Whole-Wheat Berry Gruel (Halesa), 259; Chick-Pea and Egg Bake for Sabbath (Hameen), 440; Cubes, Boneless, in Red Sauce, 484; Ground Beef Kebabs, (Kebab Digi), 136; Intestine, Large, Stuffed (Masran or Kishke), 517; Layered, Baked (Albaras), 356; Lemon-Flavored, and Rice (Orez Chamutz), 79; Meat Stew (Chouia), 390; Pan Kebabs (Kebab Digi), 135; Pie, Steamed, Bukharan (Mantu), 279; Pockets, Stuffed, with Wheat Porridge, 97; Soup with Fenugreek (Fatoot im Hilbeh), 390; Stew, Spiced (Siga Wot), 408; Stuffed Potatoes (Kavakadas), 12; Tongue, see Tongue; with Okra, see Variation, 485

Beet, Beets: and Coriander Pickle (Charkhali), 241; and Turnip Melange (Oshe Duiyoza Lav Lavu), 253; in Spiced Brine, 240; in Walnut Sauce, 240; Khuta (Sweet-and-Sour Beef and Beets), 328; Leaves in Walnut Sauce (Phali), 199; Pickled, 239; Salad (Panjar or Shalgan), 29; Soup, Sweet-and-Sour (Cholo Chamad), 95

Beidh B'laham (Egg and Meat Patties), 93

Benjamin of Tudela, 65, 91, 198, 249, 369

Berenjeno Relleno con Queso (Stuffed Eggplant with Cheese), 17

Bestil (Stuffed Potato Fritter), 508

Bestila, see Pastiya, 447

Beverages: Arak, a Liquor, 371, 388; Barley Beer (Telah), 403; Cherry Syrup Concentrate (Sharbat Albaloo), 193; Coffee, Ethiopian, 405; Honey Beer (Tech), 404; Kiddush Wine, 371; Mint Syrup Concentrate (Sharbat Serkanjibin), 192; see also Tea

Beyazit II, Sultan, viii, 3, 4, 5

Bhaji (Curried Vegetables), 340

Bhuna Haas (Baked Stuffed Duck), 335

Bichak (Stuffed Baked Tricorners), 318

Bimbrio (Quince Jelly), 33

Bissara (Fava Soup), 477

Biya Vashlee Tolma (Stuffed Apples and Quinces), 225

Boerekas (Cheese Turnovers), 54

Bonjan Salat (Spicy Eggplant Salad), 313

Boona Kalegi (Fried Chicken Liver), 337

Boranee (Spinach and Egg Fry), 139

Boranee ba Mast (Spinach and Yoghurt Salad), 179

Borekas de Nuez u de Almendra (Walnut or Almond Turnovers), 30

Boulette de Viande (Meatballs with Celery and Green Peas), 441

Boulettes de Poisson (Fish Balls), 455

Boulettes de Poisson avec Sauce (Fish Balls in Sauce), 456

Bozbashy (Lamb, Eggplant and Green-Bean Soup), 208

Brain Curry (Mugaz), 339

Bread: Afghan (Noni Afghani), 321; Bukharan (Non), 291; Chapatti, Stuffed (Puran Poli), 364; Chapatti, Whole-Wheat, Sweet, 364; Dough (Ajin), 395; Flat, Crisp (Noni Tokee), 293; Holiday (Subya), 396; Matzoh, Yemenite, 393; Pancake, Fried (Malawach), 397; Pancakes, Ethiopian (Injeera), 413; Sabbath (Dabo), 412; Sesame Loaf (Warda), 394; Wheat Cakes, Steamed (Rava Indlees), 379; Whole-Wheat (Noni Seyaw), 294; with Whole Eggs, Baked (Jachnoon), 395

Brinjal Bhurta (Smoked Eggplant Salad), 349

Brinjal Mahasha (Stuffed Eggplant and Other Vegetables), 343

Bsal bil Loubya (Bean, Onion and Beef Stew), 478

Bukharan Compote (Dried Fruit Compote), 295

Bukharan Plov (Chicken and Rice, Bukharan Style), 266

Bukhari Non (Bukharan Bread), 291

Bulemas (Spinach Rolls in Fillo), 24

Bulghur (Cracked Wheat), 66; Soup, see Note, 389; Tomato Bulghur (Gurgur), 84

Bureka (Meat-Filled Turnovers), 510

Butter, How to Make (Kebe), 403

Cabbage: Beef-Stuffed (Tolma Chorzi), 220; Leaves, Stuffed, with Pomegranate Seeds (Tolma), 222; Pickled, Pink (Gureeskaya Capusta), 242; Pickled, with Chili (Turshi Kurdi), 86; Raisin, Apple and Lamb Stuffed (Kishmish Vashli Tolma), 223; Salad, Red and White (Zalatet Kalam Smoka Uchwara), 86; Stuffed with Lamb (Tolma), 221

Cabezas de Opyo (Chicken with Celeriac), 8

Cake, Nut, in Syrup, Passover (Tezpishti), 29

Cakes, Sweet, Fried (Neyyappam), 380

Capsali, Eliyahu, Rabbi, 3

Carp in Garlic and Coriander Sauce (Zagora), 269

Carrot, Carrots: Conserve (Murabo Havidge), 191; Piquant (Mzoura), 493; Salad (Chizu Salada), 457; Salad (Tirshi), 522

Carthage, 471

Cashew fruit, see Arak, 371

Caviar Patrijani (Georgian Caviar), 201

Chai Chaymokee (Traditional Bukharan Buttered Tea), 298

Chai Kurdi (Kurdish Tea), 90

Chakapuli (Lamb and Plums in Herb Sauce), 218

Chakchouka de Matin (Breakfast Sauce), 475

Chakchouka de Saif (Summer Vegetable Melange), 498

Chalpakee Joor-Hawtee (Fried Yeast Pancake), 282

Chanakhy I (Lamb and Assorted Vegetables in a Clay Pot), 213

Chanakhy II (Lamb, Eggplant and Rice), 214

Chanakhy III (Lamb, Assorted Vegetables and Garlic), 215

Channa ka dal (split yellow lentil), see Variation, 365

Chapatti, Stuffed (Puran Poli), 364; Sweet Whole-Wheat, 364

Charkhali (Beet and Coriander Pickle), 241

Charouf bil Pisselli o Chedra (Lamb with Kishke and Peas), 516

Cheese: and Eggplant Casserole (Almodrote), 18; Eggplant and Cheese, Baked (Fritada de Berenja), 16; and Eggs (Queso con Huevo), 15; Pancake for Shavuoth (Kadey Shavuoth), 88; Pie (Khachapuri), 232, 235; Spinach and Cheese, Baked (Fritada de Spinaka), 15; Triangles (Samsadas de Quezo), 23; Turnovers (Boerekas), 54; Turnovers (Sambusak), 349

Chelo (Basic Persian Rice), 153

Chelo Nachodo (Chicken and Chick-Pea Stew with Rice), 303

Cherry Pilau, 158

Chestnuts, to peel, see Note, 7

Chicken: and Almonds in Lemon Sauce (Mukmura), 332; and Brain Soufflé (La Minnina), 486; and Carrot Stew (Gadjar Murghi Meetha), 330; and Chick-Pea Stew (Tabikha bil Houmus), 511; and Chick-Pea Stew with Rice (Chelo Nachodo), 303; and Mushroom Curry Persian Style (Khoresht Kari), 136; and Okra (Ganouia avec Poulet), 485; and Okra, Sweet-and-Sour (Bamia Khuta), 334; and Olives (Judgja bil Zeitoun), 445; and Potatoes, Spiced (Hari Kabob), 333; and Rice (Bukharan Plov), 266; and Rice (Tabit), 99; and Rice Ball (Arook), 336; (and) Rice, Egg and Yoghurt, Layered (Tachin Joojeh), 137, 138; and Rice, Slow-Cooked (Hameen II), 101; and Scrambled Eggs, 346; and Vegetable Soup, Aromatic (Koli), 372; Baked with Okra, Variation, 21; Cherry Pilau with Chicken (Albaloo Polo), 158;

Cous Cous (Judgja), 446; Cumin-Flavored, with Pasta Squares (Kulchatoy), 289; Curried, 358; Curry (Puzukku), 372; Cutlets, Calcutta (Murgi Cutlet), 331; Dumplings for Passover, Kurdish (Koobe), 69; Egg-Lemon Soup (Koto Supa Avgolemono), 39; in Onion and Tomato Sauce (Katami Chahohbili), 228, 229; in Pomegranate, Walnut and Prune Sauce (Fesenjan II), 133; in Spiced Vinegar Walnut Sauce (Katami Nigozee Satsabeli), 230; Kebab (Murgh Kebab), 309; Liver, Fried (Boona Kalegi), 337; Liver Sauté (Il Kubt Deboch), 454; Liver Sauté with Potato and Egg Garnish (Jeger e Joojeh Galie Tochim), 140; Livers, Roast (Kaliserket Kodet Ksesa), 81; Mix, Quick (Kabob Rochan), 266; Oven, Old-Style, for Sabbath (Shabat Hameen), 100; Pan Kebabs (Kebab Digi), 135; "Pigeon" Pie (Pastiya), 447; Pot-Roast (Aloo-m-Kalla Murgi), 332; Roast, 357; Roast, for Passover (Gallina al Horno), 46; Roast with Leeks (Prasa mi Kota), 47; Sabbath (Sesa Hameen), 80; Soup for Passover Dumplings (Marag Koobe), 68; Soup with Vegetables, Spiced (Marag), 327; Stew (doro wot), see Variation, 408; Stew with Green Beans and Eggplant (Joojeh Baadem Jan), 133; Stuffed, in Broth (Morgh e tu Por), 110; Stuffed with Pomegranate Seeds (Joojeh Anor), 130; Wings in Aspic for Sabbath (Murgh Mayee), 265; with Celeriac (Cabezas de Opyo), 8; with Fresh Spices, 359

Chick-Peas: (and) Calf's Foot and Veal (Hhomss bil Camoun), 481; Flour Mix and Sauce, Spiced (Shuroe), 410; Turnover, Stuffed (Sambusak), 96

Chikhirtma (Coriander-Flavored Onion Soup), 210

Chili, see under Pickles and Condiments

Chizu Salada (Carrot Salad), 467

Cholent (t'fina) see Hameen, 325; see Scheena, 438, 497

Cholo Chamad (Sweet-and-Sour Beet Soup), 95

Choraka (Squash and Cauliflower Sauté), 374

Chorba (Soup with Orzo), 476

Chouia (Meat Stew), 390

Chow (Spice Mixture), 405

Chrouf bil Karis (Lemon Lamb), 515

Chutney, see under Pickles and Condiments

Clay pot cooking, see Chanakhy I, II, III; see Deezee

Coconut Curry Soup, 355

Cocum, 355

Codrerio con Fava (Lamb and Fresh Fava Beans), 8

Coffee, Ethiopian, 405

Columbus, Christopher, 3

Compote de Fruta Seca (Compote of Dried Fruits), 32

Confections: Almond Sweet for Passover (Mustachudo), 34; Burnt Almonds (Badam Soukhte), 189; Halva (Oriental Sesame Candy), 297; Honey Almond Slivers (Sohan Asal), 188; Quince Sweets (Tajitos de Bimbrio), 60; Semolina Log Stuffed with Date Paste (Makroud), 501; Toasted

Confections (continued)
and Crumbled Sweet (Halwa Chosk), 187; Walnut and Honey Crunch (Gozinaki), 246; Walnut Fudge (Lawves), 296
Cookies: Butter (Kurbietes), 60; Rice Flour, with Poppy Seeds (Nan Berenji), 186; Stuffed (Kasmay), 87
Cooking in a Bag: Bachsh, 261; Sirkaniz, 262
Cornish Game Hen, Crisp-Fried (Varya Tabaka), 226
Cornmeal Mush (Romee), 245
Cornmeal Pancake (Mchadi), 246
Cous Cous: (Libya), 507; (Morocco), 435; (Tangieran), 465; (Tunisian), 474; Bouillon (Beef and Vegetable Soup), 491; Homemade (Semoule), 491; Judga (Chicken), 446; Royale (Jewish), 489; with Vegetables Libyan Style, 523
Cucumbers: Pickled, 102; Salad (Salata), 348; Stuffed, 345
Curry, Curried: Beef, Sheep or Goat (Alicha), 409; Chicken, 358; Chicken (Puzukku), 372; Fish (Kangi), 360; Vegetable (Sambar), 375
Custard: Egg, Baked (Galatopta), 59; Rice Flour (Halwa Bereng), 184; Toasted (Halwa Ord Tar), 185
Cyrus, 103

Dabo (Special Sabbath Bread), 412
Date and Tamarind Chutney (Indapazam), 383
Date Paste for Passover (Haroseth), 463
Deezee (Meat Roast in a Clay Pot), 127
Derma, Stuffed (Kishke), 260
Dhazmaruli Badrijani (Baby Eggplant Pickle), 243
Dolme (Stuffed Vegetables, Persian Style), 175; Bargeh (Grape Leaves), 170; Kadoo (Pumpkin), 172; Kadoo Halvoee (Pumpkin for Sabbath), 173; Kadoo Sabzi Halvoee (Pumpkin Stuffed with Meat and Herbs), 174; Sabzi (Herbal Stuffing), 171; Shereen (Sweet Stuffing), 171; with Pomegranate, 178
Domates ke Pipriya (Meat-Stuffed Peppers), 42
Domates Yena de Kezo (Cheese-Stuffed Tomatoes), 19
Donuts, Tunisian, in Honey Syrup (Yoyo), 502
Douara (Passover Variety Meat Casserole), 450
Duck: and Potatoes with Cuminseed (Kowo Rugan), 267; in Georgian Walnut Sauce (Katami Satsabeli Baga), 231; Stew (Fesenjan I), 132; Stuffed, Baked (Bhuna Haas), 335
Dumplings: Kreplach (Dushpera), 285; Meat Ravioli (Dushpera, Samarkand), 287; Pumpkin and Onion, Baked (Kadoo Bichak), 283; Red (Koobe Matfuniya), 77; Stuffed Fried (Kutel Pishra), 73; Stuffed Fried, for Purim (Samoosa Puroee), 284; Stuffed, in Soup (Koobe Hamooth), 94; Veal and Chick-Pea (Gondhi Nochodi), 109; Yellow (Koobe Maslocka), 78
Dushpera (Kreplach), 285

Dushpera, Samarkand, (Meat Ravioli), 287

Edict of Expulsion, 1492, 3, 471
Eekra (Chopped Vegetable Side Dish), 270
Egg, Eggs: and Meat Patties (Beidh B'laham), 93; and Potato Omelet (Kuku Sibzamini), 142; and Sauce, Kurdistan (Schackshouka), 82; and Sauce, Morocco Shackshooka), 437; Baked in Sand (Adma de R'Mel), 488; Carrot and Potato Omelet (Kuku Havidge), 148; Cheese and Eggs (Queso con Huevo), 15; Date and Egg Breakfast (Tochmeh Chorma), 140; Eggplant Omelet, Baked (Kuku Baademjan), 146; Green Herb Omelet (Kuku Sabzi II), 141; Ground Meat Omelet (Kuku Gusht), 143; Herb Omelet or Patty (Kuku Sabzi I), 141; Jewish (Huevos Haminados), 37; Lamb Brains Omelet (Kuku Maghz), 149; Mushrooms and Eggs (Soko Kwerstkhi), 203; Onion Omelet (Kuku Piaz), 145; Salad in Walnut Sauce (Kwerstkhi Nigozee Satsabelly), 204; Scrambled Egg and Potato Fry (Mahmoosa), 345, 346; Spinach and Egg Fry (Boranee), 139; Spinach Omelet (Kuku Esfinadge), 147; with Fenugreek, Scrambled (Hilbeh ma Beda), 392; with Sauce, Spiced (Muttacher), 376; Zucchini Omelet (Kuku Kadoo), 146
Eggplant: and Cheese, Baked (Fritada de Berenja), 16; and Cheese, Vegetarian (Moussaka), 49; and Scrambled Eggs, 346; and Zucchini Turnovers (Handrajo), 21; Baby Eggplant Pickle (Dhazmaruli Badrijani), 243; Cheese and Eggplant Casserole (Almodrote), 18; Georgian Caviar, 201; Layered (Tachin Bademjan), 169; Marinated (Ochor), 277; Meat-Stuffed (Domates), 43; Mixture, Fried (Vazuniga), 373; Pickle (Baademjan Torshi), 183; Pickled, 278; Pickle with Herbs (Leete Baademjan ba Sabzi), 182; Pio (Tapada), 22; Pie from Salonika (Pastel de Berenjena), 58; Salad (M'Raad), 426; Salad, Spicy (Bonjan Salat), 313; Slices, Stuffed, 237; Smoked Eggplant Salad, Calcutta (Brinjal Bhurta), 349; Smoked Eggplant Salad, Uzbek (Salatee Boyimjan), 251; Snails (Rodanchas), 57; Stuffed (Brinjal Mahasha), 343; Stuffed and Baked (Papoutsakia), 48; Stuffed Baked (Mhamars, Aubergines Farcies), 496; Stuffed Fried (Patrijani), 237, 238; Stuffed, Pickled (Turshi Bonjan), 315; Stuffed with Cheese (Berenjeno Relleno con Queso), 17
El Lasan bil Capar (Beef Tongue with Capers), 452
El San (Tongue Sauté with Garnishes), 451
El San bel Cares ou Cherchef (Tongue in Lemon Sauce with Artichokes), 518
Esther, Queen, 103

Fajones (Beef and White Bean Stew), 6
Falashas (Ethiopian Jews), 401, 402

Fasolada (White Bean Soup), 38
Fassoulia Beda (White Bean Stew), 419
Fatoot im Hilbeh (Beef Soup with Fenugreek), 390
Fenugreek Chutney (Halba), 350
Fesenjan, 106
Fesenjan I (Meatball Stew in Pomegranate and Walnut Sauce), 130
Fesenjan II (Chicken in Pomegranate, Walnut and Prune Sauce), 133
Fides (Angel-Hair Noodles in Sauce), 53
Fish: and Chips Complete (Poisson Complet), 487; and Sweet Red Pepper (Het bil Flafel Homar), 454; Baked (Pescado en el Horno), 468; Baked (Pesce Kotchu), 9; Balls (Boulettes de Poisson), 455; Balls in Basil Sauce (Kifte bil Haut), 520; Balls in Sauce (Boulettes de Poisson avec Sauce), 456; Balls in Simple Sauce (Albóndigas de Pescado), 469; Curry (Kangi), 360; Curry (Muchli ka Kari), 338; Fillet of, in Egg-Lemon Sauce (Piskado con Uevo i Limon), 10; Hot Spiced (Hrieme), 519; in Red Sauce (Pescado Cocho), 467; in White Sauce (Pescado en Blanco), 468; Molee, 361; panfried, 162; Salad with Coconut Milk (Anjuli), 338; Spiced (Asa Wot), 409; Yemenite (Samac), 392
Flafel (Sweet Red Pepper Salad), 460
Fool Achdar (Green Fava Beans), 424
Foolim (Crisp-Fried Fava Beans), 435
Friday Lunch Dumplings in Soup (Koobe Chamusta), 75
Fritada de Berenja (Baked Eggplant and Cheese), 16
Fritada de Spinaka (Baked Spinach and Cheese), 15
Fruit, Fruits: Compote of Dried Fruits (de Fruta Seca), 32; Dried, and Nut Mix for Passover (Halek), 189; Dried Fruit Compote, Bukharan, 295; Fresh, and Nut Mixture for Passover (Halek), 189; Passover Haroseth, 34; see also under Haroseth

Gadjar Murghi Meetha (Chicken and Carrot Stew), 330
Galatopta (Baked Egg Custard), 59
Gallina al Horno (Roast Chicken for Passover), 46
Ganouia avec Poulet (Chicken and Okra), 485
Garlic Sauce, 263
Georgian Caviar (Caviar Patrijani), 201
Georgian mortar and pestle, see Note 205
Goanese influence in Cochin, see Sambar, 375
Gondhi Berenji (Ground Meat, Rice and Herbs), 149
Gozinaki (Walnut and Honey Crunch), 246
Grape Leaves: Herbal Stuffing (Dolme Sbazi), 171; Stuffed, Kurdistan (Yaprach), 83; Stuffed, Persia (Dolme Bargeh), 170; Stuffed, Turkey (Yaprakes), 11; Sweet Stuffing (Dolme Shereen), 171
Grapes, Pickled (Torshi Angoor), 180

Great Exodus (Iraq to Israel), 66
Grebe (Pickled Mushrooms), 276
Gureeskaya Capusta (Pink Pickled Cabbage), 242
Gurgur (Tomato Bulghur), 84

Halba (Fenugreek Chutney), 350
Haleem (Lamb and Whole-Wheat Gruel), 153
Halek (Fruit and Nut Mix for Passover), 34, 189, 190
Halik (Grape Haroseth for Passover), 89
Halesa (Beef and Whole-Wheat Berry Gruel), 259
Halva (Oriental Sesame Candy), 297
Halwa Bereng (Rice Flour Custard), 184
Halwa Chosk (Toasted and Cumbled Sweet), 187
Halwa Ord, see Variation, 185
Halwa Ord Tar (Toasted Custard), 185
Haman, 103
Hameen (t'fina), 325, 438, 508
Hameen (Beef, Chick-Pea and Egg Bake for the Sabbath), 440
Hameen II (Slow-Cooked Chicken and Rice), 101
Hamim de Kastanya (Beef and Chestnut Stew), 6
Handrajo (Eggplant and Zucchini Turnovers), 21
Hanukkah, Sweet Cakes, Fried (Neyyappam), 380
Hari Kabob (Spiced Chicken and Potatoes), 333
Harissa (Hot Red Chili Paste), 434, 473, recipe 504
Hariss Temani (Beef and Green-Pea Bake for Passover), 391
Haroseth, Passover Sweets: Afghani, 322; Bukhara, 296; Grape, Kurdistan (Halik), 89; Greece, 34; Morocco, 463; Date Paste, Morocco, 463; Persia (Halek), 189, 190; Turkey, 34; see also Halek, Halik, Jaroseth
Havige Polo Chorma (Carrot Pilau with Dates), 167
Hawaish (Spice Mix), 397
Herb Fritters (Pchali), 202
Herbs and spices, Persian, 106
Het bil Flafel Homar (Fish and Sweet Red Pepper), 454
Hhomss bil Camoun (Chick-Peas, Calf's Feet and Veal), 481
Hilbeh (Fenugreek Condiment), 398, 399
Hilbeh ma Beda (Scrambled Eggs with Fenugreek), 392
Honey Dip for Yoyo, Tunisian, 502
Hrieme (Hot Spiced Fish), 519
Huevos Haminados (Jewish Eggs), 37

Il Kubt Deboch (Liver Sauté), 454
Indapazam (Date and Tamarind Chutney), 383
Injeera (Ethiopian Pancakes), 402, recipe 413
Intatisha Wot (Wild Mushroom Fry), 411
Istambulee Polo (Turkish Rice with Tomato), 163

Jachnoon (Baked Bread with Whole Eggs), 395

Jam, Jelly and Conserve: Carrot Conserve (Murabo Havidge), 191; Quince Jam (Murabo Bay), 191; Quince Jelly (Bimbrio), 33

Jaroseth (Yemen), 388

Jaroseth (Parutherium), Cochin, 379

Jeger e Joojeh Gelie Tochim (Chicken-Liver Sauté with Potato and Egg Garnish), 140

Jeremiah, 415

Jewish Paste, see Hilbeh, 398

Joojeh Anor (Chicken Stuffed with Pomegranate Seeds), 130

Joojeh Baadam Jan (Chicken Stew with Green Beans and Eggplant), 133

Judgja bil Zeitun (Chicken and Olives), 445

Kabob Rochan (Quick Chicken Mix), 266

Kadey Shavuoth (Cheese Pancake for Shavuoth), 88

Kadoo Bichak (Baked Pumpkin and Onion Dumplings), 283

Kae Atar Wot (Green-Pea Stew), 406

Kae Misr Wot (red lentil stew), see Variation, 407

Kairouan, 471

Kaliserket Kodet Ksesa (Roast Chicken Livers), 81

Kangi (Fish Curry), 360

Kartoff Mumulay (Stuffed Potato Fritters), 314

Kasmay (Stuffed Cookies), 87

Katami Chahohbili (Chicken in Onion and Tomato Sauce), 228, 229

Katami Nigozee Satsabeli (Chicken in Spiced Vinegar Walnut Sauce), 230

Katami Satsabeli Baga (Duck in Georgian Walnut Sauce), 231

Kebab Digi (Pan Kebabs), 135

Kebab Marinovat (Marinated Lamb Kebab), 308

Kebe (Butter, How to Make), 403

Keema Chowja (Stuffed Pigeon, Pan-Roasted), 268

Kemal Ataturk, 3

Kesach (black caraway seed), see Subya, 396

Khachapuri (Cheese Pie), 232, 235

Khanoom (Steamed Vegetable Pasta Roll), 290

Kharcho, see Setsamandi, 219

Khinta (Wheat Porridge with Stuffed Beef Pocket), 97

Khoreke Zabon (Tongue and Potato Fry), 128

Khoresht (Persian stew), 106: Bamieh (Beef and Okra Sauté), 113; Bamieh Lape (Meat, Okra and Yellow Split-Pea Stew), 115; Bay (Beef and Quince Stew with Pomegranate Sauce), 114; Chogondar (Beet, Beef and Fruit Stew), 116; Garch (Veal and Mushroom Stew), 117; Gremeh Lape (Tomato and Split-Pea Stew with Meat Cubes), 119; Karafs (Beef and Celery Stew), 120; Kari (Mushroom and Chicken Curry Persian Style), 136; Korme Sabzi (Veal Sauté with Herbs), 121; Nano, Jafaree, Aloo Bukhara (Lamb Stew with Mint, Parsley and Prunes), 118; Zardaloo (Veal and Apricot Stew), 117

Khorke Maghz (Veal Brain and Potato Sauté), 129

Khweli (Cheese Filling) for Khachapuri, 233

Kiddush Wine, 371

Kifte (Meatballs), 252

Kifte bil Haut (Fish Balls in Basil Sauce), 520

Kifte de Prasa (Leek and Beef Patties), 40

Kihrchiree (Mung Bean and Rice Medley), 272

Kishmish Vashli Tolma (Raisin, Apple and Lamb Stuffed Cabbage), 223

Kishke (intestines for stuffing), see Note, 212

Kishke (Osbana), Morocco, 452

Kishke (Stuffed Derma), Uzbek, 260

Klertiko (Patriot's Roast Lamb), 45

Kofta Nakhod (Meatballs and Chick-Peas), 305

Koli Soup (Aromatic Chicken and Vegetable Soup), 372

Koobe (dumpling), 66, 325: Chamo (Dome-Shaped, in Soup), 74; Chamusta (Friday Lunch, in Soup), 75; Chicken, for Passover, Kurdish, 69; Hamooth or Solet (Stuffed, in Soup), 94; Marag Koobe (Vegetable Soup with Dumplings), 71; Maslocka (Yellow), 78; Mutfuniya (Red), 77; Semolina and Rice, in Soup, 70; Shifte bi Tomate (Meatballs in Tomato Sauce), 78

Koofteh Berenji (Herbed Rice Balls in Broth), 123

Koofteh Tabrizi (Herbed Meat and Rice Balls), 111

Korma Sabzi (Herbed Meat with Prunes), 112

Koshary (Lentils and Rice), 425

Koto Supa Avgolemono (Chicken Egg-Lemon Soup), 39

Kowo Rugan (Duck and Potatoes with Cuminseed), 267

Kreplach (Dushpera), 285

Kuku (Persian Omelet): Baademjan (Baked Eggplant), 146; Esfinadge (Spinach), 147; Gusht (Ground Meat), 143; Havidge (Carrot and Potato), 148; Kadoo (Zucchini), 146; Maghz (Lamb Brains), 149; Piaz (Onion), 145; Sabzi I (Herb), 141; Sabzi II (Green Herb), 141; Sibzamini (Egg and Potato), 142

Kulchatoy (Cumin-Flavored Chicken with Pasta Squares), 289

Kulukif Tremono (Baked Zucchini Pudding), 50

Kupaty (Georgian Beef and Lamb Sausages), 211

Kurbietes (Butter Cookies), 60

Kutel Pishra (Stuffed Fried Dumplings), 73

Kwarma (Layered Beef and Vegetables), 98

Kwerstkhi Nigozee Satsabelly (Egg Salad in Walnut Sauce), 204

Lagman (Mixed Vegetables in Broth with Spaghetti), 256

Lamb: and Carrot Cutlet (Shami Kebab), 126; (and) Eggplant and Rice (Chanakhy II), 214; and Fresh Fava Beans (Codrerio), 8; and Plums in Herb Sauce (Chakapuli), 218; and Rice (Osh Plov), 264; (and) Rice and Herb Gruel (Setsamandi), 219; (and) Vegetables and Garlic (Chanaky III), 215; and Vegetables in a Clay Pot (Chanakhy I),

213; and Whole-Wheat Gruel (Haleem), 153; Balls in Prune Sauce (Shami Gondhi), 125; Barbecue, Georgian (Shashlik), 216, 217; Innards for Passover (Armiko), 45; Kebab, Marinated (Kebab Marinovat), 308; King's Rice (Shahee Polo), 307; Lemon Lamb (Chrouf bil Karis), 515; Pilau with Cubed Meat, Yellow Split Peas and Dates (Polo Gremeh Lape), 164; Ragout and Vegetables for Passover (Msoki), 482; Roast in a Clay Pot (Deezee), 127; Roast, Patriot's (Kleftiko), 45; Stew (Fesenjan I), 132; Stew with Mint, Parsley and Prunes (Khoresht Nano, Jafaree, Aloo Bukhara), 118; Turkish Rice with Tomato (Istambulee Polo), 163; with Kishke and Peas (Charouf bil Pisselli o Chedra), 516

La Minnina (Chicken and Brain Soufflé), 486

Lawves (Walnut Fudge), 296

Leek: and Beef Balls with Walnuts (Albóndigas de Prasa kon Nuez), 14; and Beef Patties (Kifte de Prasa), 40; (and) Lamb and Green-Pea Stew (Tabikha bil Karrate), 512; Rolls (Chufletikos), 11

Leete Baademjan ba Sabzi (Eggplant Pickle with Herbs), 182

Lemon Salad (Salade au Citron), 503

Lentil, Lentils: and Rice (Koshary), 425; Pilau (Adas Polo), 157; red lentil purée (Misr Allecha), see Variation, 412; Red Lentil Soup (Soupe de Lentille), 417; Red Lentil Stew (Kae Misr Wot), see Variation, 407; Stew (Adasee), 107

Lime Pickle (Achar), 382

Liver Sauté (Il Kubt Deboch), 454

Lobio (Red Bean Appetizer), 200

Lobio Soup (Red Bean Soup), 207

Mafrum (Beef-Stuffed Potatoes), 513

Mahchi (Stuffed Zucchini), 428

Mahmoosa (Scrambled Egg and Potato Fry), 345

Maimonides, Moses, 415

Makoud (Beef and Potato Pie), 480

Makroud (Semolina Log Stuffed with Date Paste), 501

Malawach (Fried Bread Pancake), 397

Mango, Green Mango Salad, 362

Manicotti or Dabla (Pastry Roses), 503

Mantu (Steamed Bukharan Beef Pie), 279

Marag (Spiced Chicken Soup with Vegetables), 327

Marag (Yemenite Bone Soup), 389

Marag Koobe (Chicken Soup for Passover Dumplings), 68

Marag Koobe (Vegetable Soup with Dumplings), 71

Marco Polo, 198, 249

Mark Dil Ga il Chimra (Pumpkin and Chick-Pea Soup), 436

Marranos (Christian Jews, Spain), 433

Masala (Spice Mixtures): Dry, for Fish, 367; Dry, for Meat, 366; Green, Basic, 366

Masran, Kishke (Stuffed Large Intestine), 517

Masto Jushak (Chicken and Vegetable Soup), 256

Matzoh, 320: and Potato Bake (Mayeena), 422; Joshawk (Passover Soup), 302; Stuffed (M'Chaqub), 524; Yemenite, 393

Mayeena (Matzoh and Potato Bake), 422

Mazeera Koobe (Cream Soup with Dumplings), 67

Mchadi (Cornmeal Pancake), 246

M'Chaqub (Stuffed Matzoh), 524

Meat: Beef, Sheep or Goat Curry (Alicha), 409; Filled Turnovers (Bureka), 510; Ground Meat Barbecue (Shoofta), 329; Kishke (Osbana), 452; Pie for Passover (Pastel de Carni), 28; Pies, Baked (Samoosa), 280; Variety Meat Casserole, Passover (Douara), 450; with Prunes, Herbed (Korma Sabzi), 112; see also Beef, Lamb, Veal

Meatball, Meatballs: and Okra Sauté in Tomato Sauce (Bamia), 421; and Rice Balls, Herbed (Koofteh Tabrizi), 111; in Tomato Sauce (Koobe Shifte be Tomate), 78; Kifte, Uzbek, 252; Stew in Pomegranate and Walnut Sauce (Fesenjan I), 130; with Celery and Green Peas (Boulette de Viande), 441; with Chick-Peas (Kofta Nakhod), 305

Menelik, son of Solomon and Sheba, 401

Mhamars (Aubergines Farcies), Stuffed Baked Eggplant, 496

Mint Chutney, 367

Mint Chutney, Sweet-and-Sour (Pudeena), 351

Misr Allecha (red lentil purée), see Variation, 412

M'Loukhia (Green Soup), 417

Morgh e tu Por (Stuffed Chicken in Broth), 110

Mosh Owaee Joor-Hawtee (Mung Bean and Rice Melange), 271

Most o Laboo (Grated Beet and Yoghurt Salad), 179

Moussaka (Vegetarian Eggplant and Cheese), 49

M'Raad (Eggplant Salad), 426

Msoki (Lamb Ragout and Vegetables for Passover), 482

Muchli ka Kari (Fish Curry), 338

Mugaz (Brain Curry), 339

Mukmura (Chicken and Almonds in Lemon Sauce), 332

Murabo Bay (Quince Jam), 191

Murabo Havidge (Carrot Conserve), 191

Murgh Kebab (Chicken Kebab), 309

Murgh Mayee (Chicken Wings in Aspic for Sabbath), 265

Murgi Cutlet (Calcutta Chicken Cutlets), 331

Mushroom, Mushrooms: and Eggs (Soko Kwerstkhi), 203; Barbecue (Soko), 202; in Walnut Sauce (Soko Nogozee), 205; Layered (Tachin Garch), 170; Pickled (Grebe), 276; Wild Mushroom Fry (Intatisha Wot), 411

Mustachudo (Almond Sweet for Passover), 34

Muttachar (Spiced Eggs with Sauce), 376

Myasnoya Kharcho (Lamb, Herbs and Rice Soup), 209

Mzoura (Piquant Carrots), 493

Nachinyonaya Forel (Stuffed Trout), 232

Nan Berenji (Rice Flour Cookies with Poppy Seeds), 186
Nebuchadnezzar, 198
Neyyappam (Fried Sweet Cakes), 380
Nimboo (small yellow lime), see Achar, 382
Nogada (Keftika), Meatballs in Walnut Sauce, 41
Noni (Bread): Afghani, 321; Seyaw (Whole-Wheat), 294; Tokee (Baked Crisp Flat), 293
Noodle Pancake (Tagarines), 423
Noodle Pie (Pastichio), 52
Noodles, Angel-Hair, in Sauce (Fides), 53

Ochor (Marinated Eggplant), 277
Ojaldres (Light, Crispy Spinach Rolls), 25
Okra, Baked, with Lemon (Bamia), 20
Okra with Sauce (Bamya), 85
Olives avec (in) Sauce, 459
Omelets, see Eggs
Onion, Onions: and Tomato Stew (Armeko), 50; Pie (Pita de Zeboya), 26; Shells, Stuffed (Oshee Pyozee), 272; Stuffed, Calcutta, 344; Stuffed, Egypt, see Variation, 429; Stuffed (Osh Pyozee), Afghan, 312
Oorow (Beef, Vegetable and Noodle Soup), 254
Operation Magic Carpet, 387
Orange and Black Olive Salad (Orange et Olive Noire), 459
Orange peel, to dry fine slivers, see Note, 159
Orez Chamutz (Lemon-Flavored Beef and Rice), 79
Osbana (Kishke), 452
Oshe Anor (Rice, Barley, Herbs with Meatballs), 151
Oshee Duiyoza Lav Lavu (Red Beet and Turnip Melange), 253
Oshee Pomeedor (Stuffed Tomatoes in Vegetable Sauce), 274
Oshee Pyozee (Stuffed Onion Shells), 272
Oshee Shula Mosh (Beef Stew with Rice, Mung Beans and Vegetables), 258
Oshee Tos Kadoo (Stuffed Pumpkin), 275
Oshemast (Spinach, Herb and Rice Stew), 150
Oshi Joor-Rawtee (Rice and Mung Beans, Afghani), 311
Osh Plov (Lamb and Rice), 264
Osh Pyozee (Stuffed Onions), 312
Ottoman Empire, 3, 387

Pachuddy Thier (Spiced Yoghurt Sauce), 377
Pancake, Pancakes: Noodle (Tagarines), 423; Scallion (Yazozee), 281; Yeast (Chalpakee Joor-Rawtee), 282
Panjar or Shalgan (Beet Salad), 29
Papoutsakia (Stuffed and Baked Eggplant), 48
Pareve, 54
Paripu Payasam (Split-Pea Sweet with Coconut Milk), 382

Parutherum (Jaroseth), 379
Pashtida (Zucchini Pie), 276
Passover dishes: Almond Sweet (Mustachudo), 34; Beef and Green-Pea Bake (Hariss Temani), 391; Beef and Matzoh Pie (Quartico), 43; Burnt Almonds (Badam Soukhte), 189; Chicken and Vegetable Soup (Masto Jushak), 256; Chicken Curry (Puzukku), 372; Chicken Soup (Marag Koobe), 68; Compote of Dried Fruits (de Fruta Seca), 32; Fruit and Nut Mix (Halek), 189, 190; Jewish Eggs (Huevos Haminados), 37; Kishke (Osbana), 452; Kurdish Chicken Dumplings (Koobe), 69; Lamb Innards (Armiko), 45; Lamb Ragout and Vegetables (Msoki), 482; Leek and Beef Patties (Kifte de Prasa), 40; Mahchi (Stuffed Zucchini, Onions, Tomatoes), 428, 429; Matzoh; Matzoh and Potato Bake (Mayeena), 422; Meat Pie (Pastel de Carni), 28; Nut Cake in Syrup (Tezpishti), 29; Potato Fritters, Stuffed (Kartoff Mumulay), 314; Rice Flour Cookies with Poppy Seeds (Nan Berenji), 186; Rice Porridge for Breakfast (Pejh), 355; Roast Chicken (Gallina al Horno), 46; Russian Salad (Salade Russe), 461; Smoky Pepper Salad (Salade Shacksooka), 461; Soup, Tunisia, 476; Soup, Uzbek, 255; Spinach Pie (Pita de Spinaka), 27; Spinach Salad (Slk Salada), 462; Stuffed Matzoh (M'Chaqub), 524; Stuffed Potato Fritter (Banatage), 499; Stuffed Potato Fritter (Pastel de Batata), 443; Sweet Red Pepper Salad (Flafel), 460; Variety Meat Casserole (Douara), 450; Veal and Mushroom Stew (Khoresht Garch), 117; Vegetable Soup (Soupe de Pesach), 436; Vegetable Turnovers, Stuffed (Samoosi Yirakot), 316; see also Haroseth
Pasta: Squares in Light Tomato Sauce (Puloni Siri), 288; Squares with Dairy Sauce (Poloni), 310; Vegetable Pasta Roll, Steamed (Khanoom), 290; see also Noodle
Pasteeya, 435
Pastel (Stuffed Triangles), 442
Pastel de Batata (Stuffed Potato Fritter), 443
Pastel de Berenjena (Eggplant Pie from Salonika), 58
Pastel de Carni (Meat Pie for Passover), 28
Pasticchio (Noodle Pie), 52
Pastiya ("Pigeon" Pie), 447
Pastry for Borekas, 31
Pastry for Handrajo, 21
Patatas Kavakadas (Beef-Stuffed Potatoes), 12
Patrijani (Stuffed Fried Eggplant), 237
Payasam (Tapioca Sweet), 381
Pchali (Herb Fritters), 202
Pea, Peas: Green-Pea Purée, Spiced (Atar Allecha), 411; Green-Pea Stew (Kae Atar Wot), 406; Split-Pea Sweet with Coconut Milk (Paripu Payasam), 382
Pejh (Rice Porridge for Breakfast), 355
Pepper, Peppers: Meat-Stuffed (Domates ke

Pipriya), 42; Smoky Pepper Salad (Salade Shackshooka), 461; Stuffed, 344; Sweet Red Pepper Salad (Flafel), 460

Pescado Cocho (Fish in Red Sauce), 467

Pescado en Blanco (Fish in White Sauce), 468

Pescado en el Horno (Baked Fish), 468

Pesoe Kotchu (Baked Fish), 9

Phali (Young Beet Leaves in Walnut Sauce), 199

Pichonka (Chopped Veal Liver), 252

Pickles, Condiments, Chutneys: Baby Eggplant Pickle (Dhazmaruli Badrijani), 243; Beet and Coriander Pickle (Charkhali), 241; Beets in Spiced Brine, 240; Carrots, Piquant (Mzoura), 493; Cooked Salad, Morocco (Salada Madbucha), 458; Cooked Salad, Tunisia, (Salade Cuite), 495; Date and Tamarind Chutney (Indapazam), 383; Eggplant Pickle with Herbs (Leete Baademjan be Sabzi), 182; Fenugreek Chutney (Halba), 350; Fenugreek Condiment (Hilbeh), 398, 399; Green Chili Chutney, Hot (Schug), 398; Lemon Salad (Salade au Citron), 503; Lime Pickle (Achar), 382; Marinated Eggplant (Ochor), 277; Mint Chutney, 367; Mint Chutney, Sweet-and-Sour (Pudeena), 351; Mixed Vegetable Pickle (Torshi Leete), 181; Olives in Sauce, 459; Pickled Beets, 238; Pickled Cabbage with Chili (Turshi Kurdi), 86; Pickled Cucumbers, 102; Pickled Eggplant, 278; Pickled Grapes (Torshi Angoor), 180; Pickled Mushrooms (Grebe), 276; Pickled Stuffed Eggplant (Turshi Bonjan), 315; Pink Pickled Cabbage (Gureeskaya Capusta), 242; Raisin Vinegar, 371; Red Chili Paste, Hot (Harissa), 504; Sour-Plum Sauce (Tqemali), 244; Turnip and Beet Pickle (Tershid Mechalal), 85; Vegetable Sauce (Satsabeli), 245; Zucchini Lemon Salad (Ajlook), 495

Pies and Turnovers: Beef and Matzoh Pie for Passover (Quartico), 43; Beef Pie, Steamed, Bukharan (Mantu), 279; Cheese Pie (Khachapuri), 232, 235; Cheese Triangles (Samsadas de Quezo), 23; Cheese Turnovers (Boerekas), 54; Cheese Turnovers (Sambusak), 349; Chick-Pea Turnover, Stuffed (Sambusak), 96; Eggplant and Zucchini Turnovers (Handrajo), 21; Eggplant Pie (Tapada), 22; Eggplant Pie from Salonika (Pastel de Berenjena), 58; Meat-Filled Turnovers (Bureka), 510; Meat Pie for Passover (Pastel de Carni), 28; Meat Pies, Baked (Samoosa), 280; Noodle Pie (Pastichio), 52; Onion Pie (Pita de Zeboya), 26; Pastry Roses (Dabla or Manicotti), 503; "Pigeon" Pie (Pastiya), 447; Spinach and Feta Cheese Pie (Spanakopeta), 56; Spinach Pie for Passover (Pita de Spinaka), 27; Spinach Rolls in Fillo (Bulemas), 24; Stuffed Triangles (Pastel), 442; Tricorners, Stuffed, Baked (Bichak), 318; Vegetable Turnovers, Stuffed (Samoosi Yirakot), 316; Walnut or Almond Turnovers (Borekas de Nuez u de Almendra), 30

Pigeon, Stuffed, Pan-Roasted (Keema Chowja), 268

Pilau, see under Rice

Piskado con Uevo i Limon (Fillet of Fish in Egg-Lemon Sauce), 10

Pita de Spinaka (Spinach Pie for Passover), 27

Pita de Zeboya (Onion Pie), 26

Plov, 250; Bukharan, 266

Plum, Sour-Plum Sauce (Tqemali), 244

Poisson Complet (Fish and Chips Complete), 487

Polo Gremeh Lape (Pilau with Cubed Meat, Yellow Split Peas and Dates), 164

Polo Havidge Loobia (Rice Pilau with Carrot and Red Kidney Beans), 156

Polo Shabati (Pilau for the Sabbath), 306

Poloni (Miniature Pasta Squares with Dairy Sauce), 310

Pomegranate Milk, see Variation, 152

Porpachina Jajik (Spinach and Sour-Cream Spread), 82

Potato, Potatoes: and Spinach Casserole, Baked (Sfongo), 19; Beef-Stuffed (Mafrum), 513; Beef-Stuffed (Patatas Kavakadas), 12; Chop, 362; Cutlets, Miniature, 313; Deep-Fried, Golden (Aloom-Kalla), 347; Fritter, Stuffed (Banatage), 499; Fritter, Stuffed (Bestil), 508; Fritter, Stuffed (Pastel de Batata), 443; Fritters, Stuffed (Kartoff Mumulay), 314; Pies, 281; Salad with Cumin (Tourchi Batata), 493; Soup, Golden (Batata bel Lamoun), 418

Poultry in Walnut Sauce (Satsabeli Bazha), 227

Prasa mi Kota (Chicken Roast with Leeks), 47

Pudding, Semolina (Semola), 32

Pudding, Zucchini, Baked (Kulukif Tremono), 50

Pudeena (Sweet-and-Sour Mint Chutney), 351

Puloni Siri (Pasta Squares in Light Tomato Sauce), 288

Pumpkin: and Chick-Pea Soup (Mark Dil Gra il Chimra), 436; and Lamb Kebob Sauté (Shifte Kadoo), 122; and Meatball Soup, Sweet-and-Sour, 96; and Onion Dumplings, Baked (Kadoo Bichak), 283; Salad (Tirshi), 522; Stuffed (Dolme Kadoo), 172; Stuffed (Oshee Tos Kadoo), 275; Stuffed, for Sabbath (Dolme Kadoo Halvoee), 173; Stuffed with Meat and Herbs (Dolme Kadoo Sabzi), 174; with Dumplings (Soup), 95

Puran Poli (Stuffed Chapatti), 364

Purim dishes: Dumplings, Stuffed Fried (Samoosa Puroee), 284; Rice Flour Custard (Halwa Bereng), 184; Stuffed Chapatti (Puran Poli), 364; Walnut or Almond Turnovers (Borekas de Nuez u de Almendra), 30

Puzukku (Chicken Curry), 372

Quartico (Beef and Matzoh Pie for Passover), 43

Quatre épices, see Note, 483

Queen of Sheba, 387

Quemam (Dry Spice Mixture), 406

Queso con Huevo (Cheese and Eggs), 15

Quince, Quinces: Jam (Murabo Bay), 191; Jelly (Bimbrio), 33; Stuffed (Biya Vashlee Tolma), 225; Sweets (Tajitos de Bimbrio), 60

Ragoût de Bamia (Beef and Okra Ragout), 479

Ragoût de Petits Pois (Beef and Green-Pea Ragout), 478

Raisin Vinegar, 371

Rava Idlees (Steamed Wheat Cakes), 379

Reshte Polo (Rice and Noodle Pilau with a Whole Chicken), 166

Rhodes, 35

Ribnoye Kharcho (Salmon and Walnut Soup), 209

Rice: Almond, Carrot, Orange Pilau (Shereen Polo I), 159; and Mung Beans, Afghani (Oshi Joor-Rawtee), 311; and Noodle Pilau with a Whole Chicken (Reshte Polo), 166; Balls, Herbed, in Broth (Koofteh Berenji), 123; Carrot Pilau with Dates (Havige Polo Chorma), 167; Cumin and Currant Pilau (Zeera Kishmish Polo), 155; Herb and Rice Pilau (Sabzi Polo), 168; Herbed, with Fish (Sabzi Polo Mohee), 161; King's (Shahee Polo), 307; Lentil Pilau (Adas Polo), 157; Mix, Old-Fashioned (Pilau Matabak), 341; Orange-Flavored (Shereen Polo II), 161; Persian, Basic (Chelo), 153; Pilau for the Sabbath (Polo Shabati), 306; Pilau with Carrot and Red Kidney Beans (Polo Havidge Loobia), 156; Pilau with Cubed Meat, Yellow Split Peas and Dates (Polo Gremeh Lape), 164; Porridge for Breakfast (Pejh), 355; Pudding for Shavuoth (Shirberenj), 184; Turkish, with Tomato (Istambulee Polo), 163; with Beef and Carrot (Shola), 263; (with) Beef (and) Carrot (Sirkaniz), 262; (with) Beef and Chicken Liver (Bachsh), 261; with Green Peas, Spiced (Pilau), 342; with Tadiq, 160

Rodanohaa (Eggplant Snails), 57

Romaniates, 4, 35

Romee (Cornmeal Mush), 245

Rosh Hashanah dishes: Eggplant Snails, Variation, 58; Pumpkin and Chick-Pea Soup (Mark Dil Gra il Chimra), 436; Rice and Noodle Pilau with a Whole Chicken, 166; Veal, Nut and Fruit Melange (Tazeen), 444

Russian Salad for Passover (Salade Russe), 461

Sabbath dishes: Beans and Beef, Cumin-Flavored (T'fina Camounia), 497, 498; Beef and Beans in Swiss-Chard Sauce (Tabikha b'Salk), 514; Beef and Potato Roast (Scheena), 438, 439; Beef, Chick-Pea and Egg Bake (Hameen), 440; Beef-Stuffed Potatoes (Mafrum), 513; Bone Soup, Yemenite (Marag), 389; Bread (Dabo), 412; Bread with Whole Eggs (Jachnoon), 395; Chicken (Sesa Hameen), 80; Chicken and Rice (Tabit), 99; Chicken and Rice, Slow-Cooked (Hameen II), 101; Chicken Wings in Aspic (Murgh Mayee), 265; Eggs Baked in Sand (Adma de H'Mel), 488; Hamim, 7; Holiday Bread (Subya), 396; Lamb with Kishke and Peas (Charouf bil Pisselli o Chedra), 516; Liver Sauté (Il Kubt Deboch), 454; Menu, Sabbath Eve Dinner, 474–475; Oven Chicken, Old-Style, 100; Potato Soup, Golden (Batata bel Lamoun), 418; Pot-Roast Chicken (Aloo-m-Kalla Murgi), 332; Rice Pilau (Polo Shabati), 306; Stuffed Chicken in Broth (Morgh e tu Por), 110; Stuffed Dumplings in Soup (Koobe Hamooth), 94; Stuffed Onion Shells (Oshee Pyozee), 272; Stuffed Pumpkin (Dolme Kadoo Halvoee), 173; Toasted and Crumbled Sweet (Halwa Chosk), 187; Wheat Porridge (Khinta), 97

Sabzi Polo (Herb and Rice Pilau), 168

Sabzi Polo Mohee (Herbed Rice with Fish), 161

Saffron, 159

Safra (Semolina and Date Cake with Honey Syrup), 525

Salad, Salada, Salade, Salata, Salatee: Beet (Panjar or Shalgan), 29; Beet Leaves in Walnut Sauce (Phali), 199; Beets in Walnut Sauce, 240; Cabbage, Red and White (Zalatet Kalam Smoka Uchwara), 86; Carrot (Chizu Salada), 457; Carrot (Tirshi), 522; Cooked, Morocco (Salada Madbucha), 458; Cooked, Tunisia (Salade Cuite), 495; Cucumber (Salata), 348; Eggplant (M'Raad), 426; Eggplant, Smoked (Brinjal Bhurta), 349; Eggplant, Spicy (Bonjan Salat), 313; Egyptian, Popular (Salade Egyptienne), 427; Fish, with Coconut Milk (Anjuli) 338; Fresh (Salade Fraîche), 492; Fresh Tomato and Basil (Bandoora), 270; Fried Chopped (Tastira Harra), 494; Grated Beet and Yoghurt (Most o Laboo), 179; Green Mango, 362; Lemon (Salade au Citron), 503; Orange and Black Olive (Orange et Olive Noire), 459; Potato, with Cumin (Tourchi Datata), 493, Pumpkin (Tirshi), 522; Russian, for Passover (Salade Russe), 461; Seasonal (Salada Fasle), 180; Smoked Eggplant (Salatee Boyimjan), 251; Smoky Pepper (Salade Shackshooka), 461; Spinach (Slk Salada), 462; Spinach and Yoghurt (Boranee ba Mast), 179; Sweet Red Pepper (Flafel), 460; Tomato and Pepper (Tomat y Pimenton), 51; Zucchini Lemon (Ajlook), 495

Salonika, 35, 37

Samac (Yemenite Fish), 392

Sambar (Vegetable Curry), 375

Sambusak (Cheese Turnovers), 349

Sambusak (Stuffed Chick-Pea Turnover), 96

Samoosa (Baked Meat Pies), 280

Samoosa Puroee (Stuffed Fried Dumplings for Purim), 284

Samoosi Yirakot (Stuffed Vegetable Turnovers), 316

Samsadas de Quezo (Cheese Triangles), 23

Satsabeli (Vegetable Sauce), 245

Satsabeli Bazha (Poultry in Walnut Sauce), 227

Sauce: Breakfast (Chakchouka de Matin), 475; Chick-Pea Flour Mix, 410; Garlic, 263; Salsa, for Kishke, 453; Yoghurt, Uzbek, 283; Yoghurt, Spiced, Cochin (Pachuddy), 377

Sausages, Beef and Lamb, Georgia (Kupaty), 211

Scallion Pancakes (Yazozee), 281

Schackshouka (Eggs and Sauce), 82

Scheena (one-dish Sabbath meals), 435, 508

Scheena (Sabbath Beef and Potato Roast), 438, 439

Schug (Hot Green Chili Chutney), 398

Semola (Semolina Pudding), 32

Semolina: and Date Cake with Honey Syrup (Safra), 525; and Rice Dumpkings in Soup (Koobe), 70; Cereal (Uppuma), 378; Log Stuffed with Date Paste (Makroud), 501; see also Cous Cous

Semoule (Homemade Cous Cous), 491

Sesa Hameen (Sabbath Chicken), 80

Sesame Candy, Oriental (Halva), 297

Sesame Loaf (Warda), 394

Setsamandi (Lamb, Rice and Herb Gruel), 219

Sevoya con Calabasa (Onion and Zucchini Sauté), 13

Sfongo (Baked Spinach and Potato Casserole), 19

Shabat Hameen (Old-Style Oven Chicken for Sabbath), 100

Shackshooka (Eggs and Sauce), 437

Shahee Polo (King's Rice), 307

Shalmaneser, 65, 198

Shami Gondhi (Ground Lamb Balls in Prune Sauce), 125

Shami Kebab (Ground Lamb and Carrot Cutlet), 126

Shampuri (long skewers for shashlik), 216

Sharbat Albaloo (Cherry Syrup Concentrate), 193

Sharbat Serkanjibin (Mint Syrup Concentrate), 192

Shashlik (Georgian Lamb Barbecue), 216, 217

Shavuoth, 67; Shavuoth dishes: Cheese Pancake (Kadey Shavuoth), 88; Rice Pudding (Shirberenj), 184; Spinach and Sour-Cream Spread (Porpachina Jajik), 82

Shereen Polo I (Almond, Carrot, Orange Pilau), 159

Shereen Polo II (Orange-Flavored Rice), 161

Shifte Kadoo (Pumpkin and Lamb Kebob Sauté), 122

Shirberenj (Rice Pudding for Shavuoth), 184

Shola (Rice with Beef and Carrot), 263

Shoofta (Ground Meat Barbecue), 329

Shorba Yavron (Assorted Vegetable Soup, 303

Shuroe (Spiced Chick-Pea Flour Mix and Sauce), 410

Siga Wot (Spiced Beef Stew), 408

Sirkaniz (Rice, Beef, Carrot Cooked in a Bag), 262

Slk Salada (Spinach Salad), 462

Sofrito (Spiced Beef and Vegetable Stew), 420

Sohan Asal (Honey Almond Slivers), 188

Soko (Mushroom Barbecue), 202

Soko Kwerstkhi (Mushrooms and Eggs), 203

Soko Nogozee (Mushrooms in Walnut Sauce), 205

Solomon, 471, 525

Solyanka (Beef, Herbs and Pickles in Tomato Sauce), 212

Soup, Soupe: Asparagus, 206; Beef and Vegetable (Cous Cous Bouillon), 491; Beef, Vegetable and Noodle (Oorow), 254; Beef, with Fenugreek (Fatoot im Hilbeh), 390; Beet, Sweet-and-Sour (Cholo Chamad), 95; Bone, Yemenite (Marag), 389; Bulghur, see Note, 389; Chicken and Vegetable (Masto Jushak), 256; Chicken and Vegetable, Aromatic (Koli), 372; Chicken Egg-Lemon (Koto Supa Avgolemono), 39; Chicken, for Passover Dumplings (Marag Koobe), 68; Chicken, with Chick-Pea, 109; Chicken with Vegetables, Spiced (Marag), 327; Coconut Curry, 355; Cream, with Dumplings (Mazeera Koobe), 67; Dome-Shaped Dumplings in Soup (Koobe Chamo), 74; Fava (Bissara), 477; Green (M'Loukhia), 417; Lamb, Eggplant and Green-Bean (Bozbashy), 208; Lamb, Herbs and Rice (Myasnoya Kharcho), 209; Mixed Vegetables in Broth with Spaghetti (Lagman), 256; Onion, Coriander-Flavored (Chikhirtma), 210; Passover, Afghan (Matzo Joshawk), 302; Passover, Tunisia (Soupe de Pesach), 476; Passover, Uzbek, 255; Potato, Golden (Batata bel Lamoun), 418; Pumpkin and Chick-Pea (Mark Dil Gra il Chimra), 436; Pumpkin and Meatball, Sweet-and-Sour, 96; Pumpkin with Dumplings, 95; Red Bean (Lobio), 207; Red Lentil (Soupe de Lentille), 417; Salmon and Walnut (Ribnoye Kharcho), 209; Vegetable, Assorted (Shorba Yavron), 303; Vegetable, for Passover (Soupe de Pesach), 436; Vegetable, with Dumplings (Marag Koobe), 71; White Bean (Fasolada), 38; Winter Noodle (Aash Rechte), 108; with Orzo (Chorba), 476

Spanakopeta (Spinach and Feta Cheese Pie), 56

Spice Mixtures: Advieh, Persian, 107; Chow, Ethiopian, 405; Hawaish, Yemen, 397; Quemam, Ethiopian, 406; see also Masala

Spinach: and Cheese, Baked (Fritada de Spinaka), 15; and Egg Fry (Boranee), 139; and Feta Cheese Pie (Spanakopeta), 56; and Potato Casserole, Baked (Sfongo), 19; and Scrambled Eggs, 346; and Yoghurt Salad (Boranee ba Mast), 179; Omelet (Kuku Esfinadge), 147; Pie for Passover (Pita de Spinaka), 27; Pies, 281; Rolls in Fillo (Bulemas), 24; Rolls, Light, Crispy (Ojaldres), 25; Salad (Slk Salada), 462

Spread, Spinach and Sour-Cream (Porpachina Jajik), 82

Squash and Cauliflower Sauté (Choraka), 374

Squash, Meat-Stuffed (Domates), 43

Stew: Bean, Onion and Beef (Bsal bil Loubya), 478; Beef and Beets, Sweet-and-Sour (Khuta), 328; Beef and Celery (Khoresht Karafs), 120; Beef and

Chestnut (Hamim de Kastanya), 6; Beef and Quince, with Pomegranate Sauce (Khoresht Bay), 114; Beef and Vegetable, Spiced (Sofrito), 420; Beef and White Bean (Fajones), 6; Beef and Whole-Wheat Berry Gruel (Halesa), 259; Beef, Spiced (Siga Wot), 408; Beef, with Rice, Mung Beans and Vegetables (Oshee Shula Mosh), 258; Beet, Beef and Fruit (Khoresht Chogondar), 116; Chicken and Carrot (Gadjar Murghi Meetha), 330; Chicken and Chick-Pea (Tabikha bil Houmus), 511; Chicken and Chick-Pea, with Rice (Chelo Nachodo), 303; chicken (doro wot), see Variation, 408; Chicken, with Green Beans and Eggplant (Joojeh Baadem Jan), 133; Ground Meat, Rice and Herbs (Gondhi Berenji), 149; Lamb, with Mint, Parsley and Prunes (Khoresht Nano, Jafaree, Aloo Bukhara), 118; Leek, Lamb and Green Pea (Tabikha bil Karrate), 512; Meat (Chouia), 390; Meatball, in Pomegranate and Walnut Sauce (Fesenjan I), 130; Meat, Okra and Yellow Split-Pea (Khoresht Bamieh Lape), 115; Onion and Tomato (Armeko), 50; Rice, Barley, Herbs with Meatballs (Oshe Anor), 151; Spinach, Herb and Rice (Oshemast), 150; Tomato and Split-Pea, with Meat Cubes (Khoresht Gremeh Lape), 119; Veal and Apricot (Khoresht Zardaloo), 117; Veal and Mushroom (Khoresht Garch), 117; White Bean (Fassoulia Beda), 419

Subya (Holiday Bread), 396

Suez Canal opening, 416

Sukkoth, Semolina Pudding (Semoule), 32

Sweetbreads in Red Sauce (Akoud), 484

Syrup: Cherry, Concentrate (Shabat Albaloo), 193; Mint, Concentrate (Sharbat Serkanjibin), 192; Sugar, 159

Tabikha bil Houmus (Chicken and Chick-Pea Stew), 511

Tabikha bil Karrate (Leek, Lamb and Green-Pea Stew), 512

Tabikha b'Salk (Beef and Beans in Swiss-Chard Sauce), 514

Tabit (Chicken and Rice), 99

Tachin, 154

Tachin Bademjan (Layered Eggplant), 169

Tachin Garch (Layered Mushrooms), 170

Tachin Joojek (Layered Chicken, Rice, Egg and Yoghurt), 137, 138

Tadiq, 153; Variation, 154

Tagarines (Noodle Pancake), 423

Tajitos de Bimbrio (Quince Sweets), 60

Tamerlane, 91, 249

Tapada (Eggplant Pie), 22

Tapioca Sweet (Payasam), 381

Tarator (Yoghurt and Cucumber Salad with Garlic), 52

Tastira Harra (Fried Chopped Salad), 494

Tazeen (Veal, Nut and Fruit Melange), 444

Tea, Bukharan, Buttered (Chai Chaymokee), 298

Tea, Kurdish (Chai Kurdi), 90

Tech (Honey Beer), 404

Teff (grain), 402, 413

Telah (Barley Beer), 403

Tershid Mechalal (Turnip and Beet Pickle), 85

Tezpishti (Passover Nut Cake in Syrup), 29

T'fina, 474, 481, 508

T'fina Camounia (Cumin-Flavored Beans and Beef), 497, 498

Tirshi (Carrot Salad), 522

Tirshi (Pumpkin Salad), 522

Tirshi (Zucchini and Potato Mash in Spice Dressing), 521

Tish-Ah B'Av dish, Pasta Squares with Dairy Sauce (Poloni), 310

Tochmeh Chorma (Date and Egg Breakfast), 140

Tolma (Stuffed Cabbage Leaves with Pomegranate Seeds), 222

Tolma (Stuffed Cabbage with Lamb), 221

Tolma Chorzi (Beef-Stuffed Cabbage), 220

Tomato, Tomatoes: and Pepper Salad (Tomat y Pimenton), 51; Cheese-Stuffed (Domates Yenas de Kezo), 19; Meat-Stuffed (Domates), 42; Stuffed, Calcutta, 344; Stuffed, Egypt, see Variations, 429; Stuffed, in Vegetable Sauce (Oshee Pomeedor), 274

Tongue: and Potato Fry (Khoreke Zabon), 128; in Lemon Sauce with Artichokes (El San bel Cares our Cherchef), 518; Sauté with Garnishes (El San), 451; with Capers (El Lasan bil Capar), 452

Torquemada, 3

Torshi Angoor (Pickled Grapes), 180

Torshi Leete (Mixed Vegetable Pickle), 181

Tourchi Batata (Potato Salad with Cumin), 493

Tqemali (Sour-Plum Sauce), 244

Tripe in Red Sauce, 484

Trout, Stuffed (Nachinyonaya Forel), 232

Turkey Stew (Fesenjan I), 132

Turnovers, see Pies and Turnovers

Turshi Bonjan (Pickled Stuffed Eggplant), 315

Turshi Kurdi (Pickled Cabbage with Chili), 86

Uppuma (Semolina Cereal), 378

Varya Tabaka (Crisp-Fried Cornish Game Hen), 226

Vazuniga (Fried Eggplant Mixture), 373

Veal: and Apricot Stew (Khoresht Zardaloo), 117; and Chick-Pea Dumpling in Chicken Soup (Abe Gusht Gondhi Nochodi), 109; and Mushroom Stew (Khoresht Garch), 117; Brain and Potato Sauté (Khorke Maghz), 129; Liver, Chopped (Pichinka), 252; Meatballs in Walnut Sauce (Nogada, Keftika), 41; Nut and Fruit Melange (Tazeen), 444; Sauté with Herbs (Khoresht Korme Sabzi), 121

Vegetable, Vegetables: Chopped (Eekra), 270; Curried (Bhaji), 340; Curry (Sambar), 375; Meat-Stuffed (Boulettes), see Cous Cous Royale, 489; Melange, Summer (Chakchouka de Saif), 498; Mixed Vegetable Sauté (Adjapsandali), 236; Sauce (Satsabeli), 245; Soup (Shorba Yavron), 303; Soup for Passover (Soupe de Pesach), 436; Stew, Mixed (Aleecha), 407; Stuffed, Persian Style (Dolme), 175, 177; Stuffed, with Pomegranate (Dolme), 178; Summer, Stuffed (Zaphulis Tolma), 224; Turnovers, Stuffed (Samoosi Yirakot), 316; see also names of vegetables

Walnut and Honey Crunch (Gozinaki), 246
Walnut or Almond Turnovers (Borekas de Nuez u de Almendra), 30
Walnut Fudge (Lawves), 296
Warda (Sesame Loaf), 394
Wheat Porridge, 98
World War II, 507

Yaprach (Stuffed Grape Leaves, Kurdistan), 83
Yaprakes (Stuffed Grape Leaves, Turkey), 11
Yazozee (Scallion Pancakes), 281

Yoghurt: and Cucumber Salad with Garlic (Tarator), 52; Sauce, 283; Sauce, Spiced (Pachuddy), 377
Yom Kippur dish, Chicken and Chick-Pea Stew (Tabikha bil Houmus), 511
Yoyo (Tunisian Donuts in Honey Syrup), 502
Yufka, 5

Zagora (Carp in Garlic and Coriander Sauce), 269
Zalatet Kalam Smoka Uchwara (Red and White Cabbage Salad), 86
Zaphulis Tolma (Summer Vegetables, Stuffed), 224
Zeera Kishmish Polo (Cumin and Currant Pilau), 155
Zerrah (beef and barley roast), see Variation, 439
Zipporah, 369
Zoch, see Note, 138
Zoroastrians, 103
Zucchini: and Eggplant Turnovers (Handrajo), 21; and Potato Mash in Spice Dressing (Tirshi), 521; Lemon Salad (Ajlook), 495; Onion and Zucchini Sauté (Sevoya con Calabasa), 13; Pie (Pashtida), 276; Pudding, Baked (Kulukif Tremono), 50; Stuffed (Mahchi), 428